W9-ASE-943

New Directions in Ethics

New Directions in Ethics

The Challenge of Applied Ethics

Edited by

Joseph P. DeMarco
Richard M. Fox
Cleveland State University

ROUTLEDGE & KEGAN PAUL

New York and London

Theodore Lownik Library
Illinois Benedictine College
Lisle, Illinois 60532

170
N 532

First published in 1986 by
Routledge & Kegan Paul Inc.
in association with Methuen Inc.
29 West 35th Street, New York, NY 10001

Published in Great Britain
by Routledge & Kegan Paul plc
11 New Fetter Lane, London EC4P 4EE

Set in Times, 10 on 12 pt
by Inforum Ltd, Portsmouth
and printed in Great Britain
by Billing and Sons Ltd
Worcester

Selection, editorial matter and Chapter 1 copyright © Joseph P. Demarco and Richard
M. Fox, 1986; Chapters 2, 4, 5, 6, 7, 8, 9, 10, 11, 12, 13, 19 copyright © Routledge &
Kegan Paul, 1986; Chapter 3 © Cambridge University Press, 1982; Chapter 14 ©
1981 by Indiana University; Chapter 15 © Michael Bayles, 1986; Chapter 16 © 1982
by The University of Chicago; Chapter 17 copyright © 1981 by The Metaphilosophy
Foundation and Basil Blackwell; Chapter 18 © William Frankena, 1986.

No part of this book may be reproduced in any
form without permission from the publisher, except
for the quotation of brief passages in criticism

Library of Congress Cataloging in Publication Data

New directions in ethics.
Includes bibliographies and index.
1. Ethics, Modern 20th century Addresses, essays,
lectures. 2. Social ethics Addresses, essays, lectures.
I. DeMarco, Joseph P., 1943–
II. Fox, Richard M., 1931–
BJ319.N48   1986   170   85–25761

British Library CIP Data also available

ISBN 0–7102–0639–9 (c)
0–7102–0847–2 (p)

CONTENTS

Contributors   vii
Preface   ix
Acknowledgments   xi

1 The challenge of applied ethics
   Richard M. Fox and Joseph P. DeMarco   1

Section I: *Contemporary ethical theory*
   Introduction   21
2 Utilitarianism and its applications
   J.J.C. Smart   24
3 A contractualist alternative
   T.M. Scanlon   42
4 Recent Thomistic ethics
   Vernon J. Bourke   58
5 Existentialist ethics
   Charles Guignon   73
6 Marxism, morality and moral philosophy
   Kai Nielsen   92
7 Pragmatic sensibility: the morality of
   experience
   John J. McDermott   113

Section II: *Fields of applied ethics*
   Introduction   137

v

Contents

8 Biomedical ethics: a precocious youth
  Mary B. Mahowald   141
9 Business ethics
  Norman E. Bowie   158
10 Reverse discrimination and equal
   opportunity
   Robert Fullinwider   173
11 The ethics of nuclear strategy
   James P. Sterba   190
12 Applied ethics and the vocation of social
   science
   Bruce Jennings   205

Section III: *The future of ethics*
   Introduction   221
13 Why do applied ethics?
   R. M. Hare   225
14 The future of ethics
   R. B. Brandt   238
15 Ethical theory in the twenty-first century
   Michael D. Bayles   249
16 How medicine saved the life of ethics
   Stephen Toulmin   265
17 Ethics, science and moral philosophy
   Marcus G. Singer   282
18 Moral philosophy and the future
   William K. Frankena   299
19 Ethical theory and moral practice: on the
   terms of their relation
   Abraham Edel   317

CONTRIBUTORS

Professor Michael D. Bayles, Department of Philosophy, University of Florida, Gainesville, Florida.

Professor Vernon J. Bourke, Department of Philosophy, Saint Louis University, St Louis, Missouri.

Professor Norman E. Bowie, Director, Center for the Study of Values, University of Delaware, Newark, Delaware.

Professor Richard B. Brandt, Department of Philosophy, University of Michigan, Ann Arbor, Michigan.

Professor Joseph P. DeMarco, Department of Philosophy, Cleveland State University, Cleveland, Ohio.

Professor Abraham Edel, Department of Philosophy, University of Pennsylvania, Philadelphia, Pennsylvania.

Professor Richard M. Fox, Department of Philosophy, Cleveland State University, Cleveland, Ohio.

Professor William K. Frankena, Department of Philsophy, University of Michigan, Ann Arbor, Michigan.

Professor Robert K. Fullinwider, Center for Philosophy and Public Policy, University of Maryland, College Park, Maryland.

Professor Charles Guignon, Department of Philosophy, The University of Vermont, Burlington, Vermont.

Professor R.M. Hare, Department of Philosophy, Oxford University, England.

Dr Bruce Jennings, Political Scientist Research Associate, The Hastings Center, New York.

Professor John J. McDermott, Department of Philosophy, Texas A & M University, College Station, Texas.

Contributors

Professor Mary B. Mahowald, Department of Pediatrics, School of Medicine, Case Western Reserve University, Cleveland, Ohio.

Professor Kai Nielsen, Department of Philosophy, University of Calgary, Calgary, Alberta, Canada.

Professor T.M. Scanlon, Department of Philosophy, Harvard University, Cambridge, Massachusetts.

Professor Marcus G. Singer, The Royal Institute of Philosophy, London, England.

Professor J.J.C. Smart, Research School of Social Sciences, Australian National University, Canberra, Australia.

Professor James P. Sterba, Department of Philosophy, University of Notre Dame, Notre Dame, Indiana.

Professor Stephen Toulmin, Department of Philosophy, University of Chicago, Chicago, Illinois.

PREFACE

In designing the present collection of essays, we planned to provide an authoritative, comprehensive up-to-date account of recent trends and developments in ethical theory as they bear upon current issues in applied ethics. We also expected the book would provide a valuable text for teachers of applied ethics, a source for scholars working in field, and a reference for professionals in the many areas where ethical issues have become a pressing concern.

The collection is indeed authoritative, we believe, because the essays in it have been written by prominent figures in each of the major schools of ethical theory and fields of applied ethics. It is reasonably comprehensive because it covers a greater number of ethical theories in far greater detail than other texts, and because it considers how theory itself is changing, or may need to change, in order to meet the requirements of application. The book is also up-to-date because the vast majority of essays in it have been written specially for this volume, while others have been revised for this publication. In a word, the essays are written by experts who survey the latest work in their fields.

In the first section of the book, leading figures in each of the schools of moral philosophy discuss recent developments within each of their theories, ways in which the theory has been or can be applied, and whether or how the theory needs to be amended to solve practical moral problems. In the second section, philosophers working in each of several areas of applied ethics survey the literature and kinds of problems which arise in their respective fields and provide examples of styles of applied ethics. They also

ix

assess the extent to which philosophical theories have been useful or deficient and point out where they think some of the solutions lie. Finally, in the third and last section, prominent ethical theorists address the question of the future of ethics, given the challenge of practical application. The first essay of the book, written by the editors, discusses the challenge of applied ethics within its historical context.

At the present time there is a widespread concern over moral issues in society, in the professions, and in public life. Because of the demand for informed opinion, many new courses, journals, books, societies and institutes on the subject of applied ethics have come into existence during the last decade or two. However, because most of this material is highly specialized and quite limited in scope, we have tried to provide an overview of the field to which teachers, scholars and concerned lay persons can refer for a reliable survey of the work that has been accomplished, explanations of the various theories being used to address moral problems, issues which have arisen in each of the special fields, and prospects for change. The many prominent scholars who have generously agreed to contribute to this volume have confirmed our belief in the need for such a work. We wish to thank them for their contributions, and we also wish to thank Basil Blackwell (Publishers), the University of Chicago Press, *Metaphilosophy*, *Nous*, *The Southern Journal of Philosophy* and *Zygon* for their permission to reprint parts of articles which appear in this volume in revised form. Several individuals contributed significantly to the preparation and typing of the manuscript: especially Cindy Bellinger and Mary Persanyi, but also Katherine Groves who provided additional help as the deadline approached. Last but not least, we want to thank our wives. Patricia Fox and Bonnie DeMarco, who read and critiqued much of the material as it was being prepared. We also want to thank the editors of Routledge & Kegan Paul, and especially Stratford Caldecott, for their helpful suggestions. The editors are equally responsible for the material contained in the book, and any errors of judgment or fact are, of course, ours.

Joseph P. DeMarco
Richard M. Fox

ACKNOWLEDGMENTS

Chapter 3 was originally published as 'Contractualism and Utilitarianism' in *Utilitarianism and Beyond* edited by Amartya Sen and Bernard Williams, Cambridge University Press 1982.

Chapter 14 is reprinted by permission of the author and of the editor of *Nous*, Vol.XV (1981): 31–40.

Chapter 15 was originally published in *The Southern Journal of Philosophy*, Vol.XXII No. 4, pp.439–51.

Chapter 16 was originally published in *Perspectives in Biology and Medicine*, 25, No. 4 (Summer 1982):736–50, by the University of Chicago.

Chapter 17 is an amalgamation, with some modification of portions of two previously published papers: 'Recent Trends and Future Prospects in Ethics', *Metaphilosophy*, Vol. 12, 1981, pp.207–23, copyright © 1981 by The Metaphilosophy Foundation and Basil Blackwell; and 'Is Ethics a Science? Ought it to be?', *Zygon*, Vol. 15, 1980.

Chapter 18 was originally published in *Two Centuries of Philosophy in America* edited by Peter Caws, Basil Blackwell 1980. Permission granted by Basil Blackwell and by Rowman and Littlefield, Totowa, New Jersey.

1

THE CHALLENGE OF APPLIED ETHICS

Richard M. Fox and Joseph P. DeMarco

For little more than a decade, philosophic ethics has been faced with a relatively new challenge: to provide theoretical frameworks within which practical moral problems can be solved. This challenge has been posed from many quarters, from outside as well as within philosophy. It is heard in the form of calls from diverse professional and policy making organizations for the study and teaching of ethics in medicine, law, business and government. Such concerns reflect the growing awareness of the many moral, social and political issues which beset the modern world: problems of war, persecution, poverty, social injustice and inequality. Crime and corruption on the one hand, and moral controversy and indifference, on the other, have called attention to an apparent lack of moral knowledge and sensitivity. In opposition to traditional beliefs, a new morality seems to have emerged, as evidenced by changing attitudes towards sex and various rights movements. New problems have also been created by scientific and technological changes, including the many issues of bioethics which focus on matters of life and death.

New philosophical concerns have been evoked especially by a growing number of moral controversies. In the past, there seems to have been more agreement about matters of right and wrong conduct and a stronger commitment to doing what was considered right, at least among persons of the same cultural background. Traditional philosophers, therefore, shared many beliefs about the rightness or wrongness of particular acts, about the appropriateness or inappropriateness of moral rules, and about the possibility of demonstrated moral knowledge. Assured by widespread moral agreement, philosophers could concentrate on finding principles which would support shared moral convictions and serve to resolve doubtful cases. Today, by contrast, there is relatively little consensus on moral issues, so that the problem of moral philosophy is not so much one of justifying moral beliefs already known or assumed to be true but, rather, one of finding a method for determining which beliefs are true. The problem is to find what counts as evidence in moral reasoning, how such evidence can be weighed, and how persons can reach consensus in cases of disagreement, ignorance or doubt.

It should not be surprising then that, in this century, the work of philosophers has focused more on problems of theory construction than on problems of application. This focus has been evident in the seemingly inordinate amount of attention given to metaethics by analytic philosophers: by their speculation over the nature, scope, and even the possibility of moral reasoning, on the one hand, and their disproportionate inattention to substantive issues, on the other. In fact, most analytic philosophers have felt that it is not the business of philosophers to address practical issues. Some of them have called into question the efficacy of moral reasoning and even the existence of moral truth. The emotivists, for example, have taken the position that there is no such thing as moral truth, and intuitionists have argued that moral truth cannot be discovered by reasoning. Relativists, in turn, have claimed that morality is a matter of individual or cultural perspective.

Despite this movement toward metaethics, there are contemporary philosophers who have proposed substantive ethical theories, and some have even questioned the distinction between metaethics and normative ethics. Those influenced by Kant have argued that moral rules can be established on the bases of universal applicability and respect for persons. Contemporary utilitarians argue that the rightness or wrongness of actions is determined by the values of consequences, and Thomists, on the basis of intentions. But, so far, no one has yet been able to fully mediate these views. Thus, skepticism over the validity of ethical reasoning and opposition between the various schools of ethical theory has created the impression that philosophy has little to offer in the way of solutions to everyday, practical concerns.

Yet since the late 1960s and the early 1970s, philosophers have been addressing contemporary moral issues, and whole new fields of applied ethics have developed. In the past ten years, there has been a vast increase in the number of conferences, societies, journals and texts devoted to the subject of applied ethics. At the same time, on the theoretical level, new models have been developed to provide procedures for making practical decisions and resolving disputes.

In many respects, the movement toward applied ethics has shown that philosophers do have something to offer by way of clarifying issues and positions, and even by showing how, or to what extent, one or another theory can be applied. Nevertheless, many critics feel that there is still a serious gap between theoretical and applied ethics. One reason for the criticism is that much of the work in applied ethics presupposes the position of one or another school of philosophy and hence does not face up to the problem of opposing philosophical views. In other cases it turns out that one or another existing theory is simply not refined enough to yield answers, even according to the principles it lays down. In still other cases, applied philosophy is done without any explicit attention to theory at all.

It is, therefore, important to investigate the relation of theoretical ethics to applied ethics, not only from the point of view of what philosophers have to offer to the solution of practical problems, but also from the point of view of seeing how philosophical ethics itself might be improved by considering problems of application. How, for example, does the question of the applicability of a theory bear upon the question of its truth? In addition to the test of internal coherence, should there also be a test of completeness, based upon a theory's ability to resolve practical disputes? How can principles be elicited from the subject-matters in which moral questions arise in order to resolve differences between theories or to construct a more comprehensive ethical view?

ETHICAL THEORY AND MORAL PRACTICE

Moral theorizing and the application of moral theory in practical moral judgment is not limited to moral philosophers. Practically everyone theorizes about values, and disciplines other than philosophy use moral theories of one kind or another to justify their activities or to resolve problems within their fields. Science, for example, is thought to be justified by its pursuit of knowledge, or a particular economic structure by its efficiency. Recent psychotherapies are founded upon ethical theories as various as hedonism and self-realization. Implicitly at least, ethical theories are being applied. Philosophy, however, retains the distinction of being the only discipline explicitly engaged in the study of ethical theory as one of its special subject-matters. Unlike practitioners or theoreticians in other disciplines, who assume the truth of one ethical theory or another without critical investigation, philosophers traditionally attempt to justify the theories they propose. Ethics is sometimes supposed to fall within the province of religion as well as philosophy, but practitioners in religion, like practitioners in other non-philosophical fields, are apt to simply assume that the principles expressed in their codes are true – although theologians sometimes attempt to justify religious beliefs on philosophical grounds. Therefore, when one seeks answers, not only to what is right or wrong in particular cases, but also to questions of correct principles, it seems only natural to turn to philosophy for answers.

The problems of moral philosophy arise quite naturally when anyone begins to reflect upon his or her moral practices, questioning the justification of actions or the reasons for judgments. Disagreement is often the source of such reflection; it also arises when people are genuinely perplexed about what they should do. In their attempts to resolve a controversy or remove doubt, they seek reasons for or against particular actions and, in so doing, they often appeal to personal codes or socially accepted rules. However, such rules may also be disputed, when, for example, there is disagreement about the acceptability of the rules, or when the accepted rules appear to conflict. An accepted rule may also seem inapplicable to a particular case, or the case may appear to be an exception, or it may not be clear which judgment the rule requires. When rules are in question, the next step is to move to higher ground, so to speak, to seek principles which will justify the rules, resolve conflicts between them, determine the range of their application, justify exceptions, or clarify their meanings. Moral reasoning does not always proceed in this way, of course, for persons may begin by appealing directly to accepted moral principles, or to contextual values, and some simply refuse to reason in support of their opinions. Traditionally, it has been the philosopher's job to sort out such responses.

Historically, philosophers have sought to examine and defend ethical principles in order to guide action and enlighten moral

judgments. Their answers to questions about the nature and justification of moral principles, therefore, may serve to distinguish the
different types of moral theory. Such answers are, for the most part,
simply highly articulated accounts of the kinds of answers anyone
might propose as an ultimate justification for his or her own actions
or beliefs. The major difference between popular opinions on ethics
and the theories of moral philosophers is that philosophers usually
try to clarify their positions and demonstrate their truth. Philosophers use logical analysis and argumentation to test whether any
principles being proposed really are the first principles of ethics and
whether any principles can be established. Philosophers also tend to
give explicit attention to the methodology employed in their examination.

Ethical theories are influenced by philosophical traditions, but
moral philosophers also arrive at their positions by analyzing the
values of the societies in which they live, or by analyzing ordinary
moral reasonings and judgments. Philosophies therefore tend to
reflect basic cultural views; yet culture is often influenced by the
views of philosophers. One expects to find Christian philosophies
among Christians, or communist philosophies among communists,
for such philosophies both express and influence the beliefs of their
adherents. The differences in the moral beliefs of different cultures
have, in fact, led many people to believe in the general relativism of
values. A belief in cultural or individual relativism, however, is not
peculiar to our time. It is a form of moral skepticism which finds
expression in all periods of philosophic history. In ancient times,
Plato, for example, tried to refute the sophists, the moral skeptics of
his day; St Augustine, at the end of the Roman Empire, argued
against 'the academics'; and in the early modern period Descartes
thought he could teach 'the infidels' how to walk with confidence in
the conduct of life.

The argument which many philosophers have used to defeat the
skeptic is relatively simple. They have argued that there must be
universal principles discoverable by reason, because otherwise
moral judgments and moral disputes would not make sense. There
would be no point in having a moral opinion, or in disputing the
opinion of another, unless one had reason to suppose that opinions
could be either correct or mistaken. If there were no principles for
determining which opinion is correct, there would be no point in
having an opinion, for a moral opinion would then be an opinion

about nothing. One way to confront such an argument would be to allow that moral judgments are really not judgments about anything, or that moral disagreements are not really logical disagreements, as, in this century, logical positivists and emotivists have claimed. They have held that so-called moral judgments are simply expressions of feeling and hence not really judgments at all.

Many philosophers have also maintained that concerning principles there is no disputing. They mean that that ultimate moral principles cannot be proved by deductive reasoning, for if they could be so proved, there would have to be still higher principles. But if there were higher moral principles, the principles being proved would not be ultimate, and the same argument applies to any supposedly higher principles. However, this argument ignores the possibility of establishing principles in other ways. For example, moral principles might be established by intuition, or by non-moral principles, or by showing that the principles in question really are ultimate. Within teleological reasoning, or reasoning according to ends and means, one might try to show, as many philosophers have, that a given value (or set of values) functions as an ultimate end, and one may even try to show *why* it is ultimate by citing certain facts about the world, or certain characteristics of human nature. Plato, for example, argues that there is no higher principle than goodness itself, because it bestows value on all other things. Hedonists have argued that, when all is said and done, the only reason anyone could give for thinking anything valuable is that it gives pleasure. But one need not suppose that there is only one ultimate principle, for there may be several, as Aristotle, for example, maintained. Indeed, the American pragmatist John Dewey held that there are different values in different contexts and, according to his ends-means continuum, that values which function as ends in some contexts function as means in others. In a system which has more than one principle, it is usually thought that some method needs to be devised for resolving possible conflicts in principle, but Thomas Aquinas appeared to believe that ultimate ends need not conflict, for he thought that a person could always be positively oriented toward several ultimate goods without ever acting in opposition to any of them.

TRADITIONAL ETHICAL VIEWS

If the arguments against skepticism are sound and there are answers to moral questions, what are the answers? Or if, philosophically, we cannot hope to propose an answer to every particular question, how in general can we go about finding answers? Many philosophers have felt that, if, as a matter of principle, we could find out what *makes* right acts right or wrong acts wrong, we would then know how to make a determination. But there is a question about whether acts are right or wrong independently of how we or anyone may happen to reason about them, or whether they are right or wrong because they correspond to right reasoning. In this century, extreme objectivists, such as the act-deontologist and intuitionist H.H. Prichard, have argued that acts are right or wrong in and of themselves, regardless of how anyone might reason about them. Some utilitarians, such as G.E. Moore, also seem to have held this position. On such accounts, intuition or reasoning is thought to be a way of *finding out* which acts are right, but intuition or reasoning does not *make* them right.

Such extreme objectivism is unusual in the history of moral philosophy, for although most moral philosophers have assumed that there are correct answers to moral questions, they have not supposed that moral truths are wholly independent of minds or ideas. Most have recognized, indeed, that moral judgments are prescriptive in nature and not simply descriptive, and hence that they must issue from some authority, even if the authority of reason itself. However, in many ancient and medieval accounts, the authority of reason was not limited to human reason, for the entire universe was thought to have a rational structure to which human reason is subordinate. In traditional theological ethics, for example, the value of things was thought to be determined by God's reason, or by God's creative act, for God was supposed to have conferred his goodness upon the world. Such moral theories were ontological in the sense that being and value were understood to be correlative terms. That is, things were thought to have value according to their level of being in a hierarchy of nature, and things could be evil, or lack value, only by failing to actualize their potentiality, or by failing to achieve the perfection of the species to which they belong. Such reasoning has been the basis of self-realization theories offered by a number of philosophers from Plato and Aristotle to Augustine and Aquinas. However, many theories which today are called self-realization theories do not have this logical or ontological foundation, for they are often quite individualistic or relativistic and do not presuppose a belief in essential natures or transcendent values.

Not all traditional philosophers held the same views, of course. In ancient philosophy, the Epicureans, for example, were materialists who believed that man's natural end is pleasure in this life and that there is nothing beyond. The stoics believed in a natural law based upon one's place in the universe, but they were more concerned with attaining peace of mind by controlling one's emotions than they were with self-realization. Indeed, most subsequent philosophies can be classified according to the extent to which they have been influenced by ancient positions: by Platonism and/or Aristotelianism, on the one hand, or by stoicism and/or Epicureanism on the other. The rationalists in the seventeenth century and the idealists in the nineteenth century were influenced mostly by Platonism, although many of these theories also contained stoic elements. The eighteen-century British empiricists were influenced mostly by Epicureanism, thinking that morality could be founded on human emotions or sentiments. Thomas Hobbes, a seventeenth-century materialist, developed a social contract theory on the basis of a hedonistic account of human motivation.

According to traditional Platonic and neo-Platonic theory, our ability to know what is right or wrong is guaranteed by the divine illumination of human understanding, and in early modern rationalistic philosophies, such as those of Descartes, Leibniz and Spinoza, by innate ideas. A belief in innate ideas, however, or ideas which all persons share by nature, need not be based on a belief in God, or on principles which transcend human thinking, for they may be based upon an analysis of the structure of human thought itself. Thus Immanuel Kant claimed that there is a first principle of practical reasoning implicit in moral reasoning – although he certainly did not deny the existence of God. This principle, often called the principle of universalizability, was supposed to be a principle according to which everyone does in fact reason when reasoning morally. Kant held that, according to this principle, moral laws are maxims which can be universally applied.

Kant opposed the thinking of the eighteenth-century empiricists who, like the Epicureans, thought morality could be founded on

8

human feelings or sentiments. However, in the nineteenth century, the classical utilitarians, Bentham and Mill, did not so much deny Kant's principle of universalizability as they did amend and supplement it by arguing that moral reasoning requires a consideration of the consequences of actions, and that consequences, in turn, can be evaluated only on hedonistic grounds. Indeed, like Kant, Bentham and Mill hoped to lay the foundations for a science of ethics by uncovering the logic of moral reasoning.

Kant believed that his principle applied to all rational beings, not just humans, and Hegel, following Kant, spoke of Reason not simply as a human faculty but as an historically developing aspect of world Spirit of Mind. This latter doctrine expresses one of the elements of nineteenth-century idealism which, like Platonism, tended to see human reason as a finite expression of the Absolute. Many of the post-Hegelian movements in the nineteenth century were, however, a reaction to one or another of Hegel's doctrines. Kierkegaard, who is sometimes thought to be the first existentialist, accepted Hegel's idea of an Absolute, but he rejected Hegel's rationalistic account of ethics, thinking that persons are united with God, not by reason, but by choice. Marx accepted Hegel's idea of dialectical historical development, but he inverted Hegel's idealism in favor of a materialism which rejected ethics as a class-bound ideology. Hegel's influence also extended into the twentieth century. John Dewey, for instance, who was also influenced by Darwinism, modified Hegel's deterministic notion of historical evolution in favor of individual freedom.

TWENTIETH-CENTURY ETHICS

Marxism, pragmatism, and existentialism continued to be prominent moral philosophies in the twentieth century, as did utilitarianism and Thomism, although all these positions have been reformulated in an attempt to answer their critics. At the beginning of this century, however, a seemingly new type of philosophy, which came to be known as analytic philosophy, was introduced by Bertrand Russell and G.E. Moore. In ethics this philosophy was characterized by its analysis of moral reasoning and the meaning of ethical terms. Although philosophers have always been concerned with moral reasoning and language, a new distinction was drawn between what came to be called metaethics and normative or substantive ethics, the former focusing on the meaning of moral language, and the latter on the use of that language in making moral judgments. Thus in *Principia Ethica*, Moore claimed that the primary question of philosophic ethics is the *meaning* of good (a metaethical issue), not what kinds of things *are* good (a substantive issue). The debates which followed during the first half of this century were largely debates on metaethical questions.

Although Moore thought that the meaning of good was the central question of ethics, he argued that good could not be defined. Because of this, he also held that goodness is not a function of any other property, or variously that goodness cannot be proved by any process of reasoning whatsoever. This is what he meant by saying that goodness must be intuited, but he thought that other moral properties such as rightness could be derived from goodness by a process of utilitarian reasoning. Other philosophers, sometimes called deontologists, thought that rightness or obligatoriness was the fundamental moral concept. H.H. Prichard held that the rightness or wrongness of each and every particular act must be intuited, on the ground that there are no other properties which make acts right. Sir David Ross also held that rightness is fundamental, but he thought that moral rules, not particular instances of rightness, must be intuited, since he believed that moral rules cannot be derived from any higher principle. Thus much of the debate focused on whether good or right is the basic concept of ethics and whether particular acts could be justified by rules or principles.

In the 1930s, the logical positivists made an impact on metaethical theory by rejecting the basic assumption of intuitionism: namely the assumption that moral terms refer to moral properties. The positivists argued that the primary function of value-terms is to express human emotions and that, because of this, moral utterances are neither true nor false. The positivists made a fundamental distinction between facts and values – between cognitive, fact-stating propositions and non-cognitive evaluations – which has plagued moral philosophy ever since.

From within a quite different philosophic tradition, the existentialist philosopher Jean-Paul Sartre argued that moral judgments could not be determined by rules or principles and that value is created by human choice. Thus, following World War II, moral philosophy seemed to be dominated by the metaethical positions of intuitionism, emotivism and decisionalism, all of which greatly restricted the place and function of reason in ethics, and the latter of which seemed to be entirely skeptical of moral truth. These views had a powerful influence upon traditional theories like utilitarianism and Kantianism. J.J.C. Smart used emotivism to support his preference for utilitarianism, and R.M. Hare combined the Sartrean idea of choosing moral principles with a Kantian requirement to universalize that decision. Indeed, in the 1950s and 1960s a new version of utilitarianism developed, called 'rule utilitarianism,' in which moral rules, of the type advocated by an intuitionist like Ross, were supposed to be justified by the principle of utility. Rule utlitarianism is a two-staged theory in which, at the first stage, moral rules are justified by utility and, at the second stage, particular actions are justified by means of the rules.

After World War II, a new kind of analysis, called 'ordinary language analysis', provided the impetus for a new movement in ethics which came to be known as 'the good reasons approach'. The main contention of this approach was that people do give reasons for their moral beliefs and actions and that some of these reasons are considered good or sufficient. Since, in ordinary discussion, it is appropriate to ask for or give reasons in ethics, it would seem that moral evaluation is not simply a matter of intuition, emotion or choice. The positivist distinction between facts and values was also called into question because it seemed that actions could be justified by social practices or, in other words, by societal facts. While metaethicists continued to debate whether or not, on the basis of promises or contracts, values can be derived from facts, John Rawls proposed a social contract theory according to which principles of justice are based upon fair consent. Rawls's theory sparked a renewed interest in substantive moral theories which extended beyond philosophic circles. Concurrently, the development of game theory, utility theory and social welfare theory also added new techniques to ethical analysis.

It was during this latter period, during and following the war in Vietnam, that applied philosophy came into existence as a distinct movement. Applied philosophy is concerned with clarifying moral issues and determining how general principles can be applied to concrete cases, whereas traditional substantive ethics was primarily concerned with defending abstract, general principles. Some of the issues of applied philosophy were in fact raised by the generation of

11

student demonstrators who in the late 1960s and early 1970s demanded 'relevance' in higher education by calling for classes on peace, environmental issues and social justice. Problems of medical ethics and business ethics also began to gain widespread attention outside the universities, and, as a result, more and more philosophers began to address such issues.

Although philosophers engaged in applied ethics have sometimes been ridiculed and even ignored by their more theoretically oriented colleagues, the growth of the applied ethics movement has posed a challenge to theoretical ethics. Existing ethical theory appears to be faced with the alternative of providing effective solutions to practical problems or remaining ineffective and perhaps even irrelevant to practical affairs. Theoretical ethics also appears to be threatened by the possibility that applied ethics may continue to grow and prosper without theoretical guidance, for the issues of applied ethics are sometimes argued within the contexts of popular debate without any explicit attempt to apply theories at all. At other times theories are applied mechanically or uncritically without any attempt to determine whether they are appropriate or correct. But this is precisely where, it appears, there is an opportunity for wedding theoretical and applied ethics: for using application as a means of testing and improving theory, and for enabling applied ethics to rise above mere casuistry or mere application to the level of philosophy itself. As things stand, applied ethics has not yet visibly benefited from the most recent developments in ethical theory, and ethical theory has not yet been visibly improved by considering problems of application.

THE CURRENT STATE OF ETHICAL THEORY

The image of a philosopher working like John Stuart Mill or John Dewey, developing a theory which addresses important social issues, is not, by and large, consistent with the activities of moral philosophers in the twentieth century. In this century, philosophers have been concerned primarily with abstract issues concerning the objectivity of moral judgments and the validity of moral reasoning. Anglo-American philosophy in particular moved away from philosophy's traditional functions of providing bases for psychological understanding and social criticism in an attempt to achieve clarity about the nature of ethics, science, and even philosophy itself. Analytic philosophers sought to distinguish philosophy from the emerging sciences of psychology and sociology for apparently much the same reasons as early modern philosophers sought to distinguish physical science from religion. However, instead of trying to show that philosophy studies a different aspect of the world, or that philosophy studies the world in a different way, analytic philosophers generally concluded that philosophy does not compete with science in studying the world at all. The prevailing view of analytic philosophers was that, while the various sciences attempt to gain positive knowledge of the world, philosophy is a metadiscipline which analyzes the language of science.

Views about ethics and even about philosophy were therefore influenced by views about science itself. Science provided the models for truth and objectivity which were used to judge other disciplines. The view of science among analytic philosophers during the first half of this century was that scientific claims are closely tied to observable data. Expressing such a view, the logical positivists argued that the very meaning of a proposition is dependent upon its possible verification or falsification in experience. They viewed ethical statements as being non-scientific because ethical statements, being emotive, are not descriptive of experience. They claimed therefore that ethical statements are non-cognitive or meaningless. On the basis of this view of science, it was simply impossible to hold that any substantive ethical theory could have objective validity.

The possibility of discovering universal moral principles was also seriously questioned by anthropologists who not only called attention to a wide variety of moral practices but also sought to explain them by a theory of cultural relativism. Given the large number of sub-groups within cultures and the vast number of individual differences within groups, it was not difficult to extend ethical relativism to individuals. What such a theory notes, of course, is that each culture or individual has opinions about what is right or wrong, but the theory provides no basis for claiming that any opinion is or even could be objectively true.

A more general supposition of science in conflict with ethics is causal determinism. Of course, the idea that physical explanation is deterministic, or that causal determinism conflicts with the ethical supposition of freedom and responsibility, was not new to this

13

century; but determinism began to win widespread acceptance in psychology and the social sciences. Freudianism and behaviorism in particular seemed to imply that human freedom is an illusion, and Marxism explicitly relegated ethics to a deterministic process, holding that ethical theory is an instrument of class exploitation.

Thus persons attempting to do substantive ethics found themselves in a hostile environment. Given the inherent difficulty of the issues and the inadequacy of existing theory, excursions into substantive ethics were practically bound to have limited success. However, more recent philosophic views of science have challenged the positivist thesis that scientific knowledge is directly linked to observation. A variety of theories in the philosophy of science have pointed to the importance of shared assumptions, cumulative efforts among scientists, and internal coherence, scope and freedom from incompleteness as conditions for the objectivity of scientific theories. In short, scientific knowledge itself is now generally viewed as being much more theory-laden than previously supposed. The objectivity of science seems to rest more on good reasons, the consistency of shared data and interpersonal agreement than upon uninterpreted observations.

These changing views of science have created a new climate of opinion in which ethical theory can be reassessed. If the theoretical interpretation of data plays such an important role in science, then one may suppose that it may do so in ethics as well – without any apparent loss of objectivity – or at least without there being less objectivity in ethics than in science. Human need, reason and agreement may be regarded as elements which give ethics an objective grounding, and the question of how ethical theories can be tested may be answered by the specification of such grounds.

Language analysis has also lost much of its previous dominance, and cultural relativism has begun to look increasingly less appealing in a world where common moral problems seem to overshadow cultural differences. The determinist theories which threatened the assumption of human freedom now appear to be incapable of adequately explaining many human activities: for example, human ingenuity in the arts and sciences, and human adaptability in developing new forms of social organization.

The demand for applied ethics, therefore, appears to have come at an appropriate yet troubling time. Some of the blocks to substantive ethics seem to have been removed – partly because of the growing interest in application – and philosophers have become less cautious in attacking practical issues. At the same time, the generation of philosophers called upon to do applied ethics has had little training in such work. On the contrary, they were typically taught that application is not an appropriate philosophical task. In applied ethics, philosophers today are trying to resolve a variety of vital issues, but there is no widely accepted theory to support their investigations. They must defend not only their substantive positions but also their theoretical approaches and sometimes even the entire enterprise in which they are involved! Questions about the objectivity of moral views, the domain of ethical theory, its methodology, and its relationship to application are still fundamental issues.

THEORY AND APPLICATION

The demands placed on ethical theory in the latter part of the twentieth century are not only different from those of previous centuries, but also from those of the early part of this century. One characteristic of ethical theory in this century is that it lost continuity with changes in society and in the various sciences. It also lost much of its continuity with traditional theories. Other sciences such as economics developed sophisticated models of rationality and choice independently of philosophical ethics, but philosophical theory generally ignored such developments. It appears that philosophers need to develop a sense of objectivity in ethics which takes into account current theoretical advances in other sciences and current social demands.

John Rawls's *A Theory of Justice*, published in 1971, was a significant attempt to construct a substantive ethical theory which recognizes these changes. The theory lays down basic principles and a methodology supporting the principles. In his method, Rawls identifies firmly held convictions, such as the rejection of slavery, as data against which theory can be tested. Such convictions may be modified by the theory, but as part of a process of mutual interaction between theory and convictions. Rawls also appeals to general principles of rationality derived from recent work in game theory and microeconomics. In general the work of Rawls signaled (1) a new confidence in substantive theory, (2) reworked conceptions of

15

objectivity and data in ethics, and (3) a view of ethical theory as a way of ordering basic convictions. Most importantly, from the standpoint of practical ethics, his theory seemed to lend itself to a wide variety of applications from medicine to business and law.

Nonetheless, Rawls's theory appears to suffer from a number of faults. First of all, the theory is presented in a highly abstract form. This is typical of traditional ethical theories, but the abstract principles of traditional theories could be given more specific interpretation because they usually reflected the social practices of their times. By contrast, Rawls defends his principles on the basis of assumptions which diverge widely from current practices. For example, he assumes full compliance with the principles he lays down, although in practice such compliance cannot be assumed. He also leaves key terms undefined or inadequately defined: questions of measurement and prediction are usually ignored. Indeed, the theory abstracts from time, assuming that application takes place instantaneously, once and for all. Full knowledge of the general findings of the sciences is assumed and the domain of the theory is restricted to a nation state. In short, Rawls's theory is not easily applied, at least as it currently stands.

In effect, in the recent history of ethics, theory has not been developed with an eye to application, and practice has not been adequately guided by theory. In the natural sciences and in economics, by contrast, application has been guided by theory, and theory has been directed toward application. In economics, much as in the natural sciences, the basic approaches and principles have been widely shared and taught to students as a common body of knowledge. Most of applied economics is based upon similar theoretical foundations in microeconomics. Different schools in microeconomics tend to use similar styles of presentation and argumentation, and economists often refer to the same basic data when defending interpretations and theories. However, in philosophic ethics, there has been a significant gap between theoretical ethics and applied ethics, and there is little consensus about principles, the relevance of data, the appropriate methods of theory construction and testing, or even what it would mean to say that a theory is objectively grounded or true.

Yet the current demand for the application of ethical theories provides an impetus for constructing new theories, or modifying older theories, which will take into account conditions of application. Such theories may be tested by their ability to resolve problems of application: by their potential for generating agreement based upon rational considerations, objective data, and generally accepted principles of action. One would expect an adequate theory to be capable of informing action consistently over time and between agents. Such a theory would enable persons to form basically similar patterns of approach to the solution of practical problems. Internal theoretical consistency or mere plausibility would not be sufficient.

Be that as it may, it is not likely that theory will provide adequate guidance for application in the near future. Under ideal conditions, theory would be used to resolve difficult cases, insure consistency, provide assurance that the correct path has been followed, and generate understanding of the basis of judgments. But current theory does not adequately serve any of these functions. It seems that, as Rawls has remarked, ethical theory is still in a primitive condition.

But work in applied fields cannot wait for theory to advance to the point of providing clear guidance. Indeed, theory will probably not advance significantly unless current investigations into practical issues reveal areas of agreement and principles on which philosophers can rely in reconstructing their theories. It may be the case that a twofold approach to ethics is required. On the one hand, philosophers may need to continue their investigations in abstract ethical and metaethical theory – but with the idea of application in mind. On the other, application may need to proceed without complete dependence on exisiting theory, but not without concern for the generalizability of its arguments and conclusions. The concerns of application naturally shift the focus away from high-level theoretical principles to lower-level principles capable of yielding concrete results. Such lower-level principles are apt to be less controversial, and they may also lend themselves to being supported by a wide variety of theories. Principles of truth-telling, promise-keeping, or self-realization, for example, may be supported by virtually every theory, and they are also bases of agreement which can be used to guide action. Such lower-level principles seem more directly applicable than higher-level principles, but the philosophic task of justifying them and determining the range of their application would still remain.

Applied ethics, unlike theoretical ethics, cannot ignore actual

17

conditions. Since applied ethics is directed toward the solution of controversial issues, it must assume disagreement and hence seek procedures for moving from disagreement to agreement. Applied ethics, therefore, must address the question of practical constraints in the form of popular or institutional obstacles to change. However, the problems of a practitioner, such as a health care professional, are different from those of an applied philosopher, for the practitioner faces such constraints directly, whereas the philosopher can consider how such constraints may be weakened or removed. In considering problems of application, the philosopher cannot simply assume existing or ideal states of affairs, for he must consider how actual conditions can be changed to bring about desirable results. Emphasis on actual conditions points up a need for interaction between philosophers, social scientists, and practitioners in other fields.

In summary, theoretical ethics and applied ethics are not likely to advance significantly if philosophers who conduct investigations on one level continue to assume that their approach is somehow vindicated by the weakness of the other. Nonetheless, for the time being, investigations into theoretical ethics and applied ethics may need to continue in relative isolation while each attempts to build upon the successes of the other. Eventually theory should gain support from consensus reached on the applied level, and applied ethics should benefit from the extension of accepted principles to controversial cases. In the process of development, theory will almost certainly become more complex, including intermediate rules which specify how principles can be applied. In moving closer to problems of application, theory may need to distinguish various phases or levels of moral reasoning in order to account for background conditions, such as institutional forms, which affect the range of reasonable choice. In general, theory needs to become more responsive to the complexities of genuine moral problems, and application needs to benefit from the general understanding, rational consistency and coordination of judgments which theory can provide.

I
CONTEMPORARY ETHICAL THEORY

INTRODUCTION

It would seem that the very idea of applied ethics supposes that there are ethics – in the form of ethical theories or statements of general principles – which can be applied. If so, what are these theories or principles, and how can we know which of them should be applied? The essays in this section attempt to answer the first of these questions by explaining the dominant ethical theories of our time, and they also go some distance toward answering the second question by surveying the arguments in support of each theory. The authors, who are leading exponents of the theories they present, explain their own points of view, but they also outline general positions and theoretical issues which divide the schools they represent, as well as differences which separate them from the advocates of other theories. They also comment on how their theories have been applied, or might be applied, to practical moral issues.

The theories explained in the following essays are dominant in the sense that they have received a considerable amount of attention from academic philosophers of the western world, and because they are living philosophies, in the sense that, whether consciously or unconsciously, they are in fact applied by large numbers of people. For example, utilitarian calculations, in the form of considering the values of consequences, or attempting to determine the efficiency or inefficiency of actions, enter into a wide variety of deliberations which pertain to government legislation, economic planning, or even strategies in war. Thomistic ethics, which, understandably, has been examined, defended and applied by Catholics more than any other group, is the basis of what many people understand as 'natural law' theory, and it has been used to support right-to-life arguments on questions of abortion and capital punishment. Contractarianism, as developed by John Locke, is thought to provide a theoretical foundation for the US Government, and it is also used to support the ideas and practices of capitalism. Existentialism has had considerable influence upon popular thinking in emphasizing the importance of individual persons and personal choice, and it has also left its mark upon recent psychology, theology and literature. Marxism, of course, in one form or another, is the official philosophy of various political parties and governments, and pragmatism is often supposed to express the attitudes and habits of English-speaking peoples – even if not always their professed moral views.

However, there are ethical theories not represented in the following essays which are often expressed in popular thinking but are not widely defended in philosophic circles today. Ethical egoism, for example, although often criticized by contemporary philosophers, is not usually defended by them, and ethical intuitionism, which flourished in academic circles during the first half of this century, is now generally supposed to be practically dead. Situation ethics, or agapism, as advocated by Joseph Fletcher, was influential among theologists in recent decades, but it has never received widespread support from philosophers.

The question of the truth of these theories may be addressed negatively by saying that, if any of them is true, all of the others must be false, since they do appear to contradict one another, at least on some issues. If utilitarianism is correct in holding that the rightness or wrongness of actions is determined only by consequences and never by intentions, then Thomism must be wrong in holding that rights and duties are determined by intentions, not consequences. If both utilitarians and Thomists are correct in holding that moral acts are absolutely right or wrong, then pragmatists and contractarians must be wrong in thinking that moral truth is relative or conventional. Or if persons have freedom of choice, as Thomists and pragmatists believe, then Marxists must be wrong in thinking that human behavior is determined.

One could go on multiplying examples of contradictions or apparent contradictions to support the thesis that most of the ethical theories advocated by philosophers must be false, but that consideration alone would not take one very far toward determining which of the theories is true, or which of them should be applied. In point of fact, all of them seem to contain some truth, since, from a descriptive point of view, all of them emphasize one or another element of popular moral thinking. If one takes an all-or-nothing view of the matter, then one will be inclined to accept one theory to the exclusion of all others. However, as the following essays amply illustrate, it is not always easy to determine exactly where one theory begins and another ends – or perhaps more precisely, where it should – since, in the process of development, practically all theories try to take into account the doctrines of seemingly opposing views. For example, given the different interpretations of utilitarianism among utilitarians, or of Thomism among Thomists, one begins to see that the elements of one theory may be absorbed into another by subordinating some principles to others, or by reinterpreting the meaning of the concepts involved. Utilitarians sometimes debate whether it is consequences pure and simple which determine the rightness or wrongness of actions, or whether it is intended or predictable consequences, while Thomists sometimes seem to take consequences seriously in applying the so-called principle of double effect. The point is that intentions and consequences may both enter into moral reasoning but perhaps in different ways, and it is certainly one of the jobs of moral philosophy to make such distinctions, under whatever name they may appear.

It is just possible, therefore, that none of the theories described in the following essays is wholly true or wholly false, but that each contains elements which must be included within a more comprehensive philosophic view. To say this, however, is not to say how such a theory should be constructed, or which elements within it will occupy the positions of first principles or subordinate rules, for these are the very sorts of issues which need to be resolved in the ongoing work of moral philosophy. These issues should point up the importance of philosophical analysis and its relevance to application: of considering various theoretical alternatives and combinations of ideas as schematizations of the ways in which moral thinking functions, and of attempting to discover how, or what extent, such schemata can be generalized or must be restricted in application.

2
UTILITARIANISM AND ITS APPLICATIONS

J.J.C. Smart

HEDONISTIC ACT UTILITARIANISM

I shall take the paradigm of utilitarianism to be hedonistic act utilitarianism, a theory that has come down to us through Jeremy Bentham[1] and Henry Sidgwick[2]. (There has been some controversy as to how far J.S. Mill's *Utilitarianism* fits this paradigm.[3]) According to this paradigm, what it is right to do on any occasion is to maximize the total happiness (now and at all future times) of all sentient creatures, whether humans, other animals, or extra-terrestrials (should we ever have to do with these last). The theory has an obvious appeal. What could be better than to maximize happiness? Any theory that was not equivalent to hedonistic act utilitarianism would imply that on occasion one should make the world less happy than it would otherwise be. By concentrating on consequences of actions the theory contrasts with theories that assess the rightness of actions by their motives (e.g. whether they arise out of respect for persons) or by whether they are in conformity with particular but nevertheless ethically ultimate rules ('Keep promises,' 'Tell the truth,' and so on) or by whether they are in accordance with essential human nature (whatever that is). The theory also contrasts with theories that say that there are basic human rights, since giving a person his or her rights need not always maximize total happiness. Similarly it contrasts with theories that stress fairness or equal distribution of happiness. This is not to say of course that a hedonistic act utilitarian, in a capacity as legislator, may not enact a system of *legal* rights or of equal distribution (not

24

of happiness but, for example, of money). The setting up of such a *legal* system may well lead to maximization of happiness.

The hedonistic act utilitarian principle, as stated above, is a criterion of right action. Utilitarianism needs to give us more than that: it needs to give us a method of ethical decision. At first sight it might be thought that the method would simply be to try to do on any occasion the act that most probably satisfies the criterion. However the most probably maximizing act may be one that gives a smaller probability of very great disaster. There is something wrong therefore with this idea. What the utilitarian should do is to maximize *expected utility*. Let A_1, A_2, A_3, . . . A_n be the possible future courses of the universe which will occur with probabilities, $p_1, p_2, p_3, . . . p_n$ respectively if I do action a. Let $V(A_i)$ be the total net happiness in A_i. Then the expected utility of a is $\sum_1^n p_i V(A_i)$.

The need to consider choices between infinite future courses of the universe might be thought to make utilitarianism impracticable. However it is plausible that the expected ethical consequences of our actions usually diminish rapidly to zero like ripples in a pond. Whether Jim marries Mary or Martha it will probably not affect the general happiness a thousand years hence. Or if it does, the probability of it mattering one way is balanced by the probability of it mattering the other way. In some cases, the relevant consequences of actions have values that do not diminish rapidly to zero, but this need not prevent utilitarian comparisons. Assuming that each future generation, even if these went on to infinity (not that this is really possible), would be on the whole happy rather than unhappy, it is clear that it would maximize utility to avoid destroying all life on earth.

As I construe it, hedonistic act utilitarianism is a *normative* theory. It is not an account of our common ethical beliefs, since it may well conflict with them, nor is it put forward as an explanation of them. Indeed if the theory did not conflict in some measure with ordinarily accepted ethical ideas there would be little practical importance in putting it forward.[4] Since hedonistic utilitarianism is put forward as a normative theory, the proponent of it must resist supposed refutations of it that depend on its conflict with common sense reactions.

UTILITARIANISM AND MOTIVES FOR ACTIONS

Hedonistic act utilitarianism says that the right action is the one that maximizes total happiness. By 'happiness' here is meant a sum of pleasures. (Unhappiness is negative happiness and displeasure is negative pleasure. I prefer to say 'displeasure' rather than 'pain,' since 'pain' is ambiguous. In one sense of these words pleasure and pain are not opposites. An itch or a feeling of loneliness can be unpleasant, but neither is a pain.) Utilitarianism as defined in terms of maximization of pleasure is a case of ethical hedonism. Ethical hedonism is a doctrine of how we ought to act and must not be confused with psychological hedonism, which is a doctrine about how we in fact act. According to psychological hedonism, which is false, we always act for the sake of our own pleasure. Unfortunately Bentham muddled up the two doctrines. Since often one can maximize the general happiness only by reducing one's own pleasure, if psychological hedonism were true we could not always do what is demanded by ethical hedonism.[5] Indeed since most of our pleasures come from satisfaction of desires for things other than pleasure, even to maximize one's own happiness one must cultivate desires for things other than one's own pleasure. I take the utilitarian principle to be the expression of an *overriding* desire or attitude (of benevolence), and this is not incompatible with the existence of subordinate desires, which in some cases may even conflict with the overriding one.[6] Our overriding attitude is what predominates 'in a cool hour,' to use Bishop Butler's expression,[7] and by which we act in such a way as to strengthen or weaken subordinate desires.

As a utilitarian, therefore, I appeal to the motive of generalized benevolence, and hope that if the theory can be stated lucidly it will appeal to those who have generalized benevolence as an overriding attitude. This may enable already benevolent persons to exercise their benevolence with clearer heads in the light of a definite ethical theory. Nevertheless the utilitarian will not suppose that his overriding attitude ought always or even generally be made the motive for action.[8] Happiness mainly comes from satisfying all sorts of more humdrum desires. Furthermore there are motives such as family affection, loyalty to an institution, and so on that can be more powerful in affecting action, and provided that on the whole they tend in the right direction then on utilitarian grounds the utilitarian will encourage actions from these motives. As Sidgwick remarked, universal benevolence is not the only right or the best motive for action. Similarly, it is not possible or even desirable, to be calculating consequences all the time, and a utilitarian will normally act according to common sense rules, such as to keep promises, so long as they tend towards the maximization of happiness. On the other hand suppose that rules conflict, or for some other reason the utilitarian does think it worth while to calculate consequences. In such a case if the utilitarian has good reason to believe that on the particular occasion in question conformity to these rules will not maximize happiness, then he or she will ignore the rules: he or she will take these as mere rules of thumb.[9]

This attitude conflicts with so-called 'rule utilitarianism' according to which we do not judge actions directly by consequences, but by their conformity with rules, these rules being judged by the consequences of everyone obeying them being better than the consequences of everyone obeying some alternative rule. 'Rule utilitarianism' is contrasted with 'act utilitarianism'. The act utilitarian will object that if he or she knows that in a particular case disobeying a generally optimific rule will maximize happiness, it would be sheer rule worship to obey the rule.[10]

An act utilitarian, on his or her own principles, will not want to think as a utilitarian all the time. Moreover he or she will have a genuine worry about whether it is right to try to persuade the general public to become utilitarians. It may be that this would merely weaken people's propensities to act in accordance with ordinary morality without making them utilitarians so that the end result would be that they would behave in a *less* utilitarian manner. It might be that even if they tried to act in a utilitarian manner they would fail to do so because of lack of skill in calculating consequences, or because of incorrect empirical beliefs. There can be something elitist about act utilitarianism. (Though I am not one of those who believe 'elitist' to be a naughty word!) In the context of nineteenth-century society Sidgwick was probably right in urging extreme tact in a utilitarian's relations with common sense morality. In the context of the late twentieth century, when there is danger of the ultimate catastrophe of nuclear annihilation, not to mention huge problems of overpopulation and famine, I am inclined to think that on utilitarian grounds a utilitarian should try to get utilitarian thinking adopted very widely. Common-sense rules may now give less of an approximation to utilitarian conduct than they used to do, at least in certain overwhelmingly important areas of application. Moreover, as Onora O'Neill has suggested to me, the early Benthamite utilitarians were felt to provide a progressive and reforming critique of existing institutions, at a time when political and economic institutions were inappropriate to an emerging industrial and social order. Unclarities about what happiness was and how to maximize it were less crucial than they have often seemed to non-utilitarian philosophers.

A utilitarian will assess the goodness or badness of dispositions and motives for actions by the utility of praise or blame of the actions. Utility of an action may not correspond exactly or at all with the utility of praise or blame of it.[11] Failure to observe this distinction may cause people to overestimate the clash between common sense ethics and utilitarianism. Thus common sense says that it is not wrong to omit to do supererogatory actions, while a utilitarian cannot admit the notion of supererogation, because nothing can be better than to maximize. However he or she can admit to a distinction between acts that are wrong but for which an agent ought not to be blamed or punished and acts that are wrong and for which an agent ought to be blamed or punished. A mother may do a wrong act misguidedly but from affection for her child. To blame her might weaken affectionate feelings in the mother and in others. Another example comes from a recent proposal by Michael Slote to modify consequentialism by replacing maximization by 'satisficing', that is, bringing about a certain level of good results.[12] Surely, the utilitarian will say, if one has a choice between satisficing and maximizing one ought to maximize.[13] Nevertheless one may often advise others or decide oneself to aim only at satisficing. Trying to maximize may be too much of a strain and the agent may give up the effort and instead act either from impulse or from conventional rules. It may therefore be useful for the agent to praise satisficers and not blame them for not maximizing. I therefore suspect that the appeal of the satisficing theory, at least for some people, may come from confusing questions of the rightness or wrongness of actions with questions of praise or blame of them. Of course satisficing is more in accordance with utilitarianism if it is taken as an economic doctrine. It is always better to have more happiness rather than less, but there is a level of wealth above which an increase produces no significant increase in happiness, or may even produce a decrease in happiness.

CO-OPERATION

Situations of the type of the well-known Prisoner's Dilemma (except for all participants being actuated by universal benevolence instead of self-interest) provide some difficulty for act utilitarianism. Consider the following simplified case. Suppose that there is an important university committee with 100 eligible participants, all of whom, if they attend, will be sure to vote beneficially on an important issue, which is such that it is important that most of the eligible participants attend. If one of the members is an act utilitarian he or she may reason that most members will behave conventionally, as they have been brought up to do, and will turn up. As he or she has valuable other work to get on with, he or she will go on to deduce that the best outcome will be achieved if he or she stays away. But what if all the 100 are act utilitarians? Perhaps there will not even be a quorum and the consequences will be very bad.

In the past I have suggested a solution of the following sort.[14] What is needed is what game theorists call a 'mixed strategy'. Supposing that each of the 100 members are act utilitarians, each member should give himself or herself a certain small probability of not attending. If $V(p)$ is the expected utility of everyone giving himself or herself the probability p of not attending, the value of p will be that for which $(d/dp)V(p) = 0$. This will indeed produce better results than either everyone attending (the rule utilitarian solution) or of no one attending. Suppose the favored value of p is 1/50, so that the best results will be achieved if exactly two members stay away. However, if each gives himself or herself a probability of 1/50 of staying away, sometimes more and sometimes fewer than two will stay away. (It is rarely that in one hundred throws of a penny 'heads' will come up exactly fifty times.) For these, and other reasons which I shall not mention, it would be better if each utilitarian could obey a rule prescribing that exactly two absent themselves from the meeting, or agree in some way to behave in this way. Arthur Kuflik has recently argued that these considerations point to the superiority of a form of rule utilitarianism.[15] However, as I have urged, there are other clear cases in which act utilitarianism seems to be superior.

The simplest and best solution might be for the 100 members to agree on two particular persons who would absent themselves. This however would require an antecedent desire to co-operate not reducible to the act utilitarian principle itself. We must suppose an independent desire to co-operate with other agents who are motivated by generalized benevolence and are also motivated to co-operate. (Here generalized benevolence must be thought of as the desire to maximize expected utility given the actual behaviour of non-co-operating agents.) I am therefore now attracted to the 'co-operative utilitarianism' recently put forward by Donald Regan. This theory is in the *spirit* of act utilitarianism and is quite different from rule utilitarianism. Indeed it reduces to act utilitarianism in those cases (which are very common) in which the agent does not need to co-operate with other agents.

(In such cases he or she may very well depend on the predictable behavior of other agents, as when travelling by aeroplane one depends on the actions of the pilot, without of course co-operating in actually flying the aeroplane.)

Regan's theory, expounded in his important book, *Utilitarianism and Co-operation*,[16] is roughly that in a situation requiring co-operation, each agent should co-operate with other co-operators so as to maximize utility.[17] The behavior of non-co-operators will be an empirical fact to be taken into account like any other. The difficulty arises from a sort of circularity in the co-operative situation. Without going into Regan's own subtle and complex analysis, let me merely remark that we could think of a group of co-operating agents who behave according to Regan's principles as a single supra-personal agent which behaves in a simply act utilitarian way.[18] After all, different parts of a single brain co-operate with one another, and it need not be objectionably metaphysical to think of a group of co-operating brains (not necessarily in causal interaction with one another) as a single spatially scattered super-brain. In cases in which co-operation is not needed, as when a rescuer dives into a river, with no other helper in the vicinity, the supra-personal agent will reduce to a single personal one and the theory will reduce to ordinary act utilitarianism.[19]

THE PROBLEMS OF MEASUREMENT OF HAPPINESS AND DESIRE

It has frequently been objected to utilitarianism that it requires us to talk of quantities of pleasure or happiness, and the meaningfulness of this has seemed dubious. A purely ordinal comparison of pleasures will not suffice – nor even would a purely ordinal comparison of whole possible future courses of the universe. This is because the notion of expected utility requires a quantitative comparison. Values of futures need to be multiplied by values of probabilities. Probabilities need to be measured too, but as will be noted below there is in principle a way of measuring subjective probabilities. It might be objected, as I have myself done in the past, that what is needed is objective probabilities, but I now think that this would be a mistake. Utilitarian decision depends on the injunction to maximize expected utility, and as far as probabilities are concerned what more would the agent have to go on than his or her own subjective probabilities? Indeed 'subjective' is a little misleading here, because these probabilities satisfy criteria of rationality.

The problem of measurement of happiness is of course related to that of the conceptual analysis of the notion of happiness. I shall take happiness to consist of a sum of pleasures (treating displeasures as negative pleasures). Pleasure is not a sort of sensation. It is true that some pleasant experiences are the havings of sensations, but other experiences can be pleasant too: for example, the experience of solving a problem. Again the pleasure of listening to music is not just the pleasure of having a succession of auditory sensations. The experience of having a pain is normally a displeasure, but it is not of course the only sort of displeasure. In the case of a person, I shall take it that a pleasure is an experience that the person would prefer to have, rather than not have, if he or she could disregard all consequences or concomitants of it.[20] In the case of non-human animals in order to apply the notion of pleasure we need some sort of analogical thinking, since the notion of preference itself gets hazy as we go down the evolutionary scale. It is hard to deny that there is some sense in which a chicken prefers the experience it gets when scratching around in a poultry yard to that it gets living overcrowded in a tiny cage. (Not just that *simpliciter* it prefers scratching around to living overcrowded in a tiny cage. One could give better behavioral evidence for this, of course.) Perhaps we could get a grip on preference for its own sake for linguistically competent humans, and extend it to non-humans by means of some sort of neurological or electro-encephalographic evidence. This is rather speculative, of course.

31

The qualification 'for its own sake' is important. A hedonist will hold that all pleasures are intrinsically good, even though some may be extrinsically bad – they may cause intrinsic displeasures. Normally a hedonist will prefer pleasures that are also extrinsically good: 'fecund' ones, as Bentham put it.

The measurement of happiness thus depends on preferences between stretches of consciousness for their own sake. Now the notion of desire for something for its own sake (and hence of preference) is a more difficult and dubious one than is the notion of desire *simpliciter*. The former also depends on the latter. So it is necessary to look at the question of measurement of desire first. First let us consider comparing the desires of a single person. (*Intra*-personal preferences.) F.P. Ramsey devised a method for measuring these. (See F.P. Ramsey's essay 'Truth and Probability'[21] and the account in Richard Jeffrey, *The Logic of Decision*.[22]) Admittedly these measurements would not be easy to carry out in practice. Moreover I think that the method should not be regarded operationistically as *defining* strength of desire, but as indirectly giving meaning to the notion *via* the hypothetico-deductive method. That desires have certain strengths should be regarded as hypotheses, though often more or less testable by Ramsey's methods.

In Ramsey's and Jeffrey's accounts one may get the impression that preferences are for truth of one proposition over another, but since the truth of any such proposition has consequences far into the future, I think that what we compare on any occasion is a weighted array of a whole branching and ever re-branching set of possible worlds going off indefinitely into the future. If someone prefers white wine to red wine on a certain occasion this may be not only due to the taste of white as compared with the taste of red but to future things too, such as the greater probability of red wine upsetting the person's stomach. An agent may assume that he or she need not take into account too many probabilistic branchings of the set of future possible worlds, because the probabilities of unconsidered future events are unaffected by the agent's action or else because although the probabilities may be affected the desiredness of different branchings of future possibilities may on average be the same. The exact instant as which a couple conceive an offspring is clearly affected by trivial decisions (e.g. exactly when to go to bed), and this will affect just which sperm in fact reaches an ovum. This will affect the particular assortment of genes from mother and father, and may have momentous consequences. Suppose that instead of Hitler a boy (or girl) with different genes had been born! You or I would not have existed if quite trivial differences had occurred in our parents' lives. Still, we don't bother about this. The probability of a trivial event having bad remote consequences is balanced by the probability of it having good ones.

Ramsey's theory gives us only a way of quantitively comparing *intra*-personal preferences. We need of course also to make *inter*-personal comparisons. We need to be able to calibrate one person's preference scale against another's. J.C. Harsanyi has proposed relying on a general similarity postulate, which has to be accepted a priori.[23] That is, it would be unwarranted to give different values to the preferences of Smith and Robinson when they are in similar situations or if they show different behavior but these differences can be allowed for.[24] Harsanyi gives the example of someone who will work for a lower wage than will another because he has a physique that makes him mind heavy work much less than does the other. Donald Davidson has argued[25] that the very process of interpreting another's language is at the same time a process of ascribing beliefs and desires to the other, and that each does this on a preponderance of agreed values and beliefs, however much in detail they may differ about these. But comparisons of strength of belief and desire are implicit in our attribution of them. So according to Davidson we need no further argument to make inter-personal comparisons.

I am not sure how far Davidson helps the utilitarian here. There is a question for Davidson about whether propositional attitudes can be ascribed to non-human animals, because his theory of ascription of propositional attitudes is so closely tied to his theory of interpretation of language. Unless the utilitarian wants to disregard animals altogether he needs a cruder and more widely applicable notion of preference. Surely a battery hen would prefer scratching in the farm yard to living overcrowded in a tiny cage, in *some* sense of 'prefer.' Perhaps this cruder notion can be got analogically from the linguistically related one.

The measurement of preference for its own sake would seem to present greater problems than that of measurement of preference *simpliciter*. We need counterfactual assumptions about what a person would prefer if he or she could ignore the concomitants or effects of stretches of pleasant or unpleasant experience. Perhaps estimates of these can be made indirectly by applying common sense psychological theories and with assumptions about actual preferences. I have already suggested that we should not think too operationistically about measurement of desire. A fortiori this should apply to preference for its own sake. The intensity of a preference or a preference for its own sake should be determined hypothetico-deductively: more like measuring the charge of an electron than measuring the dimensions of a football field.

The difficulty, of course, gets compounded by the need to extend the method to animals. One needs a notion of preference that is not that of a propositional attitude in the usual, linguistically based sense. Even if a philosopher had such metaphysical doubts about the consciousness of non-human animals, this need not make him or her much less caring about them. Consider the unhappiness caused by the overcrowding of two million chickens. Suppose that the philosopher gave a probability of one half to the hypothesis that the chickens were conscious. This would give an expected disutility equal to that which would arise from the overcrowding of one million chickens of whom it was *certain* that they were conscious. It would be thus very objectionable to let the uncertainty of metaphysical speculation weaken our solicitude for other animals.

SATISFACTION UTILITARIANISM

Perhaps influenced by developments in economics and social choice theory, some philosophers have shifted from a hedonistic form of utilitarianism (or consequentialism) to a theory in which right action is characterized in terms of maximal satisfaction of desire generally. Since our desires are for all sorts of things, not just for happiness, this has its attractions. The hedonist will say 'What could be ultimately important except happiness?' The satisfactionist will say 'What can be ultimately more important than satisfaction of desire?' Indeed not only can desire be for things other than happiness, as I have been construing it, but it need not be for experience of any sort. Consider a person who desires that something occur after his or her death. This desire may indeed be satisfied after the person's death, but though the desire will be satisfied, the person will get no satisfaction (i.e. pleasure). (A person who makes a will may of course get pleasure at the thought that his or her desire will be posthumously satisfied, but this is a different matter.) Would Sir Edmund Hillary have been satisfied with an experience just like that of climbing Mount Everest, without actually climbing the peak?

Suppose that at time *t* the intensity of a person's desire is I(*t*). Let us suppose that this desire is satisfied. Then as far as this person is concerned the consequent value thus brought about is the integral of I(*t*) with respect to *t*. R.B. Brandt has considered as a difficulty for the satisfaction utilitarian cases such as the following:[26] a lifelong atheist weakens when near to death and requests a priest. Should we consider the person's earlier desire to avoid priestcraft or should we consider the later desire for the services of a priest? I suggest that the answer that the satisfaction utilitarian should give is that if the person's atheistic period is from t_1 to t_2 and if t_2 to t_3 is the priest desiring period, and I(*t*) is the intensity of his priest avoiding desire ($-$I(*t*) the intensity of the priest getting desire) then

we should consider $\int_{t_1}^{t_2}I(t)dt + \int_{t_2}^{t_3}I(t)dt$ and if the negative value of

the second term outweighs the positive value of the first term, then (other things being equal) we should get the priest and if not we should not get the priest.

I therefore think that there is no necessity (or reason) to modify satisfaction utilitarianism to consider only 'now for now' and 'then for then' preferences, as R.M. Hare has reluctantly done in his *Moral Thinking*. [27] The theory as thus presented by Hare is modified still further by restricting the preferences to preferences for experiences that the experiencer is currently having. This brings Hare's theory closer to hedonistic utilitarianism, but not quite, because someone may prefer an experience that he or she is having without (entirely or in part) preferring it for its own sake.

In satisfaction utilitarianism as I construe it all desires are on a level, including non-utilitarian or even evil desires. Even the deontological desires of non-utilitarians should be taken into account, but only in the way in which the satisfaction utilitarian will consider all desires. The satisfaction of a non-utilitarian or evil desire is *pro tanto* good, but of course the influence of this on the total calculation is usually small: for example the satisfaction of an evil desire causes the *non* -satisfaction of countless other desires. Torturing a prisoner may satisfy a dictator's desire, but the prisoner will doubtless have a hugely greater desire not to be tortured.

APPLIED ETHICS

Utilitarian thinking has practical importance (assuming that it is adopted) in so far as it differs from common sense and traditional moral thinking. An important respect in which this is so is that utilitarian may endeavor to modify these legal and customary and of rights. This does not mean, however, that a utilitarian may not support legal and customary rules of justice and of rights. He or she may hold that such rules, enforceable either legally or by pressure of public opinion, may be extremely useful. Indeed the utilitarian may endeavor to modify these legal and customary institutions in the cause of utility, if he or she thinks that they need modifying. Jeremy Bentham did much to reform the English legal system, by continually asking of its rules and traditions 'What's the use of it?' For example, common-sense rules of punishment need re-assessing. Since punishment by its very nature involves making someone unhappy, this unhappiness has to be outweighed by more than compensating utility. Utilitarians usually argue for the useful-ness of punishment on grounds of deterrence, and of prevention (if a burglar is in prison he is prevented from burgling). Reformation of the criminal is also given as a reason, but this is often not possible, and indeed the company of other criminals in prison is likely to produce the opposite of reformation. Imprisonment will therefore have to be justified mainly by the greater utility of deterrence and prevention. A utilitarian will of course refuse to give retribution as a reason, but in a society of non-utilitarians who are, for example, liable to indulge in lynch law or private revenge, the utilitarian may see some utility in assuaging these retributionist feelings. The utilitarian's reasons for punishment will not include retribution but will include prevention of revengeful behavior in others, en-couraging respect for legal institutions, and so on. This illustrates the way in which the utilitarian will have to take account, as a social fact, of motives in others which he or she regards as disutilitarian but which as social facts affect his or her calculations. It is to be hoped that as society gets more civilized the need to pander to retributionist feelings will be less. To raise another issue, one can give some utilitarian justification for existing rules of diminished responsibility (e.g. due to insanity), but even so they could well be improved and brought into line with what would be more useful.

Utilitarianism leads to a different political philosophy from those of two influential writers, John Rawls [28] and Robert Nozick.[29] In connection with Rawls I mention the fact that he bases his theory on the principle of 'maximin'.[30] Out of various alternative actions, each with various possible outcomes, the maximin strategy is to choose the one with the most favorable worst possible outcome. In contrast, a utilitarian will maximize expected utility. A utilitarian will also disagree with Rawls's 'difference principle' – the principle of doing only that which will make the worst off person in a society better off. This can conflict with maximizing total expected utility. As for Nozick, in the preface to his *Anarchy, State and Utopia*[31] he baldly asserts 'Individuals have rights,' which takes a utilitarian's breath away, as the utilitarian will certainly not accept this axiom, and will therefore be unwilling to accept the recommendations that Nozick draws from it in the book, some of which conclusions the utilitarian will reject as inimical to the general happiness.

Utilitarianism is particularly favourable to the present expansion of concern for non-human animals. Indeed, Jeremy Bentham expressed the matter very well when he said, 'The question is not, Can they reason? nor Can they talk? but Can they suffer?'[32]

Sidgwick argued that conventional moral rules have grown up and survived, for the most part but not completely, because of their utility. However, we now live in a much more dangerous and quickly changing world than Sidgwick did, mainly because of the pace of technological change. A terrible instance of this is the rapid increase in the sophistication and destructiveness of military weapons. Developments in biology, with the possible application of techniques such as genetic engineering to humans, will obviously give rise to awesome and unprecedented decisions of social choice – if indeed decisions are made and the situation does not simply develop in an uncontrolled way. Furthermore, consider the problems connected with the population explosion (itself a product of medical and sanitary technology). It is likely therefore that useful as conventional ethical principles have been in the past, they may in the future sometimes be counter-productive. A striking example of this is the obvious inapplicability of the so-called Protestant work ethic to an age of automation and robotics.

The most urgent field for applied ethics is the arms race and the threat of nuclear war. It seems that the human race has the power to destroy itself, and perhaps all sentient animal life as well. The threat of the 'nuclear winter' is horrendous, and any who may be unlucky enough to survive a nuclear holocaust would find life in the nuclear winter, if indeed such a life is possible at all, of such a quality that even a Siberian labour camp would be luxury in comparison. But even these sorrows pale by comparison with the loss of perhaps millions of years of further evolution (whether by natural or artificial selection or biological engineering), which are likely to occur unless we silly humans destroy everything. If your main moral category is non-utilitarian you may not mind so much the end of life on earth. After all, you cannot talk of violating the rights of non-existent future persons. But we can talk of future happiness of future people, though this will be zero if there are no such people, and in all probability will be of quite unimaginable magnitude if there are such people. I think that we all need to think about the arms race, but I suggest that (other things being equal) utilitarians are likely to think better.[33]

NOTES

1 Jeremy Bentham, *The Principles of Morals and Legislation*.

2 Henry Sidgwick, *The Methods of Ethics*, 7th edition (Indianapolis: Hackett Publishing Company, 1981).

3 Some of Mill's remarks have led some critics to ascribe to him the view of rule utilitarianism that one should obey rules, though these rules are assessed by the utility of general obedience to these rules. There is also doubt as to how far Mill should be regarded as a hedonist.

4 Cf. Sidgwick, op. cit., p. 425. Sidgwick did also hold that utilitarian estimates of consequences do to a considerable extent explain the survival of common sense moral rules, and also explain the admitted limitations and need for qualification of these rules. (See p. 425 again.)

5 See also C.D. Broad on the relations between ethical and psychological hedonism in C.D. Broad, *Five Types of Ethical Theory* (London: Kegan Paul, Trench, Trubner, 1930), pp. 180–92.

6 See my paper 'Benevolence as an Over-Riding Attitude', *Australasian Journal of Philosophy* 55 (1977), 127–35.

7 See Joseph Butler, *Sermon XI*, paragraph 20. In *Fifteen Sermons and A Dissertation on the Nature of Virtue*, with Introduction, Analyses and Notes by W.R. Matthews (London: Bell, 1953).

8 Sidgwick, op. cit., p. 413 and pp. 432 ff.

Utilitarianism and its applications

9 R.M. Hare does not like this talk of 'rules of thumb', but nevertheless I have a good deal of respect for his theory of two levels of moral thinking, as expounded in his *Moral Thinking* (Oxford: Clarendon Press, 1981).

10 Cf. my paper 'Extreme and Restricted Utilitarianism', in Philippa Foot (ed.), *Theories of Ethics* (Oxford University Press, 1967). As I discovered more recently, similar objections (to Paley's form of rule utilitarianism) were put into the mouth of a hypothetical 'sophistical' utilitarian opponent by the eighteenth century anti-utilitarian moralist, Thomas Green. See the extract from Thomas Green's *An Examination of the Leading Principle in the New System of Morals* in D.H. Monro (ed.), *A Guide to the British Moralists* (London: Fontana, 1972), pp. 198–203, especially p. 201.

11 See Sidgwick, op. cit., pp. 428–9.

12 See the symposium between Michael Slote and Philip Pettit, 'Satisficing Consequentialism', *Aristotelian Society*, supp. vol. 58 (1984). Slote is a pluralist consequentialist, not a hedonistic utilitarian. His notion of satisficing is a modification of a proposal in economics by H.A. Simon. See references in Pettit, op. cit., p. 166 footnote.

13 Compare Philip Pettit's somewhat similar comments, ibid.

14 See J.J.C. Smart and Bernard Williams, *Utilitarianism, For and Against* (Cambridge University Press, 1973), pp. 58 ff.

15 See Arthur Kuflik, 'Utilitarianism and Large Scale Co-operation', *Australasian Journal of Philosophy* 60 (1982), 224–37. For an earlier critique of the mixed strategy solution see Donald Regan, *Utilitarianism and Co-operation* (Oxford: Clarendon Press, 1980), Chapter 11.

16 Donald Regan, *Utilitarianism and Co-operation*, op. cit. Indeed on p. 198 Regan rather generously suggests that in my discussion of the mixed strategy method I was 'in a hazy fashion and in a specific sort of case' groping for the co-operation utilitarian theory. I think that I was probably even more confused than this suggests.

17 Ibid., p. 11.

18 See B.C. Postow, 'Generalized Act Utilitarianism', *Analysis* 37 (1977), 49–52.

19 Each co-operative utilitarian has to identify the class of people with whom he or she is to co-operate. Could this empirical information be used by him to reason in a purely act utilitarian way? (As in David Lewis, 'Utilitarianism and Truthfulness', *Australasian Journal of Philosophy* 50 (1972), 17–19). This seems to work in the 2-person case, but in the case of *n* persons, for large *n*, each may think that he or she can do more good by acting differently, since there will still be sufficient co-operation. But if *each* reasons this way there will *not* be sufficient co-operators. So after all there does seem to be an important difference between co-operative utilitarianism and act utilitarianism. (On the

39

importance of the many person case *cf.* Derek Parfit, *Reasons and Persons* (Oxford: Clarendon Press, 1984), p. 59 at bottom.)

20 *Cf.* Sidgwick, *Methods of Ethics*, op. cit., p. 131. For a not entirely dissimilar (though more behavioristic) view see G. Ryle, *The Concept of Mind* (London: Hutchinson, 1949), pp. 108–9

21 In F.P. Ramsey, *The Foundations of Mathematics* (London: Kegan Paul, Trench, Trubner, 1931), especially pp. 177 ff.

22 Richard Jeffrey, *The Logic of Decision* (New York: McGraw-Hill, 1965), pp. 35–44.

23 J.C. Harsanyi, 'Morality and the Theory of Rational Behaviour', in Amartya Sen and Bernard Williams (eds), *Utilitarianism and Beyond* (Cambridge University Press, 1982).

24 Ibid., p. 51.

25 Donald Davidson, 'Judging Interpersonal Interests,' forthcoming. For another suggestion see Robert McNaughton, 'A Metrical Concept of Happiness', *Philosophy and Phenomenological Research* 14 (1953), 172–83, and a more recent treatment by Richard B. Brandt, *A Theory of the Good and Right* (Oxford: Clarendon Press, 1979), pp. 253–65. (See pp. 253–7 of this book for Brandt's method of measuring preferences, which depends on certain ideas from experimental psychology.) See also Lars Bergström, 'Interpersonal Utility Comparisons', *Grazer Philosophies Studien* 16/17 (1982), 284–312, especially pp. 292–6. For yet another suggestion see Bergström, op. cit., pp. 306–11. Bergström refers (among others) to F.Y. Edgeworth, *Mathematical Psychics* (London: Kegan Paul, 1881), p. 7, and to A.F. MacKay, 'Interpersonal Comparisons', *Journal of Philosophy* 72 (1975), 535–49.

26 Op. cit., pp. 247–53.

27 *Moral Thinking*, op. cit., pp. 103–4. Compare Hare's theory in his 'Ethical Theory and Utilitarianism', in H.D. Lewis (ed.), *Contemporary British Philosophy* 4 (London: Allen & Unwin, 1976).

28 John Rawls, *A Theory of Justice* (Harvard University Press, 1971).

29 Robert Nozick, *Anarchy, State and Utopia* (Oxford: Blackwells, 1974).

30 John Harsanyi in effect anticipated Rawls's method of deducing an ethical system from what a group of self-interested persons in an 'original position' would decide should be the rules. (I see little merit in this method, and I do not see what an original position, in which I am not and never have been, has to do with the price of fish. I prefer to found ethics directly on a sentiment of generalized benevolence.) However, Harsanyi reasonably rejected 'maximin' and used expected utility instead. As he has pointed out, one would not take an aeroplane trip if one were to use maximin! (There is a small probability of the plane crashing.) Using expected utility instead of maximin, Harsanyi deduced a form of rule utilitarianism, very different from Rawls's non-utilitarian system. See J.C. Harsanyi, 'Cardinal Utility in Welfare

Economics and in the Theory of Risk Taking', *Journal of Political Economy* 61 (1953), 434–5, 'Cardinal Welfare, Individualistic Ethics, and Interpersonal Comparisons of Utility', *Journal of Political Economy* 63 (1955), 309–21, and 'Can the Maximin Principle Serve as a Basis for Morality?' in Harsanyi's book *Essays on Ethics, Social Behaviour and Scientific Explanation* (Dordrecht-Holland: D. Reidel, 1976). This last paper contains a postscript replying to some objections in John Rawls, 'Some Reasons for the Maximin Criterion,' *American Economic Review* 64 (1974), 141–6.

31 Op. cit.

32 See the long footnote to paragraph 4 of Section 1 of Chapter XVII of Jeremy Bentham's *Principles of Morals and Legislation*. See also Peter Singer's criticisms of 'speciesism' in his *Animal Liberation* (New York: Random House, 1975). Concern for non-humans should also extend to extra-terrestrials, should we come across such.

33 See for example the article by Douglas P. Lackey, 'Missiles and Morals: A Utilitarian Look at Nuclear Deterrence', *Philosophy and Public Affairs* 11 (1982), 189–231. For replies to Lackey, see Russell Hardin, 'Unilateral versus Mutual Disarmament', ibid. 236–54, Gregory S. Kavka, 'Doubts about Unilateral Nuclear Disarmament', ibid. 255–60, and rejoinder by Lackey, ibid. 261–5. In assessing utilitarian arguments in this area it is important to remember that even a very small probability of accidental apocalypse can have a big effect on expected utility, and that consequences into the far future, including possibility of further evolution of the human species, must not be underestimated. Of course, a utilitarian will often be glad to see non-utilitarians working in this area too, as has my colleague S.I. Benn, in his 'Deterrence or Appeasement?', *Journal of Applied Philosophy* 1 (1984), 5–19.

3

A CONTRACTUALIST ALTERNATIVE[1]

T.M. Scanlon

Utilitarianism occupies a central place in the moral philosophy of our time. It is not the view which most people hold; certainly there are very few who would claim to be act utilitarians. But for a much wider range of people it is the view towards which they find themselves pressed when they try to give a theoretical account of their moral beliefs. Within moral philosophy it represents a position one must struggle against if one wishes to avoid it. This is so in spite of the fact that the implications of act utilitarianism are wildly at variance with firmly held moral convictions, while rule utilitarianism, the most common alternative formulation, strikes most people as an unstable compromise.

The wide appeal of utilitarianism is due, I think, to philosophical considerations of a more or less sophisticated kind which pull us in a quite different direction than our first order moral beliefs. In particular, utilitarianism derives much of its appeal from alleged difficulties about the foundations of rival views. What a successful alternative to utilitarianism must do, first and foremost, is to sap this source of strength by providing a clear account of the foundations of non-utilitarian moral reasoning.

Contractualism has been proposed as the alternative to utilitarianism, notably by John Rawls in *A Theory of Justice* (Rawls 1971). Despite the wide discussion which this book has received, however, I think that the appeal of contractualism as a foundational view has been under-rated. In particular, it has not been sufficiently appreciated that contractualism offers a particularly plausible account of moral motivation. The version of contractualism that I shall present differs from Rawls's in a number of respects. In particular, it makes no use, or only a different and more limited kind of use, of his notion of choice from behind a veil of ignorance. One result of this difference is to make the contrast between contractualism and utilitarianism stand out more clearly.

I

What a rival theory must do is to provide an alternative to philosophical utilitarianism as a conception of the subject matter of morality. This is what the theory which I shall call contractualism seeks to do. Even if it succeeds in this, however, and is judged superior to philosophical utilitarianism as an account of the nature of morality, normative utilitarianism will not have been refuted. The possibility will remain that normative utilitarianism can be established on other grounds, for example as the normative outcome of contractualism itself. But one direct and, I think, influential argument for normative utilitarianism will have been set aside.

To give an example of what I mean by contractualism, a contractualist account of the nature of moral wrongness might be stated as follows.

An act is wrong if its performance under the circumstances would be disallowed by any system of rules for the general regulation of behaviour which no one could reasonably reject as a basis for informed, unforced general agreement.

The idea of 'informed agreement' is meant to exclude agreement based on superstition or false belief about the consequences of actions, even if these beliefs are ones which it would be reasonable for the person in question to have. The intended force of the qualification 'reasonably', on the other hand, is to exclude rejections that would be unreasonably *given* the aim of finding principles which could be the basis of informed, unforced general agreement. Given this aim, it would be unreasonable, for example, to reject a principle because it imposed much greater burdens on others. I will have more to say about grounds for rejection later in the paper.

The requirement that the hypothetical agreement which is the subject of moral argument be unforced is meant not only to rule out coercion, but also to exclude being forced to accept an agreement by being in a weak bargaining position, for example because others are able to hold out longer and hence to insist on better terms. Moral argument abstracts from such considerations. The only relevant pressure for agreement comes from the desire to find and agree on principles which no one who had this desire could reasonably reject. According to contractualism, moral argument concerns the possibility of agreement among persons who are all moved by this desire, and moved by it to the same degree. But this counterfactual assumption characterizes only the agreement with which morality is concerned, not the world to which moral principles are to apply. Those who are concerned with morality look for principles for application to their imperfect world which they could not reasonably reject, and which others in this world, who are not now moved by the desire for agreement, could not reasonably reject should they come to be so moved.[2]

The contractualist account of moral wrongness refers to principles 'which no one could reasonably reject' rather than to principles 'which everyone could reasonably accept' for the following reason.[3] Consider a principle under which some people will suffer severe hardships, and suppose that these hardships are avoidable. That is, there are alternative principles under which no one would have to bear comparable burdens. It might happen, however, that the people on whom these hardships fall are particularly self-sacrificing, and are willing to accept these burdens for the sake of what they see as the greater good of all. We would not say, I think, that it would be unreasonable of them to do this. On the other hand, it might not be unreasonable for them to refuse these burdens, and, hence, not unreasonable for someone to reject a principle requiring him to bear them. If this rejection would be reasonable, then the principle imposing these burdens is put in doubt, despite the fact that some particularly self-sacrificing people could (reasonably) accept it. Thus it is the reasonableness of rejecting a principle, rather than the reasonableness of accepting it, on which moral argument turns.

It seems like that many non-equivalent sets of principles will pass the test of non-rejectability. This is suggested, for example, by the fact that there are many different ways of defining important duties, no one of which is more or less 'rejectable' than the others. It does not follow, however, that any action allowed by at least one of these sets of principles cannot be morally wrong according to contractualism. If it is important for us to have *some* duty of a given kind (some duty of fidelity to agreements, or some duty of mutual aid) of which there are many morally acceptable forms, then one of these forms needs to be established by convention. In a setting in which one of these forms *is* conventionally established, acts disallowed by it will be wrong in the sense of the definition given. For, given the need for such conventions, one thing that could not be generally agreed to would be a set of principles allowing one to disregard conventionally established (and morally acceptable) definitions of important duties. This dependence on convention introduces a degree of cultural relativity into contractualist morality. In addition, what a person can reasonably reject will depend on the aims and conditions that are important in his life, and these will also depend on the society in which he lives. The definition given above allows for variation both of these kinds by making the wrongness of an action depend on the circumstances in which it is performed.

The partial statement of contractualism which I have given has the abstract character appropriate in an account of the subject matter of morality. On its face, it involves no specific claim as to which principles could be agreed to or even whether there is a unique set of principles which could be the basis of agreement. One way, though not the only way, for a contractualist to arrive at substantive moral claims would be to give a technical definition of the relevant notion of agreement, e.g. by specifying the conditions under which agreement is to be reached, the parties to this agreement and the criteria of reasonableness to be employed. Different contractualists have done this in different ways. What must be claimed for such a definition is that (under the circumstances in which it is to apply) what it describes is indeed the kind of unforced, reasonable agreement at which moral argument aims. But contractualism can also be understood as an informal description of the subject matter of morality on the basis of which ordinary forms of moral reasoning can be understood and appraised without proceeding via a technical notion of agreement.

Who is to be included in the general agreement to which contractualism refers? The scope of morality is a difficult question of substantive morality, but a philosophical theory of the nature of morality should provide some basis for answering it. What an adequate theory should do is to provide a framework within which what seem to be relevant arguments for and against particular interpretations of the moral boundary can be carried out. It is often thought that contractualism can provide no plausible basis for an answer to this question. Critics charge either that contractualism provides no answer at all, because it must begin with some set of contracting parties taken as given, or that contractualism suggests an answer which is obviously too restrictive, since a contract requires parties who are able to make and keep agreements and who are each able to offer the others some benefit in return for their co-operation. Neither of these objections applies to the version of contractualism that I am defending. The general specification of the scope of morality which it implies seems to me to be this: morality applies to a being if the notion of justification to a being of that kind makes sense. What is required in order for this to be the case? Here I can only suggest some necessary conditions. The first is that the being have a good, that is, that there be a clear sense in which things can be said to go better or worse for that being. This gives partial sense to the idea of what it would be reasonable for a trustee to accept on the being's behalf. It would be reasonable for a trustee to accept at least those things that are good, or not bad, for the being in question. Using this idea of trusteeship we can extend the notion of acceptance to apply to beings that are incapable of literally agreeing to anything. But this minimal notion of trusteeship is too weak to provide a basis for morality, according to contractualism. Contractualist morality relies on notions of what it would be reasonable to accept, or reasonable to reject, which are essentially comparative. Whether it would be unreasonble for me to reject a certain principle, given the aim of finding principles which no one with this aim could reasonably reject, depends not only on how much actions allowed by that principle might hurt me in absolute terms but also on how that potential loss compares with other potential losses to others under this principle and alternatives to it. Thus, in order for a being to stand in moral relations with us it is not enough that it have a good, it is also necessary that its good be sufficiently similar to our own to provide a basis for some system of comparability. Only on the basis of such a system can we give proper kind of sense to the notion of what a trustee could reasonably reject on a being's behalf.

But the range of possible trusteeship is broader than that of morality. One could act as a trustee for a tomato plant, a forest or an ant colony, and such entities are not included in morality. Perhaps this can be explained by appeal to the requirement of comparability: while these entities have a good, it is not comparable to our own in a way that provides a basis for moral argument. Beyond this, however, there is in these cases insufficient foothold for the notion of justification *to* a being. One further minimum requirement for this notion is that the being constitute a point of view; that is, that there be such a thing as what it is like to be that being, such a thing as what the world seems like to it. Without this, we do not stand in a relation to the being that makes even hypothetical justification *to it* appropriate.

On the basis of what I have said so far contractualism can explain why the capacity to feel pain should have seemed to many to count in favour of moral status: a being which has this capacity seems also to satisfy the three conditions I have just mentioned as necessary for the idea of justification to it to make sense. If a being can feel pain, then it constitutes a centre of consciousness to which justification can be addressed. Feeling pain is a clear way in which the being can be worse off; having its pain alleviated a way in which it can be benefited; and these are forms of weal and woe which seem directly comparable to our own.

It is not clear that the three conditions I have listed as necessary are also sufficient for the idea of justification to a being to make sense. Whether they are, and, if they are not, what more may be required, are difficult and disputed questions. Some would restrict the moral sphere to those to whom justifications could in principle be communicated, or to those who can actually agree to something, or to those who have the capacity to understand moral argument. Contractualism as I have stated it does not settle these issues at once. All I claim is that it provides a basis for argument about them which is at least as plausible as that offered by rival accounts of the nature of morality. These proposed restrictions on the scope of morality are naturally understood as debatable claims about the conditions under which the relevant notion of justification makes sense, and the arguments commonly offered for and against them can also be plausibly understood on this basis.

Some other possible restrictions on the scope of morality are more evidently rejectable. Morality might be restricted to those who have the capacity to observe its constraints, or to those who are able to confer some reciprocal benefit on other participants. But it is extremely implausible to suppose that the beings excluded by these requirements fall entirely outside the protection of morality.

Contractualism as I have formulated it[4] can explain why this is so: the absence of these capacities alone does nothing to undermine the possibility of justifications which are relevant. I suggest that whatever importance the capacities for deliberative control and reciprocal benefit may have is as factors altering the duties which beings have and the duties others have towards them, not as conditions whose absence suspends the moral framework altogether.

II

I have so far said little about the normative content of contractualism. For all I have said, the act utilitarian formula might turn out to be a theroem of contractualism. I do not think that this is the case, but my main thesis is that whatever the normative implications of contractualism may be it still has distinctive content as a philosophical thesis about the nature of morality. This content – the difference, for example, between being a utilitarian because the utilitarian formula is the basis of general agreement and being a utilitarian on other grounds – is shown most clearly in the answer that a contractualist gives to the first motivational question.

Philosophical utilitarianism is a plausible view partly because the facts which it identifies as fundamental to morality – facts about individual well-being – have obvious motivational force. Moral facts can motivate us, on this view, because of our sympathetic identification with the good of others. But as we move from philosophical utilitarianism to a specific utilitarian formula as the standard of right action, the form of motivation that utilitarianism appeals to becomes more abstract. If classical utilitarianism is the correct normative doctrine then the natural source of moral motivation will be a tendency to be moved by changes in aggregate well-being, however these may be composed. We must be moved in the same way by an aggregate gain of suffering of a few people or by bringing tiny benefits to a vast number, perhaps at the expense of moderate discomfort for a few. This is very different from sympathy of the familiar kind toward particular individuals, but a utilitarian may argue that this more abstract desire is what natural sympathy becomes when it is corrected by rational reflection. This desire has the same content as sympathy – it is a concern for the good of others – but it is not partial or selective in its choice of objects.

A contractualist alternative

Leaving aside the psychological plausibility of this even-handed sympathy, how good a candidate is it for the role of moral motivation? Certainly sympathy of the usual kind is one of the many motives that can sometimes impel one to do the right thing. It may be the dominant motive, for example, when I run to the aid of a suffering child. But when I feel convinced by Peter Singer's article[5] on famine, and find myself crushed by the recognition of what seems a clear moral requirement, there is something else at work. In addition to the thought of how much good I could do for people in drought-stricken lands, I am overwhelmed by the further, seemingly distinct thought that it would be wrong for me to fail to aid them when I could do so at so little cost to myself. A utilitarian may respond that his account of moral motivation cannot be faulted for not capturing this aspect of moral experience, since it is just a reflection of our non-utilitarian moral upbringing. Moreover, it must be groundless. For what kind of fact could this supposed further fact of moral wrongness be, and how could it give us a further, special reason for acting? The question for contractualism, then, is whether it can provide a satisfactory answer to this challenge.

According to contractualism, the source of motivation that is directly triggered by the belief that an action is wrong is the desire to be able to justify one's actions to others on grounds they could not reasonably[6] reject. I find this an extremely plausible account of moral motivation – a better account of at least my moral experience than the natural utilitarian alternative – and it seems to me to constitute a strong point for the contractualist view. We all might like to be in actual agreement with the people around us, but the desire which contractualism identifies as basic to morality does not lead us simply to conform to the standards accepted by others whatever these may be. The desire to be able to justify one's actions to others on grounds they could not reasonably reject will be satisfied when we know that there is adequate justification for our action even though others in fact refuse to accept it (perhaps because they have no interest in finding principles which we and others could not reasonably reject). Similarly, a person moved by this desire will not be satisfied by the fact that others accept a justification for his action if he regards this justification as spurious.

One rough test of whether you regard a justification as sufficient is whether you would accept that justification if you were in another

49

person's position. This connection between the idea of 'changing places' and the motivation which underlies morality explains the frequent occurrence of 'Golden Rule' arguments within different systems of morality and in the teachings of various religions. But the thought experiment of changing places is only a rough guide; the fundamental question is what would it be unreasonable to reject as a basis for informed, unforced, general agreement. As Kant observed[7] our different individual points of view, taken as they are, may in general be simply irreconcilable. 'Judgemental harmony' requires the construction of a genuinely interpersonal form of justification which is nonetheless something that each individual could agree to. From this interpersonal standpoint, a certain amount of how things look from another person's point of view, like a certain amount of how they look from my own, will be counted as bias.

I am not claiming that the desire to be able to justify one's actions to others on grounds they could not reasonably reject is universal or 'natural'. 'Moral education' seems to me plausibly understood as a process of cultivating this desire and shaping it, largely by learning what justifications others are in fact willing to accept, by finding which ones you yourself find acceptable as you confront them from a variety of perspectives, and by appraising your own and others' acceptance or rejection of these justifications in the light of greater experience.

In fact it seems to me that the desire to be able to justify one's actions (and institutions) on grounds one takes to be acceptable is quite strong in most people. People are willing to go to considerable lengths, involving quite heavy sacrifices, in order to avoid admitting the unjustifiability of their actions and institutions. The notorious insufficiency of moral motivation as a way of getting people to do the right thing is not due to simple weakness of the underlying motive, but rather to the fact that it is easily deflected by self-interest and self-deception.

It could reasonably be objected here that the source of motivation I have described is not tied exclusively to the contractualist notion of moral truth. The account of moral motivation which I have offered refers to the idea of a justification which it would be unreasonable to reject, and this idea is potentially broader than the contractualist notion of agreement. For let M be some non-contractualist account of moral truth. According to M, we may suppose, the wrongness of an action is simply a moral characteristic of that action in virtue of which it ought not to be done. An act which has this characteristic, according to M, has it quite independently of any tendency of informed persons to come to agreement about it. However, since informed persons are presumably in a position to recognise the wrongness of a type of action, it would seem to follow that if an action is wrong then such persons would agree that it is not to be performed. Similarly, if an act is not morally wrong, and there is adequate moral justification to perform it, then there will presumably be a moral justification for it which an informed person would be unreasonable to reject. Thus, even if M, and not contractualism, is the correct account of moral truth, the desire to be able to justify my actions to others on grounds they could not reasonably reject could still serve as a basis for moral motivation.

What this shows is that the appeal of contractualism, like that of utilitarianism, rests in part on a qualified scepticism. A non-contractualist theory of morality can make use of the source of motivation to which contractualism appeals. But a moral argument will trigger this source of motivation only in virtue of being a good justification for acting in a certain way, a justification which others would be unreasonable not to accept. So a non-contractualist theory must claim that there are moral properties which have justificatory force quite independent of their recognition in any ideal agreement. These would represent what John Mackie has called instances of intrinsic 'to-be-doneness' and 'not-to-be-doneness'.[8] Part of contractualism's appeal rests on the view that, as Mackie puts it, it is puzzling how there could be such properties 'in the world'. By contrast, contractualism seeks to explain the justificatory status of moral properties, as well as their motivational force, in terms of the notion of reasonable agreement. In some cases the moral properties are themselves to be understood in terms of this notion. This is so, for example, in the case of the property of moral wrongness, considered above. But there are also right- and wrong-making properties, which are themselves independent of the contractualist notion of agreement. I take the property of being an act of killing for the pleasure of doing so to be a wrong-making property of this kind. Such properties are wrong-making because it would be reasonable to reject any set of principles which permitted the acts they characterize. Thus, while there are morally relevant properties 'in the world' which are independent of the contractualist notion of agreement, these do not constitute instances of intrinsic 'to-be-doneness' and 'not-to-be-doneness': their moral relevance – their force in justifications as well as their link with motivation – is to be explained on contractualist grounds.

In particular, contractualism can account for the apparent moral significance of facts about individual well-being, which utilitarianism takes to be fundamental. Individual well-being will be morally significant, according to contractualism, not because it is intrinsically valuable or because promoting it is self-evidently a right-making characteristic, but simply because an individual could reasonably reject a form of argument that gave his well-being no weight. This claim of moral significance is, however, only approximate, since it is a further difficult question exactly how 'well-being' is to be understood and in what ways we are required to take account of the well-being of others in deciding what to do. It does not follow from this claim, for example, that a given desire will always and everywhere have the same weight in determining the rightness of an action that would promote its satisfaction, a weight proportional to its strength or 'intensity'. The right-making force of a person's desires is specified by what might be called a conception of morally legitimate interests. Such a conception is a product of moral argument; it is not given, as the notion of individual well-being may be, simply by the idea of what it is rational for an individual to desire. Not everything for which I have a rational desire will be something in which others need concede me to have a legitimate interest which they undertake to weigh in deciding what to do. The range of things which may be objects of my rational desires is very wide indeed, and the range of claims which others could not reasonably refuse to recognise will almost certainly be narrower than this. There will be a tendency for interests to conform to rational desire – for those conditions making it rational to desire something also to establish a legitimate interest in it – but the two will not always coincide.

One effect of contractualism, then, is to break down the sharp distinction, which arguments for utilitarianism appeal to, between the status of individual well-being and that of other moral notions. A framework of moral argument is required to define our legitimate interests and to account for their moral force. This same contractualist framework can also account for the force of other moral notions such as rights, individual responsibility and procedural fairness.

III

Rawls' argument is intended to move from the informal contractualist idea of principles 'acceptable to all' to the idea of rational choice behind a veil of ignorance, an idea which is, he hopes, more precise and more capable of yielding definite results. Let me turn then to his more formal arguments for the choice of the Difference Principle by the parties to the Original Position. Rawls cites three features of the decision faced by parties to the Original Position which, he claims, make it rational for them to use the maximin rule and, therefore, to select his Difference Principle as a principle of justice. These are (1) the absence of any objective basis for estimating probabilities, (2) the fact that some principles could have consequences for them which 'they could hardly accept' while (3) it is possible for them (by following maximin) to ensure themselves of a minimum prospect, advances above which, in comparison, matter very little.[9] The first of these features is slightly puzzling, and I leave it aside. It seems clear, however, that the other considerations mentioned have at least as much force in an informal contractualist argument about what all could reasonably agree to as they do in determining the rational choice of a single person concerned to advance his interests. They express the strength of the objection that the 'losers' might have to a scheme that maximized average utility at their expense, as compared with the counter-objections that others might have to a more egalitarian arrangement.

In addition to this argument about rational choice, Rawls invokes among 'the main grounds for the two principles' other considerations which, as he says, use the concept of contract to a greater extent.[10] The parties to the Original Position, Rawls says, can agree to principles of justice only if they think that this agreement is one that they will actually be able to live up to. It is, he claims, more plausible to believe this of his two principles than of the principle of average utility, under which the sacrifices demanded ('the strains of commitment') could be much higher. A second, related claim is that the two principles of justice have greater psychological stability than the principle of average utility. It is more plausible to believe,

53

Rawls claims, that in a society in which they were fulfilled people would continue to accept them and to be motivated to act in accordance with them. Continuing acceptance of the principle of average utility, on the other hand, would require an exceptional degree of identification with the good of the whole on the part of those from whom sacrifices were demanded.

These remarks can be understood as claims about the 'stability' (in a quite practical sense) of a society founded on Rawls' two principles of justice. But they can also be seen as an attempt to show that a principle arrived at via the second form of contractualists reasoning will also satisfy the requirements of the first form, i.e. that it is something no one could reasonably reject. The question 'Is the acceptance of this principle an agreement you could actually live up to?' is, like the idea of assignment by one's worst enemy, a thought experiment through which we can use our own reactions to test our judgment that certain principles are ones that no one could reasonably reject. General principles of human psychology can also be invoked to this same end.

Rawls's final argument is that the adoption of his two principles gives public support to the self-respect of individual members of society, and 'give stronger and more characteristic interpretation of Kant's idea'[11] that people must be treated as ends, not merely as means to the greater collective good. But, whatever difference there may be here between Rawls' two principles of justice and the principle of average utility, there is at least as sharp a contrast between the two patterns of contractualist reasoning distinguished above. The connection with self-respect, and with the Kantian formula, is preserved by the requirement that principles of justice be ones which no member of the society could reasonably reject. This connection is weakened when we shift to the idea of a choice which advances the interests of a single rational individual for whom the various individual lives in a society are just so many different possibilities. This is so whatever decision rule this rational chooser is said to employ. The argument from maximin seems to preserve this connection because it reproduces as a claim about rational choice what is, in slightly different terms, an appealing moral argument.

The 'choice situation' that is fundamental to contractualism as I have described it is obtained by beginning with 'mutually disinterested' individuals with full knowledge of their situations and adding to this (not, as is sometimes suggested, benevolence but) a desire on each of their parts to find principles which none could reasonably reject insofar as they too have this desire. Rawls several times considers such an idea in passing.[12] He rejects it in favour of his own idea of mutually disinterested choice from behind a veil of ignorance on the ground that only the latter enables us to reach definite results: 'if in choosing principles we required unanimity even where there is full information, only a few rather obvious cases could be decided'.[13] I believe that this supposed advantage is questionable. Perhaps this is because my expectations for moral argument are more modest than Rawls's. However, as I have argued, almost all of Rawls's own arguments have at least as much force when they are interpreted as arguments within the form of contractualism which I have been proposing. One possible exception is the argument from maximin. If the Difference Principle were taken to be generally applicable to decisions of public policy, then the second form of contractualist reasoning through which it is derived would have more far reaching implications than the looser form of argument by comparison of losses, which I have employed. But these wider applications of the principles are not always plausible, and I do not think that Rawls intends it to be applied so widely. His intention is that the Difference Principle should be applied only to major inequalities generated by the basic institutions of a society, and this limitation is a reflection of the special conditions under which he holds maximin to be the appropriate basis for rational choice: some choices have outcomes one could hardly accept, while gains above the minimum one can assure one's self matter very little, and so on. It follows, then, that in applying the Difference Principle – in identifying the limits of its applicability – we must fall back on the informal comparison of losses which is central to the form of contractualism I have described.

IV

It is sometimes said[14] that morality is a device for our mutual protection. According to contractualism, this view is partly true but in an important way incomplete. Our concern to protect our central interests will have an important effect on what we could reasonably agree to. It will thus have an important effect on the content of morality if contractualism is correct. To the degree that this morality is observed, these interests will gain from it. If we had no desire to be able to justify our actions to others on grounds they could reasonably accept, the hope of gaining this protection would give us reason to try to instill this desire in others, perhaps through mass hypnosis or conditioning, even if this also meant acquiring it ourselves. But given that we have this desire already, our concern with morality is less instrumental.

The contrast might be put as follows. On one view, concern with protection is fundamental, and general agreement becomes relevant as a means or a necessary condition for securing this protection. On the other, contractualist view, the desire for protection is an important factor determining the content of morality because it determines. what can reasonably be agreed to. But the idea of general agreement does not arise as a means of securing protection. It is, in a more fundamental sense, what morality is about.

NOTES

1 I am greatly indebted to Derek Parfit for patient criticism and enormously helpful discussion of many earlier versions of this paper. Thanks are due also to the many audiences who have heard parts of those versions delivered as lectures and kindly responded with helpful comments. In particular, I am indebted to Marshall Cohen, Ronald Dworkin, Owen Fiss, and Thomas Nagel for valuable criticism.

2 Here I am indebted to Gilbert Harman for comments which have helped me to clarify my statement of contractualism.

3 A point I owe to Derek Parfit.

4 On this view (as contrasted with some others in which the notion of a contract is employed) what is fundamental to morality is the desire for reasonable agreement, not the pursuit of mutual advantage. See section IV below. It should be clear that this version of contractualism can account for the moral standing of future persons who will be better or worse off as a result of what we do now. It is less clear how it can deal with the problem presented by future people who would not have been born but for actions of ours which also made the conditions in which they live worse. Do such people have reason to reject principles allowing these actions to be performed? This difficult problem, which I cannot explore here, is raised by Derek Parfit in Parfit, 1976, 'On Doing the Best for Our Children', in *Ethics and Population*, edited by M.

Bayles, Cambridge, Mass.: Schenkman Publishing Company, Inc., pp. 100–15.

5 P. Singer, 1972, 'Famine, Affluence and Morality', *Philosophy and Public Affairs*, 1, pp. 229–43.

6 Reasonably, that is, given the desire to find principles which others similarly motivated could not reasonably reject.

7 Kant, 1785, *The Moral Law*, section 2, footnote 14.

8 J. Mackie, 1977, *Ethics: Inventing Right and Wrong*, Harmondsworth: Pelican, p. 42.

9 J. Rawls, 1971, *A Theory of Justice,* Cambridge, Mass: Harvard University Press, p.154.

10 Rawls 1971, sec. 29, pp. 175ff.

11 Rawls 1971, p. 183.

12 E.g. Rawls 1971, pp. 141, 148 although these passages may not clearly distinguish between this alternative and an assumption of benevolence.

13 Rawls 1971, p. 141.

14 In different ways by G.J. Warnock in Warnock, 1971, *The Object of Morality*, (London: Methuen & Co), and by J.L. Mackie in Mackie, 1977. See also Richard Brandt's remarks on justification in Chapter X of Brandt 1979.

4

RECENT THOMISTIC ETHICS

Vernon J. Bourke

Modern Thomistic ethics takes its origins in the writings of Thomas Aquinas, the thirteenth-century Dominican friar who taught at the universities of Paris and Naples. His moral philosophy is found in his *Commentary on the Nicomachean Ethics*, plus several theological works such as the *Summa contra Gentiles* and the *Summa Theologiae*.[1] The original Thomism owed much to the moral philosophies of Plato, Aristotle and the Stoics but was also indebted to the ethical ideals of the Judaeo-Christian tradition. In its emphasis on the desire for happiness (*felicitas, beatitudo*), to be achieved in a future-life contemplation of the perfect Good, it was a theistic eudaimonism. On the other hand Aquinas's ethics was somewhat naturalistic in its appeal to right reason and the precepts of natural law as norms of morality. His emphasis on the importance of good moral habits and the consequent formation of character by the cardinal and theological virtues is evident throughout the Second Part of Aquinas's *Summa of Theology*. The central role given to charity (the love of all things as God's creatures) brought Thomas's ethical thinking close, in some respects, to recent agapistic ethics. Over the last six centuries commentators and teachers of Thomistic ethics of moral theology have interpreted Aquinas's thought in a wide variety of ways.

Some scholars try to discover what precisely was Aquinas's own ethical position: for want of a better name we may call them traditionalists. Two of the best known Thomists of the twentieth century belong here: Jacques Maritain and Etienne Gilson. Both

discussed ethical problems in their many writings.[2] Maritain became noted for his view that a purely philosophical ethics could not
provide adequate guidance for living a good life. Ethics, he felt,
must be subordinated to faith in order to benefit from revealed
moral truths.[3] In general the ethical positions of Maritain and
Gilson were conservative and close to the views of Aquinas,
although some interpreters of Thomism did not agree with Maritain
on the inadequacy of philosophical ethics.

The traditional manual of Thomistic ethics includes chapters on:
the methods of moral philosophy, relation of philosophical ethics to
moral theology, the ultimate end of man, special features of moral
action (voluntariness and freedom, circumstances, roles of intellect, will and passions, norms of morality, moral law, conscience,
moral virtues and character formation, and special moral problems). Representative traditional textbooks are those of: Michael
Wittmann, A.D. Sertillanges, John Oesterle, Austin Fagothey,
Wolfgang Kluxen.

Many Thomists consider human nature to be the norm whereby
good acts are distinguished from bad ones.[4] This ethical criterion
depends on a metaphysics of substance and accident, essence and
nature, and actions as uses of the various powers of man. Every
substantial being is thought to belong to some definite species with
its own characteristic essence expressing its nature through typical
activities and responses. In the case of human beings rationality is
distinctive of the specific nature of man. Since human agents
operate in a real context of existing things, other men, and God, the
norm that is human nature encompasses the knowable relations of
the acting person to this environment. Some interpreters list these
essential relations (that must be considered in judging the appropriateness of moral activities) on three levels: in relation to God
man is a contingent being, in regard to his fellow men he is a social
being, and in relation to the goods of the earth he is a possessor.
While the classical definition of man as a rational animal is obviously operative in this criterion of ethical judgment, it is clear that
Thomists do not think that detailed rules of behavior can be
deduced from this definition alone. Empirical knowledge of the
facts of human action must ground an induction leading to ethical
generalizations.[5] Critics of this norm object to the apparent weakness of the Thomistic view of evil as a privation of good. They allege
that a more positive understanding of both physical and moral evil is

required in an ethics prepared to face the realities of human life.[6]

Another Thomistic ethical norm stresses the perfectibility of man. Early in life the human agent is a rational substance endowed with many powers enabling him to act and suffer action from others in a variety of ways. At first these powers (operative potencies) are undeveloped but with use they acquire a number of permanent dispositions (*habitus*) which qualitatively perfect each basic potency. Such habits of intellect, will, and the sensory appetites make it possible for humans to do many things more readily, promptly and perfectly than they could without habituation. Not merely motor skills, such as typing, swimming or piano playing, are involved here but also morally important intellectual, volitional and emotional habits. The ability to think with practical precision (*prudentia*), to will and do without hesitation what is good for others (*justitia*), to moderate one's feelings between extremes of too much and too little (*temperantia*), and habitually to face threats to one's well-being with reasonable firmness (*fortitude*) – these four virtues are taken by Thomists as the structure of a good moral character. (Of course there are morally bad habits, too: these are vices.) Aristotle had taught that a life in accord with these cardinal virtues is the best ethically. Aquinas used these natural virtues and also the theological virtues (faith, hope and charity) to organize his treatment of various goods and evils, so a growing number of modern Thomists see human nature *perfected by virtue* as a practical measure of good conduct.[7] A book that builds on this aretaic theme, apart from the Thomistic background, is Alasdair MacIntyre's *After Virtue: A Study in Moral Theory* (1981).

The Aristotelian influence on recent Thomists is also seen in their treatment of the right reason (*orthos logos*) theme.[8] As in the original ethics of Aquinas the rational order includes the notion of *ratio* (*logos*) as a real relation between things, so also, in modern Thomism it is an ontological view. A mother has a special relation to her child, a citizen to his country, a farmer to his property. These, and many other such ratios, form the metaphysical foundation of numerous ethical rights and duties. If A is the mother of B, then she ought to take care of B – and so should B's father. If a person is a citizen of country C, then he is morally required to promote its welfare. If farmer F is not the owner of property P, then he ought not assume property rights in regard to P. Right reason is not simply a matter of good practical thinking: such reasoning requires a basis in the interconnected realities in which the ethical agent operates. A realistic metaphysics underlies this answer to the is-ought problem.[9]

ANALYTIC THOMISM

Some Thomists are partially influenced by linguistic philosophy and have adopted an analytic modification of Aquinas's ethics. A realistic metaphysics is not stressed by this school. They reject or play down the importance of one ultimate end for all men and substitute a number of 'basic goods' for which the morally good person must strive. A typical list of such goods is: life, play, esthetic experience, speculative knowledge, integrity, practical reasonableness, and religion in the sense of holiness.[10] It is claimed that these moral objectives cannot be unified under one perfect good. They are all of equal value and must all be cherished. Critics of this pluralization of goods argue that the reasons for selecting these values as basic are not clear. The above eight values are not initially ethical goods; they are possible objectives for any kind of practical reasoning. The attempt to provide an analytic base for Thomistic ethics, say these critics, runs counter to the main features of Aquinas's ethics. Indeed John Finnis (one of the leading analytic Thomists) calls Aquinas's theory of three levels of natural inclinations (on which natural law precepts are based) 'an irrelevant schematization.'[11] Just why these eight basic goods are held to be of equal value, and how they ground ethical obligations, is not evident to other Thomists.

How far neo-Thomists may go in changing the central teachings of Thomas Aquinas, and still be called Thomists, is obviously quite a problem. At least some traditional Thomists would say that rejection of the view that God is the one ultimate end and good for man is enough to constitute a rejection of Thomism. But since the analytic approach to natural-law ethics takes its start in Aquinas's treatise on laws (*ST*, I-II, pp. 90 ff.), this school of ethics deserves mention here. It represents something of a deontological turn in Thomism.

TRANSCENDENTAL THOMISM

The ethics of Transcendental Thomism is still another move away from the older tradition. It is mainly prominent in continental Europe. This school radically modifies the metaphysics and epistemology of Aquinas.[12] Where Thomas insisted that all natural human understanding arises from grasping the universal meanings of facts gathered in sense experience, the transcendental thinkers turn to the inner presentations of consciousness for their start. In this way they are not only influenced by German idealism but also by a long-standing notion in Renaissance scholasticism that Aquinas's epistemology did not pay enough attention to spiritual experiences. Moreover, these transcendentalists have adopted the Suarezian view that each individual thing has its own unique essence: hence universal essences (such as human nature) are seen as constructs of the reflecting intellect, and as unreal. As a consequence, the ethics of transcendental Thomism differs from that of Aquinas on many points.

The best known thinker in this transcendental school is Karl Rahner. His extensive writings cover many facets of Christian thinking but he has not published a special treatise on ethics. Yet pronouncements on the role and nature of Christian ethics are found throughout his writings.[13] Rahner argues that traditional ethics has overstressed universal rules to the neglect of 'God's individual commands.' It would appear that he is more Heideggerian than Thomistic in his ethics.

Another version of this sort of ethics is represented by Josef Fuchs. He has written extensively on Aquinas's sexual ethics, on Christian situation ethics, and on values in Christian morality. His major study of natural law[14] criticizes the absolutism of earlier Thomist ethics and inisists that rule or case ethics fails to come to grips with moral action in its concrete situations.

Related to the foregoing is the work of other European Thomists who use a combination of traditional ethics with phenomenology, The present Pope, John Paul II (Karol Wojtyla), in his doctoral dissertation made a critical study of Max Scheler's phenomenology. Ten years later his *The Acting Person* (1979) stressed the role of the moral agent as central to ethical discussion. A book by W.A. Luijpen reinterpreted natural law in terms of the phenomenological approaches of Edmund Husserl and Maurice Merleau-Ponty.[15] Justice, and ethical principles in general, do not find their validity in objective realities but in values projected from man's consciousness, as thinking, willing and acting. Such a subjective philosophy rejects Aquinas's realism and especially the Aristotelian metaphysics. A similar approach is found in the ethics of Hans Reiner.[16]

AGAPISTIC THOMISM

One of the main differences between Thomas's ethics and Greek pagan moral philosophy was the Thomistic emphasis on divinely prompted love (*caritas*) as the greatest of the virtues. There was no place in the *Nicomachean Ethics* for mercy and forgiveness. But charity, says Aquinas, 'directs the acts of all the other virtues to the ultimate end.' In this sense, divine love is the 'form' of all virtue. There can be no doubt, then, as to the primacy in Thomistic ethics of the love of all things as goods created by God.[17] Such high-minded spiritual love (*agape*, *caritas*) plays an important role in the moral philosophies of all types of Thomists.

Some responses to the love-ethics of Joseph Fletcher have brought a new dimension to Thomist consideration of charity in ethics.[18] While Fletcher's situationism has been criticized for lack of precision as to the meaning of agapistic love, and for its rejection of all absolute principles except love, it has moved some Thomist writers to redefine and limit the place of moral laws in ethical judgment. Legalism is no longer in great favor, as the writings of Charles Curran indicate.[19]

A related movement features the ethical role of another theological virtue, hope. For Aquinas hope is a supernatural virtue of the human will, whereby man desires the attainment of eternal happiness with the help of God.[20] As such it follows upon faith and precedes the acquisition of the more perfect love of charity. Some recent Catholic moral theology attempts to incorporate Kant's ethical views on hope into a new version of Christian ethics.[21] Several other Kantian notions, such as the kingdom of ends and the constructive role of imagination, have led to the claim that: 'human freedom, exercized in moral endeavor, gives rise to hope in such form – that is, as an expectation about human destiny – that it can be brought to completion only in terms of human mutuality – that is, full and lasting participation in a public realm.'[22]

This new movement concentrates on the social context of ethical behavior and insists that recognition of the basic likeness of all humans is required for the perfection of moral character. Both the

63

ethics of agapistic love and that of Kantian hope stress the importance of an approved prior attitude in the moral agent and they tend
to minimize concern about the consequences of external action.

In this century Thomists have engaged in a number of ethical
controversies. One debate has centered on the autonomy of a
strictly philosophical ethics. A terminological clarification is required here. (1) Some Thomists call themselves moral theologians:
they use the data of divine revelation (scripture, Catholic tradition,
papal pronouncements) expounded with the help of some type of
philosophy, to establish a fully Christian ethics. (2) Other Thomists
develop a philosophical ethics, using natural reasoning on man's life
experiences (without the aid of religious truths but accepting the
existence of God, the immortality of the soul, and the validity of
spiritual as well as physical life, as conclusions from metaphysics
and philosophical psychology). (3) A third type of Thomist takes an
intermediate position, offering a philosophical ethics that mainly
depends on natural data and reasoning but is 'subordinated' to the
truths of Christian faith, in the sense of revealed truths (original sin,
grace, redemption, etc.) as negative norms of ethical judgment.
This third position was prominently represented by Jacques Maritain: he never called himself a moral theologian.

In general, advocates of the second position pay a good deal of
attention to Aquinas's *Commentary on the Nicomachean Ethics*
(which makes few allusions to Christian teachings) but they refer
also to many passages in Thomas's theological writings that use
philosophical arguments, even though the context is religious.[23] In
America many Thomistic ethicists have no formal training in theology and many are not clerics: they regard themselves as philosophers in the strict sense. The literature of Thomistic moral
theology is quite distinct from that produced by Thomist philosophers, some of whom are not Roman Catholics. So this three-
sided split boils down to a difference of method and initial principles. Philosophical Thomists usually admit that moral theologians
have access to higher principles and truths, and that the theologian
may well be blessed by special graces. But they point out that the
Catholic moral theologian is subject to one great limitation: he must
presuppose that his audience accepts divine revelation as interpreted by the Roman Catholic Church. The status of a Maritain
type of Christian ethics is not easy to situate.

A second controversy deals with the relative importance of the common good (*bonum commune*) as compared to the private good. At many places in his writings Aquinas had said that the common good is better than the good of one person (*Bonum commune melius est quam bonum unius*).[24] There has always been some disagreement as to the meaning of such statements but the debate reached its peak in the 1940 decade. Jacques Maritain was democratic in his socio-political thinking. He wrote much on the importance of the individual citizen – particularly in cases of oppression under totalitarian regimes. Sometimes his views were confused with those of other French personalists. In 1946 Maritain published an article on the person and the common good: it later appeared as a book in French and English.[25] This summarized his earlier views which were attacked in the same decade by Charles de Koninck.[26] Both sides in the debate were supported by other writers in Canada and the US.[27] I.T. Eschmann clarified the argument in a defense of Maritain's stance. Most Thomists would now hold that in earthly communities the common good usually takes priority but in a future life the private and the common good are not at odds.

A third dispute among Thomists concerns the ultimate end of man. At the conclusion of the *Nicomachean Ethics* Aristotle asked whether happiness consisted in the enjoyment of pleasures, the achievement of knowledge, or a reasonable life of action in accord with the virtues. As a Christian, Thomas Aquinas replied that man's highest good, toward which his life should be directed as a final goal, is a supernatural union with God. The question then arises for Thomist interpreters: is there a natural ultimate end for man, as well as a supernatural one? Should philosophical ethics consider only the natural good, while moral theology looks to the supernatural end? Some twentieth-century Thomists argue that there are two ultimate ends, while others deny that a natural end could be ultimate.[28] A few Analytic Thomists have discarded the whole claim that there is one ultimate or highest good and have replaced it, as we have seen, with several more immediate basic goods.[29]

A fourth much discussed issue deals with the role of consequences in ethical judgment. Consequentialism is, of course, one type of teleology and Thomist ethics was, until recently, quite teleological in its use of the means-end relationship. However the utilitarian calculus of results has generally been viewed with suspicion by Thomists. Yet a curious trend has appeared in recent years: a good number of writers have concentrated on what is called the 'double effect' device and they have broadened its scope into what seems like an attempt at a complete ethical theory of consequences.[30] Aquinas had taught that it is possible for one human act to have results, one of which is intended by the agent and the other quite apart from his intention.[31] What is intended is the actual end sought by the agent and, if this end is good and the other circumstances of the act are not evil, then the action is morally good. This rule is enunciated by Thomas in a discussion of the propriety of killing an unjust aggressor in self-defence. Renaissance interpreters complicated this double effect device by a theory of direct and indirect intending and they tried to apply it to many more types of moral activity than Aquinas envisioned. Recent developments of the device by Thomists such as Peter Knauer and Bruno Schueller have influenced discussion of the matter in the United States.[32]

This double effect theory has come to be known as 'proportionalism.' One advocate writes: 'What constitutes right action? It is that action which contains the proportionally greatest maximization of good and minimization of evil.'[33] The most vigorous critic of consequentialism, Germain Grisez, has said of proportionalism: ' "Choose the lesser evil" would be a workable principle only if goods and evils could be comparatively measured as proportionalism requires, but this cannot be done.'[34]

The questionable morality of modern warfare has been another cause of divided opinion among Thomists. Aquinas set forth three conditions for waging a just war: legitimate authority, a right cause, and a proper intention.[35] With the growth of sovereign nations in the Renaissance, commentators such as Francisco de Vitoria added new complexities to the justification of war. Textbooks on Thomistic ethics continued the effort to adjust the conditions for just war to the circumstances of the modern world.[36]

But most Thomists today are not pacifists. They usually attempt a middle position between pacifism and outright militarism. To the original three requirements of Aquinas they add that a justifiable war must be fought with approvable means. This implies some limitations on nuclear warfare, for instance. A recent symposium in which many contributors represent a Thomistic background shows a wide diversity of views on the morality of military service.[37]

Finally in regard to controversies, a sixth debate deals with whether any general rules of morality impose absolute obligations.

A frequent dictum in older manuals of moral theology stated that negative precepts (prohibitions) are absolutely obligatory, while affirmative rules bind only in some cases. Actually Thomas Aquinas had pointed out that practical reasoning deals with contingent matters and that the more detailed such reasoning becomes (by virtue of including changing circumstances) the more will its concluding precepts be subject to exceptions.[38] This is why Aquinas did not hold that all ethical rules are absolutely obligatory. Thomistic moral theology now tends, in some instances, to minimize the degree of obligation in ethical rules. The essays in Charles Curran's book, *Absolutes in Moral Theology?* illustrates how far this movement has gone. Reaction to it is evident in more conservative Thomist works.

Special ethical problem areas in which Thomists have been most active are: (1) bio-medical issues, (2) property and business problems, and (3) socio-political questions. Human life is a primary value which deserves special protection and care. Abortion, euthanasia and suicide are condemned as immoral practices.[39] It is well to note that these are ethical judgments about objectionable *types* of action. Judgments regarding *particular* moral decisions on such matters involve unique sets of circumstances which may sometimes absolve the moral agent from blame. It is not the work of the ethicist, as Thomists see it, to sit in judgment on the individual person who takes life, either of others or his own. The practice of artificial contraception (as distinguished from natural control of conception by avoidance of intercourse in fertile periods) is also generally deemed immoral, because sexual union is obviously designed for reproduction of members of the species.

Taking human life may be ethically permitted in three general situations: where it is necessary to kill an unjust aggressor; where one is required to defend one's country in time of war; and where a criminal has been convicted of a very serious crime. In the case of unjust aggression there must be no other available means of defense than killing, it must be done at the time of actual aggression, and the defender must have the intention of protecting his own life or that of another person. Capital punishment tends to be criticized by some Thomists as inhumane and as frequently applied unjustly. Retribution as justification for such punishment is also less supported in recent Thomist writing.[40]

Euthanasia (as a positive act of killing a person to end suffering, or to promote the good of society, or for similar benevolent motives) is considered immoral. However passive euthanasia, the allowing of a person to die by refusing to use extraordinary treatments, is not condemned. The whole problem of the definition of death is a matter of much dispute among Thomists: many think that the cessation of brain function is too narrow a criterion but some accept the Harvard definition with various qualifications. Some advocate state-approved definitions; others reject such intervention by civil authority.[41]

Thomists are also concerned with ethical problems involving property and business transactions. Aquinas clearly distinguished the right *to manage* the production and distribution of material goods from the quite different right *to use* such things.[42] The first right is private and need not be practiced by all persons; the right to use things, however, is common to all persons and cannot be reserved to just a few. As far as wealth and material possessions are concerned, there can be no rigid system of detailed ethics, for all times and places. In the future greater pluralization of ethical positions within any of the various schools of philosophy may be expected. It took Thomistic ethics a long time to adjust to modern economic and business conditions. As recently as eighty years ago, John A. Ryan was arguing for a family living wage in America of about $900 to $1200 a year.[43] But the just wage or price of one decade may be multiplied in the next. The principles of Thomistic ethics can be adjusted to changing economic conditions but open-minded prudence is also required.

The socio-political order also has many new problems. St Thomas lived in a feudal world and has often been described as a monarchist. He did think that unified control of a community is essential. But in his own religious Order of Preachers he took part in frequent democratic meetings of provincial and general chapters of the Dominicans. It cannot be said that any one system of government is typically Thomistic. Extreme forms of anarchism or totalitarianism are rejected, of course. In the US the writings of John Courtney Murray are regarded as representative of Aquinas's democratic leanings.[44]

Since the family, as a small natural group on which any stable state society is founded, is strongly defended by Thomists, problems concerning children, mutual love between spouses, marriage and divorce, receive much attention. What is called perfect divorce (separation with permission to remarry) is condemned but many older restrictions on the settlement of matrimonial problems have been removed in recent decades. Where older Thomistic treatises stressed one major purpose for marriage, the procreation and rearing of children, present thinking stresses mutual love and assistance among spouses as another important end.

Two points may finally be stressed in regard to the future of this sort of ethics. First, some Thomists are beginning to recognize that their ethics is neither wholly consequential nor wholly deontological. If we take these labels in their broadest sense, consequentialism is the theory that ethical thinking looks primarily to the predictable results of moral actions in order to decide whether they are good or evil. Utilitarianism has usually been regarded with suspicion by Thomists but there are other forms of consequentialism and Thomistic teleology is one of them. It implies a looking forward to goals and consideration of the results achieved in securing such ends. The great majority of Thomists still think that the loving contemplation of God in a future life is the highest moral good. This type of consequence theory seems essential to an updated Thomist ethics.

In the second place, Kantian duty ethics is not the only kind of prior attitude morality. No Thomist will deny that the thinking, feeling and willing which precedes performance of complete moral actions give ethical quality to the act. In other words, Thomistic ethical theory also depends a great deal on prior attitudes of consciousness in the moral agent. It is not advisable to restrict all moral activity to inter-personal transactions. Justice is not the only virtue. Right reasoning, moderation in emotional life, and courageous inner responses to serious threats – all are good but not necessarily exteriorized moral dispositions. If Thomists would make better use of the resources inherent in Aquinas's teaching on the cardinal and theological virtues, then they might be able to overcome the unfortunate deontology-teleology dichotomy and thus give a new direction to their ethics.

NOTES

1 For a survey of Aquinas's ethics see R. McInerny, *Ethica Thomistica. The Moral Philosophy of Thomas Aquinas*, Washington, D.C.: Catholic University of America Press, 1982; and V. Bourke, *History of Ethics*,

Garden City, N.T.: Doubleday, 1968, Chapter 6.

2 J. Maritain, *Neuf leçons sur les notions premières de la philosophie morale*, Paris; Tequi, 1951; *Moral Philosophy* trans. M. Suther *et al.*, New York: Scribner, 1964.

3 Maritain, *Science and Wisdom*, New York: Scribner, 1940, p. 109: 'A purely natural moral philosophy adequate to human action *could have* existed, as the state of nature could have existed, but in fact neither does exist.'

4 See the criticism of nature as norm, in D.J. O'Connor, *Aquinas and Natural Law*, London: Macmillan, 1964, pp. 16–21.

5 On ethical induction and deduction: G.D. Dalcourt, *The Methods of Ethics*, Lanham, MD: University Press of America, 1983, Chapter 9; also G.P. Klubertanz, 'The Empiricism of Thomistic Ethics,' *Proc. Amer. Cath. Philos. Assoc.* 31 (1957) 13–20.

6 More on this criticism in O'Connor, pp. 20–1.

7 Josef Pieper, *The Four Cardinal Virtues*, Notre Dame University Press, 1966; and my *Ethics: A Textbook in Moral Philosophy*, New York: Macmillan, 1966.

8 For this theme in several types of recent ethics: *The Monist* (*Right Reason in Western Ethics* issue) 66, 1 (1983), with contributions by W.K. Frankena, D.S. Theron, J.M. Rist, H. Veatch, V. Bourke, R.J. Sullivan, D.P. Dryer, G.S. Kavka, S.D. Hudson and S.F. Sapontzis.

9 On metaphysics and right reason ethics: H. Veatch, *Rational Man*, Bloomington: Indiana University Press, 1962.

10 This list of basic goods is from G. Grisez and Russell Shaw, *Beyond the New Morality. The Responsibilities of Freedom*, Notre Dame University Press, 1974, Chapter 7; almost the same list in J. Finnis, *Natural Law and Natural Rights*, Oxford: Clarendon Press, 1980, Chapters 3 and 4.

11 Finnis, op. cit. p. 95; and *Fundamentals of Ethics*, Washington D.C.: Georgetown University Press, 1982; Finnis is criticized in McInerny, *Ethica Thomistica*, pp. 52–9.

12 See R.J. Henle, 'Transcendental Thomism: A Critical Assessment,' in *One Hundred Years of Thomism*, ed. V. Brezik, Houston: University of St Thomas, 1981, pp. 90–116.

13 K. Rahner, 'On the Question of a Formal Existential Ethics,' in *Theological Investigations*, vol. II, trans, K.H. Kruger, Baltimore: Helicon, 1963, pp. 217–34; see selections from Rahner's ethics in: G. McCool, *A Rahner Reader*, New York: Seabury Press, 1975, pp. 245–77.

14 J. Fuchs, *Lex Naturae. Zur Theologie des Naturrechts*, Dusseldorf: Patmos Verlag, 1955.

15 W.A. Luijpen, *Phenomenology of Natural Law*, Pittsburgh: Duquesne University Press, 1967; for another subjectivist critique see B. Lonergan, *The Subject*, Milwaukee: Marquette University Press, 1968.

16 H. Reiner, *Gut un Böse*, Freiburg i, B: Bielefelds, 1965.

17 *ST*, II-II, 23, 8; *De Malo*, p. 8, 2; *De Caritate*, 3; of. G. Gilleman, *The Primacy of Charity in Moral Theology*, trans. W.F. Ryan and A. Vashon, Westminster, MD: Newman Press, 1959.

18 See J.G. Milhaven (pp. 70–3), R. McCormick (pp. 140–6), Charles Curran (pp. 187–93) and T. Wassmer (pp. 231–6) in *The Situation Ethics Debate*, ed. Harvey Cox, Philadelphia: The Westminster Press, 1968.

19 C. Curran, *Absolutes in Moral Theology?* Washington–Cleveland: Corpus Books, 1968, p. 20.

20 *ST*, II-II, 17, 5; *De Spe*, 1.

21 P.J. Rossi, *Together Toward Hope. A Journey to Moral Theology*, Notre Dame University Press, 1983; for the historical background: J. Collins, *The Emergence of Philosophy of Religion*, New Haven: Yale University Press, 1967.

22 Rossi, p. 31.

23 J. Fuchs, *Christian Ethics in a Secular Arena*, Washington, D.C.: Georgetown University Press, 1981; and V. Bourke, 'Moral Philosophy without Revelation,' *The Thomist*, 40 (1976) 555–70.

24 For many statements from St Thomas: I.T. Eschmann, 'A Thomistic Glossary on the Principle of the Preeminence of a Common Good,' *Mediaeval Studies* (Toronto), 5 (1943) 123–165; and 'Bonum commune melius est quam bonum unis. Eine Studie ueber den Wertvorrange des Personalen bei Thomas von Aquin,' *Med. Studies*, 6 (1944) 62–120.

25 J. Maritain, *La Personne et le bien commun*, Paris: Desclée de Brouver, 1947; trans. by J.J. Fitzgerald, *The Person and the Common Good*, New York: Scribner, 1957.

26 C. de Koninck, *De la primaute du bien commun contre les personnalistes*, Québec: Université Laval, 1943; 'In Defense of Saint Thomas: A Reply to Father Eschmann's Attack on the Primacy of the Common Good,' *Laval Théologique et Philosophique*, 2 (1945) 9–116.

27 J. Croteau, *Les Fondements thomistes du personnalisme de Maritain*, Ottawa: Université d'Ottawa, 1955.

28 Cf. G. Smith, 'The Natural end of Man,' *Proc. Amer. Cath. Philos. Assoc.* 23 (1949) 47–61.

29 G. Grisez, *Christian Moral Principles*, Chicago: Franciscan Herald Press, 1983, pp. 807–10.

30 Cf. R. McCormick, *Doing Evil to Achieve Good. Moral Choice in Conflict Situations*, Chicago: Loyola University Press, 1976.

31 *ST*, II-II, 64, 7, c: 'nihil prohibet unius actus esse duos effectus, quorum alter solum sit in intentione, alius vero sit praeter intentionem.'

32 P. Knauer, 'The Hermeneutic Function of the Principle of Double Effect,' *Natural Law Forum*, 12 (1967) 132–62; B. Schüller, 'Direkte Totung – indirekte Totung,' *Theolgie und Philosophie*, 47 (1972) 341–57; and C. Van der Poel, 'The Principle of Double Effect,' in *Absolutes*

in Moral Theology? pp. 186–210.

33 T.E. O'Connell, *Principles for a Catholic Morality*, New York: Seabury Press, 1978, p. 153.

34 Grisez, *Christian Moral Principles*, p. 160; and ch. 6.

35 *ST*, II-II, 40, 1, c.

36 On the whole problem of war and Thomistic ethics: E.B.F. Midgley, *The Natural Law Tradition*, New York: Harper & Row, 1975, pp. 43–55, 62–9, 120–31, 371–426.

37 'The Christian Soldier: A Symposium,' *Catholicism in Crisis* (Notre Dame University; II, 4 (March, 1984)).

38 *ST*, I-II, 94, 4, c; and for exceptions to certain biblical precepts, f. 100, 8, c.

39 See. G. Grisez and J.M. Boyle, *Life and Death with Liberty and Justice*, Notre Dame University Press, 1979; J. Noonan, *The Morality of Abortion*, Cambridge, Mass: Harvard University Press, 1970; and B. Häring, *Medical Ethics*, Notre Dame: Fides Press, 1973.

40 Bourke, 'The Ethical Justification of Legal Punishment,' *American Journal of Jurisprudence*, 22 (1977) 1–18.

41 Chapter 4, 'The Liberty to Refuse Medical Treatment,' in Grisez-Boyle, *Life and Death*, pp. 120; and W.C. Charron, 'Death: A Philosophical Perspective on the Legal Definition,' *Washington University Law Quarterly*, (1975) 979–1005.

42 Bourke, 'Material Possessions and Thomistic Ethics,' in *Philosophic Thought in France and the United States*, ed. M. Farber, Buffalo: University of Buffalo Publications in Philosophy, 1950, pp. 613–27.

43 See J. Noonan, *The Scholastic Analysis of Usury*, Cambridge, Mass: Harvard University Press, 1957; and J.A. Ryan, *A Living Wage*, New York: Macmillan, 1906.

44 J.C. Murray, *We Hold These Truths: Reflections on the American Proposition*, New York: Sheed & Ward, 1960.

5

EXISTENTIALIST ETHICS

Charles Guignon

A quarter of a century has passed since existentialism exploded on the American scene, filtering down to the mass culture in the form of existentialist literature, psychologies, theologies and literary theories. Its heady brew of dramatic language and vivid imagery captivated the imagination of self-styled 'outsiders', and fueled the youth rebellion of the sixties. In a short time a spate of works appeared in English attempting to formulate an existentialist ethics.[1] The appeal of existentialism lay not in any unified doctrine, but in its powerful criticisms of the complacency and hypocrisy of contemporary life, and in its stress upon individual autonomy and responsibility. Its concentration on the concrete issues of human life – on questions of freedom, commitment, the complexity of life-situations, death and authenticity – was taken by many to be an antidote to the arid and impersonal theorizing of the time.

Existentialism is best understood as a response to what Nietzsche had recognized when he proclaimed that 'God is dead.' Nietzsche makes it clear that this pronouncement does not refer merely to the decline of religion in contemporary life, but makes the bolder claim that all of the revered absolutes of Western thought, including faith in an order of nature, the dictates of Reason, and even the promise of science, have collapsed, leaving us with no taken-for-granted bases for choice and action. As a result, humans are thrown back onto themselves in a radical way. We are ultimately self-creating, with 'no excuses behind us, nor justification before us.'[2]

Today existentialism as a philosophical movement is for all practical purposes dead. Its death is due, in part, to the widespread conclusion that it breeds subjectivism and nihilism, and that it 'makes ethics impossible.'[3] More importantly, I believe, existentialism faded from the scene because it had lost its bite in contemporary life. As Richard Rorty, one of existentialism's few current defenders, says, 'Existentialism is an *intrinsically reactive* movement of thought'[4] – it gains its point from what it opposes. In America, however, existentialism seems to have been so thoroughly ingested into cultural life that it has little to react to. In our individualistic and libertarian world, it comes to appear as a commonplace rather than as a revolutionary movement. Yet existentialism lives on in the writings of some of its principal exponents who have presented powerful indictments of contemporary life and have pointed the way toward, if not an ethical theory, at least an ethos – what I will call a 'moral orientation toward life.' My goal in what follows is to examine the thought of four influential thinkers – Kierkegaard, Nietzsche, Sartre and Heidegger – and to argue that existentialism still has something worthwhile to contribute to current debates in ethics.

THE INDIVIDUAL AND THE MODERN WORLD

Most existentialists have held that it is necessary to clarify our human predicament before we can turn to formulating an ethical theory. A recurrent theme is the Sartrean claim that 'existence precedes essence,' or, in Heidegger's words, 'essence lies in existence.' The significance of this claim was first elaborated by Kierkegaard in the ironic, convoluted style that typifies existentialist writings: 'A human being is a spirit. But what is spirit? Spirit is the self. But what is the self? The self is a relation that relates itself to itself. . . ; the self is not the relation but is the relation's relating itself to itself.'[5] Kierkegaard unpacks this rigmarole by saying that a human is a combination 'of the infinite and the finite, of the temporal and the eternal, of freedom and necessity.' In other words, our human situation is characterized by a tension or conflict between two sets of needs or demands. On the one hand, there is a certain 'facticity' to life: we are finite beings, thrown into a world not of our own choosing, with inbuilt needs and drives, and limited in our range of possibilities. But, on the other hand, there is also a drive toward 'transcendence' in life: in our actions we constantly express our aspiration for some ultimate significance and justification for our existence.

To be human, then, is to be caught up in this first-order relation, this contradictory set of demands. What makes up a human, however, is not just the co-presence of these aspects; it is instead the second-order relation of taking a stand on this tension in trying to make something of our lives. Each individual tries to come to terms with the conflict built into the human situation by *acting* in the world in determinate ways, by taking over some set of self-interpretations that form a personal identity. In this sense I *am* what I make of myself in my actions: my 'essence' is defined by my 'existence,' that is, the concrete ways I act in tackling the problem posed by life.

The conception of our predicament as involving a tension or fundamental ambiguity that must be resolved by the individual reappears in most existentialist writings. According to Nietzsche, 'In man *creature* and *creator* are united'; there is both raw material to be fashioned, and 'there is also creator, form-giver'[6] with the result that we are responsible for the form our life has. In Sartre's vocabulary, we are both *en soi*, 'in-itself'; one being among others in the midst of beings; and we are *pour soi*, 'for-itself'; capable of distancing ourselves from ourselves and other beings in order to question them and decide their meaning. Hence Sartre says we always 'surpass' ourselves: having the ability to go beyond our brute givenness and envisage possibilities, we are free to decide the meaning of our lives and our world. For Heidegger, we are both 'thrown' into a world, bound up with a specific context, yet also 'ahead of ourselves' to the extent that we are 'projections' toward a future of open possibilities for interpretation and reinterpretation.

Our situation as 'thrown' into a world with no pregiven essence to realize is revealed to us in certain emotional experiences: despair (Kierkegaard), purposelessness and nihilism (Nietzsche), anxiety (Heidegger), and anguish (Sartre). These emotions reveal to us the burden we face of taking responsibility for our own lives. Needless to say, existentialists are aware that most of us generally feel no such extreme emotions, and so their task is to explain why we tend to live lives of bland complacency despite the emotional turmoil that is supposed to underlie our existence. Kierkgaard's *The Present Age*[7] served as a model for existentialist diagnoses of contemporary life. The present age, according to Kierkegaard, is characterized by a process of 'leveling down' – achieved by the 'monstrous nothing,' the 'public' – which obliterates all qualitative distinctions among people through 'the dizziness of unending abstraction.' The conformism of our time (together with its spurious 'individualism') levels everyone down to the least common denominator – to interchangeable bits in a social mosaic.

The leveling process results from society's need for norms and conventions to standardize behavior in a world in which traditional institutionalized relations have collapsed. These social norms absolve the individual from taking responsibility for his or her actions. We feel we are doing well so long as we are 'acting on principle.' Yet a principle 'is something purely external,' 'a monstrous something or other, an abstraction, just like the public.' The trouble with principles (and here we find a central theme in existentialism) is that they are universal and impersonal, whereas situations of action are particular and intensely personal. Thus, situations and actions are open to various interpretations, and can always be made to appear to fall under a principle depending on the agent's way of describing the context. For this reason, 'everything becomes permissible if done "on principle;" ' 'one can do anything "on principle" and avoid all personal responsibility.' Since principles are at best rules of thumb, they can provide guidance only for individuals who have already formed for themselves a firm moral character which monitors their interpretations of their situations and the applicability of principles. The anonymity of the 'public' and its principles, however, undermines the individual's ability to form such a character. In Kierkegaard's view, genuine social solidarity and a moral life are possible only where individuals can develop a moral orientation toward life: 'It is only after the individual has acquired an ethical outlook, in face of the whole world, that there can be any suggestion of really joining together.' An ethical outlook can be cultivated only through accepting our responsibility in interacting with the world.

Individuals succeed in evading their own responsibility for their actions because they succumb to what Olafson calls 'the objectivist illusion'[8]: the illusion that there are fixed, objective truths and values that determine what is right and wrong. No existentialist writer has criticized the objectivist illusion more extensively than Nietzsche. In Nietzsche's view, most of our 'higher morality' is just a 'herd animal morality' rooted in the needs of a herd and ultimately a matter of arbitrary convention. Nietzsche saves his harshest diatribes for Christian morality which, he thinks, is a form of 'slave morality' that arose from resentment against the ruling classes. A slave morality is the result of sheer negation, a mere inversion of the heroic noble morality. Where the masters value pride, courage, retaliation and personal merit, the slaves value humility, meekness, forgiveness, equality and social utility. Nietzsche is especially contemptuous of the form slave morality takes as utilitarianism. In promoting 'happiness,' utilitarianism ministers to the creaturely in people, dehumanizes them to the level of mere pleasure-seekers and pain-avoiders, and stifles all creativity and courage to deal with suffering.[9]

A highly individualistic and even elitist strand of existentialism emerges in the writings of Kierkegaard and Nietzsche. In Kierkegaard's view, a genuine individual is capable at any moment of 'teleologically suspending the ethical' because of his or her commitment to a personal and subjective 'absolute.'[10] And according to Nietzsche, although the herd usually has the morality it deserves, '*higher* moralities are, or ought to be, possible'.[11] For the few exceptional individuals who can face up to the purposelessness of life (as revealed in the thought of the 'eternal return of the same') Nietzsche counsels, 'Become what you are!'[12] This imperative calls for a resolute acceptance of all one has been, and for a style of life that organizes the self in such a way as 'to make a unified character out of all one has done.'[13] In the long run, Nietzsche believes, such courageous and steadfast individuals will serve humanity as a whole far better than any pallid utilitarian ideals, since the individual 'does not constitute a separate entity, an atom,' but is always a contributor to the entire species.

SARTRE AND TERRIBLE FREEDOM

The question of an existentialist ethics has tended naturally to center on the conception of human existence found in the writings of Sartre, the leading spokesman for existentialism and the most outspoken about ethical issues.[14] Like his predecessors, Sartre criticizes the 'spirit of seriousness' of ordinary people, and especially the bourgeoisie, who assume that there is a pregiven, objective set of values and obligations in the public world and that the good life consists in conforming to these objective givens. In *Nausea*,

Sartre traces the dawning awareness of this objectivist illusion in Roquentin as he painfully comes to realize that the so-called 'objective world' is in fact man-made, a product of the inertia of human customs and schematizations, with no justification or ground in 'being-in-itself.' The belief that any course of action or stance is necessitated by objective facts or values is 'bad faith,' in Sartre's view: it is a self-deception rooted in our refusal to acknowledge our ultimate freedom as self-creating beings.

In *Being and Nothingness* Sartre works out an ontology of human existence which, although it 'can not formulate ethical precepts,' can enable us to 'repudiate the spirit of seriousness.' This ontology reveals that we are, at the core, 'terrible freedom.' The conception of human existence at total, unbounded freedom has its origins in Husserl's phenomenology. For Husserl, once one realizes that all reality is constituted by the meaning-giving acts of consciousness, one sees that 'as transcendental ego I am thus the absolutely responsible subject of whatever has existential validity for me.'[15] Sartre rejects Husserl's notion of a 'transcendental ego' as one more illusion of objectivism, but nevertheless takes his start from the fact of consciousness as the source of all meanings. The '*I think, therefore I exist*' is fundamental: 'There we have the absolute truth of consciousness becoming aware of itself.' Beginning from the bedrock of consciousness as constituting activity, Sartre sets out to show that all reality is a product of our meaning-giving acts, that 'I have to realize the meaning of the world and my (own) essence . . .'

The extent to which we are 'absolutely responsible' for all being becomes apparent in some concrete examples Sartre explores in *Being and Nothingness*. Suppose a storm destroys a farmer's crops. Where does the 'destruction' come from? Surely not from being-in-itself, Sartre answers. The storm does not destroy anything; it merely modifies 'the distribution of masses of being,' just as the storms on Jupiter redistribute masses of being without that counting as 'destruction.' The change in being can *count as destruction* only for a farmer who has made his or her fundamental project the preservation and protection of the farm. In general, as Sartre argues in the chapter 'Freedom and Responsibility,' the determinate world we encounter is always a product of ways we let things count for us in our free choices of ourselves as agents in the world. A war, for example, is *my* responsibility to the extent that I choose to interpret it as a war: 'For lack of getting out of it, I have *chosen* it.' Similarly,

'I *choose* being born.' Of course my brute presence in the world is not of my own choosing, but my interpretation of how my birth *matters* to me – that is, what I think of my age, my parents, my birth-place and upbringing, and so on – is a result of my own free choices. In Sartre's view, I am always confronted by an inchoate sense of my facticity insofar as I am embodied, dealing with others, and located in a situation. But it is always up to me to *interpret* that facticity, to give it a meaning. 'Thus facticity is everywhere, but inapprehensible; I never encounter anything except my responsibility.' Even other people, who first give me a sense of who I am, are ultimately only '*opportunities* and *chances*' for my free interpreting activity. The 'entire world as a peopled-world' is founded on my choices as 'a being which is compelled to decide the meaning of being.'

At the core of our being, therefore, we are 'condemned to be free.' This ground-level freedom, which Jeanson calls 'ontological freedom,'[16] implies that any tendency to think that our actions or beliefs are compulsory is bad faith. What holds for particular interpretations and situations holds also for the 'fundamental project' or personal identity I have assumed for my life as a whole. If I choose to be an easy-going person, that choice will shape my perception of myself, my situations, others and the world as a whole. Our ultimate values are always products of the basic choices we make for our lives. But it remains the case that at every moment *I* am choosing to be such a person. I am always capable of a 'radical conversion' through which I might become dogmatic and intolerant. Therefore, to maintain the kind of character I have chosen for myself requires a constant renewal of that existential stance. To think that I really *am* anything (as broccoli really *is* broccoli) would be self-deception.

The ultimacy of our 'ontological freedom' implies that we must recognize our total *responsibility* for all our choices in dealing with moral dilemmas. In 'The Humanism of Existentialism,' Sartre considers the case of a young man during the war who has to decide whether to stay with his ailing mother or to go off to fight with the resistance. This dilemma is typical of moral dilemmas to the extent that the decision the young man faces is not merely between two kinds of action, but 'between two kinds of ethics' – an ethic of filial duty and a broader social ethic. There is no simple algorithm for choice here because the ethical framework one employs will pre-shape one's interpretation of the dilemma itself. How does the young man decide? Sartre points out that principles and values are useless because 'values are vague, and . . . are always too broad for the concrete case.' Furthermore, there is no way to seek guidance from our moral feelings, since we only find out how we *feel* about something in the process of acting. In the end, the young man can only *leap* one way rather than the other. He just 'invents,' aware that there is no basis for his choice. Ethical decisions involve 'creation and invention:' 'Man makes himself . . . In choosing his ethics, he makes himself . . .'

A Sartrean ethics therefore lays ultimate emphasis on the freedom of the individual in deciding and acting. What is problematic for such an ethics, however, is how to use this notion of 'ontological freedom' in order to draw conclusions about what we *ought* to pursue in life. Sartreans have generally held that the *fact* of freedom entails that we ought to strive to realize (1) our own practical freedom as agents, and (2) the freedom of all humankind. But it is not at all clear how such an inference is to be made.

Sartre claims, first of all, that if I acknowledge my own freedom and still act as though I were not free, this would be 'dishonest' and not 'strictly coherent.' What is questionable here is how he can make these value judgments. If all values are free creations on our part, why should I accept honesty and coherence as vaules? Moreover, even if I *did* accept these values, it is still not obvious why I *ought* to pursue my own freedom. 'Ontological freedom' signifies that we are all ultimately free – 'the slave in chains is as free as his master.'[17] Given this freedom, however, why should I care about my *actual* freedom from constraints?[18] Jeanson argues that to acknowledge our fundamental freedom and to recognize that we are usually fleeing this freedom into bad faith will lead us to see that 'we should then try to liberate ourselves,' that we should appropriate our 'factual freedom' as 'freedom-as-valued.'[19] Nevertheless, what 'self-liberation' and 'freedom-as-valued' mean here is so formal as to be uninformative. If I *am* free, how can I *want* freedom? If I do want freedom, what *sort* of freedom do I want?

Sartre's attempt to show that, in valuing my own freedom I must value the freedom of all, is also suspect. According to Sartre, 'in wanting freedom we discover that it depends entirely on the freedom of others, and that the freedom of others depends on ours.'[20] As an empirical generalization, however, this claim seems wildly implausible. Why does the slave-owner's freedom depend on the freedom of his slaves? In his analysis of 'The Existence of Others,' Sartre tries to buttress this ideal of universal freedom with a conceptual argument. My ability to feel shame as more than an inchoate sensation, he claims, presupposes that within my *cogito* I experience the 'indubitable presence' of the Other as a being who judges and appraises me. In my ability to feel ashamed, 'I recognize the justice of these appraisals . . . I am the object of values which come to qualify me without me being able to act on this qualification . . .'

To acknowledge my shame, then, is to 'accept and wish that others should confer upon me a being which I recognize.' But such self-recognition is meaningful to me only if the Other is free to judge me fairly and candidly. There is therefore a need for reciprocity and the mutual recognition among autonomous judges and evaluators, and this Hegelian concept of recognition leads de Beauvoir to conclude that 'to will oneself free is also to will the others free': 'every man needs the freedom of other men and, in a sense, always wants it . . .'[21] Nevertheless, within the confines of Sartre's Cartesian ontology, this conclusion seems unwarranted. Sartre tells us that we are always free to take a stance of 'indifference toward others,' simply ignoring their opinions. In Piotr Hoffman's words, 'shame and fear are *my* emotions, and they are thus, on Sartre's own theory, dependent upon my choice and stances . . . I could have constituted myself as a self totally oblivious to other selves.'[22]

The notion of the interdependence and 'unity of consciousnesses' in constituting a shared world leads to a deep-seated egalitarianism in Sartre's thought. From the basis of this ideal of reciprocity and the need for mutual respect he tries to show that existentialism implies universalizability: whatever rights I desire for myself I should be willing to grant to all. 'When we say that a man chooses his own self,' according to Sartre, 'we also mean that in making this choice he also chooses all men.' In each of our actions, we 'create an image of man as we think he ought to be,' and so 'at every moment I'm obliged to perform exemplary acts.'[23] But, once again, it is not clear what this noble thought is supposed to imply. If I marry Susan, does that mean I have committed myself to thinking everyone 'ought to be' married to Susan? More importantly, granting that everyone can freely constitute the meaning of others in the 'peopled-world,' why should I worry about my image or about others' opinion of me? Against Sartre's own intentions, his Cartesian picture of human existence seems to slide into a kind of solipsism and an empty ethical formalism.

There can be no doubt that Sartre's gospel of freedom can have a stirring, inspirational effect on people who feel trapped by their situations. It is because of this inspirational quality that Sartre's thought has had such an impact on an age given to conformism and scientific determinism. But there is also an insidious side to this extreme voluntarism. Alasdair MacIntyre has suggested that the Sartrean vision of the self as capable of freely leaping 'from one state of moral commitment to another,' and lacking any sense of being rooted 'within a set of social relationships,' is a picture of a self that is utterly dispersed, with no basis for coherent choice whatsoever.[24] And Charles Taylor points out that the Sartrean agent whose actions are always a matter of 'radical choice' has 'no language in which the superiority of one alternative over the other can be articulated,' with the result that 'choice fades into non-choice.'[25] Where making a decision is just a matter of plunking for one option rather than another, with no pregiven basis of values for moral deliberation, Sartre's 'terrible freedom' tends to collapse into the worst sort of slavery – the isolated self buffeted about by momentary impulses and whims.

HEIDEGGER AND SITUATED FREEDOM

Frederick Olafson sagely suggests that Sartre's conception of freedom can be modified by incorporating Merleau-Ponty's insight 'that moral community and shared evaluative standards have a place in a just characterization of the moral life, and that their role and importance can be acknowledged without prejudice to the doctrine of the primacy of choice.'[26] What Olafson fails to appreciate is the extent to which the notion of 'situated freedom' had already been worked out by Heidegger in *Being and Time*.[27] One of Heidegger's central aims was to undercut the Cartesian split between consciousness and the 'in-itself' by characterizing human existence (or 'Dasein') as a unitary phenomenon of 'Being-in-the-world.' Although Heidegger, like Sartre, insists that his ontology has no normative implications, I believe his conceptions of authenticity and authentic community have the most to offer for formulating a viable existentialist ethical position.[28]

Heidegger attempts to capture both the uniqueness of individuals and their participation in wider contexts by describing Dasein as a 'happening' caught up in a concrete world. On the one hand, human existence is 'in each case mine to be in one way or another. Dasein has always made some sort of decision as to the way in which it is to be in each case mine.' Our unique responsibility for our own lives as self-interpreting beings is revealed in the experience of anxiety which forces us to confront our finitude and the 'uncanniness' of our existence as lacking any fixed, objective ground or justification for our lives. We find ourselves 'thrown' into being, with a past behind us, yet we are also 'projecting' toward the future in the stances we take in acting in the world. What makes up our 'mineness' as individuals is not 'consciousness' as a center of intentional acts, but rather the uniqueness of our 'life-history' as a projection toward the realization of a final pattern of meaning for our lives as a whole. The expressions 'Being-toward-the-end' and 'Being-toward-death' are supposed to convey the fact that each of our lives *will* reach a culmination, and that we are ultimately responsible for what those lives add up to as a totality.

On the other hand, however, Heidegger emphasizes the way in which our actions are always situated in a cultural and historical context which we do not ourselves create.[29] At the most fundamental level of Being-in-the-world, according to Heidegger, we are agents enmeshed in a practical life-world, already involved with equipment which is organized into networks of means/ends relations by our concerns and aims as agents. Our ways of handling ourselves in ordinary situations is governed in advance by a background of intelligibility we have been initiated into in growing up into the public world of the 'Anyone' (*das Man*). Heidegger says that our dependence on the public context '*belongs to Dasein's positive constitution*,' because it is our tacit mastery of the 'preunderstanding' of the goals and forms of life in our communal world that first makes it possible for us to grasp the significance of the situations of practical action in which we find ourselves. Thus, it is not the solitary consciousness that is the source of meaning. On the contrary, 'the Anyone itself articulates the referential context of significance': that is, the meaningful practices we can and do engage in are already articulated for us by the institutions and specific relationships of the public world in which we are located.

The shared intelligibility of the public world is made accessible to us in language. Through communication, 'the articulation of being-with-one-another understandingly is constituted.' Our sense of who we are – our very identity as humans – is prescribed in advance by the vocabulary of self-description and self-evaluation 'deposited' in our language. Since language embodies a prior interpretation of what existence is all about, we first find ourselves as place-holders, so to speak, in the webs of pregiven meanings laid out in the linguistically articulated public world. This communal world is itself a product of history. 'Dasein has grown up both into and in a traditional way of interpreting itself: in terms of this it understands itself proximally and, within a certain range, constantly.' Even an 'authentic' life is 'so far from extricating itself from the way of interpreting Dasein which has come down to us, that in each case it is in terms of this interpretation . . . that any possibility one has chosen is seized upon in one's resolution.'[30] To the extent that we are always enmeshed in a linguistic and historical matrix we can never totalize or put at arm's length, the notion that there is an isolated 'consciousness' freely deciding the 'existential validity' of things loses its plausibility. In the words of Heidegger's student, Hans-Georg Gadamer, 'The focus of subjectivity is a distorting mirror. The self-awareness of the individual is only a flickering in the closed circuits of historical life.'[31]

Given his view of life as situated in an ongoing historical culture, Heidegger's ideal of 'authenticity' can involve neither realizing one's 'terrible freedom' nor 'transcending the herd' in any sense. Instead, authenticity is a distinctive way of appropriating our being as agents in the public world. But, as is well known, Heidegger is also sharply critical of the everyday way of life of 'the Anyone.' The public, he says, tends to 'level down' all possibilities, striving to preserve 'averageness' in its insistence on the importance of falling into step with daily roles and routines. Caught up in the 'turbulence' of everydayness, Heidegger suggests, we tend to be dispersed, distracted, drifting aimlessly into the standardized conventions of the public. Struggling to maintain a sense of identity in this dispersal, we also become 'entangled' in ourselves, falling into 'the most exaggerated "self-dissection" ' and self-preoccupation.

There is an inveterate tendency to self-deception in such an inauthentic life. We evade facing up to the complexities of our involvements by enacting socially approved roles, thereby blinding ourselves to the wider implications of what we are doing. Heidegger calls this evasiveness 'forgetfulness.' What is reprehensible here is not the ordinary kind of forgetting that enables us to focus on our present tasks, but a second-order forgetting in which one 'not only forgets the forgotten but forgets the forgetting itself.'[32] The business executive, for instance, cannot afford to be distracted by social concerns as she prepares her weekly profit reports. But she is inauthentic to the extent that she conceals from herself the fact that this way of organizing her identity is achieved only by blocking out the wider social consequences of her actions, and by using her professional role as an excuse for avoiding the broader responsibilities of life.

To become authentic, then, is to overcome this evasiveness and enslavement to the 'dictatorship of the Anyone.' As authentic, we face up to our own finitude (the fact that we will run out of possibilities), and through this confrontation with death we are thrown back onto our lives in a transformed way. Instead of getting lost in role-playing and self-preoccupations, the authentic individual becomes 'clear-sighted' about public possibilities and concrete situations of action. This kind of life is characterized by 'resoluteness': authentic existence is snatched back 'from the endless multiplicity of possibilities which offer themselves,' and chooses its goals with steadfastness, integrity, coherence, a willingness to be lucid about the implications of its actions, and a recognition of its belongingness to the broader context in which it lives. An authentic life is structured into the form of a coherent narrative characterized by cumulativeness, purposiveness and openness to the exigencies of the context in which it unfolds. It exemplifies the principle, 'Become what you are.'[33]

The concept of authenticity is filled out in Heidegger's discussion of 'The Basic Constitution of Historicity.' 'Historicity' refers to the actual unfolding of a life, 'from birth to death,' in its interactions with the 'happening' of its historical culture. A life characterized by authentic historicity is one that takes over what has come before as a 'heritage' pregnant with potential, and grasps its own fate as bound up with the 'sending' or 'mission' (*Geschick*) 'of the community, of a people.' An authentic individual understands his or her life as 'guided in advance in being with one another in the same world.' To be authentic is to clear-sightedly understand that one's own life is always implicated in the wider drama of striving for communal goals, and hence that 'only in communicating and struggling does the power of (our shared) destiny become free.'

A clear sense of a moral orientation toward life comes across in Heidegger's account of our historical rootedness. The linguistically articulated practices and institutions of our communal world always embody ideals and goals – such as the aims inherent in the bonds of family, friendship, a neighborhood, citizenship and the world community – that are definitive of who we are as agents implicated in a shared world. To understand ourselves as participants in this world is also to see ourselves as already committed to realizing these ideals in our lives. Authentic Dasein, according to Heidegger, will understand its task as that of reappropriating or 'retrieving' the possibilities of those who have come before in history in order to realize the 'sending' it shares with its community. Instead of drifting into the status quo of the current world, the authentic individual will 'choose its hero' and become 'free for the struggle of loyally following in the footsteps of that which can be repeated.' Heidegger's claim seems to be that the long-range goals of our civilization can be appropriated and criticized in a concrete way only from the standpoint of the paradigmatic life-stories of heroes and heroines of our past – 'paragons of virtue' such as Moses, Jesus, Buddha, Ghandi, Florence Nightingale, and so on – who exemplify ways of pursuing the purposes and aims of our social world.

An authentic individual will therefore structure his or her own life by emulating models from the past in confronting current situations of action and choice. One realizes 'the *loyalty* of existence to (one's) own self' by 'revering the sole authority which a free existing can have – of revering the repeatable possibilities of existence.' Only by identifying an exemplary way of life as a model of one's own actions can one give content to what is at stake in pursuing the values and ideals built into one's culture and in realizing one's own life as a coherent pattern embedded in an unfolding history. To sever oneself from this context is to try to be a Cartesian dimensionless point of a self, lacking any basis for coherent action.

Although the question is not central to *Being and Time*, Heidegger provides some hints about what an authentic community would be like. In our everyday, inauthentic lives, we tend to merely enact societal roles and hide behind masks, abrogating personal responsibility for what we do. Our relations to others are often manipulative as we jockey for 'social standing' and self-assertion. We '*leap in* for' others, Heidegger says, robbing them of their responsibility for their own lives. When individuals become clear-sighted about their finitude and their being-with-one-another in a communal world, in contrast, they can 'become authentically bound together, and this makes possible the right kind of objectivity, which frees the Other for his freedom for himself.' Authentic relations take the form of '*leaping ahead* of' the other, opening up possibilities for under-standing, which 'helps the Other become clear-sighted to himself' about what is of ultimate importance in life.[34]

For Heidegger, authentic human relations are possible only where individuals have broken out of the mold of conformism and self-centeredness of contemporary life. Understanding one's own finitude 'makes Dasein, as Being-with, have some understanding for the capacities for being of Others.' Authenticity 'is what first makes it possible to let the Others who are with it "be" . . ., and to co-disclose this ability to be in the solicitude which leaps forth and liberates.' The ideal community Heidegger envisages is one in which individuals with steadfast convictions and a coherent sense of what is worth pursuing join together in their shared 'sending' with mutual respect for the intrinsic dignity and capacities of each person. 'Only by authentically being-theirselves can people authentically be with one another . . .'[35]

PRACTICAL APPLICATIONS

If an ethical theory is understood as a set of principles dictating in advance how one should act in any situation, then existentialism can not (and would not want to) provide an ethical theory. In insisting on our freedom and responsibility, on the complexity of actual life-situations, on the need for experimentation in interacting with the world, and on the ambiguity and tenuousness of life, existential-ists are suspicious of pregiven prescriptions for action. They would be in sympathy with David Wiggins's remarks about those who feel dissatisfied with Aristotle's account of moral deliberation and practical wisdom:

> I entertain the unfriendly suspicion that those who feel they *must* seek more than all this provides want a scientific theory of rationality not so much from a passion for science, even where there can be no science, but because they hope and desire, by

some conceptual alchemy, to turn such a theory into a system of rules by which to spare themselves some of the agony of thinking and all the torment of feeling and understanding that is actually involved in reasoned deliberation.[36]

It is precisely this recognition of the 'agony of thinking' and the 'torment of feeling' involved in choice that distinguishes existentialism from most modern ethical theorizing.

Nevertheless, I believe that existentialism has a great deal to offer for the cultivation of what I have called a moral orientation toward life. The existentialist notion of authenticity embodies certain ideal character traits – such as courage, integrity, clear-sightedness, steadfastness, responsibility and communal solidarity – which can contribute to the formation of a character capable of making meaningful choices in concrete situations. The authentic agent might be better equipped to evaluate different ethical standpoints and their applicability to specific contexts of action than the slavish rule-follower or the cool cost/benefit calculator.

Certain policies do seem to be more consistent with an existentialist point of view than others. The non-Nietzschean strain of existentialism stresses the capacity of each individual to realize his or her potential regardless of race, religion, gender or age, and intimates that an ideal quality of life can be achieved only where all are free to realize their potential. At the same time, however, by identifying the potential for self-realization as the basis for ascribing worth to a person, existentialism would be able to make distinctions among persons, and could defend the 'right to die' of anyone who had lost the capacity to live in a meaningful way. With their respect for human dignity, most existentialists would support the individual's freedom to create his or her own life-style, and would oppose the imposition of public control over private matters such as sexual practices among mature adults and so-called 'victimless crimes.' In the area of professional ethics, existentialism offers a way of criticizing the self-deception involved in hiding behind a social role and justifying actions as necessary to 'doing one's job.' A life dedicated to lucidity and the courage to face up to the consequences of one's actions in the rough and tumble of complex situations could never find excuses in the 'spirit of seriousness' or in 'forgetfulness.'

But the fact that existentialism can offer only a mixed bag of hints about particular practices suggests that its real value for moral theory lies not in providing us with directives, but in giving us a picture of an ideal way of life and an account of how it might be formed. Since we *are* what we *do* as 'Being-in-the-world,' we create ourselves in our actions within the confines of the materials available in our world. We can choose to live in the spirit of seriousness, accepting the objectivist illusion, cowering behind the roles of the herd, and generally evading responsibility for our own lives. Or we can resolutely take over our responsibility as 'form-givers' and creators, developing self-discipline and steadfast convictions together with an openness to life's uncertainties, striving to be clear-sighted about the implications of our involvements, and acknowledging our indebtedness to the wider community. Existentialism cannot demonstrate the superiority of one stance over the other (any more than Plato or Aristotle could *prove* the superiority of psychic harmony or eudaimonia). But existentialism's distinction between inauthenticity and authenticity might be seen as proposing a modern version of what Charles Taylor calls a 'two-tiered view of the good life' which distinguishes the demands of mundane existence from a conception of a 'higher activity distinct from ordinary needs.'[37] With its rich vision of our potential as self-creators interacting with a concrete world, existentialism could contribute to making us better moral agents in confronting life's dilemmas.

NOTES

1 Frederick A. Olafson, *Principles and Persons: An Ethical Interpretation of Existentialism* (Baltimore: Johns Hopkins, 1967), Hazel Barnes, *An Existentialist Ethics* (New York: Alfred A. Knopf, 1967), and Mary Warnock, *Existentialist Ethics* (London: Macmillan, 1967). Simone de Beauvoir's *The Ethics of Ambiguity*, trans. B. Frechtman (New York: Philosophical Library) appeared in 1948. For a recent bibliography of works on existentialist ethics, see Thomas C. Anderson, *The Foundation and Structure of Sartrean Ethics* (Lawrence: The Regents Press of Kansas, 1970).

2 Jean-Paul Sartre, 'The Humanism of Existentialism,' in *Essays in Existentialism*, ed. W. Baskin (Secaucus, N.J.: Citadel, 1974), p. 41.

3 See, for instance, Warnock, Richard Bernstein, *Praxis and Action: Contemporary Philosophies of Human Activity* (Philadelphia: University of Pennsylvania, 1971), pp. 148–64, and, more recently, T.Z. Lavine, *From Socrates to Sartre* (New York: Bantam, 1984), p. 374.

4 *Philosophy and the Mirror of Nature* (Princeton University Press, 1979), p. 366.

5 *The Sickness unto Death*, trans. H.V. and E.H. Hong (Princeton University Press, 1980), p. 13.

6 *Beyond Good and Evil* in *Basic Writings of Nietzsche*, ed., W. Kaufmann (New York: Modern Library, 1968), § 225.

7 *The Present Age* (New York: Harper Torchbooks, 1962).

8 Olafson, p. 111.

9 For a good discussion of Nietzsche's views on ethics, see Richard Schacht, *Nietzsche* (London: Routledge & Kegan Paul, 1983), Chapters 6 and 7.

10 *Fear and Trembling and Repetition*, trans. H.V. and E.V. Hong (Princeton University Press, 1983).

11 *Beyond Good and Evil*, § 202.

12 *Thus Spoke Zarathustra*, trans. R.J. Hollingdale (Baltimore: Penguin, 1961), p. 252.

13 Alexander Nehemas, 'How to Become What One Is,' *The Philosophical Review* 92 (1983), 385–417, p. 417.

14 For instance, Olafson, Warnock, Barnes and Anderson (see note 1), and Francis Jeanson, *Sartre and the Problem of Morality*, trans. R.V. Stone (Bloomington: Indiana University Press, 1980). Sartre discusses his intentions of developing an ethics in the concluding pages of *Being and Nothingness*, trans. H. Barnes (New York: Philosophical Library, 1956), and sketches out his position in 'The Humanism of Existentialism.'

15 'Phenomenology and Anthropology,' in *Realism and the Background of Phenomenology*, ed. R. Chisholm (Glencoe, Ill.: Free Press, 1960), p. 138.

16 Jeanson, p. 181.

17 *Being and Nothingness*, p. 550.

18 Bernstein, *Praxis and Action*, pp. 152–5.

19 Jeanson, pp. 183, 191.

20 'The Humanism of Existentialism,' pp. 57–8.

21 de Beauvoir, pp. 70–3.

22 *The Human Self and the Life and Death Struggle* (Gainesville: University of Florida, 1983), p. 74.

23 'The Humanism of Existentialism,' pp. 37, 39.

24 *After Virtue: A Study in Moral Theory* (University of Notre Dame Press, 1981), pp. 31–3.

25 'Responsibility for Self,' in *The Identities of Persons*, ed. A. Rorty (Berkeley: University of California Press, 1976), pp. 291–2.

26 Olafson, p. 77.

27 *Being and Time*, trans. J. Macquarrie and E. Robinson (New York: Harper & Row, 1962).

28 My account of Heidegger and ethics is indebted to Douglas Kellner's 'Authenticity and Heidegger's Challenge to Ethical Theory,' in *Thinking about Being: Aspects of Heidegger's Thought*, eds, R.W. Shahan and J.N. Mohanty (Norman: University of Oklahoma Press, 1984).

29 I have discussed this conception of situatedness in my *Heidegger and the Problem of Knowledge* (Indianapolis: Hackett, 1983), pp. 85–145.

30 *Being and Time*, pp. 41, 435.

31 *Truth and Method* (New York: Seabury, 1975), p. 245.

32 *Basic Problems of Phenomenology*, trans., A. Hofstadter (Bloomington: Indiana University Press, 1982), p. 290.

33 *Being and Time*, p. 186.

34 Ibid, pp. 158–9.

35 Ibid, pp. 309, 344.

36 'Deliberation and Practical Reason,' in *Essays on Aristotle's Ethics*, ed., A. Rorty (Berkeley: University of California, 1980), p. 237.

37 'Growth, Legitimacy and the Modern Identity,' *Praxis International*, 1 (1981), 111–25, p. 112.

6

MARXISM, MORALITY AND MORAL PHILOSOPHY

Kai Nielsen

I

Neither Karl Marx nor Frederick Engels tried to construct a moral theory resembling the type we find in classical moral theories such as those of Plato, Aristotle, Kant, Bentham, J.S. Mill or Sidgwick. Indeed they made no attempt to construct a moral theory at all.[1] Marx and Engels do indeed make scattered remarks about morality but they do not try to construct a moral theory or, like Nietzsche, to forge a 'new morality' or even write anti-foundationalist treatises on moral philosophy after the fashion of Hume, Westermarck or Dewey. In this they have been followed by the great Marxist theoreticians who constitute the core of the classical Marxist tradition. (I refer here to Luxemburg, Lenin, Trotsky, Gramsci and Lukács.) The closest thing we get to anything like the articulation of a moral theory among the classical Marxists is in Leon Trotsky's pamphlet *Their Morals and Ours*, and even there Trotsky's work is in part very much a tract for the times in which he defends himself against a variety of charges including that of 'Bolshevik amoralism,' though in the course of doing so he articulates a series of theoretical claims of no small significance.[2] Indeed even *Their Morals and Ours*, interesting as it is, is hardly an exception. It is not one of Trotsky's major works; it was written near the end of his life when he was isolated and politically rather impotent and it is very taken up with the polemics of the time. However, Marx and Engels, and Lenin as well, did in passing make moral comments and they had a

92

coherent conception of the place of morals in the structure of life, that is both threatening and deeply challenging to our common conceptions of morality and the variety of views held by most moral philosophers and theologians.[3]

Other less central figures, though by no means insignificant, have in diverse ways taken up the conceptions of the Founding Fathers and have developed, challenged, modified and rejected their views in various ways. It is not part of my task here to tell this history, though I will where it is germane give some fragments of it. What I shall to do instead is to show how Marxism poses a challenge for morality, how in turn morality poses problems for Marxism, and how a variety of contemporary Marxists have responded to these problems. In doing this I shall also argue my own Marxist response to these challenges. I shall examine considerations that naturally arise when we both think carefully about the human prospect and take Marxism seriously. I shall also try to show that a Marxist is not committed to nihilism or to the belief that all moral reflection, including his own, can be nothing but ideological twaddle.[4]

II

We will start by asking the following cluster of questions, questions we will consider in various sections of this essay. Does Marxism require a moral theory and if so what sort? Can it coherently do so? Indeed, should it do so? Some Marxists have said that morality is a form of ideology and that, since any given morality arises out of a particular stage of the development of the productive forces and relations and thus (or so not a few Marxists have said) is relative to a particular mode of production and to particular class interests, there can be no objective system of moral beliefs.[5] Yet, Marx and Marxists roundly condemn capitalism. They see it as an inhuman, though historically necessary, exploitative system that must, and indeed will, be replaced by a truly human communist society which they plainly judge to be a better society than capitalist society or any of the other previous social formations. How can these two sets of beliefs go together or, if they can't, which should give way and why? We need also to ask in this context: what is ideology and is morality unavoidably ideological? Moreover, is the issue as to whether morality is ideological an epistemological thesis or some other kind of thesis? If historical materialism is true does morality, any morality at all, totter? I shall try to make some headway with these and related questions.

In addition to the social scientific theory of Marxism and to the social critique that is integral to Marxism, there has again and again in the history of Marxism been the demand for a systematic and coherent articulation of what has been called 'the moral foundations of Marxism.' This, for those dissident Marxists who take that route, has involved the claim that a Marxist moral theory be constructed. To this more mainstream Marxists have responded with a denial that anything like this is either possible or, even if it were possible, necessary.

Given such a controversy, we should ask whether there should be or even could be a Marxist ethical theory and if so what sort of an ethical theory should it be? Marxism does indeed proffer a sociology of morals and a theory of ideology but this is a very different thing from proffering an ethical theory or a foundational claim for morals. In trying to think through what is involved here, it is vital to ascertain the bearing of the theory of ideology and the sociology of morals on the question of the possibility of a moral theory or of moral knowledge. Marx certainly thought that his own social theory raised fundamental doubts about traditional moral thinking. Does Marx's anti-moralism commit him to some form of relativism in ethics or to some form of moral skepticism or nihilism that would deny the very possibility of objective moral evaluations?

These issues are under renewed discussion today particularly by social theorists and philosophers who hold progressive views and yet, at the same time, perhaps through the reading of Marx or Freud, have come to be very wary of moralistic approaches to social criticism.[6] They want to know whether Marx and Engels did in fact base their critique of capitalism on moral considerations or whether they subscribed explicitly or implicitly to any moral views or any moral theory. They also want to know to what extent, if at all, a Marxist social theory and Marxist criticisms of capitalism, no matter what Marx may have thought about the matter, require a moral critique of capitalism or even a distinctively Marxist morality?[7] Rather than requiring it, they may not even be compatible with it. It is most fundamentally this issue that we need to sort out.

III

Issues very similar to this came under intense discussion in the first quarter of the twentieth century. The *dramtis personae* here are some of the relatively major figures in the attempt to further develop or revise Marxism after Marx. Edward Bernstein, Karl Vorlander, Karl Kautsky, Georg Plekhanov, Max Adler, Otto Bauer, and Georg Lukács count centrally among their number. There, more than in contemporary discussions, the long shadow of Kant fell and the problem about the relation of fact to value – the possibility or impossibility of deriving an ought from an is – took center stage. Marx, squarely in that respect in the Hegelian tradition, tried to set that question aside and firmly rejected a fact/value dualism.[8] Edward Bernstein and Karl Vorlander tried to meld their versions of Marxism with a Kantian conception of science which, if it were to be genuine science, must be normatively neutral.[9] They took very seriously indeed Henri Poincaré's famous dictum that from premises in the indicative mood we could never draw a conclusion in the imperative mood. Although Vorlander's position was the most extreme, it is a position towards which many people who have had some philosophical training and who have become sympathetic with Marx's social criticism would, at least initially, quite naturally gravitate. Vorlander argued that socialism cannot be based on an objective normatively neutral social science or simply on political practice but must be grounded in a distinctive set of socialist values and a Marxist moral theory.

This 'ethical socialism', seconded by Edward Bernstein, was very influential with the revisionist and reformist wing of the Second International. It was opposed by what was widely taken at the time to be the 'Orthodox Marxism' of Karl Kautsky and Georg Plekhanov.[10] Surprisingly, in the light of Marx's own Hegelianism here, both Kautsky and Plekhanov accepted the Kantian fact/value distinction. But in opposition to Vorlander and Bernstein, and here closer to Marx himself, they refused to ground socialism in either moral philosophy or morality. It was sufficient for Marxist social theory to reveal the economic law of development of modern society. This is the central task of social theory and it must not, as Kautsky argued in his *Ethics and Materialist Conception of History*, if it is to remain a genuinely scientific theory, speak, as Vorlander did, of the moral point of view in *Capital*.

Both Kautsky and Plekhanov concluded that empirical trends in the world confirmed Marx's theory of history. The historical development of capitalist societies was inexorably toward socialism. But this fact (putative fact), in itself, or in relation with any other set of facts, did not enable us to conclude that we had an obligation to struggle to attain socialism or even to approve of this development. Kautsky and Plekhanov see Marx as a social scientist who tells us who we were, who we are now and what it is likely we will become. He also, and in a powerful way, condemned capitalism for the inhuman system it is, but this, Kautsky and Plekhanov claim, is not a part of Marx's scientific theory. Strictly and accurately understood it says nothing about whether the development from capitalism to socialism to communism is good or bad.

The next stage in the development of this argument came from two Austro-Marxists, Max Adler and Otto Bauer.[11] They, like the other parties to the dispute, continued to accept a Kantian conception of the autonomy of morals. They saw themselves, however, as mediators in this dispute. They sided with the 'Orthodox Marxists' in rejecting any attempt to find a moral basis for socialism. In taking this position they realized – and indeed stressed – that what brings most socialist militants to socialism in the first place and often what nourishes them and helps them remain in the struggle is a conviction about the badness (to put it mildly) of capitalism and the conviction that socialism offers humankind a better future. With the possibility of socialism there is hope in the world; without it there isn't. The choice between socialism and capitalism or a technocratic replacement of capitalism is often seen as the choice between barbarianism and a possibly decent future. These Austro-Marxists did not, for a moment, in taking their anti-moralist stance, deride these ideas or argue that they, as moral ideas, reflected an ideologically based false consciousness. But, that notwithstanding, they still sided firmly with 'Orthodox Marxism' in viewing Marx as a social scientist who is telling us, as Adler put it, that 'socialism will not be achieved because it is justified from an ethical point of view, but because it will be the result of a causal process.'[12] They were as adamant as Kautsky in repudiating any search for the moral basis for socialism in Kant, in utilitarian theory or elsewhere. Such a fashion of establishing socialism, Adler wrote, 'must be . . . energetically repudiated, and precisely from a Marxist point of view. Marxism is a system of sociological knowledge. It bases socialism on causal knowledge of the processes of social life. Marxism and sociology are one and the same thing.'[13]

This perhaps overly scientific conception of Marxist social theory was in turn resisted by Georg Lukács in his *History and Class-Consciousness*, and later by Lucien Goldmann.[14] They both, many believe, brought Marxist theory closer to its Hegelian roots. They stressed the unity of theory and practice in Marx and challenged the legitimacy of the Kantian assumption of a sharp distinction between facts and values. Like John Dewey, they rejected the standard belief that scientific inquiry dealt with the factual and could not, while remaining faithful to its vocation, make claims about what is good or bad, right or wrong. They rejected this view as an unjusti-fied dualism as well as Max Adler's view that Marxism was social science and nothing else. Such a conception utterly neglected, they argued, the very central Marxist conception of the unity of theory and practice.

Lukács and Goldmann took evaluative discourse and factual dis-course to be ineradicably intertwined and denied that there is any clear, or at least any rigid, distinction between the is and the ought. Lukács and Goldmann argue that Marx believed – and indeed rightly believed – that social theory and social critique run in tandem and, in any proper social theory, understanding, explana-tion and evaluation are so closely linked that the value judgments, including the moral judgments, which cannot but remain in any interpretive-explanatory richly descriptive discourse, are not autonomous and independent of the facts.[15] In any social theory rich enough to have explanatory value or critical thrust, statements of value, interpretations and statements of fact are indissolubly linked. We cannot atomize the situation and usefully look at these items separately, accepting the facts of Marx's social theory and rejecting the interpretations or the value judgments, or accepting the later and rejecting his factual picture of the world. We must take them as a gestalt. The conception of the science that goes with Marx's social theory and social critique cannot be the scientistic conception of a normatively neutral social science.

Neither Marx nor Marxists should give us 'the ethical founda-tions' of Marxism. Such a conception is both illusory and unneces-sary, but it also – and this is just the other side of the coin – should not seek to give us a 'cleaned up' social science which makes no moral claims. Lukács and Goldmann argue, that such a restricted social science will neither have extensive explanatory power nor have the emancipatory role of social critique. The error made in common, they argue, by the revisionists Vorlander and Bernstein, the 'Orthodox Marxists' Kautsky and Plekhanov and the Austro-Marxists Bauer and Adler, but not by Marx or Engels, was to accept the Kantian dualism of fact and value.

IV

Contemporary Anglo-American philosophers who have taken Marx seriously have for the most part fought shy of taking firm stands on the relation of fact to value. There was around a decade ago a very extensive debate about whether in any significant sense an ought can be derived from an is.[16] From the rise of analytic philosophy to about mid-century a belief in the autonomy of ethics and Poincaré's maxim had become a fixed dogma among Anglo-American philosophers. That dogma was forcefully challenged and an extensive debate followed, the result of which was inconclusive.[17] Perhaps as a result, Marxist philosophers, who are also in some way part of the analytical tradition, have been understandably reluctant to take a stand on such matters.[18]

Andrew Collier in his masterful 'Scientific Socialism and the Question of Socialist Values' captures the substance of what Lukács and Goldmann were about and indeed what Marx was about, *vis-à-vis* values, without assuming that there is no categorial distinction between facts and values or that there is an entailment relation between factual statements and fundamental evaluative utterances.[19] While avoiding Bernstein's and Vorlander's appeal to an ethical socialism and claims about distinctively socialist values, Collier does acknowledge that normative conceptions have a place in socialism.

There are a number of rather secular values, connected principally with conceptions of human flourishing and need satisfaction, that have come into common currency since the Enlightenment.[20] Certain very severe religious thinkers aside, there is by now, in societies which have gone through what Max Weber called the process of modernization, a very considerable consensus about these values: a consensus that is reflected in the thought of modernizing intelligentsia in a spectrum from Bentham to Nietzsche. (It is, of course, though often in rather inchoate forms, widely abroad in the culture.) If someone were to challenge the justifiability of this consensus either from outside this modernizing group or in a purely speculative way, I do not know how we could prove or establish those moral truisms, as I shall call them, beyond appealing to considered judgments in wide reflective equilibrium and pointing to the untenability of foundationalism.[21]

A socialist, even a Marxist anti-moralist, has those values available to him, and they will, and should, guide his practice. What divides him from the liberal or indeed from most conservatives as well, is his political sociology. That is to say, his disagreement with them is about the facts – about what is the most perspicuous representation of the facts – and about what in a particular historical situation, including most importantly our situation, is possible (empirically feasible).

Liberals typically would have it that fundamental political disagreements are deep moral or normative disagreements – often tragic disagreements – that cannot be rationally resolved. Collier argues that this is false. Fundamental political disagreements, he carefully argues, turn finally on factual disagreements about what is the case and most importantly about what can become the case. Such disagreements can, at least in principle, be resolved, though the strength of various ideological defenses make their rational resolution extremely difficult. But there is neither conceptual imprisonment nor an ultimate disagreement over fundamental values here. To so view political argument is to misunderstand it.

Even if we cannot derive fundamental moral judgments from plain matters of fact, it does remain the case – and this is what is actually important – that we can, do and indeed should, base moral judgments on the facts. In most situations, for a person about to step off a curb, the fact that there is a car coming is a good reason to stop. The value judgment 'You ought to stop' is based on the fact that there is a car coming.

No matter how autonomist we are about ethics we have to realize that repeatedly in everyday life value judgments are based on the facts. Marx's analyses of capitalism and other social formations, his remarks about how social change takes place and the relations of power between the classes, and his claims about how these relations could change and what could replace them all give us at least a putatively perspicuous representation of the facts and what is empirically possible. If so then for people who accept what I have called moral truisms, the set of factual-cum-theoretical claims that Marxists make are of the utmost moral relevance. In speaking of 'moral truisms' I am referring to the belief that human autonomy is a good thing, that suffering and degradation are bad things, that it is a good thing for people to stand in conditions of fraternity and mutual respect, that it is a good thing for people to live lives in which their needs are met and their wants are satisfied (which are neither self-destructive nor harmful to others) and it is a good thing that people stand in relation of rough equality in which one person or group of persons cannot dominate others. For people who accept these beliefs (as almost all of us do) the Marxist factual claims, if true, are of a not inconsiderable moral relevance. A Marxist critique of society proceeds not by way of presenting new moral tablets but by way of showing people with ordinary human feelings and moral beliefs how societies really function and what the world could become with the development of the productive forces.[22]

Marxist social science is also, as we have seen Lukács and Goldmann stressing, an emancipatory social science functioning as critique, but its critique (including its motivating import to change the world), Collier stresses, is by way of telling it like it is and by showing us what the human possibilities are.[23] For neutral spectators, it would have only explanatory value; it would not serve as a guide for what to do or what to struggle against. But human beings are not neutral spectators. They are agents who intervene in the world and react to the world, who care about their lives and the lives of others. For people who have tolerably mundane commonsensical moral beliefs, the Marxist picture of the world is emancipatory. The important thing, Marxists rightly believe, is to see if it is *an approximately true and comprehensive picture of the world*. If that picture is approximately true, the moral evaluations will take care of themselves. We do not need to spell out a distinctive set of socialist values or give a Marxist foundationalist account of morality.

V

What, however, are we to make of Marx's claim that historical materialism breaks the staff of morality and his repeated claims that morality is through and through ideological? *The Communist Manifesto* echoes earlier remarks in *The German Ideology* to the effect that morality is ideology, that morality in capitalist society, along with law and religion, is a collection of disguised bourgeois prejudices masking and rationalizing bourgeois domination in class society. The thing to do, according to Marx, is to strip morality of all the mystification created by moralizing and to come to see morality for what it is, namely as an ideology in which the class interests of the dominant class are, through mystification, insinuated as being in the interests of the society as a whole. People are seduced by moral ideology into accepting their domination as their rightful or at least inescapable station with corresponding duties, to which they should subordinate their wants and interests.[24] Yet Marx and Engels's suspicion of moralizing, their hostility towards moral theorizing, and their reception of the ideological nature of morality went hand in hand with their readiness, throughout their lives – in their pamphleteering, in their theoretical work and in their private correspondence – to perfectly unselfconsciously make moral evaluations which they gave no sign at all of regarding as ideology, as class biases or as subjective. This would lead us to think that their accounts of morality are contradictory. Without abandoning historical materialism or any of Marx's strong and, I believe, basically correct claims about the ideological functions of morality, I will attempt in the reminder of this essay to establish that Marx's claims are neither contradictory nor incoherent and are indeed powerful and plausible claims that deserve serious consideration.

An acceptance of the perspective on morality I have portrayed does not entail, or even suggest, a rejection of the reality of moral conceptions, though historical materialism does entail the denial of their causal primacy, particularly where epochal social change is at issue. (But this, note, is not to deny them any causal efficacy.) Far from believing in the unreality of moral notions Engels did say baldly in *Anti-Duhring* that it cannot be doubted that there has been progress in morality. These considerations, however, are not decisive, for it is perfectly natural to reply that, if Marx and Engels had thought through the implications of historical materialism and of their sociology of morals (including their beliefs about ideology) they would have rejected a belief in the objectivity of morals or of the possibility of moral truth claims. Their accounts of historical materialism and ideology are incompatible with a belief in moral knowledge. This is the central issue with which I must come to grips.

Morality, on any Marxist account, must be part of the superstructure and hence, it is natural to say, it must be ideological. And if morality is ideological, it cannot be objective, since ideological beliefs cannot be justified. All we can do is explain how moral beliefs arise. (Keep in mind here that an ideology is typically a system of illusory beliefs reflecting in a disguised way the interests of a determinate class.)

What we need first to recognize is that it is consistent with historical materialism to distinguish, within the moral realm itself, between ideological beliefs and non-ideological beliefs and that, on Marx's own account, it is not true that all forms of consciousness, including all forms of self-consciousness, are ideological.[25] If they were Marx would have hoisted himself by his own petard.

Being superstructural is only a *necessary* condition for being ideological. It is *not sufficient*. There can be superstructural beliefs which are not ideological. While all ideological beliefs are super-structural not all superstructural beliefs are ideological.[26] In many, but not all, contexts, the following moral beliefs (expressed in the five sentences below) are non-ideological, though this is not to deny, what is plainly true, that they *can* be embedded in moral theories or in moralities which are ideological. But from the fact that they *can* be so embedded it does not follow that they *must* be so embedded.

1 Pleasure is good.
2 Health is good.
3 Freedom is good.
4 Servitude is bad.
5 Suffering is bad.[27]

These beliefs can be held in such a way that they are not supportive of any particular class interests. They neither directly favor the interests of the dominant class nor the interests of the challenging exploited class. These beliefs need not mystify social reality: they need not express false consciousness or false beliefs, and they need not rest on rationalizations. Moreover, they are beliefs which would not be extinguished, if we came to know what caused us to hold them. They need not be beliefs which are expressive of dominant class interests or of any class interests. This can be seen to be true because it would be reasonable to continue to hold those beliefs in a classless society. They would not wither away with the ending of capitalism, the complete disappearance of all elements of a capitalist mentality, the withering away of the state and the achievement of communism. If the moral theories in which they are embedded are ideological, as they typically are, it is crucial to recognize that these moral beliefs themselves can have a life of their own outside these ideological theories. There is no good reason to believe that these moral beliefs are *per se* ideological.

VI

A Marxist sociology of morals shows that moral beliefs have a tendency to function ideologically. But it is not committed to the thesis – a strange kind of *a priori* thesis, probably rooted in some questionable moral epistemology – that they all do or all must. Indeed, acceptance of that thesis would make nonsense out of many, though surely not all, of the critical remarks Marxists direct against capitalism. Consider, for example, claims about the de-humanizing effects of capitalist work relations. They are plainly moral beliefs, though in the way I pointed out in the previous section, they are moral beliefs based on factual beliefs articulated by and argued for by Marxist social theory. To accept such an *a priori* thesis about all moral beliefs being necessarily ideological and distorting of our understanding of ourselves would render all such remarks ideological and unjustifiable. We should keep firmly in mind in this context that it is one thing to deny that Marx's social science is a treatise on social ethics or a moral critique and it is another thing again to deny legitimacy to the moral remarks that are liberally distributed throughout his scientific work simply on the grounds that they are moral judgments or value judgments.

What we need to see is how a fuller accounting of what it is for a belief to be ideological makes it evident how some moral beliefs can be superstructural without being ideological. It is our various publicly articulated forms of self-consciousness that are the primary subject matter of ideology. It is here where we have that which in class societies is necessarily ideological. But it is not the case that any belief or any self-conception a person has must be ideological, though such beliefs, in class societies, are ideology-prone. Ideological beliefs are most paradigmatically the *public* conceptions we have about ourselves; they are in their most paradigmatic instances *the socially* sanctioned self-images. They typically are conceptions on the social level which, like purely individual rationalizations, involve mystification. Typically they are the social rationalizations of the ruling class, but sometimes these public conceptions have such a publicly approved status only within a challenging class. But what is crucial for us to see here is that not all ideas or ideals *must* involve such a collective rationalization and mystification of social relations. Moreover, this is not true of all ideas or beliefs as such, even when they are, as moral ideas must be, superstructural.

It cannot be the case that all our beliefs about man and society are ideological because we all must suffer from some grave epistemological malady. This is not even a coherent possibility, for, if it were so, nothing conceptualized could count as an unmystified idea. The very notion of an 'ideological belief' would be unintelligible, for then we could not even recognize that certain belief-systems mystify social reality.[28] Indeed, only if we can draw a conceptual distinction between 'a mystified idea' and 'an unmystified idea' could we go on to show how pervasively ideological most moral thinking actually is.

It is vital to avoid turning ideology or being ideological into an *epistemological* category about how or what we can know, or about what can be true or false. Ideologies are our *public* conceptions of ourselves and should not be taken as referring to *all* our beliefs or even to all our self-images or philosophical or moral conceptions. Ideology is not a term referring to an all-inclusive range of cognitive or affective phenomena.[29] Rather ideology is the *official currency* of self-consciousness in class societies. This explains why the extant moralities – the moralities of the various tribes and classes – will all be ideological.

Most private forms of cognition are also very likely to conform in one way or another and, to a greater or lesser degree, to the ideology of the class society in which the person lives and sometimes is a member. But it does not follow that all individual or even all group thinking must so conform to an ideological pattern. There is conceptual and epistemological space for moral conceptions and beliefs which are non-ideological. These remarks show why Marxism itself need not be ideological.

VII

There remain 'relativistic problems' about Marxism *vis-à-vis* ethics which might show that if historical materialism is true morality totters. I think it is evident enough that a Marxist need not endorse any version of *ethical* relativism, namely the doctrine that an action or practice X is morally right in society S if and only if X is permitted (approved) by the conventions of S or by the dominant class in S. Historical materialism is a thesis about what generates and sustains moral beliefs in a society and the related Marxist doctrine of ideology explains how moral beliefs function in class society. It is probably the case that these doctrines do not commit one to any assertion about what is right or wrong. But, whether or not that is so, they do not commit one to saying that, because a moral belief is deemed right by the conventions of the society or by the ruling or dominant class in the society, that moral belief is therefore right in that society or indeed in any society. At most, it would require the historical materialist to say that if it is *believed* to be right by the ruling class of that society, it will generally be believed to be right in that society. But that anthropological observation is perfectly compatible with denying that it is therefore right in that society, or with a skepticism about whether we could ever determine what is right or wrong period. And that, whatever it is, is not ethical relativism.

Moreover, if a Marxist committed himself to ethical relativism, he would have to say that if Society S were a capitalist society and action X were a revolutionary act designed to overthrow capitalism that he, the Marxist, would be committed to believing that it is wrong to do X in Society S, for X is not approved by the conventions of S or by its ruling class, unless (perhaps) he could show that the production relations in S no longer suit the productive forces. But no Marxist need say that. He could, and in my view should, stick to the innocuous and trivial thesis in descriptive ethics that such acts would be generally *believed* to be wrong in Society S and he could use historical materialism and its correlated theory of ideology to explain why it was believed to be wrong. But this is to assert nothing at all about what is right or wrong, let alone to assert that, if it is generally *believed* to be wrong in Society S, it is wrong in Society S.

To assert anything like this ethical relativist thesis is entirely contrary to the spirit of Marxism and is not required by historical materialism. Historical materialism sees the dominant moralities in a society as cultural 'legitimizing' and stabilizing devices in that society. They are devices functionally required by a given mode of production. But to make such a claim is not to imply anything about what is or is not right, or to claim that what is functionally required by a given mode of production ought to obtain.

However, ethical relativism is not the only kind of relativism there is. There is also metaethical relativism. It is the view that there are no objectively sound procedures for justifying one moral code or one set of moral judgments against another moral code or another set of moral judgments. For all we can ascertain, two moral codes may be equally 'sound' and two moral claims may be equally 'justified' or 'reasonable'. There is no way of establishing what is 'the true moral code' or set of moral beliefs. Indeed it may not even make sense to say that there could be a true moral code. Someone who believes that historical materialism commits her to metaethical relativism, and who also accepts historical materialism, will also claim that, if historical materialism is true, judgments of what is right or wrong, just or unjust, become mode-of-production dependent. Taking metaethical relativism and historical materialism together, she will assert that there is no possible Archimedian point in morality – there is nothing that could be properly called a 'true morality' – and thus it is not even possible for there to be an objective certification of moral principles. There is no method that all rational, properly informed and conceptually sophisticated people must accept for fixing moral belief.

VIII

Does historical materialism actually entail or contextually imply the non-availability of an Archimedian point or cluster of developing Archimedian points in moral philosophy? Neither the diversity of actual moral beliefs nor the diversity of methods for establishing moral beliefs will show that no Archimedian point is possible. Such diversities do not show that all are equally sound. Moreover, the relative appropriateness of certain moral conceptions to historically determinate modes of production would not show that there could not be progress towards the greater adequacy of a mode of production over previous modes of production, or that perfectly objective judgments could not be made. We could show that certain norms were appropriated to capitalism and still quite consistently assess capitalism as a general advance over feudalism and as less advanced than socialism.[30] There is no inconsistency at all here in making these diverse assessments. We could not only show that certain norms were functionally appropriate to certain modes of production but that whole modes of production – later more developed modes of production – make possible a way of organizing social life that is better than previous organizations which were also functionally appropriate to their modes of production.

Historical materialism is clearly committed to contextualism, not relativism or subjectivism. It does not rule out a belief in moral progress. Indeed, it would appear at least to commit one, as Engels was committed, to a belief in moral progress through the development of moral ideas from one mode of production to another as the productive forces develop and as we gain a greater control over the world and a more extensive rationalization of our lives.

We should also recognize that the causal genesis of moral beliefs does not undermine their validity. We can recognize that people have moral beliefs because of the distinctive production relations of the society in which they live without thereby thinking that their moral beliefs must be unjustified and subjective.

An elementary distinction can be drawn between the cause of a person (class, society) holding a certain belief and the evidence for that belief or, alternatively, between the reasons for which one believes and the reasons which justify belief. A fundamental tenet of Marxist class analysis is that one's class position, one's particular location in a specific type of economic structure, strongly conditions one's outlook, moral and otherwise. But it is a simple truth of logical analysis that the origin of a belief is not relevant to its evaluation as true or false. Thus, there is nothing inconsistent in a Marxist maintaining (say) both that the value judgments of the proletariat are socially determined and that they tended to be more veridical than the judgments of other classes.[31]

We need to distinguish between the origin of moral beliefs, their rationale and their justification.

We need, however, to be careful about applying such genetic

fallacy arguments in such an unequivocal way. As Richard Miller points out, it is not always the case that 'ideas are debunked simply by tracing their origins to social interests.'[32] It was false to say, as was said above, that the origin of a belief is not at all relevant to its evaluation as true or false. Miller points out that tracking moral beliefs can be vitally important. He gives the following example:

> . . . a strong duty to be hospitable to strangers is accepted by traditional Eskimoes because of a common interest in such hospitality in a semi-nomadic society where any family may be struck down in the constant battle with Nature. This explanation does not debunk. If anything, it justifies.[33]

Here, pointing to the origin of the moral belief reveals a rationale that otherwise might not have been obvious, but it is also true that simply pointing to the origin of the belief does not even start to justify. Moreover, and more relevantly to the standard genetic fallacy arguments, we cannot simply prove a belief to be mistaken by pointing to its origin. But if the belief can be shown to have a rationale, then we have at least some start on a justification. If we can exhibit a rationale, we have at least a *prima facie* case for claiming it is justified. The fact that our moral outlook is dependent on general economic conditions does not show that there is no independent justification for that outlook. There might not be one, but that could not be determined by simply finding out how moral outlooks arise.

The above notwithstanding, it still does look like historical materialism may be committed to a metaethical relativism in the following rather distinctive sense: if historical materialism is true there could be no ground for asserting a trans-historical set of moral principles. As Engels stressed, we cannot justifiably say that there is a set of *eternal* moral principles. However, we may be able to say that at time t1 in context X such and such moral principles are correct, and that at time t2 in context Y that such and such moral principles are correct, and that at time t3 in context Z such and such principles are correct. These judgments are general and can be made across modes of production. Moreover, historical materialism allows, though it may not require, the judgment that there is rational progress from t1 to t2 to t3 such that it is, *ceteris paribus*, better for human beings to go through that development rather than remain fixed at t1. This shows a moral understanding, a moral way of viewing things, which, is non-relativist, contextual, and yet compatible with historical materialism. If such moral progress is an illusion, historical materialism does not and does not attempt to show that it is. There is no good reason to believe that if historical materialism is true morality totters.

NOTES

1 The closest thing to an extended account in one work comes in Karl Marx, *Critique of the Gotha Programme*, C.P. Dutt (ed. and trans.), (New York, NY: International Publishers, 1938), and in Frederick Engels, *Anti-Duhring*, Emile Bruns (trans.), (New York: International Publishers, 1939), chapters IX–XI.

2 Leon Trotsky, *Their Morals and Ours* (London: Plough Press, 1968). The original publication date of the Russian text was 1938.

3 Though I demur from some of his key conclusions, it should be remarked that Richard Miller brilliantly brings out what Marx is up to here. Richard Miller, *Analyzing Marx*, (Princeton University Press, 1984), pp. 15–97.

4 Kai Nielsen, 'Justice as Ideology,' *Windsor Yearbook of Access to Justice*, vol. 1 (1981), pp. 165–78.

5 David Levin provides a powerful and sophisticated example of such a defense. David S. Levin, 'The Moral Relativism of Marxism,' *The Philosophical Forum*, vol. XV, no. 3, (Spring 1984), pp. 249–78.

6 Anthony Skillen, *Ruling Illusions*, (Sussex: Harvester Press 1977) and Richard Norman, *The Moral Philosophers*, (Oxford: Clarendon Press, 1983), pp. 173–201.

7 This may sound paradoxical to some. How could a Marxist set aside things that Marx said and still remain a Marxist? Very easily indeed, for there are many things that Marx said that are hardly central to his core theory and indeed some of the things he said may be incompatible with it. There is no need for a Marxist to go around defending everything Marx believed. But he must make some judgments about what is canonical to Marx's theory (say historical materialism, the theory of classes, the labour theory of value) and concerning these matters there is, of course, room for intelligent dispute. That is why there is a perennial dispute over what is essentially Marxist. The worry about whether a Marxist critique of capitalism requires for its rounding out a moral critique and perhaps even a moral theory is the worry about whether the theory really is incomplete without it or whether the insights embedded in the canonical core would be undermined or in any way compromised if such an ethical rounding out were made. For a

masterful discussion of the notion of a canonical core see Marx Wartofsky, 'The Unhappy Consciousness,' *Praxis International* (1981), pp. 288–306. For three significant attempts to weld an ethical critique to Marxism see Maximilien Rubel, *Rubel on Karl Marx: Five Essays*, Joseph O'Malley and Keith Algozin (eds and trans 1.), (Cambridge University Press, 1981), pp. 26–81. Svetozar Stojanovic, *Between Ideals and Reality*, (New York: Oxford University Press, 1973) and Douglas Kellner, 'Marxism, Morality and Ideology,' *Marx and Morality* in Kai Nielsen and Steven Patten (eds), (Guelph, ON: Canadian Association for Publishing in Philosophy, 1981), pp. 93–120.

8 See the stress on this by Lucien Goldmann and Bertell Ollman in their discussions of Marx on morality. Lucien Goldmann, 'Y a-t-il une sociologie marxiste?', *Les Temps modernes*, vol. 13 (1957), pp. 729–51 and Bertell Ollman, *Alienation*, second edition, (Cambridge University Press, 1976), pp. 41–51.

9 Kurt Vorlander, *Kant ünd Marx* (Tubingen: 1926). Edward Bernstein, *Evolutionary Socialism*, Edith Havey (trans.) (New York: Shocken Books, 1961).

10 Karl Kautsky, *Ethik und materialistiche Geschichtsauffassung* (Stuttgart: 1926) and Georg Plekhanov, *Selected Philosophical Works*, (Moscow: 1961).

11 Max Adler, *Der soziologische Sinn der Lehre von Karl Marx* (Leipzig: 1914) and Otto Bauer, 'Marxismus und Ethik,' *Die Neue Zeit*, vol. 24 (1905–6), pp. 485–99.

12 Max Adler, *Kant und der Marxismus*, p. 141.

13 Ibid.

14 Georg Lukács, *History and Class-Consciousness*, Rodney Livingstone (trans.), (London: Merlin Press, 1968). See note 8 and Lucien Goldmann, *The Hidden God*, Philip Thody (trans.), (London: Routledge & Kegan Paul, 1964), Chapter 5, and his *The Human Sciences and Philosophy*, Hayden V. White (trans.), (London, Jonathan Cape, 1969).

15 This has also been argued powerfully from the liberal side by Isaiah Berlin and Charles Taylor. Isaiah Berlin, *Concepts and Categories*, (Oxford University Press 1980), pp. 103–42 and 'Rationality of Value Judgments,' *Nomos* VII, Carl J. Friedrich (ed.), (New York: Atherton Press 1964), pp. 221–3. Charles Taylor, 'Neutrality in Political Science,' in *Philosophy, Politics and Society*, (third series), P. Laslett and W.G. Runciman (eds), (Oxford: Basil Blackwell, 1967), and 'Interpretation and the Sciences of Man,' *The Review of Metaphysics*, vol. 25 no. 1 (September 1971).

16 On the traditional autonomist side perhaps the most significant figures were R.M. Hare, Karl Popper and J.L. Mackie, the chief non-autonomist challengers were John Searle, Charles Taylor, Max Black

and Philippa Foot. A reasonable sampling of the significant literature is brought together in *The Is/Ought Question*, W.D. Hudson's (ed.), (London: Macmillan 1969). But see also the two essays by Charles Taylor cited in footnote 15, Richard Norman, 'Seeing Things Different-ly,' *Radical Philosophy*, No. 1 (January 1972), pp. 6–13 and Philippa Foot, 'Morality as a System of Hypothetical Imperatives,' *Philosophical Review*, vol. 81 (July 1972), pp. 305–16.

17 See the references in the previous footnote.

18 I both review the literature and take an autonomist stand in my 'On Deriving an Ought from an Is: A Retrospective Look,' *The Review of Metaphysics*, vol. XXXII, no. 3 (March 1979), pp. 487–514. (Useful additional biblographical references occur in the first two footnotes.) I also try to show, in a way that meshes well with Andrew Collier's Marxist arguments, that non-derivability (the core autonomist claim) entails no significant substantive conclusion for we still in moral reasoning back up our moral judgments by an appeal to facts. See also on this, Peter Singer, 'The Triviality of the Debate Over "Is/Ought" and the Definition of "Moral",' *American Philosophical Quarterly*, vol. 10 (January 1973), pp. 51–6.

19 Andrew Collier, 'Scientific Socialism and the Question of Socialist Values,' in *Marx and Morality*, Kai Nielsen and Steven Patten (eds,), (Guelph: Canadian Association for Publishing in Philosophy, 1981), pp. 121–54 and his 'Positive Values,' *The Aristotelian Society* supplementary vol. LVII (1983).

20 I am not here giving to understand that these values were invented by the Enlightenment. There were certainly such beliefs floating around before and they were sometimes passionately held by some people. But that cluster of values came to have a very deep and pervasive consensus only after the ethos of the Enlightment took hold.

21 Kai Nielsen, *Equality and Liberty* (Totawa, NJ: Rowman & Allenheld 1985), Chapter 2. Norman Daniels, 'Wide Reflective Equilibrium and Theory Acceptance in Ethics,' *The Journal of Philosophy*, vol. 10 (1979), pp. 256–82 and his 'Reflective Equilibrium and Archimedean Points,' *Canadian Journal of Philosophy*, vol. 10, no. 1 (March 1980), pp. 83–104. Jane English, 'Ethics and Science,' *Proceedings of the XVI World Congress of Philosophy* (1979).

22 This is convincingly argued by Andrew Collier in his 'Positive Values.'

23 Ibid.

24 Anthony Skillen and Andrew Collier skillfully bring out this side of Marx and Marxism in Skillen, 'Marxism and Morality,' *Radical Philosophy*, vol. 8 (1974) and Collier, 'Truth and Practice,' *Radical Philosophy* 5 (1973) and in his 'The Production of Moral Ideology,' *Radical Philosophy* 9 (1974).

25 This has been well articulated by John McMurty in his *The Structure of*

Marx's World-View (Princeton University Press, 1978), pp. 123–56.

26 Ibid.

27 I do not mean to give to understand that these moral beliefs are little nuggets of eternal moral truth to be uncovered after all the layers of ideology have been peeled away. The very notion of 'moral truth' is not unproblematic. What these are, are moral truisms that take somewhat different readings in different contexts; still each of these utterances are not without a common content, e.g. health means something different from culture to culture but *not* completely different. If you want to call these 'eternal moral truths' you can but this is using an enriched moral language for the commonplace. There is no good reason to go on like that.

28 Alasdair MacIntyre, 'Ideology, Social Science and Revolution,' *Comparative Politics*, vol. 5, no. 5 (April 1973), pp. 321–42.

29 McMurty, op. cit., pp. 123–56.

30 'Advanced' here, for Weberian reasons, might cause trouble. Much of the sense here (a sense Weber would sanction) can be cashed in terms of the greater development of the modes of production of certain societies and thus the capacity for those societies to more fully satisfy human wants and needs.

31 William Shaw, 'Marxism and Moral Objectivity,' *Marx and Morality*, Kai Nielsen and Steven Patten (eds), (Guelph: Canadian Association for Publishing in Philosophy, 1981).

32 Richard Miller, 'Marx and Morality,' *Nomos*, vol. XXVI (New York University Press, 1983), pp. 18–19.

33 Ibid.

7

PRAGMATIC SENSIBILITY: THE MORALITY OF EXPERIENCE

John J. McDermott

In the almost three-millennia-long, contested, controversial and vaunted history of philosophy in Western civilization, no tradition has been more misunderstood and more maligned than that of American pragmatism. A practical cause of that misunderstanding has been the long-standing condescension of European thinkers to American thought, an activity often given lamentable support by American intellectuals, who ignore the warning of Emerson and would rather court the whited sepulchers of the past than pay attention to new wisdom.[1]

In a modern replay of the ancient biblical refrain as to what good can come from Nazareth, or the later lament that a prophet is without honor in his or her own country, American thinkers, especially philosophers, tend to look elsewhere for insight than to the classical American philosophers. This jeremiad awaits further analysis in another setting and the possibility of that is propitious, for we are witnessing a bona fide renascence of interest in classical American philosophy, as attested by the publication of Critical Editions of the *Works* of C.S. Peirce, William James, John Dewey and George Santayana, with scholarly editions of the writings of Josiah Royce and George Herbert Mead a welcome accompaniment. Commentaries on each of these major American philosophers are increasing in quality and quantity.[2] Yet, their contribution to ethics is still comparatively hidden. The present essay attempts to plot a course for a rejuvenation of the original way in which some of the classical American philosophers looked at the moral question, especially as found in the thought of William James and John Dewey.

113

I: Contemporary ethical theory

Our first task is to allay suspicion and to fend off misconceptions. A pragmatic approach to philosophy is not a vulgar replay of British utilitarianism. A pragmatic ethics is not a gross manipulation of means for the sake of ends. A pragmatic approach to life is not a caricature of a contemporary version of *realpolitik*. Yet, those of us who are interested in classical American philosophy, must admit that the terms pragmatic and pragmatism are sullied beyond redemption. No less an oracle than the *New York Times* referred to Richard Nixon as a pragmatist. Obviously, if Mr Nixon is, in fact, a pragmatist, the rest of us are called upon to be something else, something better. But in the historical and genuine sense of that term, Mr Nixon and his assorted cohorts are not pragmatists, for pragmatism in its philosophical lineage is dead-set against personal aggrandizement, arrogance, manipulation and the corruption of traditional ethical values. Further, pragmatic ethics is quite the reverse of any form of self-indulgence, being extremely sensitive to human aspiration, human need and being deeply committed to a fructuous future, gained by stepping warily and creatively through and over the obstacles to human growth.

In James Mark Baldwin's *Dictionary of Philosophy and Psychology*, the fundamental contentions and lineaments of pragmatism, inclusive of paragraphs by Charles Sanders Peirce and William James, are presented as follows:

> *Pragmatic anthropology*, according to Kant, is practical ethics.
> *Pragmatic horizon* is the adaptation of our general knowledge to influencing our morals.
> (2) The opinion that metaphysics is to be largely cleared up by the application of the following maxim for attaining clearness of apprehension: 'Consider what effects, that might conceivably have practical bearings, we conceive the object of our conception to have. Then, our conception of these effects is the whole of our conception of the object.' (C.S.P.)
> The doctrine that the whole 'meaning' of a conception expresses itself in practical consequences, consequences either in the shape of conduct to be recommended, or in that of experiences to be expected, if the conception be true; which consequences would be different if it were untrue, and must be different from the consequences by which the meaning of other

114

conceptions is in turn expressed. If a second conception should not appear to have other consequences, then it must really be only the first conception under a different name. In methodology it is certain that to trace and compare their respective consequences is an admirable way of establishing the differing meanings of different conceptions. (W.J.)[3]

The fundamental point in the text, which is reiterated constantly by James and Peirce,[4] has to do with effects and consequences as the bottom line of the worthiness of judgments, propositions, truth-claims or decisions. The classical philosophical tradition in ethics, with the exception of utilitarianism, has been tied to either an a priori source for ethical decisions, or a redoubt of permanence, such as a fixed human nature or a natural law governing all events and evaluations. Pragmatism, to the contrary, stresses the open-ended and novelty-ridden character of our experience, which in turn renders all judgments tentative. Obviously, the future stretches into infinity such that one cannot wait indefinitely to make a decision. The obligation is to be wary of the immediate future and to weigh one's decisions always in the light of possible novelty, both near and far. Once the decision has been made, a persistent monitoring of the ability to sustain that decision is necessary, especially as its ramifications unfold in the context of future experience. This is what is meant when James says that truth is what 'works,'[5] namely, when we are confident in our judgments, not once and for all, but rather *en passant*, through the flow of experience.

One criticism of the pragmatic approach to decisions as sketched above has to do with the worthiness of tradition-saturated values. The argument is that a pragmatic attitude would always keep its eye on the future and have to begin anew each time one was faced with a decision or an evaluation. The question of tradition is a thorny one, filled as it is with both a hoary and an illustrious bequest. It is tradition which for centuries honored male chauvinism, blind obeisance to dehumanizing authority and patterns of superstition. Yet, it is also tradition which has yielded the Bill of Rights, the Constitution and a host of allied warnings to avoid the mistakes of the past. John Dewey approached this problem directly, for he knew that the past was a teacher of both truth and malfeasance. Invoking the history of our experience, Dewey sorted out those experiences which were 'funded,' by which he meant that they carried the weight of past wisdom into our present and projected themselves into our future. From these 'funded experiences,' we can glean 'warranted assertibility'[6] such that human slavery is evil. For Dewey, the overwhelming testament of human history on this issue is such as to make it unnecessary, unwise, and morally capricious to ever again open the issue of human slavery as worthy of reconsideration. Similar judgments can be made about the Holocaust and about the dramatically evil results of absolute creeds, be they religious or political, as attested everyday by the systematic madness that afflicts the beleaguered nation of Lebanon.

The message here is that pragmatism does not spawn a vicious ethical relativism in which human values have no historical roots. Dewey is quite clear on this issue as he states in a remarkable text on the most adventitious relation betweeen traditional, funded values and the emergence of new situations.

> We are not, then, to get away from enjoyments experienced in the past and from recall of them, but from the notion that they are the arbiters of things to be further enjoyed. At present, the arbiter is found in the past, although there are many ways of interpreting what in the past is authoritative. Nominally, the most influential conception doubtless is that of a revelation once had or a perfect life once lived. Reliance upon precedent, upon institutions created in the past, especially in law, upon rules of morals that have come to us through unexamined customs, upon uncriticized tradition, are other forms of dependence. It is not for a moment suggested that we can get away from customs and established institutions. A mere break would doubtless result simply in chaos. But there is no danger of such a break. Mankind is too inertly conservative both by constitution and by education to give the idea of this danger actuality. What there is genuine danger of is that the force of new conditions will produce disruption externally and mechanically: this is an ever-present danger. The prospect is increased, not mitigated, by that conservatism which insists upon the adequacy of old standards to meet new conditions. What is needed is intelligent examination of the consequences that are actually effected by inherited institutions and customs, in order that there may be intelligent consideration of the ways in which they are to be intentionally modified in behalf of generation of different consequences.[7]

116

One further clarification and dispensation of a misconception with regard to pragmatism awaits us, before we develop the metaphysics which sustain a morality of experience. Pragmatism was never intended to be a full-blown philosophical system. James is quite clear that he conceived of pragmatism as a *method* for settling epistemological and metaphysical disputes. It is clearly invoked as a way of clearing the philosophical world of the claims of 'foundationalism,' by which many philosophers claimed to arrive at apodictic certitude, never to be questioned or challenged. James was adamantly opposed to any form of philosophical closure. In his chapter on 'What Pragmatism Means,' James lays out the parameters of the pragmatic method.

> Pragmatism represents a perfectly familiar attitude in philosophy, the empiricist attitude, but it represents it, as it seems to me, both in a more radical and in a less objectionable form than it has ever yet assumed. A pragmatist turns his back resolutely and once for all upon a lot of inveterate habits dear to professional philosophers. He turns away from abstraction and insufficiency, from verbal solutions, from bad a priori reasons, from fixed principles, closed systems, and pretended absolutes and origins. He turns towards concreteness and adequacy, towards facts, towards action, and towards power. That means the empiricist temper regnant, and the rationalist temper sincerely given up. It means the open air and possibilities of nature, as against dogma, artificiality and the pretence of finality in truth.
>
> At the same time it does not stand for any special results. It is a method only. But the general triumph of that method would mean an enormous change in what I called in my last lecture the 'temperament' of philosophy. Teachers of the ultrarationalistic type would be frozen out, much as the courtier type is frozen out in republics, as the ultramontane type of priest is frozen out in protestant lands. Science and metaphysics would come much nearer together, would in fact work absolutely hand in hand.[8]

If pragmatism is a method and one which denigrates previous philosophical attempts at absolutism or foundationalism, what does one say about how it is to be in the world? In short, does pragmatism presuppose a metaphysics? The answer is a resounding 'yes'. It is what James calls radical empiricism[9] and what Dewey refers to as

117

immediate empiricism.[10] The problem for both James and for Dewey was to find a way to cut between the competing and regnant philosophies of their time, that is the decades from 1880 until 1910. The reference here is to Anglo-American idealism, led by the thought of F.H. Bradley and Josiah Royce, on the one hand, and by Associationism, with its roots in Locke and Hume and its flowering in James Mill and late nineteenth-century psychology. Parenthetically, the utilitarianism of Bentham and John Stuart Mill, with its wooden, quantitative assessment of ethical values is a child of Associationism, having the same lock-step view of human activity.

As early as 1897 James announced a break with these philosophical approaches to knowing and being. Citing it as an attitude, he called for the development of radical empiricism.

> Were I obliged to give a short name to the attitude in question, I should call it that of *radical empiricism* . . . I say 'empiricism' because it is contented to regard its most assured conclusions concerning matters of fact as hypotheses liable to modification in the course of future experience; and I say 'radical,' because it treats the doctrine of monism itself as an hypothesis. . .
>
> He who takes for his hypothesis the notion that it (pluralism) is the permanent form of the world is what I call a radical empiricist. For him the crudity of experience remains an eternal element thereof. There is no possible point of view from which the world can appear an absolutely single fact.[11]

In 1909 William James lays out the parameters of a radically empirical metaphysics, one which retroactively explicated the full import of his telescoped version of pragmatism in his book of that name in 1907.

> Radical empiricism consists first of a postulate, next of a statement of fact, and finally of a generalized conclusion.
>
> The postulate is that the only things that shall be debatable among philosophers shall be things definable in terms drawn from experience. (Things of an unexperienceable nature may exist *ad libitum*, but they form no part of the material for philosophic debate.)
>
> The statement of fact is that the relations between things, conjunctive as well as disjunctive, are just as much matters of

direct particular experience, neither more so nor less so, than the things themselves.

The generalized conclusion is that therefore the parts of experience hold together from next to next by relations that are themselves parts of experience. The directly apprehended universe needs, in short, no extraneous transempirical connective support, but possesses in its own right a concatenated or continuous structure.[12]

William James wrote most of his essays on radical empiricism from 1904 until 1907. In a remarkable dovetailing of philosophical outlook, John Dewey published his own version of this new metaphysics during the same years. For Dewey, the analysis of experience was the centerpiece of this new endeavor.

The criticisms made upon that vital but still unformed movement variously termed radical empiricism, pragmatism, humanism, functionalism, according as one or another aspect of it is uppermost, have left me with a conviction that the *fundamental* difference is not so much in matters overtly discussed as in a presupposition that remains tacit: a presupposition as to what experience is and means . . .

Immediate empiricism postulates that things – anything, everything, in the ordinary or non-technical use of the term 'thing' – are what they are experienced as . . .[13]

The key assumptions in the positions of James and Dewey are as follows: (a) our experience as taken or had directly, that is perceptually and not filtered through conceptual schema, is cognitive in the fullest and deepest sense of that word, a knowing; (b) that the relations which bind our experiences of objects, one to the other, are equally as experienced as the objects themselves; (c) the flow of experience is its own epistemological mean, if we but pay attention to the relations which gather and regather the flow in its continuous, although open-ended movement. Consequently, James and Dewey bequeathe to us a dubiety about the possibility of finality, closure, and any effort to designate decisions and values in a way which precludes the press of experience. For Dewey, the ontology of our human situation is that it is problematic. By this he means that to be human is to be in an irresolute situation in so far as ultimate meaning is sought but never realized. For James, the world can never be grasped as whole or as finished for each of us has an original, although not exclusive perspective and every other perspective lacks the perspective of all others. And James joins with C.S. Peirce in the belief that all experience is riven with chance and novelty as a permanent condition.

William James is the architect of contemporary consciousness, for it is he who introduces process as the major metaphor for our understanding of how we are in, of and about the world. Substances, products, become secondary and ministerial to the flow. *How* we live is more central than is *what* we have, know and define. Dewey refines this notion of James by placing it squarely within the context of a naturalistic metaphysics. Dewey describes our fundamental situation as the transaction of the human organism with the affairs of nature, such that we make our way hand over hand, through the travails which beset us in our everyday experience. It is crucial for us to correctly diagnose this transaction so that we ascertain the problem, the potential resolution, the negative fallout and the possibility of survival into the future. Further, the rhythm of these transactions constitutes the aesthetic fiber of our being in the world, a rhythm which yields the quality of our personal life. In short, it is *how* we transact with the environment which is more revealing of our humanness than the whatness of that environment. The systolic and diastolic rhythm of our heartbeat is a prime analogate for the way in which we come and go, win and lose, crest and fall in our daily activities.

At first blush and as described above, the metaphysics of James and Dewey seems to be reminiscent of the Greek and the Roman stoics, thereby eliciting a similar moral philosophy, characterized by the homage to *apatheia*, the stoic word for continuity with the rhythms, rewards and penalites of response to the call of nature. The similarity between the stoic philosophy and that of James and Dewey is initially true, for both traditions have a deep respect for the wiles and gifts of nature as well as for the necessary burden put upon human activity not to offend the way in which the world sets up, naturally, for better or for worse. In this regard, James has a telling text:

> Woe to him whose beliefs play fast and loose with the order which realities follow in his experience; they will lead him nowhere or else make false connexions.[14]

This attitude of James is endorsed by Dewey in his classic work, *Experience and Nature*:

> Man finds himself living in an aleatory world; his existence involves, to put it baldly, a gamble. The world is a scene of risk; it is uncertain, unstable, uncannily unstable. Its dangers are irregular, inconstant, not to be counted upon as to their times and seasons. Although persistent, they are sporadic, episodic. It is darkest just before dawn; pride goes before a fall; the moment of greatest prosperity is the moment most charged with ill-omen, most opportune for the evil eye. Plague, famine, failure of crops, disease, death, defeat in battle, are always just around the corner, and so are abundance, strength, victory, festival and song. Luck is proverbially both good and bad in its distributions. The sacred and the accursed are potentialities of the same situation; and there is no category of things which has not embodied the sacred and accursed: persons, words, places, times, directions in space, stones, winds, animals, stars.[15]

Of the stoic philosophy and that of James and Dewey, the analogy is indeed initially great, for both traditions have an extraordinary sense of the ways in which human beings are bound to the rhythms of nature, writ both large and small. A closer diagnosis, however, reveals that the pragmatic epistemology and metaphysics of James and Dewey carries with it a bundle of assumptions, attitudes and beliefs which are separate from and novel to the entire Graeco, Hebrew, Roman, Christian and Modern philosophical approaches to the fundamental questions of human life. Taking the moral questions as our point of reference, we isolate the following themes in the philosophy of James and Dewey, as touchstones for a radical reconstitution of an approach to ethics: (a) transiency; (b) pluralism; and (c) meliorism. We will then attempt to illustrate how this pragmatic metaphysics generates an approach to complex ethical questions, especially those found in modern medicine.

TRANSIENCY

The first of the three major characteristics in the diagnosis of human experience as presented by James and Dewey is that of transiency. We distinguish transiency as a more radical notion than that of the journey motif made famous by Homer, Virgil, Dante and Goethe in western literature and by the great Chinese masterpiece, *The Journey to the West*. Transiency is a distinctive American metaphor, for it connotes trekking on behalf of a better future, but it has no transcendent goal or end in sight. The flow of experience has its ridges, its plains, its mountains and streams. The flow of experience warns, cajoles and rewards as we make our way. A transient has no final resting place, for the journey is its own message, its own meaning. American thought, American life, especially in its pragmatic formulation is deeply anti-eschatological, that is, opposed to post-historical judgments retroactively conveying meaning to the activities and affairs of temporal experience. It is this attitude which sustains the American commitment to the sanctity of individuals and to the sanctity of everyday events.

In the classical world view, human life had a proper and natural place. Modern physics and modern cosmology has cast this assumption into a state of grave doubt. Contemporary thought is more likely to hold that the human organism is a phase, a passing through of the eons of cosmic DNA. Post-Copernican consciousness, having finally arrived in the twentieth century, convinces us that our meaning is chipped out of the flow of experience, rather than being an inherited award by a benevolent nature. For those for whom the world will be redeemed, once and for all in some paradisiacal future, the doctrine of transiency is immensely frightening. The evidence, however, for such a rescue from the snares of time does not exist. For others of us, for whom the everyday is constitutive of all that we have and is the only reality with which we can communicate, the doctrine of transiency turns out to be the bottom line of authenticity. Relegating the disasters of the present to the potential redemption of an unknown, uncharted and non-empirical future is the height of self-deception.

The moral question which dogs us in our human activity is forever sullied if we live a life of self-deception. To the contrary, the task is to face up to the deepest paradox in our lives, namely, that our decisions are of paramount importance, though they have no ultimate future to sanction them. It turns out that the integrity of our lives is directly proportionate to the time-bound character of human acts, having no subsequent redemptive accolades to rescue them from the ravages of the everyday. Why do I do what I do? Why do I care for you? Is it the hope of a reward for me in some other place, at some other time? Or is it because I assess the situation as deserving and needful of my help, my care? This distinction is not a minor or trivial ethical issue. It strikes at the heart of being human, for to be generous, loving, caring for its own sake, appropriately mocks the aggrandizement of a reward system in some alleged immortal future. Many years ago, a student confronted me, face-to-face and said, 'If you believe in immortality, you cannot understand pragmatic ethics nor can you understand the philosophy of John Dewey.' He was perceptive and correct. Dewey affirms this position as early as 1906.

> An empiricism that acknowledges the transitive character of experience, and that acknowledges the possible control of the character of the transition by means of intelligent effort, has abundant opportunity to celebrate in productive art, genial morals, and impartial inquiry the grace and the severity of the ideal.[16]

Dewey's phrase, 'the severity of the ideal,' is well taken. In order for us to convert the experience of the everyday into something rich, glowing and symbolically pregnant, we must keep the ideal ever before us, moment by moment. It is not that the ideal is set apart as a transcendent float, but rather the ideal is embodied in the potentialities and possibilities which reside in all of experience. If in fact we are transients without a fixed end in sight, then the over-arching moral imperative is to be ever alert, or in Dewey's phrase, always on the *qui vive*, like the nostrils of a pure bred animal. We should never barter the present for a future, about which we have no evidence. The present is the exacting scene of our being in the world and it is the present which demands our attention and our affection. The sacred is not an endowment from afar, as though external forces have decided the quality of our experience by indirection. No, the sacred is the way in which we find ourselves in the world, our values, our needs and above all, our things which accompany us on this journey whose only message is the quality of our life, day by day.

For some, to see ourselves as transients rather than as participants in some fixed scheme, is chilling, even depressing. Yet, from a wider vantage point, such an attitude is liberating for it places the meaning of our lives in our own hands. If we see ourselves as creators rather than as followers, our experience takes on a texture of possibility too often closed off to those of us whose eyes are fixed on an eternal meaning. The pragmatic approach is clearly temporalistic and finite, thereby placing enormous emphasis on the moral gravity of all our activities. Following James, we are really able to build a personal world.

> In our cognitive as well as in our active life we are creative. We *add*, both to the subject and to the predicate part of reality. The world stands really malleable, waiting to receive its final touches at our hands. Like the kingdom of heaven, it suffers human violence willingly. Man *engenders* truths upon it.[17]

Transients though we be, the moral task is clear. It is to have our experiences straight-out and straight-up, negative and positive. It is to care, touch, sense, reconnoiter, plan, rebound and penetrate the fabric of our experiences. It is to taste the nectar of the journey, for, after all, what else is there to do or to know?

PLURALISM

The second moral characteristic which emerges from our pragmatic diagnosis of experience is that of pluralism. Often associated with political or religious considerations, pluralism, at bottom, is a moral stance of the most grave significance. We do not refer to pluralism as a way-station until agreement and unity of creed, doctrine, custom and ideology can be achieved. Such an approach is but a furtive way to ultimate closure in blatant disregard for the complex and irreducible human perspective on values, beliefs and ways of living one's life. In the pragmatic tradition, pluralism comes to mean something entirely different. Put bluntly, pluralism is here to stay, for it is a constituting strand in the fabric of the human condition.

It is not an accident or a fall from grace that we have many religions, several social-political ideologies and a countless host of rituals, pertaining to birth, adolescence, marriage, death and the cosmological context in which we find ourselves. Despite the vast range of differences in these beliefs and rituals, it is of note that they each carry with them a moral imperative. Some things *should be* done. Some things *must* be done. Some things *should not* be done. Some things *must not* be done. It is significant that these proscriptions have a different content from one culture to another and, in fact, many prescriptions for ethical conduct are proscriptions in another culture. All human beings, however, are called upon to honor the tradition and the set of values which they inherit at their birth.

It is *difficult* to sort out the vast panoply of traditions, especially in that some of them appear to modern culture to have barbaric and dehumanizing effects. One thinks here of the ancient Meso-American Mayan civilization which regularly chose young virgins to be dropped off a cliff into sure death below as an acknowledgment of a fertility ritual. And it was the same Mayans who insisted on the beheading of the losing captain in a game of sport similar to our basketball. Other instances abound. Yet, before our revulsion becomes too self-righteous, it is we in the twentieth century who have indulged the Holocaust, Hiroshima and Nagasaki, and speak glibly about a *just* nuclear war. Further, it is we of the twentieth century who have participated in the unnecessary deaths of some 100,000,000 people, all for reasons of obdurate racial, religious, and ideological conflict.

Obviously, the commitment to pluralism does not entail the approval or adoption of anti-human activities, no matter the sanctioning ritual. Nor does a positive response to pluralism enjoin us to accept any aggrandizing and imperialistic moves on the part of these different commitments, for bullying and conquest are precisely what is ruled out by a pluralistic world-view. Rather, the acceptance of pluralism connotes a willingness to understand and perhaps endorse a variant of life-styles, beliefs and values, though they may be at odds with our own. Moral pluralism is at the center of political pluralism and it demands a constant summit meeting among the people of the world, so that only intractable conflicts remain. In our judgment, intractable conflicts are rare, for most of our difficulties emerge from misunderstanding, condescension and arrogance, none of which are salutary for building a genuine moral community throughout the world.[18] Once again, James says it best. This time in his 'Overview' to *A Pluralistic Universe*,

> Pragmatically interpreted, pluralism or the doctrine that it is many means only that the sundry parts of reality *may be externally related*. Everything you can think of, however vast or inclusive, has on the pluralistic view a genuinely 'external'

125

environment of some sort of amount. Things are 'with' one another in many ways, but nothing includes everything or dominates over everything. The word 'and' trails along after every sentence. Something always escapes. 'Ever not quite' has to be said of the best attempts made anywhere in the universe at attaining all-inclusiveness. The pluralistic world is thus more like a federal republic than like an empire or a kingdom. However much may be collected, however much may report itself as present at any effective centre of consciousness or action, something else is self-governed and absent and unreduced to unity.[19]

MELIORISM

Given our transiency and our commitment to a pluralistic attitude toward the activities and versions of human life, globally, the question remains as to just what is the moral demand made upon us. Here too, the pragmatic response lacks the stentorian persuasion of the moral imperatives which have blasted their clarion call down through the centuries. Modest, but deep, pragmatic morality calls upon us to live a life of meliorism, that is, a life in which we effect no ultimate solutions, yet strive to make things better. There is a homely ring to that latter phrase, the making of things better, which belies its importance. Human beings have a tendency to go for the jugular, to want to clean it up, once and for all. Lamentably, it is rare that any human problem can be totally resolved, and if it is, the wages of the resolution are often more damaging than the original problem. More likely, by far, is it that we can ameliorate a situation, by bringing a sense of healing, perspective and comparative context, which last shows us that others have been in worse shape and survived.

The most salutary virtue in the application of meliorism, that is, the attempt to make things better rather than the attempt to solve them once and for all, is that of hope. Surely charity is always desirable, although of late it has been polluted by self-interest and chicanery, especially among evangelical religions. The third theological virtue, that of faith, is especially treacherous for it more and more is characterized by exclusivity, intolerance and even violence against the heterdox or non-believers. The virtue of hope, when combined with a willingness to see that hope realized in a concrete, human way by means of melioristic activity is our best strategy for a healing future in a world pockmarked with natural and human threats and disasters. John Dewey states the case for a pragmatic attitude which would be creative, constructive, ameliorative and committed to human growth and a better future.

Pragmatism thus has a metaphysical implication. The doctrine of the value of consequences leads us to take the future into consideration. And this taking into consideration of the future takes us to the conception of a universe whose evolution is not finished, of a universe which is still, in James' term, 'in the making,' 'in the process of becoming,' of a universe up to a certain point still plastic.

Consequently reason, or thought, in its more general sense, has a real, though limited, function, a creative, constructive function. If we form general ideas and if we put them in action, consequences are produced which could not be produced otherwise. Under these conditions the world will be different from what it would have been if thought had not intervened. This consideration confirms the human and moral importance of thought and of its reflective operation in experience . . . One will understand the philosophy of James better if one considers it in its totality as a revision of English empiricism, a revision which replaces the value of past experience, of what is already given, by the future, by that which is as yet mere possibility.[20]

Taken as mooring points for the pragmatic approach to the intrinsic morality in our experience of the world, transiency, pluralism and meliorism provide a setting which is characterized by care and by flexibility in the making of moral choices. Aware of the past but also deeply sensitive to the emergence of consequences, the pragmatic approach, when genuine and informed, avoids the twin pitfalls of ethical absolutism and ethical expediency. Although these dangers to intelligent moral choice lurk in every area of our lives, nowhere are they more apparent and more tempting than in the activities of modern medicine, recently beset by a transformation of values and options due to the advent of medical high technology. The response to these developments in medicine has been a spate of articles and textbooks on medical ethics. The ethical systems and approaches adopted are repetitive and predictable, namely, natural law ethics, utilitarian ethics and de-ontological ethics. Each of these is given a contemporary flavor, usually in the analytic mode of contemporary philosophy. It is striking that Stoic ethics, existentialist ethics and pragmatic ethics[21] are rarely mentioned and then only in passing. An occasional effort at phenomenological diagnosis of bodily experience is the single exception to the traditional philosophical resources.

The major difficulty with classical ethical theories is their inability to deal with the extraordinary permutations of individual situations and their rigidity about the future, holding that it will resemble the present. For better or for worse, in our contemporary technological society, even the near future explodes with novelty, much of it nefarious as, for example, the emerging 'side-effects' of miracle drugs. The pervasive medical ethical questions of abortion, euthanasia, truth-telling, confidentiality and the allocation of scarce resources have become dramatically more complex as medical technology outraces our ability to adjust our goals, values and decisions. Organ transplants, ventilation therapy and a host of new drugs have made it possible to keep human beings alive who only a decade ago would die a natural death. Some wanted to live, some wanted to die, whereas others such as neo-nates and comatose patients had no say on whether to live or die. As these cases become public, we are struck by the dazzling array of personal differences, idiosyncracies and needs which differ from case to case, making it very troublesome to use a general theory for purpose of decision and accountability. We now present two recent paradigmatic cases, both of which illustrate the damaging and foolhardy effort to cling to a principle, at the expense of the patients and their families. These cases also demonstrate the massive danger in failing to take into account the potential future consequences as a central factor in making the decision.

Baby girl S, the first born to her parents, had a high lumbar meningomyelocele, hydrocephalus, and paralysis and deformities with the condition from her work, refused to sign the acquainted with the condition from her work, refused to sign the operation permit for back closure. Her husband supported her position, but the physicians and hospital staff obtained a court order for a series of operations. The parents openly expressed their feelings to the staff, and in turn the staff was hostile to them. After surgery, complications were numerous and the child's brain was damaged severely, but Mr. and Mrs. S resolved to do their best for their baby. They took her home hoping that they had been wrong (as they knew they could have been) and that the best choice had been made. As complications arose, they brought the baby into the hospital several times for further treatment. Each time, they felt the hostility of the staff whom they would have liked to avoid but couldn't. When the baby died at 10 months of age, they were questioned by physicians and the police about whether they had deliberately delayed seeking treatment for 'heavy breathing' (diagnosed at autopsy as pneumonia) until their baby was near death.

Subsequently, two healthy children were born, but Mrs. S had to work to help pay the large debt incurred in the care of the first baby. She was away from the children much of the time and was always tired when she was at home. Her husband felt neglected, and the children developed behavioral disorders. When one of the children was diagnosed as suffering from maternal deprivation, Mrs. S was hospitalized for treatment of severe depression. She later reported, 'It was just more than I could take.' She and Mr. S felt that their first baby should have been 'helped to die.' They considered that much of the suffering of their baby, themselves, and their other children was senseless and destructive. They doubted that they or their living children would ever fully recover from the court-ordered treatment of their first child.[22]

Mrs. J was a 45-year-old housewife with a husband on disability due to diagnosed coronary artery disease, a 16-year-old son with a delinquent record, and a 5-year-old mentally retarded daughter with inoperable congenital heart disease. Mrs. J was admitted to the hospital in severe respiratory distress. She had noticed shortness of breath with strenuous exercise 8 years prior to admission, which increased in severity over the next several years. She neglected her own medicinal needs because she was caring for her disabled husband and daughter. Two months prior to admission her symptoms worsened, and by the time of admission she was no longer able to perform her household duties, slept kneeling in a chair, and drank only fluids for nourishment.

On physical examination she was breathing rapidly. The patient was told by the doctor that it was necessary to insert a nasotracheal tube and control her ventilation with a volume-cycled ventilator, to begin intensive respiratory therapy, and to transfer her to the intensive care unit. The patient pleaded: 'Please let me go home. We have no money to pay you. I have to go home to take care of my daughter and husband.' The physician considered her behavior inappropriate, the result of a mental state created by the low oxygen and high carbon dioxide levels indicated by laboratory tests. He telephoned her husband, who agreed that his severely ill wife should be treated and signed all the consent documents. . .

The total hospital bill was $250,798. The husband signed the house mortgage and his life insurance policy over to the hospital. The family would live on welfare and Medicaid assistance. The average monthly bill for oxygen in the home alone was $275.

Nine months after the patient's discharge from the hospital, her husband died from a heart attack. Her son, who needed money to support the family, was arrested for armed robbery 1 month later. The daughter died six months after the father. One year after the operation, the respiratory-crippled woman was able to pursue her activities of daily living. However, 4 years after the surgery, Mrs. J finally succumbed to the complications of her illness. The cause of death was respiratory failure.[23]

These cases, alas, are not unique, for at this reading they are being duplicated in thousands of homes and hospital rooms throughout the nation. Never before has the question of human quality of life been subjected to such public scrutiny and subsequent revision. Never before have so many people rejected life-saving technology, whether it be permanent ventilation, transplants or kidney dialysis. Yet countless more seek these regimens which prolong life, although often with severe penalty as found in the artificial heart patients. No ethical panacea is available, which would make all of these cases and situations palatable. This is especially true of those who offer philosophical theories that are neither grounded nor tested in the heat of actual, everyday experience. This warning applies to all practitioners of professional ethics, the author included, but it is especially telling for medical ethics. As the cases cited above demonstrate with a vividness and a sadness, the imposition of a rigid ethical principle can spell contentment for the originator and disaster for the recipient.

No more than the classical ethical theories can pragmatic ethics offer a resolution of these issues. Yet, the pragmatic approach being more cautious, less convinced of a single right way, more cognizant of baleful consequences and more open to an experimental, even ad hoc response, does provide a more potentially fruitful point-of-departure with regard to the decisions that must be made. Looking back to the two medical cases just cited, it is obvious that an amalgam of the three mooring points for a pragmatic ethics would have provided a more salutary development in both instances.

Surely Mr. and Mrs. S had enormous affection for their first-born baby daughter, yet they had an instinct that on their human journey, it was best not to keep her alive, for her own sake and for theirs. As the outcome of the case decisively showed, the child was to be a clot, a trap in the journey, a ten-months-long way-station which irrevocably wrecked the future of the entire family. Had a sense of passing through, of *transiency* [24] been at work, the hospital staff would have realized that and provided the sustenance to enable the family to continue on its way, wounded but not decimated.

In our second case, it is striking that the wishes of Mrs. J were summarily dismissed, although they proved to be chillingly accurate only four years later after the total destruction of the family. A dispute between the respiratory therapist and the physician involved allegedly moral positions, taken monistically, each hostile to the other with neither showing any regard for the wider, *pluralistic* constellation in which the needs and moral stance of Mrs. J would be taken into account.

Both cases are startling in their absence of any *melioristic* sensibility, for all of the participants from the professional side are articulating, defending and imposing their point of view, independent of what is *better* for the patient and the family. This is in blatant disregard of the physician's motto, *primum non nocere*, a maxim which requires first of all that we do no harm. Meliorism goes one step further, urging us to make things better, not for ourselves, but for our patients and for those whom we serve.

The pragmatic method can live with a variant of styles, so long as they are not absolute and allow for options under the press of experience. It is difficult to live with a belief in the ultimately irresolute. More seriously, it is dangerous to live with confidence that complex moral issues have ultimate, final, absolute resolutions.

The passing of time is the source of our joy, our celebrations and our suffering. Time is a taskmaster, and in time, time will exact our end. We know of no one who has beaten time at its own game. 'Come and play,' says time, yet remember that the game will conclude. Pragmatic ethics and the radically empirical metaphysics which it articulates understands the parameters of the game. Transient, multi-faceted and inexorably finite, our nectar is in the human journey. Seeing to the quality of that journey is our moral burden and, occasionally, our delight.

NOTES

1 Cf. Ralph Waldo Emerson, 'Introduction to Nature,' *The Complete Works of Ralph Waldo Emerson*, vol. I (Boston: Houghton, Mifflin Company, 1903), p. 3.

2 Cf. John J. McDermott, 'The Renascence of Classical American Philosophy,' *Streams of Experience: Reflections on the History and Philosophy of American Culture* (Amherst: The University of Massachusetts Press, 1985), Appendix. This is a bibliographical essay pertaining to both primary and secondary sources.

3 James Mark Baldwin (ed.), *Dictionary of Philosophy and Psychology*, vol. II (New York: The Macmillan Company, 1901), p. 321.

4 Cf. 'Pragmatism and Pragmaticism,' *The Collected Papers of Charles Sanders Peirce*, Charles Hartshorne and Paul Weiss (eds), vol. V (Cambridge, Mass: Harvard University Press, 1934), and William James, *Pragmatism: The Works of William James*, Frederick Burkhardt (ed.), (Cambridge, Mass: Harvard University Press, 1975); William James, *The Meaning of Truth: The Works of William James* (Cambridge, Mass: Harvard University Press, 1975).

5 The finest explication of James's theory of truth and the meaning of 'works' is to be found in H. Standish Thayer, 'Introduction,' *The Meaning of Truth*, *op. cit.*, pp. xi-xlvi.

6 Cf. John Dewey, 'Propositions, Warranted Assertibility, and Truth,' *The Journal of Philosophy*, vol. XXXVIII (March 27, 1941), 169–86, and Gail Kennedy, 'Dewey's Logic and Theory of Knowledge,' *Guide to the Works of John Dewey*, Jo Ann Boydston (ed.), (Carbondale: Southern Illinois University Press, 1970), pp. 61–97.

7 John Dewey, *The Quest for Certainty: The Later Works*, vol. 4 (Carbondale: Southern Illinois University Press, 1984), pp. 217–18. The de-

velopment of 'Dewey's Ethics' is summarized by Herbert Schneider (Part I) and Darnell Rucker (Part II) in a *Guide to the Works of John Dewey, op. cit.*, pp. 99–130.

8 William James, *Pragmatism: Works* (Cambridge, Mass: Harvard University Press, 1975), p. 31. For a further elaboration of James's meaning of pragmatism, cf. William James, 'The Pragmatist Account of Truth and Its Misunderstanders,' *The Meaning of Truth: Works, op. cit.*, pp. 99–119.

9 Cf. William James, *Essays in Radical Empiricism: Works* (Cambridge, Mass: Harvard University Press, 1976).

10 Cf. John Dewey, 'The Postulate of Immediate Empiricism,' *The Middle Works*, vol. 3, pp. 153–67. Dewey's comparable essays to James's radically empirical metaphysics are best found gathered in John Dewey, *The Influence of Darwin on Philosophy and other Essays in Contemporary Thought* (New York: Henry Holt, 1910).

11 William James, 'Preface,' *The Will to Believe: Works*, pp. 5 and 6.

12 William James, 'Preface,' *The Meaning of Truth: Works, op. cit.*, pp. 6–7.

13 John Dewey, 'The Postulate of Immediate Empiricism,' *op. cit.*, p. 158.

14 William James, *Pragmatism: Works, op. cit.*, p. 99.

15 John Dewey, *Experience and Nature: The Later Works*, vol. 1, p. 43.

16 John Dewey, 'Experience and Objective Idealism,' *The Middle Works*, vol. 3, p. 144.

17 James, *Pragmatism*, p. 123. In any given society, however, individuals are often felt called upon to oppose the governing ritual. This takes 'genuine courage,' which for Dewey is always 'moral.' Cf. John Dewey, 'The Virtues,' *Ethics: The Middle Works*, vol. 5, p. 370. '*Moral Courage and Optimism* – A characteristic modern development of courageousness is implied in the phrase "moral courage," – as if all genuine courage were not moral. It means devotion to the good in the face of the customs of one's friends and associates, rather than against the attacks of one's enemies. It is willingness to brave for sake of a new idea of the good the unpopularity that attends breach of custom and convention. It is the type of heroism, manifested in integrity of memory and foresight, which wins the characteristic admiration of to-day, rather than the outward heroism of bearing wounds and undergoing physical dangers.' It is of note, that in his otherwise brilliant book, *After Virtue* (University of Notre Dame Press, 1981), Alasdair MacIntyre, makes no mention of either James or Dewey. Surely James's essay on 'The Moral Philosopher and the Moral Life' is a premier piece relevant to *After Virtue*. Cf. William James, *The Will to Believe: Works*, pp. 141–62, where James attempts 'to show that there is no such thing possible as an ethical philosophy dogmatically made up in advance.'

18 One thinks here of C.S. Peirce's life-long commitment to a 'community

of inquiry' and, above all, of Josiah Royce's indefatigable effort to provide the lineament, rationale and sustenance for a world community. Cf. Josiah Royce, 'The Hope of the Great Community,' *The Basic Writings of Josiah Royce*, John J. McDermott (ed.), vol. II (University of Chicago Press, 1969), pp. 1145–63.

19 John J. McDermott (ed.), *The Writings of William James* (University of Chicago Press, 1977), pp. 806–7.

20 John Dewey, 'The Development of American Pragmatism,' *The Philosophy of John Dewey*, John J. McDermott (ed.), vol. I (University of Chicago Press, 1981), pp. 50–1.

21 Pragmatic ethics is not the focus but it is present, *malgré lui*, throughout the excellent book by Albert R. Jonsen, *et al.*, *Clinical Ethics* (New York: Macmillan, 1982). This book is akin to the early modern tradition of Roman Catholic casuistry, which like the Jewish Talmud, has instinctive pragmatic insights and methods.

22 Ronald Munson, *Intervention and Reflections, Basic Issues in Medical Ethics* (Belmont, California: Wadsworth, 1979), pp. 117–18.

23 Kathleen A. McCormick and Faye G. Abdellah, 'Respiratory Failure: Technological Care in the Home and Hospital,' *The Machine at the Bedside: Strategies for Using Technology in Patient Care*, Stanley Joel Reiser and Michael Anbar (eds) (New York: Cambridge University Press, 1984), pp. 321–2.

24 We use transiency here to signal the need to confront death. Physicians have no business keeping human beings alive if death is appropriate and liberating. Cf. John J. McDermott, 'The Stethoscope as Talisman: Medical Technology and Loneliness,' forthcoming, and John J. McDermott, 'The Inevitability of Our Own Death: The Celebration of Time as a Prelude to Disaster,' in *Streams of Experience: Reflections in the History and Philosophy of American Culture* (Amherst: University of Massachusetts Press, 1986), pp. 157–168.

II

FIELDS OF APPLIED ETHICS

INTRODUCTION

In this section, philosophers working in applied ethics discuss the problems of their respective fields. The first two essays, on medical ethics and business ethics, review the developments of these rapidly expanding fields and explore the role which ethical theory has played within them. In the next two articles, the authors argue in support of particular answers to questions of national and international importance: reverse discrimination and nuclear war. The last essay points up the fundamental role of the social sciences in applied ethics and argues that the social sciences can contribute to our understanding of values as well as facts.

These essays are not meant to cover all the fields of applied ethics, but they do cover several of the most important ones, and they do illustrate how theoretical ethics have been applied. The reader may notice that even if not explicitly mentioned the assumptions or principles of one kind of ethical theory or another are implicit in the styles of argumentation, the very questions posed, or in the specification of goals to be achieved. The reader may also notice the extent to which theory seems to be ignored and questions are addressed intuitively or on the basis of popular beliefs or social norms. Such popular beliefs or practices need not conflict with theoretical principles; the question is whether popular controversies can be adequately (or consistently) resolved without theory.

Mary B. Mahowald's summary of the development of medical ethics concludes with an appraisal of apparent weaknesses within the field. She believes that improvement awaits greater interaction

137

between theoreticians and practitioners because, at present, many medical practitioners feel they are capable of making correct moral judgments in medicine without the benefit of theory, while those who support the application of theory have had only limited success in their attempts to resolve practical disputes. Nonetheless, Mahowald notes that there is a growing concern over questions of ethics in hospitals and medical schools. Although the teaching and practice of medical ethics is often conducted by persons who have had no special training in ethics, the input of philosophers and of philosophical studies of ethics has greatly increased.

After surveying the recent growth of business ethics, Norman Bowie cites guidelines which have been proposed by the NEH-sponsored Committee for Education in Business Ethics. These guidelines state that 'ethical theories were unsuccessful as pedagogical devices' and that 'ethical theory should be introduced relatively late in the course.' Bowie believes that these conclusions were drawn because, in business ethics courses, ethical principles were often applied in a simplistic, mechanical way. The solution, he finds, lies in the use of middle level or bridge concepts which can link ethical principles to particular cases. By using such principles, he thinks, ethical theory will play a much more important role in standard courses on business ethics.

James P. Sterba believes that philosophers have an important role to play in the application of moral values to policy questions on the use and maintenance of nuclear weapons. However, he finds it surprising that only a few philosophers have addressed themselves to such an enormous problem. The center of the debate has been on whether or not having or using nuclear weapons is morally justified, and the philosophers who address this issue have usually concluded with a simple 'Yes' or 'No': there has been little discussion of how to reduce conflict, or how to reach a settlement of international issues. Some philosophers, overwhelmed by the possibility of nuclear destruction, have declared it immoral to hold nuclear weapons or threaten their use. Others have argued that the risk of unilateral disarmament outweighs the risks of a policy of nuclear deterrence. In all of this, the role of traditional ethical theory has been minor, and, aside from the specification of very general goals, not much attention has been directed to the question of how such goals can be reached.

In his essay on reverse discrimination, Robert K. Fullinwider makes it clear that the debate over quota for minorities and women has not directly involved a consideration of traditional ethical theories but has focused upon the meaning and status of compensation: the question of who owes what to whom. Is it right to compensate some for the supposed wrongs of others? Fullinwider explores present conditions and typical, prejudicial behaviors in arguing that quotas are temporarily necessary as a means of achieving equal opportunity, even if the individuals actually harmed are not compensated for their loss. Thus, implicitly, he seems to dismiss a rule-deontological approach which would require retributive justice in favor of a consequentialist approach based upon quantitative or representative gains.

Lastly, in his article on the vocation of the social scientist, Bruce Jennings provides a transition from the present section on applied ethics to the next section on the future of ethics, for he holds that both moral philosophy and social science must change in order to improve applied ethics. Although he thinks that many people in the social sciences are still operating on the basis of positivist assumptions which have been generally abandoned in recent philosophy, he also thinks that the boundaries between the disciplines are beginning to blur and that connections are being formed between ethics and social science. Jennings views the role of the social sciences as essentially interpretive: as articulating an understanding of human agency within a social context and not simply providing uninterpreted facts or data for evaluative review.

In these accounts of applied ethics, the reader may notice that, to date, traditional ethical theories have played an inconclusive role in the development of applied fields, and yet, in the opinion of the contributors to this section, theory is needed in application. Although some philosophers may be convinced that one or another existing ethical theory is adequate for this purpose, the writers of this section tend to believe that existing theory must be amended, or at least supplemented, in order to do the kinds of jobs required. One possible procedure in applied ethics would be to curtail highly abstract philosophical theorizing and attend more closely to the lower level generalizations of popular debate, building theory from the bottom up, so to speak, rather than from the top down, and hence temporarily ignoring or at least tolerating apparent inconsistencies in principles or rules. Another possible procedure would be to continue investigations on the theoretical and applied levels

139

while modifying the one in the light of the other, seeking connections between the two. But, if the authors in this section are correct, ethical theorists can no longer simply ignore the problems of application, and persons working in applied ethics can no longer continue to operate effectively without taking theoretical considerations into account.

8

BIOMEDICAL ETHICS: A PRECOCIOUS YOUTH

Mary B. Mahowald

Medicine and philosophy have been at different points on parallel tracks for some time now, at least as far as jobs and prestige are concerned. Previously esteemed, both have experienced a period of disenchantment by the public. Positions have become scarcer, and financial incentives have declined. As Stephen Toulmin suggests, medicine may have saved the life of philosophy by rescuing the discipline from total absorption in the unreal world of metaethics.[1] Philosophers in turn have become more involved in the life of medicine, holding regular appointments in medical schools, conducting 'ethics rounds' in hospitals, serving on institutional review boards and government committees addressing ethical problems in health care and health research.

Important differences remain of course. The content and method of medical or health care practice are almost exclusively empirical and case-oriented. Philosophers, in contrast, continue their devotion to analysis of concepts and arguments. During the past decade, mutual need and attraction on the part of members of both disciplines have prompted a rather fruitful, ongoing relationship epitomized in the birth and development of biomedical ethics.

GENERATION, NAMING, DEVELOPMENT

The offspring of medicine and philosophy goes by other names as well. Van Rensselaer Potter first applied the term 'bioethics' to ethical issues regarding population and environment, but the term 'bio' has clearly been interpreted to extend beyond biological issues to those involving health care.[2] 'Medical ethics' has a long history if the term 'medical' is construed as applicable to anyone involved in health care. But its meaning may be restricted to those who are 'medical' in the narrower sense, namely, physicians. Veatch maintains that 'medical ethics' connotes the broader view, and proposes the term 'physician ethics' for the narrower perspective.[3] The terms 'health care ethics' and 'clinical ethics' explicitly indicate recognition that diverse professions are involved in health care issues, and more specific terms such as 'nursing ethics' and 'social work ethics' are used to identify the professional perspective from which ethical questions may be addressed. If we assume the broader concept of 'medicine,' and wish to incorporate the biological component as well, the term 'biomedical ethics' serves our purpose.

Any of the preceding designations points to the necessity of dealing with this subject interdisciplinarily. Since we are addressing problems that arise at the interface between ethics and biomedicine, we obviously need input from both sides. Moreover, since disciplines such as theology, law and the social sciences also deal with these issues, we can hardly ignore the relevance of their contributions. The success of those institutes or centers of biomedical ethics which have been most influential during the past decade, the Hastings Center (1969), and the Kennedy Institute (1971), owes partly at least to their commitment to interdisciplinarity. Less prestigious but also influential is the Society for Health and Human Values, formed in 1969 through support from the United Ministries in Higher Education. This group, which plans yearly meetings in conjunction with medical meetings, initiated publication of the *Journal of Medicine and Philosophy* in 1975. The Committee on Medicine and Philosophy, formed in 1974 from within the ranks of the American Philosophical Association, is smaller in membership but more populated and respected by philosophers. Few non-philosophers are even aware of this organization; fewer still attend its meetings, usually held in conjunction with meetings of the American Philosophical Association. Fortunately, a number of well-regarded philosophers belong to both the Society for Health and Human Values and the Committee on Medicine and Philosophy.

Early experts in biomedical ethics came from religious studies or theology rather than philosophy. In 1954, Joseph Fletcher, an ordained Episcopal minister, published *Moral Problems in Medicine*[4]; this was a dozen years before his better known and controversial *Situation Ethics*.[5] In 1970, Paul Ramsey, another Christian theologian, published *The Patient as Person*, a text representing a religious deontological perspective.[6] Jesuit theologian Gerald Kelly,[7] and Augustinian Charles McFadden[8] were early exemplars of the traditional Catholic interpretation of natural law, while later moral theologians such as Richard McCormick, S.J.[9] and Charles Curran[10] advanced more liberal interpretations of that tradition. Philosophers arrived in the fray somewhat later. One of their first forays came in 1973 at Case Western Reserve University in Cleveland, where Samuel Gorowitz and his colleagues taught a course called 'Moral Problems in Medicine.' Material developed for pedagogical purposes led to publication of the first philosophical anthology in biomedical ethics.[11] Recently (1984) revised and updated, this continues to be more philosophically demanding than its competitors.

The proliferation of undergraduate courses in biomedical ethics is now a commonplace, as philosophers scramble to upgrade their own background and maintain currency about the issues, so that they may aptly respond to the need for good teachers in this area. Simultaneously, undergraduate programs in nursing and allied health fields have assigned faculty to the teaching of such courses. There is some concern that these, and courses taught by practitioners in professional schools, will be superficial in ethics content, perhaps confusing ethics with moral proselytizing or values clarification.[12] Possibly the most important contribution that philosophers may make in this regard is to work with the instructors of such courses. A significant ongoing activity of the Hastings and Kennedy Centers has been the conduct of summer programs or workshops in ethics for theoreticians and practitioners; these provide remedial and enriching opportunities for members of different disciplines. More substantial and extended 'updates' have been available for philosophers through fellowship programs funded by the National Endowment for the Humanities. Some of these emphasize clinical experience, as in the Program on Human Values and Ethics at the Univerity of Tennessee Center for the Health Sciences. Others emphasized personal research in an interdisciplinary context (e.g. Hastings) or seminar-type experience (e.g. NEH Summer Seminars for College Teachers).

II: Fields of applied ethics

In an overview published by the Institute on Human Values in Medicine, Pellegrino and McElhinney document the unprecedented growth of ethics teaching in medical schools and nursing schools during the past decade. Contrasting the present situation with the early 1970s, they claim that 'almost every school of medicine and many schools of nursing are teaching courses in ethics and, in addition, some other aspect of human values or the humanities.'[13] The Institute's survey of 122 medical schools shows 1,064 faculty members teaching in the area of 'human values,' with almost half of these physicians. Most of the teaching by physicians is informal, i.e., they function mainly as small group leaders, conference participants, or discussants at 'ethical rounds.' This mode of teaching is entirely consistent with the way clinical medical education is usually conducted. *Bona fide* humanists, i.e. philosophers, theologians, historians, and teachers of literature, comprise only about 10 per cent of the total number of faculty involved in teaching 'human values.' Of these only one out of five actually devotes more than 25 per cent time to such teaching. Institutions which have hired philosophers as regular faculty have been commended for 'practicing what they preach.'[14]

A move by philosophers into the clinical setting is not without its drawbacks, as well as its challenges. The first two years of medical school are often a memory feat, the next two years an endurance contest. Moreover, medical students are at a point in their lives where they have zeroed in on a very specific goal, namely, to be a doctor. They are naturally drawn to subjects which will equip them to do that, and philosophy is not one of these. But a growing number of experienced physicians and administrators are convinced that the best way to develop good physicians is to develop thoughtful people who are clear about fundamental principles of medicine, and committed to continual update of their medical knowledge. A recent report of the Association of American Medical Colleges strongly sanctions this approach, arguing for an emphasis on active rather than passive learning, and for reduction in course hours so as to provide more opportunity for independent learning.[15] The recommended revisions clearly favor broader inclusion of ethics into the medical curriculum.

Recently, a new kind of expert in biomedical ethics has emerged. This is the individual who is fully prepared in philosophy and in his or her health care speciality, e.g., the physician-philosopher or

144

nurse-philosopher. While these individuals are rare, their number is increasing, and their credibility in both philosophical and medical communities is a decided advantage. For example, Howard Brody, a physician-philosopher at Michigan State, has written a book which is uniquely appealing to medical students because it is written from their perspective. While case-based, and somewhat complexly organized, Brody's *Ethical Decisions in Medicine* incorporates careful philosophical analysis leading to specific, well-supported conclusions.[16] It stands as an attractive alternative to the inconclusive speculations of 'pure' philosophers, and the isolated, detailed histories of 'unique' cases by practitioners.

Brody was one of a group of physicians and ethicists who met at Dartmouth College in July 1983 to 'survey the current status of the teaching of medical ethics.' The group concluded that the field is 'now sufficiently developed, and the need for the application of ethical knowledge and skills in medicine sufficiently compelling to justify a recommendation that all medical schools require basic instruction in the subject.'[17] What is particularly intriguing and challenging about this report is its account of specific goals appropriate to the teaching of ethics in the medical school setting. By the end of their training, the authors maintain, physicians should:

1 Be able to identify the moral aspects of medical practice.
2 Be able to obtain a valid consent or a valid refusal.
3 Know how to proceed if a patient is only partially competent, or is incompetent, to consent to or refuse treatment.
4 Know how to proceed if a patient refuses treatment.
5 Be able to decide when it is morally justified to withhold information from a patient.
6 Be able to decide when it is morally justified to breach confidentiality.
7 Know how to manage patients with poor prognoses, including patients who are terminally ill.[18]

Such specifications of practical skills as behavioral goals is unusual, to say the least, in the teaching of philosophy. Some philosophers are likely to disown the preceding list as quite unrelated to their discipline. But goals 1, 5, and 6 are surely intellectual skills that philosophers as such may cultivate in their students. The other goals, 2, 3, 4, and 7, are inevitably related to an understanding of other concepts ('valid consent,' 'competence,' and 'death') which it is the business of philosophy to help clarify.

As might be expected, proliferation of courses has led to proliferation of textbooks. Most of these are issue-oriented anthologies with brief introductory sections dealing with ethical theories and recurrent concepts. Since ethical questions arise at the cutting edge of research, currency in the field requires continual updating. Hence, the best of the earlier collections have already been revised and republished.[19] Collections differ in the extent to which they incorporate selections by philosophers, theologians, lawyers, social scientists, basic scientists and health caretakers. Some have unique, useful features such as Shannon's introductory review of Roman Catholic ethics,[20] and Reiser's historical material.[21] Several of the newer anthologies are compiled specifically for nurses, or for non-physician practitioners, and several of the newer issue-oriented texts (not anthologies) are written to represent a specific religious perspective.[22]

Medical journals have clearly increased their coverage of topics in ethics, publishing articles by philosophers, some of which have been quite influential.[23] Similarly, physicians occasionally contribute to philosophical conferences on biomedical issues, and team up with philosophers in addressing these issues for publication.[24] General philosophy and ethics journals frequently carry articles in biomedical ethics,[25] and a number of journals focus exclusively on such topics.[26] *The Hastings Center Report*, published since 1970, has become a widely read interdisciplinary bimonthly journal devoted to issues in professional ethics, most of which are biomedical. This journal also provides regular case studies and commentaries, collected every few years and published as a separate volume; these are extremely useful in teaching practitioners on an *ad hoc* basis. For philosophers the *Report* suffers the inevitable limitation of its intentionally popular, non-technical style. Matters of philosophical substance are more substantially treated in philosophy journals.

There are also many books focusing on specific issues or topics, such as abortion, death and dying, concepts of health, paternalism, decisions regarding disabled infants, reproductive technologies and institutional review boards.[27] The *Encyclopedia of Bioethics*, published in 1978, continues to be a significant resource, covering the full range of concepts and issues, with supplementary bibliographies to assist researchers in updating the material provided there.[28] While updates may also be pursued through computerized searches of philosophy and clinical journals, there is now a special Bioethics File which is particularly helpful in this regard. In multiple volumes available from the US Government Printing Office, the President's Commission for the Study of Ethical Problems in Medicine and Biomedical and Behavioral Research has provided another significant resource, on topics such as informed consent, decisions to forego treatment, definitions of death, genetic counselling and engineering and access to health care.[29] These volumes too are essentially interdisciplinary, useful for philosophers as well as non-philosophers not only in their own content but also in the sources they cite.

ISSUES OLD AND NEW

Long-standing issues in biomedical ethics continue to be important not only for teaching, but also as ways through which to test or illustrate ethical theories and concepts. Unfortunately, less attention is given to everyday issues such as truth-telling and confidentiality, than to the more dramatic ones which usually involve life and death decisions. Advances in neonatology and prenatal diagnosis have prompted reconsideration of late abortions, as permitting termination of pregnancy without termination of fetal life.[30] The same technologies have exacerbated questions regarding nontreatment of disabled infants. Euthanasia continues to be debated but there is more discussion now of whether artificial feeding may be discontinued in terminal patients.[31] Although there is general acceptance of the concept of whole brain death, some argue that cessation of cognitive function, i.e. higher brain death, is a preferable definition.[32] Possibilities for extending life now include artificial hearts and interspecies transplant, renewing the issue of experimental treatment, and raising further questions of personal identity.

The identity problem is also raised in the context of new techniques of reproduction. In vitro fertilization, combined with ovum and embryo transfer, make it possible for a child to have three biologically related parents, none of whom may actually raise their offspring. Social alternatives raise further questions – e.g., ova, sperm, and embryos may be donated or sold; embryos may have

147

inheritance rights; women may 'rent' their wombs, accepting payment for pregnancy and childbirth in order to provide another
person or couple with an adopted child. The payment factor has
suggested analogy with prostitution, and reinforced the criticism
that human beings (children) are thus treated as property of other
persons.[33] Through 'surrogate mother' arrangements, single men or
women, as well as lesbian or homosexual couples, may acquire
biologically related offspring. 'Double standard' arguments, those
claiming unequal treatment of men or unmarried individuals, are
articulated by those who affirm that the right to one's biological
progeny is fundamental for all human beings. Nonetheless, the
judicial council of the American Medical Association stipulated in
1984 that consent of both the woman and 'her husband' are required
for artificial insemination.[34] Marriage is thus construed as a relevant
consideration for reproductive interventions.

In addressing many of these questions, social and political attitudes are clearly influential. For example, 'Right-to-life' advocates
have aligned themselves with issues regarding disabled neonates,
claiming that infanticide is the logical and inevitable extension of a
liberalized abortion policy. The general trend towards smaller
families, motivated variously by concerns about overpopulation,
economic motives, and the effectiveness of contraception, has
provoked a 'premium baby' mentality, which supports not simply
the right to reproduce, but an alleged right to perfect or nearly
perfect offspring. Along these lines there is the legal and medical
possibility of abortions performed solely because the child is not of
the desired sex. A new technique in prenatal diagnosis, chorionic
villi tissue sampling, makes this possible as early as the eighth week
of gestation, when abortion is more acceptable to some.[35]
Amniocentesis, the usual technique through which chromosomal
sampling is accomplished, can only effectively be done during the
second trimester of pregnancy, when abortion is considerably more
hazardous both physically and emotionally.

At times the crucial role played by philosophers in biomedical
ethics is the critique of language described by Wittgenstein. Meanings of person, health and disease, life and death remain controversial; yet such concepts must be clarified if fruitful dialogue is to take
place concerning their implications. Where new and popular terms
(e.g. 'pro-choice' and 'pro-life,' 'test tube babies,' 'orphaned
embryos,' 'surrogate motherhood') are inaccurate or misleading,

the philosopher's task is to 'overcome the bewitchment of intelligence' by pointing out the confusions entailed by such linguistic uses.[36] Analysis of the professional/other relationship is another area in which philosophers have contributed to biomedical ethics, in some cases proposing new models – such as Bayles's fiduciary model,[37] and Thomasma's conscience model.[38] Both of these point to the inadequacy of the traditional paternalistic model, as well as the producer/consumer model, or patient autonomy model. Both stress moral rights as well as responsibility on both sides of the professional/other relationship. An emphasis on patient autonomy is also reflected by substitution of the term 'client' for 'patient,' as in the new Code of the American Nurses Association.[39] In contrast, the code of the American Medical Association has retained its use of the term 'patient.'

MATURATION – THEORETICAL SOURCES AND CRITICISM

One sign of the coming of age of biomedical ethics is the development of literature addressing the theoretical basis of medicine, e.g. Thomasma and Pellegrino, *A Philosophical Basis of Medical Practice*,[40] and the foundations of medical ethics as distinct from other fields of applied ethics, e.g. Veatch, *A Theory of Medical Ethics*.[41] Thomasma and Pelligrino's account, although nuanced and updated, is largely consistent with the orientation of the medical profession throughout history. It imputes a unique, beneficent role to the physician, as Hippocratic healer. In contrast, Veatch exemplifies an emphasis consistent with American public opinion and much of the writing of ethicists: a critique of the Hippocratic tradition and insistence on patient autonomy.

Noticeably absent from Thomasma's and Pelligrino's work is the jargon of contemporary or classical ethical theory. Instead, the authors purport to develop a philosophy of medicine based on medical practice (Pelligrino is a physician), rather than one resulting from the imposition of an existing philosophy on medical practice. Epistemologically, this involves 'explanation of how scientific theories of diagnosis, prognosis, and therapy can be derived from, and applied to, individual living human bodies.'[42] Ontologically, both the theory and practice of medicine derive from a focus on the living human body, which the physician attempts to heal through correct clinical judgments. That attempt, according to Thomasma and Pellegrino, implies three ethical axioms applicable to a 'living body in need of help': 'Do no harm; Respect vulnerability of patients; Treat all patients as equal members of the human race.'[43]

In stressing patient vulnerability, these axioms scarcely address those categories of 'patients' who are in fact healthy rather than ill, e.g., pregnant women, or others whose recourse to physicians is elective rather than coercive (e.g. through routine check-ups, cosmetic surgery, etc.). Moreover, it is not at all clear that respect for patient autonomy is acknowledged within the axioms, although perhaps treating 'all patients as equal members of the human race' implies this. Thomasma and Pellegrino do discuss moral agency as applicable to physicians as well as patients, and delineate responsibilities for both in the medical relationship.

In *A Theory of Medical Ethics*, Veatch defines the Hippocratic tradition as 'the directive to benefit the patient according to the physician's ability and judgment.'[44] His own contract/covenant model is an attempt to overcome the excessive individualism and paternalism which that principle entails. The foundation of his theory is a triple contract which starts with universal agreement on basic ethical principles. This agreement provides the framework for a contract between society and each profession, which in turn is the context for a contract between professional and patient. As Veatch develops them, the principles that emerge from the original social contract are utilitarian (beneficence) and deontological (contract keeping, autonomy, honesty, avoidance of killing, and justice). Although conflicts among deontological principles are to be resolved so as to minimize violations, the principle of beneficence is never to take precedence over the deontological principles. Veatch's rendition is comparable to the principles defended by Tom Beauchamp and James Childress in *Principles of Biomedical Ethics*, a widely read summation of utilitarian and deontological perspectives, as expressed through the principles of beneficence, autonomy, non-maleficence and justice.[45] In both books, the principles are similar to W.D. Ross's *prima facie* duties. Unlike Ross, however, Veatch does not admit to intuitionism as their foundation. Beauchamp and Childress only partially and indirectly acknowledge that source.

Philosophically, perhaps the weakest link in Veatch's chain of reasoning is his effort to ground ethical principles without benefit of an epistemological model. Instead, he maintains that competing models of discovery and invention produce convergent support for the same principles. In an important review of the work, L.W. Summer has argued that this convergence hypothesis is incorrect.[46] Since the competing models may themselves be false, the conclusion supported by both is hardly established through mere convergence.

In contrast to Veatch's book, and epitomizing a tendency to strip biomedical ethics of technical philosophical accoutrements, is the recent work of a religious ethicist (Albert Jonsen), physician (Mark Siegler) and attorney (William Winslade), entitled *Clinical Ethics*.[47] For medical students or professionals, the most striking feature of this book is its resemblance in size and format to one which they often carry in their pocket as a source of necessary information about medications. Jonsen and his colleagues have succeeded in reducing medical ethics to a 'look-up' formula. For each of the different issues commonly encountered by clinicians, a brief medical description, legal counsel, and ethical commentary is provided. Lest it be thought that this amounts to a *reductio ad absurdum*, the strengths of this approach need to be acknowledged. First and most obvious is the fact that busy clinicians are more likely to read and use a work of this type than those which are less accessible in size and content. Second, the book in fact recognizes that different disciplines have relevant input regarding ethical quandaries in real situations. And third, the authors recognize what philosophers have often missed, namely, that the great range of medical conditions which characterize clinical practice demand different approaches to different situations.

Jonsen and his colleagues distinguish three types of disease situations which call for distinct responses. These are identified by the acronyms ACURE, CARE and COPE. ACURE stands for an acute, critical, unexpected (disease), responsive (to treatment), and easily diagnosed; this is the basic model for emergency care. The acronym CARE stands for a critical, active (condition), recalcitrant (to treatment), eventually leading to death; this is the paradigm for critical care. COPE refers to a chronic (condition which calls for) outpatient (treatment to provide) palliative, effective (care); this is the model for ambulatory practice.[48] The authors proceed to explore the implications of patient preferences, quality of life criteria, and external factors, all of which are relevant to ethical decisions in the health care setting. They thus provide a useful manual for clinicians.

Probably the most convincing evidence that biomedical ethics has matured is that philosophers have begun to be self-critical of their own involvement in the field. This is different from the earlier scoffing attitude of rigid analytic philosophers who viewed medical ethics as a bastard offspring, illegitimately conceived by philosophers who have been unfaithful to, or unworthy of, their own tradition. Two intriguing examples of this criticism come to mind. The first is an article by Cheryl Noble, philosopher turned lawyer, who castigates philosophers for pretending moral expertise in addressing questions of applied ethics. 'Moral problems are everybody's business,' Noble writes, but philosophers have increasingly claimed that they alone possess the intellectual skills to solve such problems.[49] Philosophers Peter Singer, Thomas Nagel, Richard Brandt and Ronald Dworkin all come under Noble's attack, as does the rather prestigious journal *Philosophy and Public Affairs*. In response to her critique, Singer defends the philosopher's special role by outlining its advantages for addressing moral issues: general training in logical arguments and detection of fallacies, understanding of moral concepts, or meta-ethics, and of moral theories, and opportunity to 'think full-time about ethics.'[50]

Basically, Noble is concerned about an elitism among philosophers, a defect that is at least reducible through genuine interdisciplinarity. Of course, *genuine* interdisciplinarity is difficult to achieve, since it entails admission of limitation on the part of the interdisciplinary contributors. Philosophers may be less likely than others to withdraw or share their claim of expertise for several reasons: 1 they are particularly concerned with abstract or non-empirical content, accessible as such to other intellects; 2 they generally lack the knowledge base of colleagues whose expertise is scientific or clinical; 3 such colleagues are often quite capable of functioning logically, with apt understanding of moral concepts and frameworks, and some at least make time to apply these analytic skills to moral problems. As for the 'full-time status' of philosophers who 'do' medical ethics, such philosophers have many other professional responsibilities that fill their days (e.g. committee work, curricular development, administrative tasks, teaching, grading, etc.).

Another philosopher who is critical of contemporary ethicists, while retaining the status of ethicist herself, is Colleen Clements, an assistant professor of psychiatry at the University of Rochester Medical Center. Typical of Clements's criticisms is an article coauthored with Roger Sider, MD, entitled 'Medical Ethics' Assault upon Medical Values.' Therein, Clements contends that

the currently dominant school in medical ethics, that of a patient autonomy-rights model based in rationalist philosophy and liberal political theory, has been used to subvert values intrinsic to medicine, that it has done so without adequately establishing the merits of its case, and that the unfortunate result has been the attempted replacement of the historic medical value system by an ill-fitting alternative.[51]

To overcome such subversion, Clements proposes a model based on 'adaption, function, and best interest,' a model she claims consistent with the Hippocratic tradition, and so with medical values.[52] Autonomy or formalism (which Clements apparently equates) is an inappropriate foundation upon which to build medical ethics. The concluding statement is suggestively exhortatory: 'When we (*sic*) as physicians act in the best interests of our patients, we do so with the firm hope that, when the time comes, our physicians will do the same for us.'[52] The 'we' suggests that Clements identifies more with the institution of medicine than with philosophy. Indeed, such identification or cooption is a possibility that must be reckoned with by philosophers who function 'full time' within the medical 'establishment.' While such philosophers draw a salary from the institution, their essential role is as critic of the institution. To fulfill that role, they must in some sense remain 'outsiders' among the 'insiders.' Socrates is an obvious model for the philosopher in such a position. For some, such as Arthur Caplan, a move from the clinical situation to a bioethical think tank (the Hastings Center) is the hemlock-taking that allows fidelity to philosophy. For others, such as Ruth Macklin (Albert Einstein), it remains possible (while difficult) to maintain philosophical identity in the clinical situation.

Despite Clements's claim to the contrary, there are significant sources in medical ethics that do not rely primarily or exclusively on the principle of patient autonomy for their criticisms of medical practice. We have already mentioned two of these: Thomasma and Pellegrino's *The Philosophical Basis of Medical Practice*, and

II: Fields of applied ethics

Clinical Ethics by Jonsen, Siegler and Winslade. Both reflect an emphasis on the traditional medical value of beneficence; both avoid discussion of 'formalist' ethics. In addition, Jonsen's work considers the 'best interest' of the patient *before* patient preferences, invoking a case-based method similar to that followed by most physicians, and recommended by Clements.[53] The difference, perhaps, between this approach and Clements's is that the latter would ignore patient preferences entirely.

Clements labels her method 'Natural Law – Naturalistic Ethics,' correlating its components with traditional medical values. Both views are based on empirical norms, recognized as promoting 'adaptive functioning' of the human organism. Both involve an intimate connection between facts and values, between 'is' and 'ought.' 'Doing what is best in terms of these norms,' sometimes over the objection of the patient, is 'the proper application of ethics.'[54] Such a view is powerfully and frighteningly paternalistic. It is also quite distinct from ethics as taught by most Roman Catholic theologians, whose tradition is allied with natural law theory.[55]

Summarily, the views of Colleen Clements typify the precocity of contemporary biomedical ethics. While overstated, her criticisms are partly valid, comparable to those articulated by adolescents who recognize the real defects of the adult world. Like them, however, she seems clearer and more reliable in what she opposes than in what she proposes. 'Adaptive functioning' remains an extremely vague criterion.

Similarly, biomedical ethics is an adolescent, sharp and accurate in its criticisms but still weak in its theoretical and practical proposals. Centuries of ethical theorizing have yielded little agreement among philosophers, and has hardly engaged clinicians. To insure a fruitful union, philosophy must surrender its claim to exclusive expertise in ethics, and biomedicine must acknowledge its dependence on philosophy.

NOTES

1 Cf. Stephen Toulmin, 'How Medicine Saved the Life of Ethics,' *Perspectives in Biology and Medicine* 25, 4 (Summer 1982), p. 736.
2 Van Rensselaer Potter, *Bioethics, Bridge to the Future* (Englewood Cliffs, N.J.: Prentice-Hall, 1971), pp. vii-viii.

3 Robert Veatch, *A Theory of Medical Ethics* (New York: Basic Books, 1981), p. 16.

4 Joseph Fletcher, *Moral Problems in Medicine* (Princeton University Press, 1954).

5 Joseph Fletcher, *Situation Ethics* (Philadelphia: Westminster Press, 1966).

6 Paul Ramsey, *The Patient as Person* (New Haven: Yale University Press, 1970).

7 Gerald Kelly, *Medico-Moral Problems* (St Louis: Catholic Hospital Association, 1958).

8 Charles McFadden, *Medical Ethics*, 6th Edition (Philadelphia: F.A. Davis, 1967).

9 Richard McCormick, *Health and Medicine in the Catholic Tradition* (New York: Crossroad Publishing Company, 1984).

10 Charles Curran, *Contemporary Problems in Moral Theology* (Notre Dame: Fides Publishers, 1970), pp. 97–158.

11 Samuel Gorovitz *et al.* (eds), *Moral Problems in Medicine* (Englewood Cliffs, N.J.: Prentice-Hall, 1976).

12 Cf. Mary B. Mahowald and Anthony P. Mahowald, 'Should Ethics Be Taught in a Science Course?' *Hastings Center Report* 12, 4 (August 1982), p. 18.

13 Edmund D. Pellegrino and Thomas K. McElhinney, *Teaching Ethics, the Humanities, and Human Values in Medical Schools: A Ten-Year Overview* (Washington, D.C.: Institute on Human Values in Medicine, Society for Health and Human Values, 1981), p. 2.

14 Lynn Kahn, 'Philosophers Prime Physicians for Ethical Dilemmas,' *Hospitals* (September 16, 1982), p. 166.

15 Cf. Panel on the General Professional Education of the Physician and College Preparation for Medicine, *Physicians for the Twenty-First Century*, The GPEP Report (Washington D.C.: Association of American Medical Colleges, 1984), pp. 10, 11.

16 *Ethical Decisions in Medicine*, 2nd edition (Boston: Little, Brown & Company, 1981).

17 Charles M. Culver, *et al.*, 'Basic Curricular Goals in Medical Ethics, *New England Journal of Medicine* 312, 4 (Jan. 24, 1985), p. 253.

18 Cf. ibid., pp. 254–4.

19 E.g., Tom Beauchamp and LeRoy Walters, *Contemporary Issues in Bioethics*, 2nd edition. (Belmont, Ca.,: Wadsworth Publishing Company, 1982); Robert Hunt and John Arras, *Ethical Issues in Modern Medicine* 2nd edition (Palo Alto: Mayfield Publishing, 1983); Ronald Munson, *Intervention and Reflection*, 2nd edition (Belmont, Ca.: Wadsworth Publishing, 1983).

20 Thomas Shannon (ed.), *Bioethics* (New York: Paulist Press, 1976), pp. 3–10.

II: Fields of applied ethics

21 Stanley Reiser *et al.*, *Ethics in Medicine* (Cambridge, Mass: The MIT Press, 1971), pp. 3–76.

22 E.g., Martin Benjamin and Joy Curtis, *Ethics in Nursing* (New York: Oxford University Press, 1981); Natalie Abrams and Michael Buckner, *Medical Ethics* (Cambridge: The MIT Press, 1983); Martin E. Marty, *Health and Medicine in the Lutheran Tradition* (New York: Crossroad Publishing Company, 1984); Kenneth Vaux, *Health and Medicine in the Reformed Tradition* (New York: Crossroad Publishing Company, 1984).

23 E.g., James Rachels, 'Active and Passive Euthanasia,' *New England Journal of Medicine* 292, 2 (Jan. 9, 1975), pp. 78–80.

24 E.g., Bernard Gert and Charles M. Culver, 'The Justification of Paternalism,' *Medical Responsibility*, Wade Robison and Michael Pritchard (eds.) (Clifton, N.J.: Human Press, 1979), pp. 1–14; Stuart Youngner and Edward Bartlett, 'Human Death and High Technology: The Failure of the Whole Brain Formulations,' *Annals of Internal Medicine* 99, 2 (Aug. 1983), pp. 252–6.

25 E.g., *Ethics, Journal of Value Inquiry, Journal of Social Philosophy, Philosophy in Context, Philosophy and Public Affairs.*

26 E.g., *Journal of Medicine and Philosophy, Man and Medicine, Journal of Medical Ethics, Bioethics Quarterly.*

27 E.g., L.W. Sumner, *Abortion and Moral Theory* (Princeton: Princeton University Press, 1981); Robert Veatch, *Death, Dying and the Biological Revolution* (New Haven: Yale University Press, 1976); Arthur Caplan *et al.* (eds.), *Concepts of Health and Disease* (Reading, Mass.: Addison-Wesley Publishing Company, 1981); Rolf Sartorius (ed.) *Paternalism* (Minneapolis: University of Minnesota Press, 1983); Robert Weir, *Selective Nontreatment of Handicapped Newborns* (New York: Oxford University Press, 1984); Michael Bayles, *Reproductive Ethics* (Englewood Cliffs: Prentice-Hall, 1984); Ronald Cranford and A.E. Doudera (eds.), *Institutional Ethics Committees and Health Care Decision Making* (Ann Arbor: Health Administration Press, 1984).

28 Warren Reich (ed.), *Encyclopedia of Bioethics*, 4 vols. (New York: Free Press, 1978).

29 All of these are published by the United States Government Printing Office: *Defining Death*, July 1981; *Making Health Care Decisions*, 3 vols., Oct. 1982; *Splicing Life*, Nov. 1982; *Securing Access to Health Care*, 3 vols., 1983; *Screening and Counselling for Genetic Conditions*, Feb. 1983; *Deciding to Forego Life-Sustaining Treatment*, March 1983; *Implementing Human Research Regulations*, March 1983.

30 Cf. Mary B. Mahowald, 'Concepts of Abortion and Their Relevance to the Abortion Debate,' *Southern Journal of Philosophy* 20, 2 (Summer 1982), pp. 195–207.

31 E.g., Willard Green, 'Setting Boundaries for Artificial Feeding,' and

Gilbert Meilaender, 'On Removing Food and Water: Against the Stream,' *Hastings Center Report* 14, 6 (Dec. 1984), 8–13.

32 Cf. Youngner and Bartlett, note 24 *supra*.

33 Cf. Mary B. Mahowald, 'Surrogate Mothers and Parental Rights,' *Hastings Center Report* 14, 3 (June 1984), p. 43.

34 Cf. *Current Opinions of the Judicial Council of the American Medical Association* (Chicago: American Medical Association, 1984), p. 3.

35 Nadine Brozan, 'Fetal Health: New Early Diagnosis Studied,' *New York Times* (Mar. 9, 1985), p. 18.

36 Ludwig Wittgenstein, *Philosophical Investigations*, trans. by G.E.M. Anscombe (New York: Macmillan Company, 1953), 109.

37 Michael Bayles, *Professional Ethics* (Belmont, Ca.: Wadsworth Publishing, 1981), p. 68–86.

38 David Thomasma, 'Beyond Medical Paternalism and Patient Autonomy: A Model for the Physician-Patient Relationship,' *Annals of Internal Medicine* 98, 2 (Feb. 1983), pp. 243–8.

39 *Code for Nurses with Interpretive Statements* (Kansas City: American Nurses' Association, 1976), pp. 3 ff.; cf. note 33 *supra*.

40 David Thomasma and Edmund Pellegrino (New York: Oxford University Press, 1981).

41 Cf. note 3 *supra*.

42 Thomasma and Pellegrino, p. xii.

43 *Ibid.*, pp. xiii, 186.

44 Veatch, *A Theory of Medical Ethics*, p. 10

45 2nd edition (New York: Oxford University Press, 1983).

46 L.W. Summer, 'Does Medical Ethics Have Its Own Theory?' *Hastings Center Report* 12, 4 (Aug. 1982), pp. 38–9.

47 (New York: Macmillan Publishing Company, 1982).

48 *Ibid.*, pp. 17–46.

49 'Ethics and Experts,' *Hastings Center Report* 12, 3 (June 1982), p. 7.

50 'How Do We Decide?' *Hastings Center Report* 12, 3 (June 1982), pp. 9–10.

51 *Journal of the American Medical Association* 250, 15 (Oct. 21, 1983), p. 2011.

52 *Ibid*, p. 2015.

53 Jonsen equates the 'best interests' of the patient with the principle of beneficence, as expressed by the Hippocratic maxim: Be of benefit and do no harm. *Ibid.*, p. 11.

54 Clements and Sider, p. 2014.

55 E.g., Benedict Ashley, O.P. and Kevin O'Rourke, O.P., *Health Care Ethics, A Theological Analysis*, 2nd edition (St Louis: Catholic Hospital Association, 1982).

9

BUSINESS ETHICS

Norman E. Bowie

One might date the birth of business ethics as November, 1974 – the date of the first conference on business ethics at the University of Kansas and cosponsored by the Philosophy Department (Richard De George) and the College of Business (Joseph Pichler). The proceedings of that conference were subsequently published as a book, *Ethics, Free Enterprise, and Public Policy: Essays on Moral Issues in Business*. Shortly thereafter, Executive Secretary of the American Philosophical Association, Norman Bowie, prepared a proposal to the National Endowment for the Humanities for a three-year grant to allow philosophers, business school professors, and business persons to draft guidelines for business ethics courses. NEH funding was obtained and work began in 1977.

Before tracing the history of the field since these two events in the middle 1970s, the ten-year period from late 1974 to late 1984 should be put in its proper perspective. The field of business ethics was not created *ex nihilo*. Plato and Aristotle both discussed, albeit briefly, matters of business ethics; Plato identified the proper function of business – a view very much in line with the twentieth-century economist Milton Friedman. Aristotle provided an account of economic institutions and at least a partial account of economic justice. Other references to economic institutions can be found in the history of philosophy, e.g. the theory of the just price and debates about usury. With the rise of the industrial age and the advent of 'big business' in the late eighteenth and nineteenth centuries respectively, the philosophical consideration of economic institutions including business evolved rapidly. Some of the philosophizing was quite crude, as with the 'philosophy' of social Darwinism. Some of the philosophizing was highly critical, as with Marxism. But some philosophizing was quite supportive as was generally the case with the pragmatist John Dewey. In general, most of the discussion by 'pro's,' 'anti's' and 'moderates' occurred at a fairly abstract level. *Vis-à-vis* business institutions, the discussion occurred at a meta-level and focused more on economic systems than on business per se. References to business practice were used to buttress larger theses about economics. This discussion has continued unbroken in political philosophy. Most political philosophy courses contain a section on economic systems with reference to, or selections by Marx, Nozick, and Rawls – to name but a few. Although most business ethics courses also contain a section, and most business ethics books a chapter, on these broader issues of economic justice, the focus of business ethics has been more narrowly drawn on business practice. In the US, something like a free enterprise system has been more or less assumed and discussion has proceeded on a micro-level – on the practices of firms and on the behavior of individuals within the firm. This narrowing of focus has been both applauded and severely criticized. The critics argue that by narrowing the focus, philosophers are selling out to the system. On the other hand, many who have taken the narrower path, argue that a proper ethical analysis of business practice requires a suspending of judgment on the larger issues. Indeed, these persons argue, greater understanding at the micro-level is relevant in the assessment of the macro-issues. Moreover, if that micro-analysis requires an interdisciplinary approach, a Marxist attack on capitalism usually won't provide the required access to the research and opinions of scholars who are not philosophers. In many ways the whole imbroglio is a tempest in a teapot. An adequate analysis of business ethics requires that both the macro- and the micro-issues be addressed. However, since most academics are far more familiar with the macro-issues, this essay will focus on the micro-issues within business ethics, i.e., it will focus on the behavior of firms and on the actions of individuals who work in them.

Even at the micro-level, business ethics didn't appear *ex nihilo* in 1974. Many Catholic philosophers had been at work on micro-questions since the Middle Ages. That work didn't stop but rather continued through the Industrial Revolution in a straight line to the

1950s and 1960s. Perhaps the best known Catholic philosopher is Clarence Walton the former President of Catholic University, who wrote the book *Corporate Social Responsibilities* in 1967. That book on competing theories of the moral purpose of the firm can be read with insight today. Other Catholic philosophers who have contributed to the field before 1974 include Thomas Garrett, W.L. LaCroix, and Theodore Purcell. Before focusing on the last decade, the pioneering efforts of these individuals deserve recognition.

The report of the NEH sponsored Committee for Education in Business Ethics (CEBE) reported its findings by the end of 1980. By that time the first three business ethics texts by philosophers had been published: Vincent Barry's *Moral Issues in Business*, Tom Beauchamp and Norman Bowie's *Ethical Theory and Business*, and Thomas Donaldson and Patricia H. Werhane's *Ethical Issues in Business: A Philosophical Approach* (all 1979). A society 'Society for Business Ethics' had formed and Thomas Donaldson was elected as its first president. The society publishes a newsletter and sponsors colloquia at all three divisional meetings of the American Philosophical Association. Moreover, the CEBE report was to be supplemented by a detailed business ethics course description written by Richard De George and a booklet containing syllabi for the teaching of management ethics prepared by The Society of Values in Higher Education.

It might be interesting to see how subsequent developments in the field have squared with the recommendations of that CEBE report. The Committee adopted the following guidelines:

1   All business ethics courses should have three components:
   a   A section describing some of the fundamental ethical concepts which could be used to analyze cases in business ethics. Analyses of Harm/Avoidance, Equity, Obligation, Justice, Fidelity, Dignity (Self-Respect) have been prepared.
   b   A section describing some of the most widely held ethical theories and some comment on the application of these theories to problems in business.
   c   A section of cases with philosophical analyses.
2   Since our own experimental course indicated that traditional ethical theories were unsuccessful as pedagogical devices for achieving the aims of the course,

ethical theory should be introduced relatively late in the course. Best results are obtained by introducing students to central moral concepts like justice, honesty and autonomy early in the course.

3 All courses should contain cases on whistle-blowing.

4 Every course should contain a discussion of business codes of ethics.

5 Consideration of the relation between business practice and moral responsibility is essential in each course.

6 Team teaching represents the ideal for a course in business ethics.

7 Measuring changes in student attitude is not an essential goal in a course in business ethics.

8 Prerequisites for a course in business ethics are not required.

9 In business schools, courses in business ethics need not be kept separate from courses in business law.

10 The possession of certain degrees is not required to teach a course in business ethics. Interest is one of the most important qualifications.

11 However, as a means for upgrading standard qualifications CEBE recommends (a) training courses, (b) fellowship support so that philosophers might study business, and (c) promotion of the notion of a second degree.

With respect to the content of business ethics courses, nearly all of them contain items b and c in recommendation 1 and most contain (a) as well. Any delay in introducing (a) into the courses can be understood in light of recommendation 2. The traditional pedagogical approach in applied ethics was to use utilitarianism and some version of deontology (usually Kantianism) as tools for resolving problems in medicine, business, government and the professions. Since most standard ethics texts in the middle 1970s contained large doses of utilitarianism, Kantianism, and meta-ethics, students were taught the normative ethics without meta-ethics. But many found this approach unsatisfactory pedagogically. To any given problem, students would respond in 'rote' fashion – 'seek the greatest good for the greatest number,' or 'respect persons.' As a result discussions in applied ethics often appeared shallow. Students knew the definitions of the traditional theories without understanding the subtleties that they would have gotten in standard ethics courses at that time – recall the debate as to whether act and rule utilitarianism ultimately came to the same thing.

Although it is extremely hard to trace cause and effect here, as applied ethics courses grew, both standard ethics courses and research in ethics began to shift focus. There was an increased emphasis on these middle-level ethical bridge concepts – bridge concepts because they fill the space between specific issues and the two general ethical theories. Rawls's *A Theory of Justice* directed attention toward the concept of justice without any help from applied ethics. Indeed, Rawls's book may have helped make applied ethics respectable. But it is equally likely that examples from business and the professions supported theoretical work on rights and virtue. Alasdair MacIntyre was an early participant at a business ethics conference and his famous work *After Virtue* discusses business practice at length – albeit critically. Well-known theoreticians like Alan Gewirth and R.M. Hare devoted considerable time and space in applying their own theories to problems of business and professional ethics. I know of few theoreticians in ethics who ignore applied ethics. The issues of applied ethics are intellectually respectable – at least as long as they are addressed by those who have made their mark as theoreticians.

Even the analysis of the two traditional normative theories – utilitarianism and deontology – has proceeded along lines parallel with discussions in applied ethics. Economic theory abandoned psychological utility theory for revealed preference theory – in part to escape charges that using such concepts as "satisfaction" committed economists to value judgments and hence made economics 'unscientific.' Lately philosophers have tended to follow their economic colleagues by substituting preference for satisfaction. However, most philosophers have differed from most economists on the issue of whether or not all preferences are of equal value – or at least of equal value except for the intensity with which the preferences are held. Since the task of public policy on utilitarian theory is to enact policies which produce the greatest good for the greatest number, whether or not all preferences are deemed worthy of being considered is an important moral question. For example, should the preferences of the members of the Ku-Klux-Klan for discrimination against Blacks and Jews be counted at all – even if the opposite preferences of others will win out. Theories about the moral evaluation of preferences are widely discussed – especially in the work of Ronald Dworkin and Amartya Sen. This work is of great interest to those who use utilitarian moral theory to evaluate the free enterprise system in general and business policy in particular. Writers in business ethics are not satisfied with the view that American business practices are justified because they efficiently maximize consumer preferences. Rather, such writers are concerned with how such preferences are formed and with minority preferences that might be ignored. Neither in the theoretical work in utility theory nor in the applied research in business ethics are preferences taken as given. The moral evaluation of preferences is one of the more exciting areas of contemporary research – both in ethical theory and in business ethics.

With respect to deontology, the direct contribution of business ethics is the emphasis on role morality (Bowie's *Business Ethics* (1982) begins with role morality as the first building block in a theory of business ethics). Often deontologists are criticized for having a theory based on an abstract unrealistic individualism. For example, rights theorists emphasize the rights that individuals have against institutions but lose sight of the fact that individuals are in part the individuals they are because of the roles individuals play within institutions.

Also deontological discussions of the principles of respect for persons have been enriched by discussions in applied ethics. Philosophers writing in feminist theory are providing the heaviest input. But writers in business ethics have their contribution to make. At first the early research was on the concept of whistle-blowing. By now there is a fair consensus among writers in business ethics both on the definition of whistle-blowing and on the conditions for justified whistle-blowing. Recently the discussion has shifted to employee rights. Questions concerning employee rights present great opportunities for interdisciplinary research. The publication of *In Search of Excellence*, the publicity given to the means of redressing declines in American productivity, the study of Japanese management, and the interest of organization theorists in corporate culture all enrich and are enriched by philosophical analyses of employee rights. Although the uncritical euphoria which accompanied *In Search of Excellence* is subsiding, philosophical contributions have yet to achieve their full recognition. The right of management to move or close a plant and the employment at will doctrine

163

Theodore Lownik Library
Illinois Benedictine College
Lisle, Illinois 60532

are no longer considered self-evident truths. Research efforts in business ethics are directed to strategies for employer/employee cooperation – strategies which recognize the rights and respect the integrity of both parties. I would expect much fruitful analysis in this area over the next decade and I am sure philosophers working in business ethics will make an important contribution to that analysis.

Thus, books on ethical theory no longer resemble the books on ethical theory in 1974. Both within utilitarianism and deontology the content of the discussion has shifted. Moreover, the discussion has been broadened to include in depth analyses of these so called bridge concepts of justice, dignity, rights, virtue and harm. In part that shift of emphasis is a result of the activity in applied ethics. Moreover, the discussion has progressed sufficiently far so that we can say that there is no longer any excuse for a student to respond to a case study in business ethics by saying, 'All you have to do is produce the greatest good for the greatest number' or 'All you have to do is to respect persons.' Business ethics texts provide a more sophisticated analysis of the two traditional theories and contain an analysis of the important bridge concepts as well.

For example, the concept of moral rights functions as a bridge concept between the fundamental deontological principle of respect for persons and a number of problems that arise in business ethics. The overreaching concern might well be, 'How does one respect persons in the business context?' Now a number of philosophers have already argued that unless persons are viewed as rights bearers, they can't be shown respect. For example, Joel Feinberg asks us to imagine a world, Nowheresville, which is just like our own except for the fact that none of its inhabitants have any rights ('The Nature and Value of Rights,' *The Journal of Value Inquiry*, Vol. 4, 1970, pp. 243–57). Feinberg easily convinces us that such a world is morally impoverished and the inhabitants of Nowheresville cannot treat each other with dignity and respect. This analysis anchors one end of the rights bridge in the deontological principle of respect for persons.

Within the business context, the concept of fundamental rights enables us to morally evaluate both business law and business practice. Generally an employee is employed at will. He or she may be fired for any reason – good or bad, moral or immoral, or indeed for no reason at all. A not very subtle argument would show that persons employed at will lack a right to their job and that without such a right employees lose an essential element of self-respect. Employees, similarly, are not shown respect when management simply treats them on a par with capital, land, and machines in a calculation as to whether or not a plant should close or move. Without rights to their job, and rights to be consulted about major decisions which affect that job, employees are on the same level as machines, land, and capital and hence they are not shown the respect persons deserve. This analysis anchors the other end of the rights bridge within business practice.

As these bridge concepts are developed and as traditional ethical theory is subsequently enriched, we might be able to say that the second recommendation of CEBE no longer holds; the traditional ethical theories might well be introduced fairly early in the course.

An analysis of the major texts in the field indicate that recommendations 3–5 have largely been adopted. Actually there is a much wider consensus on what should be covered in a business ethics course than anticipated in the CEBE report. Although nearly every author (authors) has a topic which is fairly unique to him or her, there is a remarkable consensus on content. It is interesting to speculate as to whether or not this consensus will remain. As the field of business ethics grows, business professors teaching management theory, labor relations, and business law will begin to produce books on business ethics. Given the fact that cooperation between business professors and philosophers is recent and still rare, there is some prima facie reason to think that these books will look considerably different from their philosophical counterparts. Philosophers can only hope that the contributions of philosophers to business ethics will not go unrecognized in these new texts.

However, philosophers have already made a difference in the curricula of America's business schools. Ethical issues were typically treated within the context of business law or in courses on business and society. As a result they were not treated adequately. The legal questions tended to dominate the law courses. Courses in business and society weren't really courses in business ethics at all. Perhaps they are more adequately described as courses which serve the task of consciousness raising for business persons. In these courses business students are traditionally introduced to the writings of Marx, Ralph Nader, and others who are critical of business. In this way, students become acquainted with the thoughts of business critics. But little in the way of ethical analysis gets done.

Whatever the value of such courses, business and society courses are different from business ethics courses and are likely to remain so.

This leads to the possibilities for interdisciplinary research. I predict that over the next decade, a number of the major business schools will appoint a full-time philosopher or theologian to their faculty. Harvard has taken the lead here with the appointment of Kenneth Goodpaster. Such appointments would follow the successful precedent of medical colleges.

Interdisciplinary research will not be limited to the appointment of philosophers to business school faculties. Cross-fertilization will take place in the journals as well. Since 1980 two journals edited by philosophers have been created, *Journal of Business Ethics* and *Business and Professional Ethics Journal*. Both journals are interdisciplinary. *Journal of Business Ethics* frequently publishes the proceedings of various conferences on business ethics; for example, the 16th Conference on Value Inquiry, 'Ethics and the Market Place: An Exercise in Bridge-Building or On the Slopes of the Interface.' *Business and Professional Ethics Journal* has the policy of having all articles written by academics criticized by non-academics. In addition to these two journals, mention should be made of *Business and Society Review* – a journal published by Arthur Rosenfeld which also discusses items on business ethics. Finally, nearly all the scholarly and popular business publications carry articles on business ethics. *The California Management Review* seems to have some such articles in nearly every issue.

In addition to the formal appointments to business school faculty, philosophers and business professors frequently cooperate in the planning of conferences, symposia, and the appearances of guest speakers. Special mention should be made of the Center for Business Ethics, at Bentley College, directed by Michael Hoffman. Hoffman is a philosopher by training, although both the Center and his appointment are at a business college. Although there are more than a dozen centers on applied ethics affiliated with universities around the country, the Bentley center focuses exclusively on business ethics. It has sponsored a number of major conferences on topics in business ethics which have involved the participation of business persons in a major way. The Center which is affiliated with a philosophy department and most emphasizes business ethics is the Center for the Study of Values at the University of Delaware.

However, nearly all centers for applied ethics have programs and research related to business ethics – including the prestigious independent applied ethics center – the Hastings Center. An extensive list of centers and institutes concerned with business ethics may be obtained from CORPORATE ETHICS: A Review of Selected Corporate Policies and Practices published by Instructional Design, Development, and Evaluation, School of Education, Syracuse University, Syracuse, New York 13210.

In addition to the books, articles, and conferences, bibliographies are being compiled. The most extensive bibliography is the third in a series published by The Center for the Study of Applied Ethics, The Colgate Darden Graduate School of Business Administration at the University of Virginia. Unfortunately the bibliography ends with the year 1980. A volume encompassing 1981–5 is scheduled for publication in late 1986 or early 1987.

If courses, conferences, and journals focusing on business ethics exist, can programs be far behind? Actually programs already exist. The Department of Philosophy at Bowling Green State University has the longest-running and best-known MA programs in applied ethics. Persons interested in business ethics are certainly welcome in that program. However, the only graduate program in business ethics per se has been created by Loyola University of Chicago. The program is administered by the Philosophy Department but is offered in conjunction with the School of Business, the School of Law and the Institute of Industrial Relations. Of the ten required courses, six are in philosophy (four in ethics).

Finally, some mention should be made of business ethics seminars which occur within the corporate setting. One of the pioneers in this field is Charles Powers whose career has spanned both business and academia. For the past few years however, Mr Powers has not been in academic life. The most active academic seminar leader is Professor Donald Jones of Drew University who has published a book, *Doing Ethics in Business: New Ventures in Management Development* (1982). Recently philosophers have joined other academics in offering seminars or workshops in the corporate setting. For example, Professor Neil Luebke of Oklahoma State has been working with Phillips Petroleum. As business persons are exposed to the work of philosophers, perhaps these isolated instances will become a trend.

Despite the important research that has been done and the

167

interdisciplinary cross-fertilization that has been started, business ethics is still in its infancy as a discipline. Moreover, business ethics is an infant that many believe suffers from birth defects – some of them serious – possibly fatal. In considering the possible defects in business ethics, I pass over the intemperate and uninformed criticism of Peter Drucker (a criticism which has caused great mischief despite the fact that it is intemperate and uninformed). Others have adequately criticized Drucker.

Business ethics courses – as well as ethics courses in general – have been criticized because they don't change people's behaviour. *The Wall Street Journal* in an editorial of August 6, 1979, made just this criticism. However, surely CEBE was correct when it did not include changing people's behavior as one of the goals of the course. Although CEBE did recommend a greater sensitization to ethical issues, it concluded that even measuring changes in student attitude is not an essential goal of the course.

Why? In general educators do not want to be accused of indoctrination. Professors will lead horses to water but they won't even try to make them drink. In courses on art or music theory, students are taught those elements of music theory which would provide greater sophistication of taste. Faculty should be judged on how well they teach those essential elements and not on how many students switch from the Beatles to Bach. But why? To answer that question gets to the heart of the issue of what constitutes the purpose of higher education. Most persons believe that a dispassionate consideration of the evidence and the development of autonomous rational persons are central values of higher education. It is not that universities don't adopt value positions; they do. Rather, with respect to the content of any course, the priority is given to the presentation of balanced information in a rational way. Making students more ethical pales beside that goal and to the extent that trying to make people more ethical interferes with the values of the university, then it ought to be abandoned. The Wall Street critique illustrates a lack of understanding of the purpose of a university and what it stands for. Of course, business ethics instructors hope that their students will become more ethical, but making people more ethical is not the prime reason for giving the courses.

A far more serious criticism is presented by those who think that the field of business ethics is not sufficiently interdisciplinary, more specifically that philosophers systematically ignore empirical data on ethics from the social scientists. Up to a certain point, there is good philosophical warrant for this. As we philosophers say, 'What Is Doesn't Tell Us What Ought To Be.' On the other hand, we philosophers also say that 'Ought Implies Can.' Perhaps in this context a better expression is 'What Is Helps Define What Can Be Which In Turn Helps Define What Ought To Be.'

In a yet unpublished paper, the critic William Frederick has drawn the dispute between the social scientists and the philosopher ethicists far more sharply:

Clearly, the behavioral and socialization realities on both sides lead unavoidably to confrontation and clash of embedded values . . . Now enter the philosophic ethician, speaking the voice of sweet reason and urging the adoption of abstractly attractive ethical principles and categories. As well ask Niagara to stop falling or the salmon to stop spawning. Embedded values *will drive* organizations and individuals along certain pathways. Neither drive is likely to be deflected by an appeal to philosophic reason or wisdom, however attractive the alternatives may appear to be. Here we find the real difference between a philosophic and a social science approach to ethical analysis. The latter deals with the reality – the observed fact – of value conditioning within a sociocultural context, not with the wishfulness that humans committed to one set of values would yield to another, more attractive, set or to the moral reasoning or principles inhering in philosophic categories. For social science, the locus of the ethical problem is in the value systems that drive individuals, organizations, and societies along certain pathways and toward certain destinations and to reason ethically in certain ways and according to certain culturally- and genetically-induced principles. . .

Although I think Frederick's analysis is excessively deterministic, his analysis would strike a responsive chord in many, and it is certainly not enough that ethicists point out various flaws in Frederick's reasoning. Frederick's analysis rests on a number of contentions about philosophical research in ethics. He argues that philosophers in business ethics: 1 ignore the role played by culture in the formation of the human person: 2 basically ignore the role played by genetic factors in the determination of human behavior: 3 basically ignore the evidence of child psychologists and psychologists, e.g. Piaget, Kohlberg, and Rokeatch, about value formation and the growth of moral reasoning. As a result of this ignorance one shouldn't be surprised if philosophers are criticized for making judgments about corporations and business persons which seem 'removed from reality.' Business persons operate within a corporate culture and their ethical decisions are constrained in ways that ethical theorists ought to understand (they analyze the conditions of responsibility) but frequently seem not to understand (because they do not know much about corporate cultures).

Perhaps a good way to conclude this review of ten years of business ethics is to look at some of the research by philosophers that mitigates Frederick's criticism but also to point out directions for further research in the decade ahead.

Philosophers have not ignored the corporation *qua* corporation. Indeed, in a controversial analysis, Peter French has argued that a corporation has sufficiently analogous charactertistics to moral persons that it makes sense to hold corporations *qua* corporations morally responsible. French's view has been subjected to a barage of criticism and French has at least modified his view if not given it up. Tom Donaldson has produced a book in business ethics whose organizing theme is the corporation.

But the insights of non-philosophers with respect to corporate entities has been pretty much ignored. There has been little analysis of Maccoby's *The Gamesman*, nor of Theory X, Theory Z management styles, nor of quality of life circles. There has been little overt discussion of corporate culture.

An emphasis on the purpose of corporations and on the business philosophy of corporations might have many beneficial results. Business ethics is not a series of anecdotes about 'bad' business persons or about business persons who have the wrong principles. Rather it is in part an attempt to point out the clashes and conflicts that result between persons within corporations and between corporate perspectives and the perspectives of others outside the corporate setting.

Moreover, a focus on the corporation itself might advance the discussion of a number of important issues. Does the notion of a corporate culture enhance French's contention that corporations are sufficiently like moral persons? Would the notion of corporate culture give support to Professor Goodpaster's contention that corporations as corporations can take the moral point of view?

Even if there is a consensus on the definition of whistle-blowing and on the conditions for justified instances of whistle-blowing, given the value structure of corporations can we expect whistle-blowing to increase? Should more whistle-blowing be encouraged? What changes in organization structure can be made which would make whistle-blowing virtually unnecessary?

Although some attention has been given to role morality, much work still needs to be done on the concept of loyalty and the legitimacy of competing role demands. Borrowing from Rawls's analysis of procedural justice, what mechanisms can be evoked to resolve conflicts between the demands of the job and one's other obligations? Where do the demands of individual moral principles fit in? How can the individual maintain his or her moral integrity in large organizations without at that same time encouraging a kind of anarchy that would make organizations highly unstable and inefficient?

What about attitudes? How can and how should workers be encouraged to be concerned with product quality and with giving an honest day's work? Employee theft and employee absenteeism are serious problems, but surely moral exhortations against stealing and skipping work are futile. We need to know why employees steal or stay home and only then can we decide whether employee theft ought to be curbed by secret surveillance, e.g. one-way mirrors, or by higher pay. In the absence of the empirical facts as to why employees steal, discussions about privacy rights often have an unrealistic ring.

There are other issues which have not yet been addressed by philosophers which can only be discussed within the context of the purpose of the corporation and the philosophy of business. Except for some brief discussions on international bribery and investment in South Africa, there has been little analysis on multinationals. Corporate takeovers and 'greenmail' have yet to be subjected to philosophical treatment. From the proper perspective both could be grist for the philosopher's mill.

Finally, philosophers might suggest different metaphors for discussing corporate activity. Perhaps metaphors like 'game,' 'war,' 'the jungle' and 'poker' should be replaced. Perhaps analysis will show that cooperation is as important as competition if a corporation is to be both responsible and successful.

I am certain that this list of future research topics is far from complete. What is significant is that the list is so oriented to interdisciplinary issues. The integration of applied ethics and theoretical ethics is already under way. Perhaps the time is fast approaching when philosophers working in ethics (whatever the adjective that precedes 'ethics') will see themselves as a community of scholars that has the task of enriching our society's understanding of its major institutions.

10

REVERSE DISCRIMINATION AND EQUAL OPPORTUNITY

Robert K. Fullinwider

The United States began, in the mid-1960s, an extensive assault on racial and sexual discrimination. The omnibus Civil Rights Act of 1964 (as amended in 1972) and Executive Order 11246 (as amended in 1968) were major legislative and regulatory initiatives. Some of the programs and policies that evolved from these initiatives generated enormous controversy even among those opposed in principle to racial and sexual discrimination. These programs and policies appear to, or actually do, permit or require businesses, professional schools, municipal agencies, and other institutions to give special favorable weight to the race or sex of minorities and females. Such favorable treatment, on the view of its critics, transgresses the very principle of non-discrimination established in the 1960s.

Can race and sex properly be used as factors in hirings, promotions, layoffs, school admissions, and similar choices? Do programs of preferential treatment have, or lack, moral, legal, and constitutional foundations?

As could be expected, public debate on this matter has been extended and acrimonious. Likewise, a voluminous literature has grown up in the law journals commenting on judicial and executive interpretation of the law and Constitution. But somewhat less expectedly, there has also been an outpouring of writings by academic philosophers, most of it appearing in academic philosophy journals. Few other public policy controversies – one thinks of the abortion controversy, or of the newly growing controversy about nuclear deterrence – have generated such a direct philosophic engagement.

II: Fields of applied ethics

The philosophical literature dates, roughly, from two seminal essays by Judith Jarvis Thomon and Thomas Nagel published in the same 1973 issue of *Philosophy & Public Affairs*. The two essays mark out distinct approaches to the reverse discrimination controversy. In 'Preferential Hiring,' Thomson relies on a principle of compensation to defend racial and sexual preferences; in 'Equal Treatment and Compensatory Discrimination,' Nagel argues that preferential treatment is permitted, although not required, by justice and best defended by appeal to forward-looking considerations. Roughly speaking, the backward-looking approach favored by Thomson has, in the last decade, become less popular than the forward-looking approach recommended by Nagel.

I

Initially, defenses of preferential treatment rooted in appeals to compensation seemed attractive.[1] They promised to tie preferences to a very deep and widely shared moral conviction: that justice requires past wrongs be righted; that where wrongful injury has been done, a duty exists to make restitution. When conjoined with our society's history of flagrant denial of basic rights and opportunities to blacks and women, this deep conviction suggests a powerful claim for the legitimacy of giving preferences to blacks and women. Preferential programs yield to blacks and women what they are owed.[2] However, philosophical writings offered no sophisticated account of compensation. They were content to exploit our intuitions through reliance on simple examples or simple principles. Bernard Boxill introduced the reader to the concept of compensation with a story of a stolen bicycle that must be returned.[3] Judith Thomson relied on the principle that he who wrongs another owes him compensation.[4] These simple examples or principles generally command our agreement, but they do not quite apply to the programs they are supposed to justify. They need to be augmented and elaborated. As the elaborations are made, the compensation defense becomes more applicable to the programs in need of justification, but at the same time loses the direct intuitive appeal from which it begins.

The *simple model* of compensation, around which our common intuitions focus, contains four elements related thus: (1) an agent,

(2) acting wrongfully, (3) causes injury or harm (4) to a victim. In any case of compensation there are three crucial questions: *Who* owes *what* to *whom*? The formula of the simple model tells us how to construct an answer: the wrongful actor owes, the victim is owed, and what he is owed is restoration to his pre-injury condition (or to some approximation of this). So, to look at a concrete example, in Boxill's story the individual who wrongfully took the bicycle is duty-bound to return it (undamaged) to its original possessor.

This simple model does not directly match the circumstances in which preferential treatment is being practiced. Consider the complications that arise in trying to answer in regard to preferential programs the three questions implied by any compensation claim.

1 *Who owes?* Those who bear the costs of current preferential programs are generally those white, male applicants or workers denied positions, awards, or promotions they otherwise would have received; yet the wrongs for which compensation is owed were not the personal wrongs of these individuals but were corporate wrongs, namely, legislatively enacted and judicially enforced discrimination supported by social custom. How is the community (the debtor according to the simple model) warranted in transferring the costs of its debt to nondebtors? One strategy is to argue that white males are not wholly 'innocent' parties; thus, just as persons complicit in an agent's wrongdoing may have to share responsibility, so too white male applicants or job-holders can properly be assessed the costs of the community's programs of preferential treatment. Thomson, for example, argues that it is 'not inappropriate' that the costs of the programs fall on white males since they have profited from the wrongful discrimination imposed by the community.[5]

Now, the shift from 'he who wrongfully harms another must pay' to 'he who benefits from someone else's wrongs must pay' is a major variation from the simple model, and it is far from clear that there is any consensus at the level of intuition supporting the latter principle. We are apt to judge one thing where benefits were received knowingly and willingly and another thing where benefits were unavoidable and unwanted. We are apt to feel more disposed toward a required return of a benefit where it is easily transferable from the recipient back to its original possessor, and less disposed where it has become intermixed with other things and can't simply be transferred back to where it once lay. Bernard Boxill has insisted

175

that *merely* receiving benefits produced by injustice is enough to make one personally liable to compensate the victim of injustice, but this claim doesn't have much intuitive plausibility and the example he uses to support it carries little force. Suppose, he says, that a surgeon transplants a heart into Harry from Dick's corpse without getting permission from Dick's next-of-kin. When Harry recovers, he is bound, according to Boxill, to make 'suitable reparation' to Dick's family.[6] But I doubt readers will have the same intuitions about this.

The proposition that all white males have benefited from racial and sexual discrimination is offered fairly casually in the literature. It seems, perhaps, too obviously true to need arguing. However, it is not enough that all white males have benefited from discrimination. If they are liable to make compensation, then they must have received *net* benefits. Now, this observation forces us to a prior question: how are we to understand gain and loss when it comes to matters of compensation? As a first approximation, it seems reasonable to impute gain from discrimination to an individual who is better off than he would have been had discrimination never occurred, and to impute loss to an individual who is worse off than he would have been had discrimination never occurred. Given this account, it will not be obviously clear that all white males are or were net gainers from either racial or sexual discrimination.

Take racial discrimination. Employment segregation, by artificially limiting the flow of labor to good jobs, resulted in higher wages for those jobs than might have obtained had labor flowed freely to opportunities. Whites who competed for these jobs benefited. By the same token, crowding of blacks into menial work likely depressed pay for unskilled labor below what it might have been in the absence of segregation. Both blacks *and whites* who competed for this work suffered economic losses. Many urban and rural lower-class whites may lead, or have led, lives materially worse than they would have led had racial discrimination not existed; and they have passed their disadvantages to their children just as have deprived blacks. At least materially, these whites have not been net beneficiaries of racial discrimination. Perhaps other gains – intangible and psychological – can be included to alter this picture of net deficit and confirm the generalization about all white males as beneficiaries, but more argument is needed here than is commonly given.

2 *Who is owed?* Programs of preferential treatment confer their

benefits on those minority and female individuals who happen to apply for affected positions and who are qualified above some threshold. Do such programs actually compensate victims of discrimination? That is to say, do we have reason to feel confident that qualified minority and female applicants who happen to apply for affected positions are themselves victims of past discrimination? Judith Thomson in her 1973 article declared it 'absurd to suppose that young blacks and women now of age to apply for jobs have not been wronged.'[7] Likewise, Bernard Boxill in his 1984 book insists: 'We *know* that all blacks, lower class, middle class, and upper class, have been wronged by racial injustice.'[8]

As these two claims are framed, they raise yet another question about the nature of compensation: do we compensate a person for being *wronged* or being *harmed*? This is an important question because it is possible to be wronged without being harmed. Suppose an enemy spreads vicious lies about my behavior. He clearly wrongs me in doing so. But suppose no one believes the charges (they are too transparently lies), I do not fear they will be believed, no damage is done to my business, and I suffer no anxiety about my future. It is hard to see any way I have been *harmed* by the lying attack. This is not to say the lies had no effect on me. They made me angry and indignant. The lies *hurt* even if they did not *harm*.

Now, leaving aside the issue of punitive damages, which has to do with retribution rather than restitution, it does not appear I have a claim against my attacker for compensation, although I surely have a claim for public retraction and apology.

Boxill's recent attempt to rehabilitate the compensation defense of preferential treatment exhibits how inattention to these questions – Are hurts harms? Do we compensate wrongs or harms? – can result in elusive arguments. Blacks 'deserve compensation for the wrongful *harms* of discrimination,' declares Boxill.[9] Do *all* blacks then deserve compensation? All have been *wronged* by discrimination, he argues. Discrimination materially damages the life prospects of many blacks; in addition, those blacks who 'escape discrimination,' who are 'spared' discrimination, nevertheless 'feel threatened and insulted' at the discrimination against other blacks.[10] All blacks are 'wronged and *liable to be wrongfully harmed*,'[11] 'wronged and *probably harmed*,'[12] 'wronged and *possibly harmed*'[13] by racial discrimination. These claims do not amount to the proposition that all blacks have been harmed, which is the ground Boxill himself establishes for compensation.

Are insult and threat to be construed as harms? Discrimination attacks the 'self-confidence and self-respect' of blacks,[14] but attack can toughen as well as weaken. We want to be careful about implying that discrimination has turned all blacks into psychological cripples. (Likewise we want to be wary of similar generalizations about women.) *Hurt*, *harm*, and *wrong* need to be clarified and given appropriate places in a compensation argument.[15]

3 *What is owed*? Finally, even if we concede that every black or woman has been harmed by discrimination, it is still not clear we can adequately defend preferential treatment programs in the name of compensation. The simple model tells us to make good the victim's loss. Consequently, we would expect compensation practices to exhibit *proportionality*, matching benefit to loss. Those most harmed would receive more compensation than those least harmed. Many critics of preferential treatment view it as virtually reversing the expected proportionality. Preferential programs benefit those qualified blacks and women who happen to be making job searches, requests for transfer or promotion, or applications to school. These will be disproportionately younger individuals. If we suppose that younger, qualified blacks and women have been least victimized by discrimination, then 'a policy of preferential treatment directed toward groups as a whole will invert the ratio of past harm to present benefit, picking out just those individuals for present preference who least deserve compensation relative to other members.'[16] Preferential programs seem *perverse* as compensation schemes.

Now, none of the problems raised for the compensation defense amounts to a barrier that cannot be argued around. It could be claimed that preferential treatment programs should be viewed as one part of a total compensation package, other parts of which may never have enough political support to get implemented. It could be argued that preferential treatment is designed to yield compensatory justice for *groups* rather than individuals.[17] It could be claimed that whether or not all blacks and women have been harmed by discrimination, enough have to make it administratively efficient to prefer applicants according to skin color or gender. It could be argued that the presence or absence of fault on the part of white male applicants is irrelevant because preferential treatment programs should be viewed on a model of strict liability.[18] And yet other elaborations of greater or lesser plausibility can be made in the compensation argument.

These elaborations will by and large, though, move the compensation argument away from the simple model about which our intuitions are firm. As the elaborations diverge from the simple model, we lose an important basis for agreeing on policies. Where the basis in common intuitions fades away, theory must do the work of persuasion. A theory of compensation that successfully assimilated preferential-treatment-as-compensation to extensive and well-understood compensation and restitution practices already in place (in torts, product safety, quasi-contract, and so on) would carry great weight. By further showing how these practices reflect widely accepted principles of justice, such a defense might well compel assent. The problems with the compensation defenses that have been offered by philosophers has been their failure to advance beyond reliance on very simple examples and ad hoc principles upon which to build their arguments.

One reason we may remain skeptical of getting any broadly compensatory defense to 'fit' the policies of preferences that actually exist is that such a defense is at variance with the justifications these policies offer for themselves. Let us turn to an actual use of preferential treatment.

II

In 1973, American Telephone and Telegraph Company (AT&T) and the Federal government entered into a consent decree that required extensive changes in the company's employment practices.[19] Among other things the decree called for extensive use of preferences, primarily gender preferences.[20] It is instructive to look at the conditions that gave rise to the consent decree and at the government's specific aims in imposing it.

In 1970, AT&T employed over 800,000 persons (excluding Bell Labs and Western Electric), more than half of whom were women.[21] This ratio between men and women in overall employment was not reflected, however, through the various job classifications in the company. Eighty per cent of the women were in three classifications: operator, clerical, secretarial. This was no accident. Explicit sex segregation was the practice at AT&T. Men and women applicants were given different entrance exams and channeled into different career paths. 'Men's jobs in outside crafts, inside crafts, and management paid more, of course, than 'women's' jobs as clerk, operator, secretary, or inside sales representative, and carried greater advancement opportunities.

Even when men and women happened to do the same job, women were paid less. At Michigan Bell, the inside craft job of switchroom helper was performed by women, but at the other Bell companies the job was 'frameman' and was performed by men. When AT&T entered into the consent decree in 1973, it had to raise switchroom helper salaries substantially to bring them into line with those for framemen.

Women made up 1 per cent of career management positions. The company recruited management personnel from two sources. It promoted workers from craft jobs – male jobs – into management ranks, and it also recruited college students into management training programs – recruitment that excluded women.

In deliberations before the Federal Communications Commission and the Equal Employment Opportunities Commission in 1971 and 1972, AT&T defended its failure to put women in craft and management jobs. Women 'weren't qualified' for craft jobs, the company averred. Women couldn't be given management positions because they 'weren't mobile,' because they 'think differently from men,' because there would be 'suspicions of favoritism' in male superiors promoting women subordinates. Women were 'not interested' in craft and management jobs.

AT&T's defense of its maldistribution of men and women revealed deep-seated conceptions about the nature of women and men and the work they were fit for. Relations between men and women were viewed as primarily sexual or matrimonial, thus the natural suspicion of favoritism should a male superior promote a female subordinate. Women were viewed as having limited career aspirations and as being incompetent at craft work.

A vivid illustration of how 'women's work' was perceived as a less serious matter than 'men's work' was provided by the different responses Bell companies made to the same kind of complaints made by men and women. A company study of male workers' complaints – that their pay was too low, their skills underutilized, and the prospects of advancement too few – recommended speeding up promotions, increasing pay, and tailoring jobs to skills. Another study of similar complaints by operators recommended that the company in question stop hiring women who complain and seek women who were 'more realistic about their goals' and 'not looking for a glamorous career.'[22]

The ambitions of men to get ahead and earn more were taken seriously by AT&T; the similar ambitions of women were not. Women were expected to be 'realistic' because their primary vocation was to be homemakers and not breadwinners. It was a fault in women to 'look for glamorous careers.'

The consent decree entered into by AT&T, under the threat of extensive litigation, was designed to change the company's employment practices. Among other things, it required the company to set broad hiring and promotion 'targets' for fifteen job classifications. Fulfillment of the targets meant the company would on many occasions have to give sexual preferences. Provision was made for this in the consent decree. The prevailing union-management agreement called for promotion of the 'most senior' from among the 'best qualified.' When strict adherence to this agreement failed to produce enough of the right sex, the consent decree provided for an 'affirmative action override,' in which a person of the right sex could be selected from among 'basically qualified' workers. Hiring goals required similar deviation from standard selection criteria.

The operations of the consent decree produced a considerable amount of preferential selection of women.[23] This resulted in a lot of disgruntlement among male workers.[24] One worker expressed his feelings this way:

one thing that really bothers me is moving up in the company. I am white, male, 25. I am not a brain, but average. I have a lot of drive and want to go ahead. I have just been notified there is some kind of freeze which will last 3 or 4 months. (Note: frequently, when a target couldn't be met, all promotions would be frozen until a person of the right sex could be found.) In that time, if I am passed over, the company will go to the street. This is not fair. I work for the company, but my chances are less than someone on the street.[25]

However, the operations of the consent decree did not uniformly work against men. The decree included male 'targets' in clerical and operator jobs. This meant that some women were denied positions because of their sex. One such woman, Bertha Biel, unsuccessfully sued in Federal court when she was denied a promotion. In the words of the Court:

> In October 1973 the Company had one job class II opening to be filled for the remainder of the year. It had not met its intermediate goals for that year since no males had sought the opening. Accordingly, it filled its last opening for the year by hiring a male not previously employed by the Company.[26]

Like her male colleague (let's call him 'Bert'), the company passed Bertha over and went 'to the street' in order to fill a sexual quota. She could with justice echo Bert's own lament: 'It's not fair!'

What was accomplished at the cost of this unfairness? By 1979, the gender profiles of job classifications at the company had changed significantly. For example, between 1973 and 1979 there was a 38 per cent increase in the number of women employed in the top three job classifications (officials and managers), while there was only a 5.3 per cent increase in the number of men. Women made significant strides in sales positions, increasing in numbers by 53 per cent (a growth rate seven times faster than that of white males), and in inside crafts, increasing by 68 per cent (white males were decreasing by 10 per cent). In the outside crafts, the number of women grew by 5,300 while the number of men declined by 6,700.

On the other hand, AT&T increased the proportion of men in clerical and operator positions. It did this by meeting male hiring and promotion targets, and by making clerical positions entry jobs for men. In 1973, 17 per cent of men hired in the Bell companies entered through clerical positions, while 83 per cent entered through craft positions. In 1979, 43.7 per cent of men hired entered through clerical positions, while only 56.3 per cent entered through crafts. Overall, the percentage of men in clerical roles grew from 5.9 to 11.1 per cent.

At the end of 1972, AT&T employed 415,725 women (52.4 per cent of all employees); at the beginning of 1979, it employed 408,671 women (50.8 per cent of all employees). This overall decline was not inconsistent with the principal aim of the consent decree, which was to break down and destroy the 'culture of sex segregation' at AT&T. One signal fact at the company dominated management attitudes, job organization, physical layout, equipment design, work-rules, and employee expectations: that there were 'men's' jobs and 'women's' jobs. The purpose of the consent decree, with its targets and affirmative action overrides, was to

182

destroy this fact and the institutional inertia surrounding it. Women would be force-fed in significant numbers into positions from which they had previously been excluded; men would be assigned to 'women's' jobs.

Through this shock treatment enough women would become lodged in nontraditional jobs to effect lasting changes in the work environment, creating a more hospitable climate for women, and making unbiased employment practices truly possible.

If the government had simply required AT&T to eliminate its formal job segregtion and to change its employment practices to make them facially unbiased, it is likely that in 1979 the gender profiles of job classifications at the company would have looked remarkably similar to those in 1970. Two reasons suggest this conclusion. First, everything about the company was stacked against women's success in nontraditional jobs even if non-biased procedures were nominally adopted. The introduction of token women into alien and non-supportive work environments would have produced a high rate of failure and attrition, simply confirming the already prevailing belief among management that women would not succeed in 'men's' jobs and were out of place in them. Second, the period 1973–9 was not a period of growth but a period of employment decline for the company. Consequently, women would have been competing for very few positions, and getting but few of those. In 1979, AT&T would still have been a thoroughly segregated place to work, although giving lip service to equality of opportunity and bemoaning its inability to find 'qualified women.'

Even with the best of will, nominally unbiased procedures would not have produced a truly unbiased workplace. The *aspiration* to treat women fairly would have foundered against institutional *habits* reflecting a very different and long-standing *reality*: sex segregation. The strategy of the consent decree was not to change the reality by changing the habits but to change the habits by changing the reality.

Now, the underlying justification for preferential treatment that we can extract from the principal aim and the operations of the consent decree is forward-looking. The aim of law and policy is to achieve equality of employment opportunity, understood as selection without bias.[27] The use of preferences is a tool to this aim. The apparently paradoxical nature of using deliberate biases to undermine bias is dissipated by offering a credible account of an institution and its habits that reveals deep blockages to achieving truly unbiased selections, blockages not dislodgeable without resort to the drastic measure of preferential treatment.

This forward-looking justification, made in terms of promoting equality of opportunity, has a number of virtues apart from its mirroring the avowed aims of the laws and regulations under which the AT&T consent decree was formulated. First, if we view preferential programs as essentially compensatory or restitutive, then that portion of the consent decree requiring male quotas appears indefensible and out of line with the remaining aspects of the decree. On the forward-looking defense, this particular feature of the consent decree makes sense; it works to undermine the existence of 'men's' jobs and 'women's' jobs. Second, the fact that preferential programs benefit the best qualified blacks or women instead of the most injured constitutes an embarrassment for the compensatory defense, but not for the defense in terms of equal opportunity. If the aim is to reform institutional habits, then it is irrelevant that those whose presence can most effectively accomplish this change are themselves relatively advantaged.

The forward-looking defense does not have to find some special deservingness in the beneficiaries of preference, since it does not view them as receiving their benefits by right. They are given preferences because it serves the larger aim. Likewise, the forward-looking defense does not have to search about to find reasons why those who lose out under preferential programs deserve their fate. At AT&T, both Bertha and Bert lost out, and for the very same *impersonal* reason: being in the wrong place at the wrong time.

Now, no individual will be particularly happy at losing out on a job or promotion as a result of a program of preferences; Bert lamented his circumstances and Bertha went to court. Nevertheless, the equal opportunity defense of such a program allows us to justify it to losers in terms of values they cannot easily disavow. If an individual declares he just wants the promotion coming to him, he's not interested in equal opportunity, then he is in no position to complain that denying him the promotion violates his right to equal opportunity. On the other hand, if the loser bases his complaint on the value of equality of opportunity, he must concede that if a preferential program is truly necessary to create conditions for equal opportunity *for all*, adopting the program is not arbitrary and does not simply sacrifice his interests for some gain unrelated to his own values.

The equal opportunities defense has merit from a more abstract point of view as well. In many political theories, equality of opportunity ranks as a primary value. Its pursuit has high priority. Alan Goldman, a vigorous critic of preferential treatment by race or sex, nevertheless offers a theoretical defense of such treatment in terms of equality of opportunity:

> The rule for hiring the most competent (he says) . . . (is) justified as part of a right to equal opportunity . . . (which would be rationally willed by all actual members of society). Since it is justified in relation to a right to equal opportunity, and since application of the rule may simply compound injustices when opportunities are unequal elsewhere in the system, the creation of more equal opportunities takes precedence when in conflict with the rule for awarding positions. Thus short-run violations of the rule are justified to create a more just distribution of benefits by applying the rule itself in future years.[28]

In short, if preferences would create a situation that would 'result in fewer violations of rights in the future,' they would be justified.[29] Goldman himself does *not* support giving preferences on the basis of race or sex, but this is because he believes that *as a matter of fact* 'strict enforcement' of anti-bias regulations short of preferential treatment will succeed in creating genuine nondiscrimination. Given his principles, Goldman could repudiate the use of preferences at AT&T only by holding that the institutional habits of the company were not so recalcitrant as to require the drastic measures imposed by the consent decree.

Finally, the forward-looking defense being considered here has two further features. First, it suggests that preferential programs will not have an unlimited duration. The program need persist only until *enough* minorities or women are lodged in place to create appropriate changes in attitudes and habits. Proportional representation has no independent value: at best it is a proxy for the level of women and minorities sufficient to effect the desired changes. The consent decree at AT&T ended after six years. Although the company was far from having proportional representation of women in its assorted job classifications, nevertheless enough women had been moved into nontraditional positions to *institutionalize* the expectations and the reality of women's presence in management, crafts, sales, and so on.

Moreover, the forward-looking justification does not imply that preferential programs are appropriate at every institution. Where institutional habits are *not* so frozen that facially unbiased procedures would be ineffective, there is no reason provided by the equal opportunity defense for giving anyone a preference because of race or sex. The possibilities of creating equality of opportunity without resort to preferences will vary according to the type of institution, its location, its history or lack of history of segregation, its prospects for growth or decline, and so on. The circumstances we actually encounter may suggest the need for preferential treatment of women but not minorities, of minorities but not women, of both, or of neither.

The equal opportunity defense of preferences is not the only possible forward-looking justification. Preferences might be defended as serving other goals. A frequent defense of preferentially admitting blacks to medical and law schools is the anticipation that this will eventually improve the delivery of medical and legal services to the black community.[30] Richard Wasserstrom has argued that including substantial numbers of blacks in otherwise white educational programs enriches the educational climate by adding new perspectives on social issues, and that preferential admissions can serve this end.[31] Many have argued for the need to create female and black role models in the professions, the university, and the corporation as inspirations for other women and blacks to aspire to careers they otherwise would have feared to enter.[32] These and other forward-looking defenses may or may not individually offer as much justification for preferential programs as the equal opportunity defense of the AT&T consent decree; but they can all probably be assimilated one way or another into a broader equal opportunity aim: to break down the barriers that impede the free access of blacks and women into all aspects of economic, political, and social life.[33]

NOTES

1 A word of caution is necessary about the word 'compensation.' It is used in different senses in the literature being discussed here. Thomson uses

it more or less synonymously with 'restitution' or 'reparation,' to mean making good on damage or harm caused by wrongful action. Sometimes, however, the term is used by writers in its generic sense, which means simply to make up for some lack or deficiency. Bernard Boxill, in 'The Morality of Reparations,' *Social Theory and Practice* 2 (Spring 1972), *contrasts* compensation with reparation, calling the former a 'forward-looking' device for alleviating disabilities however they came about (p. 117). However, in his recent book, *Blacks and Social Justice* (Totowa, NJ: Rowman & Allanheld, 1984), he uses 'compensation' to refer to the same backward-looking practice encompassed by 'reparation.' The reader is advised to take care when encountering 'compensation' and 'compensatory' in a work. I use the term throughout this essay as Thomson used it, to refer to a practice that looks back to a wrongful action or deed producing harm.

2 In addition to the works of Thomson and Boxill, see Anne C. Minas, 'How Reverse Discrimination Compensates Women,' *Ethics* 88 (October 1977), pp. 74–79, and Howard McGary, Jr., 'Justice and Reparations,' *Philosophical Forum* 9 (Winter-Spring 1977–78), pp. 250–63.

3 Boxill, 'The Morality of Reparations,' p. 119.

4 Thomson, 'Preferential Hiring,' *Philosophy & Public Affairs* 2 (Summer 1973), p. 380.

5 Ibid., 383. Similar contentions are made by Boxill and McGary.

6 Boxill, 'The Morality of Reparations,' p. 121.

7 Thomson, 'Preferential Hiring,' p. 381.

8 Boxill, *Blacks and Social Justice*, p. 164.

9 Ibid., p. 153; emphasis added.

10 Ibid., pp. 151, 152.

11 Ibid., p. 152; emphasis added.

12 Ibid., p. 150; emphasis added.

13 Ibid., p. 151; emphasis added.

14 Ibid., p. 152.

15 Apology rather than compensation is the appropriate response to insult. Some may value preferential programs less for what they actually accomplish than for what they symbolize: public acknowledgment and expatiation of past wrong.

   As to the question about wrong, harm, and hurt: it isn't as if there are no resources at hand for working out answers about their places in compensation. Several hundred years of Anglo-American legal practice have grappled with the kinds of harm and injury the law ought to cognize, the responsibility and liabilities of various parties involved, the appropriateness of various kinds of restitution, and so on. Philosophers, however, had not made much use of this resource.

16 Alan Goldman, *Justice and Reverse Discrimination* (Princeton, NJ: Princeton University Press, 1979), pp. 90–1.

17 See Boxill, *Blacks and Social Justice*, pp.153 ff.

18 A suggestion made by Tom Beauchamp at a talk at Union College, May 1975.

19 A consent decree is an agreement, supervised by a court, in which the government refrains from pressing legal charges to a full decision if the company complies with the terms agreed to.

20 Although the decree also affected minority hiring and promotions, its main effect was on women. I confine my discussion of the AT&T case to this main effect.

21 The details in the next several paragraphs are drawn from Robert Fullinwider, *The AT&T Case and Affirmative Action* (Dover, MA: Case Publishing Company, 1981).

22 Judith Long Laws, 'The Bell System,' in Phyllis A. Wallace, ed., *Equal Employment Opportunity and the AT&T Case* (Cambridge, Mass: MIT Press, 1976), p. 159.

23 I estimate in excess of 45,000 instances between 1973–9. See *The AT&T Case and Affirmative Action*, p. 5, for the grounds of this estimate.

24 The company's affirmative action efforts under the decree resulted in thousands of grievances and two dozen lawsuits.

25 Herbert R. Nothrup and John A. Larson, *The Impact of the AT&T-EEO Consent Decree* (Philadelphia: The Wharton School, University of Pennsylvania, 1979), p. 78.

26 *Telephone Workers Union v. N.J. Bell Tel.*, 584 F. 2d 31 (1978), at 32.

27 Title VII, Civil Rights Act of 1984, 42 U.S.C. 2000e-2; Executive Order 11246 (as amended), 42 U.S.C. 2000e; Revised Order No. 4, 41 C.F.R. 60)2ff.

28 Goldman, *Justice and Reverse Discrimination*, p. 165. The interpolated section comes from p. 29. See pp. 23ff.

29 Ibid., p. 193. A similar argument is found in Thomas Nagel, 'Equal Treatment and Compensatory Discrimination,' *Philosophy & Public Affairs* 2 (Summer 1973), in the footnote at the bottom of p. 362. Nagel reports a suggestion by Adam Morton that the defense of preferences lies in their ability to contribute to a more just situation in the future. Another writer who anticipates the form if not the details of the equal opportunity argument is Marlene Gerber Fried, 'In Defense of Preferential Hiring,' *Philosophical Forum* 5 (Fall-Winter 1973–74), pp. 308–19.

30 See Nagel, 'Equal Treatment and Compensatory Discrimination,' p. 361.

31 Richard Wasserstrom, 'The University and the Case for Preferential Treatment,' *American Philosophical Quarterly* 13 (April 1976), pp. 165–60.

32 See, e.g., Michael Martin, 'Pedagogical Arguments for Preferential Hiring and Tenuring of Women Teachers in the University,' *Philo-*

Reverse discrimination and equal opportunity

sophical *Forum* 5 (Fall-Winter 1973–74), pp. 325–33.

33 This essay was written during a period of support from the National Endowment for the Humanities for work on equal opportunity in American social policy.

11

THE ETHICS OF NUCLEAR STRATEGY

James P. Sterba

The recent attention that focused on the resumption of strategic arms talks between the United States and the Soviet Union dramatizes the importance to the world community of improved relations between the superpowers. Whether these talks will actually improve relations between the superpowers, however, depends in large part on the goals and strategies that the participants bring to them, and these in turn depend, at least in part, on the application of moral values and principles to the use and threatened use of nuclear weapons – which is just where philosophers can make an important contribution.

Yet surprisingly, only a few philosophers have rallied to the task. Despite the fact that most philosophers today tend to congratulate themselves on the practical turn taken by moral philosophy since the late 1960s, only a few have yet to address what may be the most important moral problem of our times: Whether the use or threatened use of nuclear weapons can be morally justified?

THE USE OF NUCLEAR WEAPONS

Not surprisingly, those philosophers who have addressed this question, like Douglas Lackey, Anthony Kenny, Gregory Kavka and myself, have tended to agree that any massive use of nuclear weapons would be grossly immoral.[1] For consider the massive use of nuclear weapons by the United States or the Soviet Union against industrial and economic targets. Such a use, according to the US

Office of Technology Assessment, could destroy between 70–80 per cent of each nation's industry and result in the immediate death of as many as 165 million Americans and 100 million Russians respectively.[2] Or consider a massive use of nuclear weapons against only ICBMs, submarine and bomber bases. According to the US Office of Technology Assessment such a use could wipe out as many as 20 million Americans and 28 million Russians respectively.[3]

Moroever, those who did not perish in such attacks would face serious – even life-long – dangers. To cite a report by the International Physicians for the Prevention of Nuclear War:

> Many exposed persons would be at increased risk, throughout the remainder of their lives, of leukemia and a variety of malignant tumors. The risk is emotional as well as physical. Tens of thousands would live with the fear of developing cancer or of transmitting genetic defects, for they would understand that nuclear weapons, unlike conventional weapons, have memories – long, radioactive memories. Children are known to be particularly susceptible to most of these effects. Exposure of fetuses would result in the birth of children with small headsizes, mental retardation, and impaired growth and development. Many exposed persons would develop radiation cataracts and chromosomal aberrations.[4]

And as if these consequences were not enough, it has been estimated by Carl Sagan and others that such massive attacks are very likely to generate firestorms which would cover much of the earth with sooty smoke for months, creating a 'nuclear winter' that would threaten the very survival of the human species.[5] As a result, it is not surprising that philosophers have tended to agree that there is no foreseeable end that could justify a massive use of nuclear weapons.

But what about a limited use of nuclear weapons against tactical and strategic targets? Unfortunately, philosophers have not sufficiently attended to such a use. Yet practically it would be quite difficult for either superpower to distinguish between a limited and a massive use of nuclear weapons, especially if a full-scale conventional war is raging. In such circumstances, any use of nuclear weapons is likely to be viewed as part of a massive use of such weapons, thus increasing the risk of a massive nuclear retaliatory strike.[6] Henry Kissinger once proposed that in a limited nuclear war a nation might announce that it would not use nuclear weapons of more than 500 kilotons explosive power unless an adversary used them first. Unfortunately, however, neither the United States nor the Soviet Union has a system of instantaneous damage assessment to determine whether such a limit was being observed. In addition, war games have shown that if enough tactical nuclear weapons are employed over time in a limited area, such as Germany, the effect on noncombatants in that area would be much the same as in a massive nuclear attack.[7] As Bundy, Kennan, McNamara and Smith put the point in their recent endorsement of a doctrine of no first use of nuclear weapons:

> Every serious analysis and every military exercise, for over 25 years, has demonstrated that even the most restrained battlefield use would be enormously destructive to civilian life and property. There is no way for anyone to have any confidence that such a nuclear action will not lead to further and more devastating exchanges. Any use of nuclear weapons in Europe, by the Alliance or against it, carries with it a high and inescapable risk of escalation into the general nuclear war which would bring ruin to all and victory to none.[8]

For these reasons, it would seem that even a limited use of nuclear weapons generally would not be morally justified, all things considered.

Yet while endorsing a near prohibition of the use of nuclear weapons, philosophers are deeply divided concerning the moral legitimacy of threatening nuclear retaliation to achieve nuclear deterrence. On the one hand, philosophers, like Lackey and Kenny, although for different reasons, endorse complete unilateral nuclear disarmament, while, on the other hand, philosophers, like Kavka and myself, endorse different forms of threatening nuclear retaliation to achieve nuclear deterrence.

UNILATERAL NUCLEAR DISARMAMENT

Douglas Lackey's most recent endorsement of unilateral nuclear disarmament is based in part upon a comparison of the expected consequences of following a strategy of unilateral nuclear disarmament with the expected consequences of following what Lackey calls victory or detente strategies. A victory strategy, according to Lackey, assumes that nuclear weapons can be used to obtain victories over opponents. It is committed to: (a) possessing nuclear weapons; (b) possessing as many kinds of nuclear weapons as possible; (c) being prepared to use them first; (d) being committed to using them, at least in limited quantities, when the chips are down; (e) aiming these weapons at all sorts of targets, including the enemy's strategic forces; (f) arranging for every possible sequence of use, and (g) building a physical defense against nuclear attack if possible.

By contrast, a detente strategy has as its main purpose to prevent nuclear war by permitting both sides to possess an effective nuclear deterrent. It is committed to (a) possessing nuclear weapons; (b) building only the few weapons needed to assure second strike capacity; (c) committing the nation to 'no first use,' (d) making it possible to back off from nuclear threats; (e) aiming nuclear weapons away from the opponent's strategic forces; (f) arranging for minimum flexibility in the sequence of use; and (g) forswearing any attempt to construct physical defenses.

To determine the probability of the various outcomes under each of these three strategies, Lackey combines the probability estimates that both proponents and opponents of each strategy would give to those outcomes. For example, Lackey claims that proponents of a victory strategy estimate the probability of limited nuclear war to be 10 per cent under their strategy while opponents estimate that probability to be 60 per cent. Similarly, Lackey claims that proponents of unilateral nuclear disarmament estimate the probability of a counterforce strike at 4 per cent under their strategy while opponents estimate that probability to be 50 per cent. Unfortunately, Lackey's procedure of simply averaging opposing probability estimates of various outcomes under each strategy and showing that such averaging favors unilateral nuclear disarmament is not likely to gain much acceptance among proponents of the other strategies since presumably proponents of the other strategies would argue that their estimates of the probabilities are the ones upon which we should rely.

Furthermore, Lackey's averaging procedure does not even support his own endorsement of unilateral nuclear disarmament. For Lackey admits that the expected consequences of following a detente strategy combined with 'city-avoidance' may be better than the expected consequences of following a policy of unilateral nuclear disarmament.[10] Thus finding himself unable to support unilateral nuclear disarmament over a detente with city-avoidance strategy with a consequentialist argument, Lackey offers a nonconsequentialist one.[11] He contends that a detente with city-avoidance strategy would achieve its deterrent effect by placing innocent civilians at risk. Lackey allows that under a detente with city-avoidance strategy the placing of innocent civilians at risk would be unintentional; he simply maintains that it would still be a morally illegitimate means for achieving nuclear deterrence.

Yet what Lackey fails to see is that while part of the deterrent effect of a detente with city-avoidance strategy is surely achieved by placing innocent civilians at risk that part is not needed to ground the use of the strategy; it is simply an unnecessary and unintentional side-effect. For just as would-be criminals might be deterred in part by the unintentional risks the threat of punishment places upon their family and friends without such a deterrent effect undercutting the justification for threatening punishment, so likewise would-be aggressors might be deterred in part by the unintended risks the threat of nuclear retaliation against military targets places upon innocent civilians without that deterrent effect undercutting the justification for threatening nuclear retaliation. In each case the relevant question is whether that part of the deterrent effect that results from the unintended risks imposed upon innocent parties is needed to justify use of the threat. In the case of a detente with city-avoidance strategy, there is no such need because the threat that strategy imposes on military forces alone suffices to justify its use. Accordingly, Lackey's nonconsequentialist argument does not support his endorsement of unilateral nuclear disarmament.

In contrast with Lackey's endorsement of unilateral nuclear disarmament, Anthony Kenny's most recent endorsement is not even partly based upon a comparison of the expected consequences of a range of possible nuclear strategies.[12] Rather Kenny's endorsement of unilateral nuclear disarmament is based upon a comparison of unilateral nuclear disarmament with a strategy that appears to be presently endorsed at least in the United States and Great Britain. That strategy Kenny describes as one of 'giving a blank cheque to our own leaders to commit mass murder in the event of war.' Kenny allows that endorsing unilateral nuclear disarmament would involve accepting risk of nuclear blackmail; he simply argues that such a risk is not as terrible as the risk of nuclear war under a 'blank cheque' strategy.

Yet while there are good grounds for condemning a blank cheque strategy, Kenny has not shown that a strategy of unilateral nuclear disarmament is morally preferable to other possible strategies for achieving nuclear deterrence – strategies that differ in morally significant respects from a blank cheque strategy. For example, when I suggested to Kenny at a recent conference held at the University of St Andrews, Scotland that Trident and Poseidon submarines could be armed with more accurate Trident II missiles, thereby constituting a survivable force with relatively precise nuclear weapons, Kenny appeared to have no objection to threatening to use such a force to achieve nuclear deterrence.

STRATEGIES OF NUCLEAR DETERRENCE

Yet even if we were to reject unilateral nuclear disarmament on the basis of the objections that have been raised against Lackey's and Kenny's defenses of the view, we would still need to determine what are the moral limits to the pursuit of nuclear deterrence.

Gregory Kavka, in his most recent article, attempts to determine these limits by arguing in favor of the following two principles:
1 *The Revised National Defense Principle.* It is permissible for a nation to do whatever it reasonably believes is necessary for national self-defense, provided such measures do not impose disproportionate risks or harms on other parties.
2 *The Revised Threat Principle.* It is impermissible to disproportionately threaten and impose risks of death upon large numbers of innocent people.[13]

In defending the first principle, Kavka considers whether there might be a stronger defense principle that rules out a policy of nuclear deterrence because it imposes an unacceptable risk on innocent civilians. Kavka argues against such a possibility on the ground that we can justify imposing risks on people who are 'morally innocent' if they happen to be a threat to our lives. Kavka further contends that, even if people are not a threat to our lives, we can still justify imposing risks on them if they belong to a group that is imposing a threat to our lives. To justify this further claim Kavka compares Russian civilians to a mad attacker, claiming that both are

195

'partially responsible.' However, this comparison is faulty because what justifies our defending ourselves against a mad attacker is not that such an attacker is partially responsible, since almost by definition a 'mad attacker' is not responsible at all for her attack. Rather what allows us to defend ourselves against such an attacker is that she is a threat to our lives. It is just this feature that is absent in the case of the Russian civilians, and its absence seems to undercut any possible justification for threats of retaliation directed specifically against them.

In defending the Revised Threat Principle, Kavka considers whether a strong prohibition against threats might be based upon the Wrongful Intention Principle: if an act is a wrong, intending to perform it is also wrong. Kavka argues that a stronger prohibition against threats cannot be justified in this fashion because the Wrongful Intention Principle fails when applied to a conditional intention adopted solely to prevent the occurrence of the circumstances in which the intention would be acted upon. For Kavka, United States policy of threatening massive nuclear retaliation is justified, provided that the United States adopts a conditional intention to retaliate with a massive use of nuclear weapons only to prevent the occurrence of those circumstances in which it would so retaliate.

Unfortunately, this line of argument would also serve to justify the threats commonly employed by armed robbers! For robbers, in threatening 'Hand over your money, or I'll shoot,' usually hope to avoid just those circumstances in which you don't hand over your money, and they do shoot. However, it is clear from an earlier article[14] that Kavka is primarily concerned with situations in which people adopt a conditional intention *in order to prevent an unjust offense*, and certainly such motivation would typically be lacking in cases of armed robbery. Nevertheless, when Kavka comments upon what is distinctive about those situations in which he thinks the adoption of conditional intentions is justified, he only refers to the effects such intentions have that are independent of the intended acts actually being performed – that is, to their 'autonomous effects.' Consequently, if a strategy of nuclear deterrence is to avoid condemnation on the basis of the Wrongful Intention Principle, it must be for reasons other than the mere presence of autonomous effects.

Presumably Kavka would claim that what distinguishes a nation's legitimate threatening from a robber's illegitimate threatening is that the beneficial autonomous effects that flow from legitimate threatening by a nation are not matched, even proportionately, by the beneficial autonomous effects that flow from the threats standardly employed by armed robbers. Yet at the same time Kavka wants to separate the justification for the act of threatening nuclear retaliation from the justification for the act of carrying out such retaliation. For, contrary to the Wrongful Intention Principle, Kavka thinks that the act of threatening nuclear retaliation which involves an intention to retaliate under certain conditions can be morally justified even when the act of carrying out that retaliation cannot be morally justified.

To illustrate how the act of intending to do x can be evaluated differently from the act of doing x, Kavka asks us to consider the following situation:

> You are offered a million dollars to be paid tomorrow morning, if at midnight tonight you intend to drink a vial of toxin tomorrow afternoon that will make you very sick for a day. If you believe the offer and believe that the offerers can really tell whether, at midnight, you have the requisite intention, you would clearly have a good reason (in fact, a million good reasons) to form that intention. Suppose that you do so and bank the money the next morning – cashing in the desired autonomous effect of your intention. Would it then be rational for you to carry out your intention and drink the toxin? Surely not. If not, we have a divergence between the rationality of forming a problematic intention and the rationality of carrying it out.[15]

Yet how is a person to form an intention to do something it would be irrational or immoral for her to do? In particular, how are a nation's leaders to form the intention to unleash a massive nuclear retaliation against industrial and economic targets when, as Kavka admits, carrying out such a retaliation would be grossly immoral? Notice that in order for a nation's leaders to form an intention to retaliate with a massive attack they must expect that they would in fact carry out such an attack under certain conditions. So how could they expect that they would actually perform such a morally horrendous deed?

Kavka's answer is that they could form the requisite intentions and thereby expect to carry out the morally horrendous deed only by making themselves into the morally corrupt sort of persons who would be willing to carry out such a deed under the appropriate circumstances. Similarly, in Kavka's toxin example, only by making oneself into an irrational sort of person who would in fact drink the vial of toxin would one qualify to collect the million dollar prize.

Yet the problem with resorting to morally corrupt or irrational agents to achieve certain results is that there is no reason to think that agents who have committed themselves to acting in a morally horrendous or irrational manner in one context, might not be willing to do the same in other contexts, sometimes with disastrous consequences. In fact, it would seem that only by behaving similarly in other contexts can they become agents clearly capable of forming the intention to act in a morally horrendous or irrational manner in some particular context.

Moreover, Kavka does not take seriously the possibility of achieving nuclear deterrence by other means. For example, suppose a nation possesses a survivable nuclear force capable of massive nuclear retaliation but its leaders only threaten to use this force in limited counterforce retaliatory strikes. Why would not such a policy of limited nuclear retaliation be morally preferable to a policy of massive nuclear retaliation? Presumably, Kavka's objection to such a policy is that it is not morally distinct from a policy of massive nuclear retaliation since it still places the lives of many innocent civilians at risk.[17] But while it is true that the policy of limited nuclear retaliation does place the lives of innocent civilians at risk, the risk involved is much less than it would be under a policy of massive nuclear retaliation. This is because a policy of limited nuclear retaliation provides a much more credible deterrent than a policy of massive nuclear retaliation which depends as we have seen upon the possibility of creating agents who are capable of making immoral threats.

However, my own view is that we are morally required to endorse an even more limited policy for pursuing nuclear deterrence than these objections to Kavka's view might suggest.[18] To see why this is the case, consider two possible stances a nation's leaders might take with respect to nuclear weapons:

1   A nation's leaders might be willing to carry out a nuclear strike only in response to either a nuclear first strike or a massive conventional first strike on itself or its principal allies.

2　A nation's leaders might be willing to carry out a massive conventional strike only in response to either a nuclear first strike or a massive conventional first strike on itself or its principal allies.

Now assuming that a nation's leaders were to adopt both 1 and 2 then threats of nuclear retaliation could not in fact be made against them! For a threat must render less eligible something an agent might otherwise want to do, and leaders of nation's who adopt both 1 and 2 have a preference structure that would not be affected by any attempt to threaten nuclear retaliation. Hence, such threats could not be made against them either explicitly or implicitly.

Now if we take them at their word, the leaders of both superpowers seem to have adopted both 1 and 2. As Caspar Weinberger recently characterized United States policy:

> Our strategy is a defensive one, designed to prevent attack, particularly nuclear attack, against us or our allies.[19]

And a similar statement of Soviet policy can be found in Mikhail Gorbachev's recent appeal for a return to a new era of detente.[20] Moreover, since 1982 Soviet leaders appear to have gone beyond simply endorsing 1 and 2 and have ruled out the use of a nuclear first strike under any circumstances.[21]

Assuming the truth of these statements it follows that the present leaders of the United States and the Soviet Union could not be threatening each other with nuclear retaliation despite their apparent attempts to do so. This is because a commitment to 1 and 2 rules out the necessary aggressive intentions that it is the purpose of such threats to deter. Leaders of nations whose strategy is a purely defensive one would be immune from threats of nuclear retaliation. In fact, leaders of nations who claim their strategy is purely defense yet persist in attempting to threaten nuclear retaliation against other nations whose proclaimed strategy is also purely defensive eventually throw into doubt their own commitment to a purely defensive strategy. For these reasons, I claim that attempts to threaten nuclear retaliation under present conditions would not be morally justified.

Of course, the leaders of a superpower might claim that threatening or bluffing nuclear retaliation would be morally justified under present conditions on the grounds that the proclaimed defensive strategy of the other superpower is not believable. Surely this stance would be reasonable if the other superpower had launched an aggressive attack against the superpower or its principal allies. But neither United States intervention in Nicaragua nor Soviet intervention in Afghanistan nor other military actions taken by either superpower are directed against even a principal ally of the other superpower. Consequently, in the absence of an aggressive attack of the appropriate sort and in the absence of an opposing military force that could be used without risking unacceptable losses from retaliatory strikes, each superpower is morally required to provisionally place some trust in the proclaimed defensive strategy of the other superpower.

At the same time, I think that it would still be morally legitimate for both superpowers to retain a retaliatory nuclear force so as to be able to threaten or bluff nuclear retaliation in the future should conditions change for the worse. For as long as nations possess nuclear weapons, such a change could occur simply with a change of leadership bringing power to leaders who can only be deterred by a threat or bluff of nuclear retaliation. For example, suppose a nation possesses a survivable nuclear force capable of inflicting unacceptable damage upon its adversary, yet possession of such a force alone would not suffice to deter an adversary from carrying out a nuclear first strike unless that possession were combined with a threat of limited nuclear retaliation or a bluff of massive nuclear retaliation. (With respect to massive nuclear retaliation, bluffing would be required since leaders who recognize and respect the above moral constraints on the use of nuclear weapons could not in fact threaten such retaliation.) Under these circumstances, I think that the required threat or bluff would be morally justified. But I also think that there is ample evidence today to indicate that neither the leadership of the United States nor that of the Soviet Union requires such a threat or bluff to deter them from carrying out a nuclear first strike.[22] Consequently, under present conditions, such a threat or bluff would not be morally justified.

Nevertheless, under present conditions it would be legitimate for a nation to maintain a survivable nuclear force in order to be able to deal effectively with a change of policy in the future. Moreover, if either superpower does in fact harbor any undetected aggressive intention against the other, the possession of a survivable nuclear force by the other superpower should suffice to deter a first strike because neither superpower could be sure whether in response to such strike the other superpower would follow its moral principles or its national interest.

Of course, if nuclear forces were only used to retain the capacity for threatening or bluffing in the future should conditions change for the worse then surely at some point this use of nuclear weapons could also be eliminated. But its elimination would require the establishment of extensive political, economic and cultural ties between the superpowers so as to reduce the present uncertainty about the future direction of policy, and obviously the establishment of such ties, even when it is given the highest priority, which it frequently is not, requires time to develop.

In the meantime, a nuclear force deployed for the purpose of being capable of threatening or bluffing in the future should conditions change for the worse should be capable of surviving a first strike and then inflicting either limited or massive nuclear retaliation on an aggressor. During the Kennedy-Johnson years, Robert McNamara estimated that massive nuclear retaliation required a nuclear force capable of destroying one-half of a nation's industrial capacity along with one-quarter of its population, and comparable figures have been suggested by others. Clearly, ensuring a loss in this neighborhood should constitute unacceptable damage from the perspective of any would-be aggressor.

Notice, however, that in order for a nation to maintain a nuclear force capable of inflicting such damage, it is not necessary that components of its land-, its air- and its sea-based strategic forces all be survivable. Accordingly, even if all the land-based ICBMs in the United States were totally destroyed in a first strike, surviving elements of the United States air and submarine force could easily inflict the required degree of damage and more. In fact, any one of the 37 nuclear submarines maintained by the United States, each with up to 192 warheads, could almost single-handedly inflict the required degree of damage. Consequently, the United States submarine force alone should suffice as a force capable of massive nuclear retaliation.

But what about a nuclear force capable of limited nuclear retaliation? At least with respect to United States nuclear forces, it would seem that as Trident I missiles replace less accurate Poseidon missiles, and especially when Trident II missiles come on line in the next few years, the United States submarine force will have the capacity for both limited and massive nuclear retaliation. However, until this modernization is complete, the United States will still have to rely, in part, on surviving elements of its air- and land-based strategic forces for its capacity to inflict limited nuclear retaliation. And it would seem that the Soviet Union is also in a comparable situation.[23]

In sum, I have argued for the following:

1   Under present conditions, it is morally justified to possess a survivable nuclear force in order to be able to quickly threaten or bluff nuclear retaliation should conditions change for the worse.

2   If conditions do change for the worse, it would be morally justified at some point to threaten a form of limited nuclear retaliation.

3   If conditions worsen further so that a massive nuclear first strike can only be deterred by the bluff or threat of a massive nuclear retaliation, it would be morally justified to bluff but not threaten massive nuclear retaliation.

Now by following this proposed policy under present conditions, a nation would also be able to achieve nuclear deterrence, when necessary, without threatening or bluffing nuclear destruction. When this occurs, nuclear deterrence would be the foreseen but not the intended consequence of possessing a survivable nuclear force to be able to threaten or bluff nuclear retaliation should conditions change for the worse.[24]

Obviously, this proposed policy requires further development. For example, it needs to be supplemented by an account of how bluffing with nuclear weapons can be institutionalized in a society.[25] Nevertheless, the policy does reflect the concern of proponents of unilateral nuclear disarmament, like Lackey and Kenny, to reduce reliance on nuclear weapons and the threat of nuclear retaliation and the concern of proponents of nuclear deterrence, like Kavka, to be protected from nuclear attack and nuclear blackmail. And if anything is certain, it is that future work by philosophers in this area will continue to reflect both of these concerns.

NOTES

1 Douglas Lackey, *Moral Principles and Nuclear Weapons* (Totowa, 1984), Anthony Kenny, 'Better Dead than Red' in *Objections to Nuclear Defense* edited by Nigel Blake and Kay Pole (London, 1984). Gregory S. Kavka, 'Nuclear Deterrence: Some Moral Perplexities,' in *The Security Gamble* edited by Douglas Maclean (Totowa, 1984) and also in *The Ethics of War and Nuclear Deterrence* edited by James P. Sterba (Belmont, 1985); James P. Sterba, 'How to Achieve Nuclear Deterrence Without Threatening Nuclear Destruction,' in *The Ethics of War and Nuclear Deterrence*.

2 *The Effects of Nuclear War*, Office of Technology Assessment (Washington, D.C. 1979), pp. 94, 100.

3 *The Effects of Nuclear War*, pp. 83, 91.

4 Eric Chivian and others, *Last Aid* (San Francisco, 1982).

5 Carl Sagan, 'Nuclear War and Climate Catastrophe: Some Policy Implications,' *Foreign Affairs* (1983) pp. 257–92.

6 Sidney Lens, *The Day Before Doomsday* (Boston, 1977) pp. 78–9; Spurgeon Keeny and Wolfgang Panofsky 'MAD verse NUTS' *Foreign Affairs* (1981–2), pp. 297–8; Ian Clark, *Limited Nuclear War*, (Princeton, 1982), p. 242.

7 Lens, P. 73.

8 McGeorge Bundy, George F. Kennan, Robert S. McNamara and Gerald Smith, 'Nuclear Weapons and the Atlantic Alliance,' *Foreign Affairs* (1982), p. 757. It should be noted that Bundy, Kennan, McNamara and Smith believe that their endorsement of a doctrine of no first use of nuclear weapons *may* involved increased spending for conventional forces in Europe. Others, however, have found NATO's existing conventional strength to be adequate to meet a Soviet attack. See David Barash and Judith Lipton, *Stop Nuclear War* (New York, 1982), pp. 138–40; Harold Brown, *Department of Defense, Annual Report* (1981).

9 Lackey, especially Chapter 5.

10 Lackey, p. 229.

11 Lackey, p. 229.

12 Kenny, 'Better Red then Dead.' Kenny's earlier argument for unilateral nuclear disarmament is very similar to his present one. See 'Counterforce and Countervalue,' in *Nuclear Weapons and the Christian Conscience*, ed. Walter Stern (London, 1961).

13 Kavka, 'Nuclear Deterrence: Some Moral Perplexities,' in *The Security Gamble* pp. 156–7.

14 Kavka, 'The Paradoxes of Deterrence,' *The Journal of Philosophy* (1978).

15 Kavka, 'Deterrent Intentions and Retaliatory Actions,' in *The Security*

Gamble pp. 156–7.

16 Kavka, 'The Paradoxes of Deterrence,' pp. 295–7.

17 Kavka, 'Nuclear Deterrence: Some Moral Perplexities,' pp. 135–6.

18 Sterba, 'How to Achieve Nuclear Deterrence without Threatening Nuclear Destruction,' but see also 'Social Welfare vs. National Defense,' in *Social Conflict* (1985) edited by R.G. Frey and 'Justifying Nuclear Deterrence: The Right and the Wrong Way', (Special Issue) *Peace and Change* (1985).

19 Casper Weinberger, 'Why We Must have Nuclear Deterrence,' *Defense* (1983) p. 3.

20 *The New York Times*, May 9, 1985.

21 See Leonid Brezhnev's message to the UN General Assembly on June 2, 1982.

22 See Jerome Kahan, *Security in the Nuclear Age* (1975), Sidney Yens, *The Day Before Doomsday* (1977); Henry Kendall and others, *Beyond the Freeze* (1982); George Kistiakowsky, 'False Alarm: The Story Behind Salt II,' *The New York Review of Books* (1979); Les Aspin, 'How to Look at the Soviet-American Balance,' *Foreign Policy* (1976); Gordon Adams, 'The Iron Triangle,' *The Nation* (1981). Much of this evidence is reviewed in 'How to Achieve Nuclear Deterrence Without Threatening Nuclear Destruction.'

23 *Soviet Military Power*, US Department of Defense (Washington, D.C., 1983); David Holoway, *The Soviet Union and the Arms Race* (New Haven, 1983); Andrew Cockburn, *The Threat* (New York, 1983) Chapter 12.

24 For a development of this line of argument, see 'How to Achieve Nuclear Deterrence Without Threatening Nuclear Destruction.'

25 I have provided a sketch of such an account in 'Between MAD and Counterforce: In Search of a Morally and Strategically Sound Nuclear Defense Policy,' *Social Theory and Practice* (1986).

12

APPLIED ETHICS AND THE VOCATION OF SOCIAL SCIENCE

Bruce Jennings

The study of ethics is currently undergoing a remarkable period of transition and renewal. Eclipsed for decades by specialized areas such as the philosophy of science and the philosophy of language, ethical theory has now reclaimed its place as one of the most active and intellectually exciting branches of philosophical inquiry. This renewal has touched the study of ethics at many different levels. Recent work in metaethics has provided new ways to vindicate the rationality of moral discourse and to explore the philosophical foundations of ethical theory. It has persuasively challenged received doctrines of logical positivism and emotivisim whose dominance in Anglo-American academic philosophy during the middle decades of the twentieth century had directed most philosophers' attention away from the traditional questions of substantive ethical theory. By different routes logical positivism and emotivism had both come to the same conclusion, namely, that ethical claims are not subject to rational discussion or to public, intersubjective standards of agreement and evaluation. Telling criticisms of these doctrines, and their eventual overthrow, have provided a good deal of the philosophical warrant for the new work in ethical theory that has blossomed in recent years.

Moreover, at the level of normative ethics where particular moral principles, ideals, and virtues are formulated for the evaluation of individual conduct and social institutions, moral philosophy has also opened up a variety of new lines of investigation. Important and innovative theoretical positions have been developed on topics such as justice, human rights, equality, and moral obligation. Moral philosophers have increasingly turned as well to the study of traditional normative works – such as Aristotelian, natural law, Kantian, and utilitarian theories – not simply as matters of historical or antiquarian interest, but rather with the intention of revitalizing these older traditions of discourse and of using them to help restore our moral bearings in the contemporary world.

Finally, the current renewal of moral philosophy has been stimulated by the rise of applied or practical ethicals, where various ethical principles and ideals are brought to bear on practical decisionmaking and the resolution of moral dilemmas in specific institutional settings, such as governmental policymaking or the provision of professional services to clients. Generally speaking, these studies – which typically focus on a detailed examination of particular cases and trace the institutional, social, and cultural sources of value conflicts – aspire to provide an understanding of what is involved in translating a general, theoretical principle into a specific course of conduct. At its best applied ethics can help us explore the human significance of abstract, universal moral rules when those rules are embodied in concrete social relationships.

If we turn from these recent trends in moral philosophy to the intellectual, theoretical, and methodological currents prevalent in the social sciences, we find an analogous state of ferment and flux. Undeniably, the twin legacies of positivism and emotivism have proved more tenacious in the social sciences than they have in philosophy, where not only metaethics but also philosophy of science itself have undermined them. Nonetheless, even in the mainstream social sciences a kind of post-positivistic reconstruction has taken hold – to a greater extent in political science, sociology, and anthropology; to a lesser extent in economics and psychology. The notion that social scientific inquiry can attain and should strive for nomological-deductive explanations (and predictions) of human behavior and social phenomena has been widely questioned, as has the notion that social scientific knowledge can be achieved through the analytic deployment of value neutral concepts. As a result, many social scientists are coming to realize that their proper business is not so much the explanation of human behavior as it is the explication or interpretative understanding of human action; not so much the discovery of laws describing the casual relationships among objects as the recovery of meaning in the symbolically and institutionally mediated relationships among subjects. As these shifts in orientation and perspective have taken hold, familiar boundaries separating descriptive and normative discourse, and *mutatis mutandis* disciplinary boundaries separating ethics from social science, have begun to blur and break down.

For these reasons, among others, new linkages are being formed between ethics and social science at many different levels. Like geological plates shifting to overlap in new ways, descriptive social scientific analysis appears to be increasingly value-laden while normative ethical analysis becomes increasingly fact-laden. Applied studies in ethics are one fault line where the shifts are most evident and potentially most significant in their consequences. However, many standard accounts of the nature, logic, and methodology of applied ethics seriously misconstrue the relationship between the ethics and social science and fail to appreciate the implications that this relationship has for both disciplines.

Accordingly, in this essay I propose to re-examine the role that social scientific inquiry, conceived of as an interpretative rather than an explanatory or scientific mode of analysis, can and should play in studies of applied and professional ethics. Taking its proper role in these studies as a point of departure, I want then to raise some more general questions about the ends of social scientific inquiry and about the ethical vocation animating a commitment to the advance of social scientific understanding and knowledge.

APPLIED ETHICS AND SOCIAL INTERPRETATION

Studies of applied and professional ethics do not constitute simply one more subdiscipline within academic philosophy. They involve an attempt to forge a new kind of interdisciplinary synthesis. Their characteristic impulse has been to break down the barriers separating specialized bodies of knowledge, and to demonstrate the pertinence of ethical analysis to the practical problems and concerns of the larger society.

No doubt it would be a mistake to overestimate the effects these studies have had in improving the moral quality of professional conduct or public policy. But it would be no less a mistake to underestimate their impact. Many of the most central and troubling public issues of recent years – such as international human rights, sexual and racial discrimination, abortion, capital punishment, and the distribution of economic resources – have been marked by the fact that the debates surrounding them have not simply taken place in the more or less standard ideological terms of partisan politics, but have also involved explicit appeal to specific ethical theories drawn from various philosophical and theological writings. And in the area of health care and biomedical research, applied studies in ethics have had a particularly direct impact, leading to reforms that have quite radically altered the law and informal norms concerning the definition of death, patients' rights, and the treatment of research subjects. In these cases and others, the public issues and controversies can scarcely be described, let alone understood, without a thorough familiarity with the ethical theories and categories underlying them.

Thus, increasingly, applied ethics has become an intellecutal force to be reckoned with in the life of our society. Through applied studies moral philosophers have regained their public voice. When viewed in comparison with the situation of Anglo-American moral philosophy throughout roughly the first half of the twentieth century, this state of affiars is new and, to some, unsettling if not actually inappropriate. But in terms of a larger historical perspective, the current situation may be better regarded as a return to normalcy following a period of excessively scholastic and inbred philosophical discourse.

Applied ethics is now entering the second stage of its development. In its initial stage, during the past ten years, philosophers and others who undertook work in applied ethics were not overly concerned with second order or meta-level questions about the nature of their enterprise. They were impatient to grapple with pressing moral dilemmas and social issues directly; they were preoccupied with combating naive but deeply entrenched skeptical, relativistic, and scientistic attitudes prevalent among their intended non-philosophical audiences. Early work in applied ethics labored hard to show first that various problems of professional decision-making and public and social policy were not only scientific, technical, or political problems, but that they also had significant ethical or value dimensions, which could only be properly understood and resolved with the aid of conceptual and philosophical analysis. Second, these studies cast about for ways to demonstrate that they could in fact offer practical advice and specific guidelines for helping to resolve these problems. Demonstrating this to skeptical professionals and to equally skeptical colleagues in mainstream philosophy was not easy because applied ethicists seemed to occupy a nebulous zone halfway between the theoretical rigor of their academic disciplines and the experienced, practical judgment of the professional and political worlds they sought to influence. As William May has aptly put it, the applied ethicist 'carries water from wells he has not dug to fires he cannot find. He does not appear to be an intellectually serious figure.'[1] To overcome this rather Chaplinesque persona, at once comic and pathetic, applied ethicists pressed a number of important claims – that philosophical training in ethics gives applied ethicists special analytic skills and conceptual 'tools' that decisionmakers and professionals with different kinds of training lack; that 'good reasons' can in principle be adduced to guide the choice of one alternative course of conduct in particular circumstances; that prescriptive and proscriptive moral rules can be deduced from universalistic moral principles; and that through reasoned moral deliberation and reflection, fair-minded individuals can reach a practical consensus on morally appropriate standards of conduct and policy goals.

These claims have been widely accepted, and, as I mentioned earlier, applied ethics has achieved a good deal of institutional and social support. Now that their intellectual legitimacy has been more securely established, studies of applied ethics have entered a second, more methodologically self-conscious stage of development. Both proponents and critics are paying closer attention to the nature of applied ethics and to its underlying methodological, sociological, and psychological assumptions. In particular, critics have begun to raise serious questions about the model of 'application' that explicitly or tacitly underlies much work in applied ethics and about the relationship between moral principles or rules on the one hand, and concrete moral decisionmaking in specific institutional settings on the other.

I believe that many of these criticisms are compelling, but they need to be taken one step further and supplemented by a reappraisal of the role that social scientific understanding has been assumed to play in conditioning the application of moral principles or rules to moral action in particular social, cultural, and institutional contexts. That is to say, those models of application which I think are most problematic have tended not only to misconstrue the relationship between moral principles and moral decisionmaking, but

209

they have also tended to relegate the social scientific component of applied ethics to a naively descriptive role. Social scientific inquiry, to the extent that it has been used seriously to inform studies of applied ethics, in fact does a good deal more than simply describe the institutional pressures and constraints impinging upon moral decisionmaking and moral agency. It provides an interpretation of the context of action which helps us understand and appreciate the process through which intentions are formed, possibilities are defined, and moral principles and ideals themselves are made meaningful in the social perceptions and self-understandings of acting subjects. If this is the case, it suggests that certain models of application are misguided not only because they mistake the logical relationship between principles and conduct, but also, and more importantly, because they rest on an insufficiently rich account of the relationship between theory and practice – moral rules and the lived interpretation of those rules.

The model of application most prevalent in applied ethics is the so-called engineering model.[2] It likens application in ethics to application in engineering and applied science. This model is made up of three presuppositions. First, that ethical theory constitutes a distinct body of knowledge comprised of universal moral principles grounded in rational foundations or reasonably well established metaethical strategies of justification. Mastery of this body of knowledge can be gained through appropriate disciplinary training. Second, the application of this body of knowledge takes place through the logical deduction of action-guiding conclusions (prescriptions and proscriptions) from general principles in light of relevant empirical facts. And third, the reasoning process involved in deriving specific ethical conclusions from general ethical principles can and should be impartial and disinterested. That is to say, the reasoning involved in ethical application is itself value-neutral and divorced from the substantive ethical perspectives contained in the general principles that are being applied.

I think there are several reasons why the engineering model has been taken up as a way of describing what is going on in many studies of applied ethics.

To begin with, this model provides a ready-made, respectable niche in the prevailing intellectual division of labor in our culture. Engineers and applied scientists who are widely – although probably mistakenly – perceived as applying knowledge in accordance with this model, can readily persuade potential users of their services that they have something practical and important to offer. Professional practitioners also commonly perceive themselves as technically applying the knowledge base of their profession in more or less this way. Thus by organizing their work along lines suggested by the engineering model and by presenting themselves as philosophical specialists akin to specialists in other scientific and technical fields, applied ethicists have been able to create a persona for themselves that is both familiar and valued. All this may have little to do with the conceptual merits of the engineering model, but it has a great deal to do with the politics of applied and professional ethics – with gaining access to and credibility in professional and policy settings; with social legitimation based on professionalized expertise; and with holding one's own in social and policy debates involving expert elites from other fields and disciplines.

In addition, the engineering model has helped to reinforce the claims made on behalf of applied ethics mentioned above. It has provided a way of showing how reasonable deliberation and dialogue about ethical and value questions can be achieved. It also shows how some measure of moral compromise and consensus can emerge among individuals who are initially at odds, if they are honest and open-minded enough to acknowledge that they do share some general moral principles and values, and if they can get the facts straight, and if they can reason clearly and perceive the logical implications of their general moral beliefs. Equally important, the engineering model, particularly its emphasis on use of value-neutral and theory-neutral deductive reasoning, seems to protect applied ethicists from the charge that they are improperly engaged in some form of moral indoctrination. In this connection it is interesting to note that those who pursue studies of applied ethics are almost always referred to as 'ethicists,' almost never as 'moralists.' According to the engineering model, applied ethicists are like independent insurance agents. They do not necessarily proffer any one single ethical theory but thoroughly understand several. Their real contribution lies in their theory-neutral skills and in their ability to help others sort through various theories and weigh their practical implications. Again, these considerations tell us little about the philosophical adequacy of the engineering model as a conception of application, but they do reveal something real and quite troubling about the legitimation demands placed on moral discourse in our

211

liberal, pluralistic society.

Finally, the engineering model has a certain, perhaps unconscious, appeal because it contains a significant residue of the logical positivist legacy. Earlier I suggested that the recent renewal of interest in applied ethics was related to metaethical challenges to philosophical positivism, and I do think this is true in the sense that positivism's denial of the cognitive significance of ethical terms had to be overcome, or at least set aside, before the study of applied ethics could prosper in the culture of academic philosophy. But what has actually taken place is a more qualified and partial rejection of the positivist legacy. The engineering model of applied ethics draws its strength and appeal from that legacy through its formalism and through its construal of application as a deductive operation linking universal principles to demonstrable conclusions via the medium of observable empirical facts. One must not push the analogy between the engineering model of applied ethics and the covering law model of scientific reasoning too far, of course, but I do think that the family resemblance between these two models does partially account for the appeal that the engineering model has enjoyed. Or at least it may help to explain why a number of philosophers have been predisposed to adopt the engineering model, particularly when other social pressures and forces have also made it expedient to do so.

Critiques of the conception of application that I have called the engineering model are becoming more and more numerous as applied and professional ethics enters the second phase of its development. Summarizing and developing these critiques here would take us too far afield, so I want to concentrate on the role the engineering model gives to social scientific inquiry in applied ethics because that problematic feature of the model has been relatively neglected. Where I differ from some other critics of the engineering model is that I do not think rejecting it requires a wholesale rejection of the study of applied and professional ethics as such. For while the engineering model is often used by applied ethicists as a second-order methodological account of their enterprise, it does not in fact accurately describe what these studies are doing. The engineeering model, I contend, is best seen as an ideology of applied ethics and not as an accurate reconstruction of the nature of applied ethical analysis.

In his recent critique of applied ethics Alasdair MacIntyre indicates one reason why the engineering model (he does not use this term) cannot be a satisfactory reconstruction of what applying ethics involves.[3] The engineering model presumes that the moral principles or rules to be applied are specified prior to and independently of their application to human action in particular social contexts. Applied ethics, therefore, putatively consists of a three-step operation with the following logical sequence: (a) universal principles are formulated and theoretically grounded; (b) a particular social or institutional context, consisting of institutional structures embedding the motivations and intentions of individual agents, is empirically described; and (c) moral principles are applied to alternative courses of action possible within that context.

However, as MacIntyre points out, this account will not do because moral principles specified independently of their application to particular situations can only be formal and contentless. The power that moral principles have to structure and direct human choice and action must come about in one of two ways. Either formal, empty principles take on their content through successive applications and interpretations in particular contexts or cases, or else prior to specific application they take on substantive content from ethical theorizing that builds upon substantive sociological, psychological, and anthropological assumptions. In either case the logical sequence presumed by the engineering model is confounded, and two other crucial components of the model are destroyed as well. These are the notion that the reasoning process involved in application is itself theory- and value-neutral, and the notion that social scientific inquiry in applied ethics contributes merely ancillary descriptive information that affects the content of the conclusion reached but not the process of reasoning from principles to conclusions itself.

When principles take on content from the process of being applied to specific choices and actions in particular contexts, we move back and forth between our understanding of the context and our understanding of the principles. Neither pole is prior or self-sufficient. We interpret the principles in light of the context; and the context in light of the principles. Hence, the social scientific interpretation of the institutional patterns, shared meanings, and intentions which constitute that context are not simply involved at the second step when the principles are about to be applied. That interpretation is inherently involved in constituting our understanding of the principles themselves. Similarly, the process of application inevitably involves more than merely value-neutral deductive operations; it is itself a process of interpretation – a reconstruction of meaning and possibility that is simultaneously prescriptive and descriptive in nature.

On the other hand, if the general more principles to be applied derive their substantive content from concomitant elements of philosophical anthropology and social theory woven into the ethical theory as a whole, the process of applying these principles can scarcely be said to be value-neutral either. Nor, in this case, can we remain indifferent to the relationship between the social scientific interpretation of the context within which these principles are applied and the more general social and anthropological interpretations embedded in the ethical theory.

If these considerations are correct, they suggest at least one important observation about the significance of applied ethics and its relationship to other dimensions of ethical inquiry, normative ethics and metaethics. The engineering model has tended to construe applied ethics as derivative of and parasitic upon foundational theorizing. That view blinds us to the constructive role that applied ethics plays in the development of ethical theory. Applied ethicists in principle need not, and in fact do not, simply carry water from wells only ethical theorists have dug; they help dig those wells themselves and are beginning to help identify where we should all stop digging in dry holes.

SOCIAL SCIENCE AS A VOCATION

The preceding remarks have taken us some way, I hope, in the direction of a better understanding of the complex relationship between normative and social scientific inquiry as they interact in the domain of applied ethics. I have suggested that there is a parallel and a connection between the intellectual ferment now taking place in the discipline of moral philosophy and in many areas of the social sciences, a ferment that is leading us to rethink some long-standing assumptions about the separation of facts and values and about the impermeability of the membrane separating normative from descriptive inquiry. Once we get beyond the blinders imposed by the engineering model we can see that applied ethics is a site where the normative interpretations of moral principles, ideals, and concepts and the social scientific interpretation of human action and the contextual preconditions for its meaning are not two rigidly distinct modes of understanding. Indeed, these two modes of understanding can be, and often are, complementary and mutually illuminating.

However, this is not always or necessarily the case. It is not for nothing that social science and moral philosophy have often been at odds with one another, especially in the twentieth century. To get at one important source of these tensions, let me return to a point I raised but did not develop above. Various criticisms of the engineering model of applied ethics suggest that we must be attentive to the relationship between the character of our social scientific understanding of the context within which moral principles are to be applied and the general social scientific assumptions contained in the ethical theory which gives those principles their moral content. Applied ethical analysis runs into trouble, and indeed becomes profoundly incoherent, when the sociological, psychological, and anthropological accounts contained in these two levels of the analysis are antithetical to one another.

One way to develop this point is as follows. In general, ethical theories contain a philosophical anthropology and social theory that hold open to humankind the possibility of autonomous, rational, and responsible moral agency and personhood. In the western tradition, theories of human nature that radically deny this possibility are usually tied to a rejection of the enterprise of moral philosophy itself.

During the past century, when the modern social scientific disciplines began to form and to develop their distinct theoretical perspectives which are still largely operative today, the tension between ethical theory and the social sciences was exacerbated by the basic picture of the human individual in modern society that the social sciences presented. The main point at issue between them became the meaning and pertinence of those traditional conceptions of autonomous, rational, and responsible agency upon which ethical theory has been based. By and large, the social sciences have given us a disturbing and systematic account of the social, psychological, and even biological facets of the human condition. In that account, the categories of autonomy, rationality, and responsibility have been replaced, at least in part, by a set of categories designed

215

to accentuate the external, material, or irrational determinants of human behavior. Developed in response to the massive social changes provoked by nineteenth-century capitalism and the rise of the bureaucratic nation-state, the social sciences have radically transformed the western image of humanity and have greatly increased our awareness of the ways in which individuals are subject to the play of forces that are largely beyond their understanding and control. The social sciences, therefore, have tended to shatter the conceptual framework of ethical theory, either by reinterpreting its basic categories so that their meaning is altered beyond recognition or else by dispensing with those categories altogether. In the world described by the social sciences, the traditional notion of autonomous moral agency is at best exceedingly problematic and at worst incoherent. And yet it is precisely this traditional notion that seems to be coming back into its own with the current renaissance of ethical theory and applied ethics.

Now, one of the reasons why I believe applied ethics has flourished and can continue to flourish is that concomitant reorientations taking place in the social sciences have made the contemporary climate of social science a good deal more receptive to the traditional categories of moral agency than it was twenty or even ten years ago. In large measure, the rise of interpretive approaches to social scientific inquiry in fundamental opposition to older positivistic and behavioralistic approaches accounts for this change of climate and for this new receptivity. Interpretive social science has not overthrown the deterministic picture of the social world, but it has mitigated the extremism of that vision. It has given us reason to believe that the older categories of autonomy, rationality, and responsibility remain serviceable for the purposes of our contemporary social self-understanding.

For interpretive social inquiry, human beings are essentially makers of meaning; they are purposive agents who inhabit symbolically constituted cultural orders, who engage in rule-governed social practices, and whose self-identities are formed in these orders and through those practices.[4] Although it does not always come out explicitly in the work of interpretive social scientists, a certain ethical commitment, a sense of social science as a vocation, is linked to this perspective. On this view, the well-being – indeed the very personhood and humanness – of human beings depends upon the integrity and coherence of those cultural orders of meaning and social practices through which individuals act, and by so doing, realize the possibilities of their own development and self-realization.

Ethical theory and applied ethics, I submit, have fundamentally the same concerns. An essential part of the ethical mission of social science is to nurture and articulate this understanding of human agency in its social context and to expose structures of domination which warp that agency and stunt its possibilities. It is on this basis that a mutual partnership between the study of social science and the study of ethics must be sought. In this partnership with ethics, and especially applied ethics, the social sciences will not simply add a few facts to a normative stew. They will recover their sense of their own proper vocation, and prod ethics to recover its vocation as well.

NOTES

1 William F. May, 'Professional Ethics: Setting, Terrain, and Teacher,' in *Ethics Teaching in Higher Education*, Daniel Callahan and Sissela Bok (eds) (New York: Plenum Press, 1980), p. 239.
2 For further discussion of the engineering model see Arthur L. Caplan, 'Mechanics on Duty: The Limitations of a Technical Definition of Moral Expertise for Work in Applied Ethics,' *Canadian Journal of Philosophy*, Supplementary Volume VIII (1982), pp. 1–18.
3 Alasdair MacIntyre, 'Does Applied Ethics Rest on a Mistake?,' *The Monist*, Vol. 67 No. 4 (1984), pp. 498–513.
4 Cf. Bruce Jennings, 'Interpretive Social Science and Policy Analysis,' in *Ethics, the Social Sciences, and Policy Analysis*, Daniel Callahan and Bruce Jennings (eds) (New York: Plenum Press, 1983), pp. 3–36.

III

THE FUTURE OF ETHICS

INTRODUCTION

Although, within the last twenty years or so, there has been a renewed interest in substantive ethical theory, there has also been disagreement among philosophers over substantive principles and methodology. Some philosophers have held that rules and principles are logically prior to particular judgments, thinking that rules and principles determine which particular judgments are correct, whereas others have felt that rules and principles are simply summary statements of particular judgments independently made. Thus there has been little consensus, not only about which ethical theory is true, but also about how to test the truth of ethical theories. Faced with the rise of applied ethics, however, substantive ethics has been challenged to meet the test of application: the test of seeing whether, how, and to what extent ethical theory can be applied, or of seeing what, if anything, ethical theory can contribute to the resolution of practical moral issues. Whether existing moral theory is adequate, or how it may need to change in order to become so, is the major question addressed in this section.

. In the first essay, R.M. Hare argues that the recent concern with practical application is not altogether new and that much of the current criticism of traditional moral philosophy has been misdirected. He believes that existing moral theory, particularly utilitarianism, can enlighten investigations into contemporary moral issues, and that, when people confront such issues in a manner that is free of prejudice, the pattern of their argumentation will provide support for the theory he holds. Hare views ethical theories as hypotheses which may be either confirmed or disconfirmed,

221

thinking that applied ethics can reveal the weaknesses of some hypotheses and provide assurance for the extension of others to new situations. R.B. Brandt supports Hare's rejection of intuitionism but rejects his reliance on the logic of ordinary discourse. Brandt develops his conception of rationality in ethics, insisting that the future of ethics rests upon a rational preference theory. Moral conclusions, Brandt maintains, must be judged according to the desires of a fully rational person, which he defines, partly at least, by reference to theories in empirical psychology.

Michael Bayles, by contrast, thinks that existing ethical theory is unhelpful in application because it is based upon a set of oversimplified and unrealistic assumptions including the restriction of theory to normal human beings, national boundaries, and one or a few supposedly universal moral principles. In addition to questioning such assumptions, Bayles believes that ethicists must enter into cooperation with social scientists in order to develop a more fruitful approach. In a manner not wholly unlike that of Bayles, Stephen Toulmin questions the usefulness of abstract ethical principles and supports the examination of particular cases. He argues that medicine helped to save ethics from the sterile debate over absolutism vs. relativism by focusing attention on actual cases and objective interests. Toulmin advocates, therefore, a return to casuistry, or to an Aristotelian approach to practical reasoning.

Marcus Singer regards the development of applied ethics as possibly the rise of a new science independent of philosophy. He sees no reason why ethics cannot divide into two separate branches: one capable of becoming a science based on commonly accepted assumptions, and another, more traditionally philosophic, which continues to question these assumptions. Thus Singer seems to accept both the more abstract and general approaches to ethics advocated by Hare and Brandt and the more concrete and specific approaches advocated by Bayles and Toulmin, but as independent types of activity which may sometimes overlap.

William Frankena looks upon ethical theories from the standpoint of moral education. He believes that the application of ethical theory requires attention to institutionalized social morality as well as to personal ideals and therefore assesses alternative theories according to their implications for general education. In the last essay, Abraham Edel agrees that current ethical theory and current practices in moral philosophy are inadequate to the task of resolving

222

practical issues. However, he points up a number of new directions for the development of ethics which hold promise of yielding fruitful results. On Edel's view, the principles of traditional ethical theories need not conflict, for they may find application in different contexts. Ethical principles may be used to enlighten decisions, but they should not be viewed as intuitively valid first principles which are antecedent to or independent of social practices and institutions.

If there is one word to characterize these essays, one would be tempted to say that they are all pragmatic – although not all in the same respect. In a way, that should not be surprising, because they are all concerned with practice, or with practical issues, or simply with ethics, which has traditionally been called practical philosophy. But, within the rationalist tradition, some philosophers seem to have supposed that the principles of ethics could be discovered or known independently of practice or application: by intuition, for example, or by an analysis of the nature of persons. Others, within the empiricist tradition, have argued that there are no normative principles but only descriptively true generalizations. However, pragmatists, unlike either traditional rationalists or empiricists, have generally refused to regard either general principles or particular judgments as absolute or incorrigible, for they have supposed that theory must sometimes be amended to conform to particular judgments and that particular judgments must sometimes be amended to conform to theory.

Thus, when Hare speaks of moral theory as an example of an hypothetico-deductive system, he seems to mean that moral theory can be verified or falsified in practice, by seeing whether it conforms or fails to conform to actual moral reasoning. Yet he also seems to think that the principles advocated by such a theory may be used to guide actions in particular cases.

All of the philosophers writing in this section are concerned about how ethical theories can be used, of course, and this is, broadly speaking, a pragmatic concern. William Frankena, for example, is specifically concerned with how ethical theories can be used in education, and several writers point up the importance of social acceptance and institutionalization. But some are more pluralistic or contextualistic than others in supposing that there may be different principles, or even different procedures, which are appropriate in different situations, and that, perhaps, no overriding

223

principles can cover all cases.

One conclusion which can be drawn from these discussions of the relation between theoretical and applied ethics is that ethical theorists need to take a much closer look at the various fields in which moral problems arise, and this is precisely what the people working in applied ethics are doing. However, the authors in this section are not in total agreement about the relevance of philosophical ethics to the solution of appied issues. R.M. Hare seems to believe that philosophic ethics is directly relevant and useful, whereas Toulmin and Singer appear to think that applied ethics may develop independently of philosophical theory. Edel, on the other hand, appears to regard ethical theory and moral practice as correlative, each capable of enlightening the other. Yet nearly all of these philosophers envisage a much closer relationship between philosophy and other academic disciplines, on the one hand, and philosophy and moral practitioners, on the other.

13

WHY DO APPLIED ETHICS?

R.M. Hare

It is becoming quite common nowadays to see writers, whether popular or academic, speaking of a happy period which has just dawned, in which philosophers actually try to say something relevant to practical issues. This rather patronizing pat on the back is not really intended as a compliment to our profession. It is intended, rather, as a rebuke to those in the recent past who, allegedly, did *not* say anything relevant to practice. As one who came into philosophy in the 1940s with the dominant motive of doing something to help us resolve practical moral problems, I may perhaps be forgiven for finding this a little irritating. My first published philosophical contribution to a practical issue (that of what the duties of citizens are when their governments are acting immorally) was delivered first in Germany, then on the BBC Third Programme, and published in *The Listener* in 1955,[1] and since then I have published many papers on practical topics. I do not think that I am alone in this among moral philosophers. It is true that some of them have confined their attention to ethical theory; but their theoretical contributions, none the less, may have been valuable indirectly in helping those of us who *were* applying theory to practice to improve the theory. On the other hand, they may not have been valuable, if the theoretical work was poor, as it may have been for reasons I shall be discussing. But what the writers I am complaining about fail to say is that there can be no helpful intervention of philosophers, as philosophers, in practical issues unless the philosophy is well done. It is not easy to make any useful application of theory to practice unless one has a viable theory, or at least a firm and coherent grasp of the theoretical moves.

Why do people, and why do I, do applied ethics? One reason they do it is to make themselves more popular. They are in receipt of public money, and they think they will incur the public's displeasure if it can see no obvious helpful results from their researches. A better reason is that we want to find answers to moral questions and think that philosophy might help. I have found, since I first took up moral philosophy in the hope of tackling some acute moral problems that had confronted me during the Second World War, that it does help. It helps first of all by yielding clarifications on minor points of detail which, nevertheless, can generate major confusions. More importantly, it helps, if one does it well, by the clarification of moral language in general – its meaning, its uses and its logic. This is what I meant when I spoke of a viable ethical theory. I think I have one. Other theorists, I am sure, think the same of their own theories. The practical applications of these different theories are what make the theoretical disputes between us of practical importance. There are other theorists who are unlikely to say much that is of practical help. This can be for at least two different reasons. The first is that their theories are of an intuitionist sort which makes appeal to common moral convictions or consensus. These theories will be of little help because on any issue that is in the least contentious there are no common convictions and no consensus to appeal to. Try appealing to common intuitions about the abortion controversy, for example. I do not believe that even prolonged reflection on these intuitions will yield an equilibrium; what we need are firmly established rules of argument based on an understanding of the words we are using when we ask moral questions.

The second handicap which afflicts some moral philosophers can have the same consequence and worse. They may think that there is just no hope of finding an ethical theory – that is an account of the logic of the moral concepts – which will yield rules of reasoning. In default of that, all we can do is exchange intuitions from our pluralist armoury; but then there is no reason why, failing any way of testing the intuitions in argument, the exchange should ever stop. When there are conflicting intuitions battling for control of the conduct even of a single thinker, these philosophers can offer him no comfort or help beyond the armchair comment that such tragedies are one of the facts of life. Philosophers really would deserve a pat on the back if they succeeded instead, as they can if

226

their theory is sound, in showing people how to sort out these conflicts.

There are, then, ways in which philosophers can help resolve practical issues by applying theory to them. But the benefit is mutual. Having taken part in a great many discussions, in working parties and seminars, with people from other professions who face moral problems (doctors and psychiatrists for example) I have been struck by the way in which, in trying to apply theory to these problems, one gains confidence in certain parts of the theory but sees the need for improvements in others.

It often happens in such discussions that I am not the only philosopher present. There may be, for example, somebody also who is, not a non-descriptivist Kantian utilitarian[2] like me, but a descriptivist intuitionist deontologist, perhaps pretending to be a Kantian. These theoretical differences are largely, though not wholly, independent of any differences on the practical issues. Before we start arguing, our unphilosophical opinions may or may not coincide. But when we do start arguing, it is likely to turn out that I am able to give Kantian utilitarian reasons for my opinions, and the other philosopher is not able to give any reasons at all. He just appeals to the consensus of those present, which, unless the working party has been stacked, may not be forthcoming. When he does produce reasons which seem to have any force with those who did not initially share his opinions, they turn out to be utilitarian reasons – appeals for example to the bad consequences of some policy.

A splendid example of this kind of thing occurring in a more august body is to be found in the report of the British Home Office working party on Obscenity and Film Censorship, chaired by Bernard Williams.[3] In his philosophical capacity, he is well known for the single-minded integrity (in his eccentric sense of the word) of his persecution of utilitarians, which rivals St Paul's of the Christians before his conversion. But the arguments of the Williams Report are utilitarian from start to finish, as has been pointed out by Ronald Dworkin in a review of the Report, and by myself.[4] The key chapter in the report is called 'Harms?', and is a masterly cost-benefit analysis of various proposed legislative measures for the control or decontrol of pornography. Whether this presages any Damascus-road conversion of Williams to utilitarianism I doubt; but it illustrates my point that when anti-utilitarians produce arguments on practical issues they are usually utilitarian ones. The Williams Report is a really excellent piece of work, and it is a pity that, being a bit in advance of public opinion, it has not been acted on.

I could not honestly say the same for the report of another British working party headed by a philosopher, the Warnock Report on Human Fertilization and Embryology,[5] which recommends new legislation for the regulation of in vitro fertilization and the treatment of embryos. My impression is that Mary Warnock and her working party, unlike Bernard Williams and his, did not set out to find solid arguments leading to conclusions that could be rationally defended. Rather, they looked around among the conflicting opinions that were current in the working party and outside, and tried to find recommendations which would arouse the least dissent. That, no doubt, is why Warnock had so much better a press than Williams, and is likely to be acted on by the legislature. But if you look at the actual report, you will find again and again, in almost every paragraph, judgments which are mere affirmation without any argument. Many of these have struck the public, and have struck me, as perfectly sensible. But if you ask why they are sensible, you will not get any answer from the report. It is significant that on the issues on which the report has been seriously challenged – that is, the issues which are most controversial and on which help would be most valuable – the disputes that have followed the publication of the Report have been left unresolved by anything in it. This illustrates very well what I said about intuitionists. The issues I am referring to are those concerning the legalization of surrogate motherhood and the time-period after which embryos should be given legal protection.

It might be claimed in favour of the Warnock approach that, if philosophers want to influence public opinion, it is more likely to be successful than that of Williams. I am reminded here of what Plato says in the *Republic*[6] about the difficulties philosophers face in politics. And no doubt Mary Warnock did her usual marvellous job as a practical adviser to government. And she has shown elsewhere (for example in her writings on education) that she is capable of giving reasons (most of them broadly utilitarian) for her views. But she seems to have made almost no *philosophical* contribution to this report, although such help is badly needed in this area.

Williams, on the other hand, has not yet had much influence; but

228

if anybody now or in the future wants to understand the issues on the control of pornography and make up his mind rationally what should be done about them, Williams has provided a wealth of genuinely philosophical assistance. I would say that his time will come. The only trouble is that events and technology do move on, and may require new discussions and measures; for example, 'video nasties' have come on general sale on the black market in Britain since the Williams Report was published.

I am sure that there will be some philosophers (perhaps the majority) who will claim that they fall into neither of the two classes I have mentioned: the Kantian utilitarians like me, and the intuitionists who cannot provide any reasons for their opinions. All I can say in reply is that in my reading of the philosophical literature on practical issues (although I have not read enough of it to speak with authority) I have found that nearly all writers appeal to moral intuitions to a degree which quite destroys their claim to rational assent; and that where reasons are given, they are either covertly utilitarian reasons, or are invalid (e.g., because of suppressed premisses), or else rest on foundations for which themselves no reasons are given. I could also, if space permitted, give my justification for discarding the prevalent dogma, emanating from recent *soi-disants* 'Kantians', and bottle-fed to nearly all beginner students, that Kant and the utilitarians are at opposite poles of moral philosophy and cannot mix. I have shown elsewhere how they can be synthesized.[7]

So, then, one of the main benefits that ethical theory can get from a dose of real practical controversy in the company of practitioners of other disciplines is that we are brought to see the poverty of intuitionism and the appeal to conviction and consensus. Some philosophers, however, react to this experience, not by trying to find a viable theory which *will* yield arguments that can be defended, but by doubting the practical value of theory altogether. They join the pluralist anti-philosophers that I mentioned earlier. This is even more likely to happen in the case of someone who has not had much serious down-to-earth contact with practical issues, but whose education in applied philosophy has been limited to the class-room. It is perfectly true that discussion of practical issues with students may be inconclusive. It may even be corrupting, if badly handled by a philosopher who does not know the theoretical moves well enough to guide students through them to conclusions which they can rationally accept. The students may come to think that absolutely *any* moral opinion can find *some* ethical theory to buttress it. That, to my mind, is not an argument for abandoning theory, but for seeking the best theory, which involves serious discussion of the theoretical issues with one's students. It might also be thought (wrongly) to be an illustration of what Aristotle says,[8] that the young are not suitable audiences for such lectures, because they lack practical experience. Certainly one does not find this happening with an audience of experienced practitioners, unless they have become too exasperated by the antics of bad philosophers. But nor, *pace* Aristotle, does one with the young either, if they are made acquainted in a serious way with the problems.

I may mention lastly another and even more pernicious kind of anti-philosopher, consisting of those whose motives for engaging in these discussions are not really philosophical at all. They have some deep unquestioned conviction, usually religious or political in origin, about, say, contraception or social justice, and, having learnt some philosophy, are prepared to make any eristical move they can think up, not to test the conviction, but to support it. One is reminded of the famous remark about the way politicians use statistics as a drunkard uses a lamp-post, not for illumination but for support. Some of these are good philosophers who have done excellent work in other fields; but when they come to applied ethics they are not prepared to expose to scrutiny opinions which they are certain are correct.

It might be thought from what I have said so far that my recommendation to philosophers engaged in practical discussion would be the following: discard all appeals to antecedent moral convictions; ascertain the facts from the practitioners; devise, by the theoretical methods available to the moral philosopher (essentially the methods of philosophical logic or conceptual analysis), a viable ethical theory yielding rules of sound reasoning on moral questions; and then reason from the facts in accordance with the rules and try to get the practitioners to follow the reasoning and accept its conclusions. This might be a possible approach to start with, but it suffers from certain disadvantages and is not what I am going to recommend. From experience I have come to see that a much more dialectical approach, in almost the true Platonic sense, is likely to be more fecund.

To begin with, the practitioners do not like to be given a theoretical lecture on moral philosophy, especially if they think you are trying to prove practical conclusions about which they have antecedent doubts. This difficulty will be increased if they are made aware, as they should be, that there are rival theories in moral philosophy which might not yield the same conclusions. But the biggest disadvantage of this procedure is that it cuts the philosopher off from a very important source of useful information. This is information about the moral opinions of those with experience of the issues. To paraphrase what Aristotle said about virtue, we have to examine it not merely in a logical way, but on the basis of what people say about it.[9]

You might suppose that I would never think that important, after what I have said about the futility of appeals to convictions. But what I am now going to recommend is not an *appeal* to convictions, but rather a study of them in the hope that we might learn something about the concepts, including the moral concepts, that the practitioners are using. It was J.L. Austin above all from whom we learnt that those doing conceptual analysis will make fewer mistakes if they study the words whose use they are investigating in their proper habitat. I am sure that Wittgenstein would have said the same about the study of words *in use*. I have come to see that this is especially true in moral philosophy, but that in moral philosophy there is a peculiar hazard to be avoided. That is the hazard I was warning against when I said that we cannot usefully *appeal* to moral convictions however widespread, especially on issues which are controversial. The 'moral majority' does not have the last word.

What I am recommending is not that we should produce arguments of the following form, as many do: everybody but a few cranks and Buddhists thinks that meat-eating is all right, so it must be all right. I am recommending something quite different. This is that we should look at the opinions of people, and ask whether, if our theory about the uses of words and the rules of reasoning which they determine were correct, these are the opinions we could expect them to hold. The method is essentially Popperian: It tests an ethical theory by seeing whether it yields predictions which are false. The predictions are about the moral opinions people will hold; and the basis of them is a series of assumptions about the preferences, their factual beliefs, including beliefs about other people's preferences, the meaning and thus the logic of the moral words they are using, and the correctness and clarity with which they follow this logic. People come to their moral opinions as a result of a number of factors, not all of them rational, and they may be led astray. But one of the factors is the meaning and use of the moral words they are employing; and these generate the rules of reasoning which, if they understand the words, they will follow, perhaps without articulating them.

There is a difficulty here which is common to all such hypothetico-deductive procedures. We are basing our prediction on a number of assumptions; and we can only test one of these assumptions at a time, by taking the others as given. In the present case what we are trying to do is test the assumption about the meaning and logic of the moral words as people use them. We therefore have to take as given the other assumptions just listed. But in fact we may have other evidence for the truth of these, so this is not a fatal objection to the method. We may have evidence, that is, that the people we are examining have certain factual beliefs and preferences, and are to some degree clear-headed and logical.

Given these other assumptions, we can test the single hypothesis that their use of the moral words is as we have assumed. Thus, on the basis of purely anthropological facts and assumptions about the people we are examining, we can test a hypothesis in ethical theory, though not, of course, any substantial moral hypothesis.

There is, however, a possible objection to this procedure which we must now consider. We have been assuming that substantial moral opinions are one thing, and logical theses about the uses of moral words another. Ethical naturalists[10] deny this, but I shall not concern myself with them here. A more serious difficulty is posed by those who challenged us to say how we would discriminate between theses which people hold as a matter of logic (hold as analytically true) and their substantial moral opinions.[11]

If we were not able to make this distinction, then there would be a loophole in the procedure I have been describing. Given information on their moral opinions about particular matters, and the other assumptions I mentioned, we might be able to test hypotheses about (to put it vaguely at first) their ways of moral thinking. But which of these ways were logically imposed, and which of them were substantial moral theses or rules, we should not be able to say.

I propose to leave this difficulty for another occasion, remarking merely that even if we could not perform the required discrimination, as I think we can, we should still be able to make considerable progress in ethical theory by the method advocated. For, on the basis of information about people's opinions on particular matters, and the other assumptions mentioned, we should be able to test hypotheses to the effect that our subjects held some combination of rather high-level moral principles and rules for the use of words or the meaning of concepts. It would remain to sort out these things from each other (which can be done). But at least we should have tested hypotheses in a combination of moral anthropology and conceptual analysis – hypotheses capable of shedding considerable light in ethical theory. What we should not have tested, let alone proved, would be any other substantial *moral* theses. This is what differentiates the proposed method from any form of intuitionism.

We might give the following as an example of the application of the method. Suppose we are trying to test the thesis of universalizability (part of ethical theory). We find that people (for example King David when reproached by the prophet Nathan)[12] do apply to themselves moral judgments which they have just been making about other cases they think similar in the relevant particulars. From the fact that they make these moral judgments, in conjunction with assumptions of the sort mentioned above, we infer that the thesis of universalizability (that is, the thesis that, as people use words like 'wrong' they hold it inconsistent to make varying moral judgments about relevantly similar cases) is compatible with the observed facts of usage.

If other instances are produced with which it is claimed that the thesis is incompatible, then the thesis will have to be tested again on those cases, and its defender will have to show that the cases are in fact not incompatible with it. This, in all the cases I have seen produced, can be done; the cases are only thought to be incompatible with the thesis because those who produce them are confused. But I am not here defending the thesis – only illustrating the method.

So the moral opinions of people are not a test of *moral* truth: they are, rather, a test of what I called a viable ethical (i.e., *metaethical*) theory. If we find people holding moral opinions different from what the rules of reasoning generated by the theory would justify, this does not in itself refute the theory. But it does raise the question of what *other* factor in their thinking could have led them to those opinions. As I said, the factor need not be a rational nor even a respectable one. They may simply have got their facts wrong, in which case, we hope, they will alter their opinions when they get them right. But it may be that they have deeply ingrained prejudices which are not amenable to reason, like some of the philosophers I mentioned just now. I am sure that this is true both of some of the opponents of legalized abortion and of some of its defenders. Or it may be that they just have not thought very clearly and so have got into a muddle. All these factors, ignorance, prejudice and muddled thinking, can reinforce one another.

However, I am not so pessimistic as to think that people, especially educated people, will always fall into these traps. Of such people, the 'moral majority' is not actually a majority, even now. Let me give an example of how public opinion, by sound reasoning, albeit inarticulate, can come to reject a moral opinion that it rationally ought to reject. It is by no means the only example I could give. Before the First World War, the ruling classes of all the major European powers were swayed by a kind of nationalism (misnamed 'patriotism') whose outcome in action led directly to the war. The public, having seen the appalling sufferings caused, came to the conclusion that any set of moral principles that allowed such policies must have something wrong with it.[13] On the question of *what* was wrong, and what principles should take the place of those rejected, the public has not yet made up its mind. Some think they should be pacifists; others, like myself, think that there is a kind of patriotism which we can recommend to the citizens of all countries, not just our own (universalizing our prescriptions), and which will permit the use of force in resisting aggression, but not for national self-aggrandisement. That question is still being argued, as is the related question of what difference it makes that nuclear weapons are now available.

Nevertheless this is, so far as it goes, an example of how the public can, in the course of a generation, reach new moral convictions, or at least reject old ones, on rational grounds. And the grounds are ones which, when fully set out, are completely in accord with my own utilitarian ethical theory. I think that the application of the same style of reasoning could sort out the questions that remain, given more certainty about the facts than we yet possess. But for now all I want to claim is that this is an illustration of the mutual benefit that comes to theory and practice by their interaction. The conclusion (the rejection of nationalism) is one that we should expect people to come to, given their understanding of the moral concepts as set out in the theory, and given also their knowledge of the facts, a reasonable freedom from muddle and prejudice, and their ordinary non-moral preferences, such as the preference not to undergo the kind of sufferings that the two world wars entailed. So the theory has to that extent been tested. That is the benefit for theory. The benefit for practice is that, having provisionally, in Popperian style, tested the theory, we can go on using it in trying to solve the problems that remain.

So then the approach that I favour when discussing moral questions with the practitioners of other disciplines is not the somewhat condescending one that I described earlier, but rather something like this. First of all, find out from the practitioners as much as they know about the facts which generate the moral problems. Then discuss the moral problems with them in a perfectly open way, trying to find out what they think, and the reasons they give. It is my experience that one learns a lot by doing this. The practitioners may not be moral philosophers; but they have had in the course of their work to grapple with the problems; they do understand how to use the moral words, though they may not be able to give a philosophical account of their use that will stand up. So they can be expected to have thought rationally about the problems to the extent that they were free of prejudice and muddle (it would be implausible to accuse them of ignorance, because it is their own field and they have their noses in the problems). The doctors, for example, that I have met on working parties measure up very well to these expectations, unlike many people outside their disciplines who pontificate publicly about such questions. Admittedly, one occasionally meets very prejudiced irrational people; but I have not met them in the working parties I have served on.

Having elicited the opinions of our colleagues and the reasons they give for them, we can then ask to what extent a sound process of reasoning, based on the logic of the concepts that they are using, would yield those opinions. If opinions differ, as they will, then we can go further, and ask which of the opinions would be supported, and which rejected, by such a reasoning process. By the time the argument has reached this stage, it should be possible to explain one's reasoning to the non-philosophers, because they will have learnt something about philosophy in the process, just as the philosopher will have learnt something about medicine. Ideally, opinions will at this point start to converge as the reasons for them become clear, and you may even be able to present a unanimous report.

To sum up then, the chief benefits that ethical theory can get from an immersion in practical issues are two: first, the exposure of the pretensions of intuitionists (whether they call themselves that or not), who think that appeals to convictions or to consensus can carry any weight; and secondly, the testing of ethical theories about the meanings of moral words and the rules of moral argument which they generate, by seeing whether people's actual conclusions, when they are reasoning in favourable conditions, free from ignorance, muddle and prejudice, tally with what sound argument, in accordance with these rules, would justify. In this way we can hope to establish, at least provisionally, a theory which can then be applied to new problems. Since the testing of the theory will have involved no appeal to any substantial moral convictions, but only to the empirical, non-moral (if you like anthropological) fact that people hold them, we can retain the hope that the same kind of application to new problems, in addition to shedding light on the problems and so helping with practice, will also further test the theory. It is a virtuous spiral.

NOTES

1 'Ethics and Politics,' *The Listener*, October 1955.
2 For justification of the term 'Kantian utilitarian' see my *Moral Thinking* (Oxford University Press, 1981), p. 4.
3 Home Office, *Report of the Committee on Obscenity and Film Censorship*, chairman Bernard Williams (HMS Cmnd. 7772, 1979). Reprinted without appendices by Cambridge University Press.
4 R.M. Dworkin, 'Is there a Right to Pornography', Oxford Journal of Legal Studies 1 (1981); R.M. Hare, 'Arguing about Rights', *Emory Law Journal* 33 (1984).
5 Department of Health and Social Security, *Report of the Committee of Inquiry into Human Fertilization and Embryology*, Chairman Dame Mary Warnock, HMSO Cmnd. 9314, 1984.
6 Plato, *Republic* 496a ff.
7 See note 2 above and *Moral Thinking*, passim.
8 Aristotle, *Nicomachean Ethics* 1095a 2 ff.
9 Aristotle, *Nicomachean Ethics* 1098b 9 ff.
10 On naturalism see my *The Language of Morals* (Oxford University Press, 1952). Chapter 5 and 'Descriptivism' (*Proc. of British Academy*

49, 1963), reprinted in my *Essays on the Moral Concepts* (London: Macmillan, 1972).

11 On difference between moral and logical or linguistic theses, see my *Moral Thinking*, pp. 10 ff. and *Freedom and Reason* (Oxford University Press, 1963), pp. 30 ff.

12 For David and Nathan, see 2 Samuel 12.

13 On attitudes to war, see my 'Philosophy and Practice: Some Issues About War and Peace,' in *Philosophy and Practice*, ed. A.P. Griffiths, Royal Inst. of Philosophy Lectures 18, Supp. to *Philosophy* 59 (Cambridge University Press, 1985).

14

THE FUTURE OF ETHICS

R.B. Brandt

In discussing 'the future' of ethics I shall confine myself to the next twenty years. In talking of 'ethics' I shall confine myself to the central, most significant problems, about which philosophers are better qualified to think than non-philosophers. I shall suppose that the thinking of the next twenty years in this area will be much influenced by advances in the psychology and physiology of motivation, perhaps advances in the understanding of the development and effects of cultural forms such as moral codes, by better understanding of the basis and logic of rational decision theory, and by a clarified and better argued theory of knowledge or, better, of justified belief. We cannot now know what these advances will be, and hence to some extent speculation about what the concerns of moral philosophies will be twenty years from now is uncertain. What does seem certain is that philosophers, being rational, will be thinking about the strategically central issues.

Let me begin by identifying what strike me as dead, or obsolescent, theories in moral philosophy. The first is that we can get some normative principles from the analysis of ordinary language, or alternatively, that we can show by examining ordinary language that there is no such thing as truth or justification in ethics. I suppose R.M. Hare is the outstanding example of what I take to be the obsolescent theory, at the present time. There have been ideal observer theories, and interest theories, and so on and on. I suggest it is a waste of time to try to establish ethical principles by reflection on the meaning of ethical terms. The terms have no definite meaning in ordinary use; to the extent to which they do have a meaning it appears to differ from person to person, place to place, and time to time; and even if we knew what ordinary people meant by these words, nothing important would follow. I mention this theory only to leave it.

The second dead theory is non-naturalistic intuitionism, the theory that some synthetic ethical propositions are self-evident and can form the epistemological basis of ethics. This view is hardly defended today, and I propose to ignore it.

If we drop these two theories, we may be accused of having removed all possibility of a sound epistemological basis for ethics, of the sort enjoyed by the sciences. For if we reject the idea that ethical terms have meanings which can be related to observation statements, we seem to have removed the possibility that observation can provide any logical support for ethical beliefs. (Professor Hare's prescriptivism does not allow ethics to be an empirical science, as the ideal observer theory does; but it is very close.) Ethics could still boast well-supported principles if we allow the *a priori* synthetic; if we drop this possibility too, we seem to have given up at least any foundationalist epistemology for ethics.

There are, however, some other options. One is a kind of coherence theory for ethics, which is illustrated by Professor Rawls's conception of 'reflective equilibrium', and appears to be the guiding idea behind many discussions of normative problems like infanticide, euthanasia, and capital punishment at the present time. Whatever one may think of the ultimate acceptability of this type of reasoning as an 'epistemology' for ethics, there can be no question that the pattern of thinking has been a very helpful one for clarifying normative problems. What has been demanded for thinking about normative problems is that a person identify the principles to which he is willing to appeal in defense of his stance on a given problem, that he answer charges that he is employing obscure concepts (e.g., if he argues that some kind of action is 'unnatural'), that he be prepared to accept the implications of the principles on which he relies in defense of one stance for all the other issues on which he has ethical opinions, and that he make whatever revisions are necessary in order to have a consistent whole. A person who honestly tries to meet these demands is highly likely to come out with views on ethical problems very different from, and much more sophisticated than, those with which he began. That is something, and possibly it is all there is to be had by thinking about ethics.

III: The future of ethics

As a complete account of how to reason in ethics, and why, however, this view is not very satisfactory. The requirements of clear concepts and consistency of general principles may seem unquestionable; but it does seem that some larger account, of the purpose or good of ethical reasoning, is needed for justification even of these. Much more is this so of a further requirement, usually made, that one's ethical principles be free of any taint of self-interest. More important, however, is the status of what appears to be the basic test of a person's tentative set of ethical principles, whether he can *accept* their implications, especially for concrete cases. Actually, acceptance of implications for concrete cases is not quite the basic 'test', since sometimes a person will prefer to revise his appraisal of some concrete cases in view of the principles to which he would be committed if he did not do so. The proposal is rather like what Goodman once recommended for inductive logic: that we amend a general principle which implies particular judgments we are unwilling to accept, and that we reject particular judgments which violate a general principle we are unwilling to amend. The view seems to be that, in case of choice between two sets of normative beliefs, we prefer the one we find it easier to accept as a whole. This is Rawls's conception of 'reflective equilibrium', and it will be obvious why I call it a 'coherence theory of ethics.' (I am of course assuming that a person will have a background of logical and factual beliefs, which will often be important as premises linking general ethical principles with their concrete implications.) But we have to ask ourselves what is the status of ethical beliefs in reflective equilibrium. It seems quite clear that different persons, and different societies, will probably arrive at quite different sets of principles, in reflective equilibrium. Further, it seems we know that many ethical principles seem persuasive to people because of having interiorized the ethics of their own culture. More important, we need to ask whether an ethical belief in reflective equilibrium is more likely to be true than whatever was held in the first place. After all, where will coherence with our other beliefs take us, if we do not know that some of them are true or justified initially? I believe the most serious defenders of the coherence theory of justification today would agree that the logical force of coherence with other beliefs is zero unless the system contains an ample set of *reports of experience*, something that moral philosophers defending coherence hardly claim. A system of ethical

240

beliefs in reflective equilibrium is what it is, but it is not obvious why such a set of beliefs should be credible for the person, why he ought to believe them. One might say that, if we have rejected the first two theories, the ones I discarded as properly dead, reflective equilibrium is all we can get and that the ideal is of great practical importance.

I think, however, that there are other options (and that Rawls's theory, construed in a proper way, is one of them), and that these should be, and will be, explored fully in the years to come. I have in mind various theories which have made *rational preference*, in some sense or other and in some conditions or other, central to ethical evaluations. Let us look into this conception.

There can, I think, be agreement about what kind of thing philosophers want to appraise. First, wants, desires, goals, aspirations, and above all what is wanted to some extent for itself. Since before Socrates philosophers have wanted to know whether aspiration to enjoyment, power, glory, wealth, or virtue is justified, with or without reference to consequences. Moreover, if several types of situation are worthwhile, they have wanted to know what is the proper order of priority or weight. Second, given an answer to the first question, there is another question: what to do. The Greeks discussed this question under the heading of 'the practical syllogism.' They considered, however, only the special case of some action's being a necessary or a sufficient condition of the state of affairs properly preferred. But matters are not so simple. Often we don't know for certain what the effects of a given course of action will be; we have to go on probabilities. Moreover, we sometimes know that the system of goals, rank-ordered, which we now accept is not the same as the one we shall accept next week. So how do we deal, rationally, with probabilities, and with known disparities between preference-orderings at different times? Third, there are moral commitments which people have, or at least closely related, charactertraits which people may have. To have a moral commitment is to have an aversion to an act-type, to view it as out of bounds, not to be taken seriously as an option for action; normally, when a person has such an aversion, he tends to feel guilty if he himself behaves in the forbidden way and tends to dislike others who do so. Traits of character are, I think, relatively stable patterns of motivation; hence they include moral commitments (but definitionally may not include tendencies to feel guilt or disapprove of

241

others) but reach farther, since generosity is a trait of character but hardly a moral commitment. At any rate these things – desires for states of affairs, actions somehow based on desires, and moral codes and traits of character – require appraisal. Such appraisal seems to be the target of normative ethics in the broad sense.

It will be helpful at this point if I insert a thumbnail sketch of a theory I have recently urged. I have supposed that we know a good deal – and where we do not have the knowledge, it is knowledge I suppose we can count on coming to have some time in the not too far distant future – about the role that *beliefs* play in motivation: not only in the process of decision-making but in the process of formation of basic desires and aversions, or of the actual complex set of these which a person has. My suggestion then was that, if we thought of *justified beliefs* (not necessarily true ones, but currently justified ones) as plugged into the motivational process wherever beliefs play a causal role, we should be able to say what a fully informed – I for various reasons chose to use the term 'fully rational' – person would want or be averse to, would do, given his wants and aversions, and in particular what he would do if faced with a decision which kind of moral code to support for the society in which he expected to live – which one, or perhaps none at all. I suggested that if we could identify this, we would know where available information would take us in criticizing the valuations we want to appraise, and that this might answer our appraisal problems in so far as they can be answered by information of an objective sort.

An objection may be raised to the relevance of such conclusions for the problems of ethics. The objection does not bear merely on my suggestion; it bears equally, I believe, on proposals about what a 'rational' person would do – proposals that have been made, say, by Rawls, Baier, and Gauthier. For, it may be asked, what does knowing what a 'rational' person, in any one of these senses espoused by different philosophers, would want or do show about what is good or right? In order to show, say, that 'A fully rational person would want that p' is relevant to 'p is good', one needs to have a further argument to the effect: 'Something is good if and only if a fully rational person would want it.' And to get this argument, don't we need to go back to familiar territory: the analysis of 'good', synthetic a priori propositions, or a coherence theory of justification?

I do not believe so. To see that, let us consider what would follow if the psychological theory, often held last century, of psychological hedonism were true. Let us suppose we know that it is true of all persons that they want something for itself if and only if and to the extent that they think it will be pleasant for them. If this theory is true, then no one wants wealth or power just for itself; it is not true of anybody that he wants wealth for itself but not pleasure. But now suppose someone says: 'It is true, perhaps, that no one ever wants wealth for itself, but how does this bear on the question whether it is *good* in itself? You need another argument, one to show that something is good in itself only if it can be desired for itself. And how will you do that?' Aristotle, I think, would have been impatient with this reply. If it is shown that human nature is such that something isn't and can't be desired at all, what could be the point of raising the question whether it is good or fittingly desired?

Of course, it is one thing to rule out a certain logically possible target of desire by showing it is not a causally possible object of desire, whereas it is another thing to suggest that something is not a fitting object of desire – even when some people in fact desire it – because a fully rational or fully informed person would not desire it. How does it follow that something is not desirable, from the fact (purportedly) that a fully informed or rational person would not desire it? Well, it would, of course, if we *decided to construe* 'Is X desirable?' as 'Would a fully rational person want X? Such a construction is, of course, a replacement – a replacement of an obscure question by, apparently, a clear and better one. If we think such a replacement is in order, we might ask a critic why he insists on asking a question which no one really understands? It is true that the question whether to replace an old question by a newer one, or to keep the old obscure one and insist that it is the question to be answered, is itself a normative question, and you may say that, since it is, we should be paralyzed and refuse to make a move. (It is rather like suggesting, however, that since a decision to make a cost-benefit analysis is itself an action which must be justified by a cost-benefit analysis, and so on indefinitely, it is never quite clear in a given situation that it is worthwhile to stop and make a cost-benefit analysis.)

Let me review some of the credentials of 'Would a fully rational person want, or do so-and-so?' (including in the last, support a moral code of a certain type) as a question on which we should concentrate attention, in the area of practice.

1   It is (or can be, when spelled out more carefully) clear, and can be answered by well-known objective methods.
2   It is normatively neutral.
3   It does not advise a person to want/do just whatever he is already inclined to want/do; in other words, the answer to it can provide practical guidance.
4   Information that you would do/want so-and-so if you were fully rational will commend that to you – make you more favorably disposed toward it then you would otherwise have been.
5   I suggest there is no relevant question which can be raised about what to do/want which would be excluded by the proposed question, and which, in fact, the proposed question is not helpful in understanding and answering.
6   I suggest there is nothing clear that we could say with the older unreconstructed terminology of ethics which we cannot say with the language of the proposed question.

A thoughtful person has to make up his own mind whether he is content with the proposed conceptual scheme. My belief is that persons who reflect on the matter will decide that they no longer have use for the unreconstructed terminology, and that, when not construed in the suggested way, it no longer raises a question they want to raise.

All the above suggestion is pretty empty if it should turn out that we have no way of knowing what a fully informed – rational – person would want or do, or support in the way of a moral system. Some of our 'knowledge' on such matters is pretty common-sense, but some of it is not, and in so far as it is not what we say is dependent on the progress of psychological theory and experiment. There is nothing wrong with that; much of philosophy cannot be done when torn from the context of the knowledge and conceptual framework of the science of the day.

The views of philosophers like Rawls, Baier, and Gauthier are somewhat less dependent on the content of empirical psychology. The same is true of Professor Gewirth's theory. These theorists employ somewhat different conceptions of 'rationality', and one thing philosophers of the future will presumably explore fully is what is going on when such different conceptions are put forward. Let us look briefly at this.

The most influential conception of 'rationality' among social sciences is simply a requirement on a person's preferences (dispositions to choose between options): that they be *transitive, complete* (determined for all possible states of affairs and especially gambling offers), *continuous* and *strongly independent* (we need not worry about the definition of the last two). Such a preference-ordering permits the assignment of numbers to each outcome, unique up to a linear transformation. If a person's preference-ordering meets these conditions, it follows that his choices will maximize expected utility, in the sense that his choice among options will always maximize the sum of the products of the utility numbers X the subjective probability of the outcome if the action is performed. While this conception is widely accepted, it is by no means sacrosanct. Some writers feel there are types of situations in which it would be irrational to demand transitivity in a person's preference ordering. Again, the condition of continuity must be rejected if some outcomes, such as death or loss of honor, have infinitely high value, so that no reward would be deemed equal to the smallest risk of one of these. The theory may strike some as incomplete because it does not exclude time-preferences, say assigning a low value to an outcome tomorrow although the same outcome for today would be assigned a high value, and when it is known that tomorrow's preference-ordering will assign the outcome the same high value it is given for today in today's scheme. Again, it sets no restriction on the preferences themselves; but there is a long tradition to the effect that some desires are irrational, say a desire for posthumous glory.

These requirements on a person's preference are certainly different from the *definition* of 'fully rational action' which I have employed, although it is possible that an action fully rational in my sense would turn out, given facts of psychology, would meet these requirements. Neither my definition nor these requirements can be identified with the meaning of 'rational' in ordinary speech, which is as 'vague as the meaning of 'moral'. Writers on decision theory speak freely of their 'intuitions' about rational action, and it is logically possible that they view rationality as a nonnatural property about which they have self-evident knowledge. I suggest, however, that they do not, and further that they do not regard their 'intuitions' as analyses of the ordinary-language meaning of 'rational.' As far as I can see, what they call 'intuitions' are no more than reports of what a writer thinks he would recommend to others to do, or thinks he would do himself if he had to adopt a policy for laying bets – perhaps if he were fully rational in my sense. There is nothing wrong with this; but if such reports are the epistemological basis for principles of rational decision theory, it would be helpful to make that clear. There is also no harm in employing the pejorative term 'irrational' to strategies one would reject; but it should be clear that the principles are not intended as reports of the ordinary meaning of 'rational.' As Luce and Raiffa remark in commentary on The Prisoner's Dilemma, one does not get anywhere 'by a play on the words "rational" and "irrational".' Indeed, I suggest it would be clarifying all around if the term 'rational' were dropped from English, and each writer explained simply which policy for behavior he thinks everyone should adopt, and then give his reasons why anyone should be interested in adopting it.

Various writers depart from both these conceptions of rationality. For instance, Professor Baier writes[1], explaining why it is rational to follow the rules of an equitable morality even when it conflicts with self-interest: 'If we bear in mind the nature of the enterprise of Reason and the role reasons play in it, then it is clear that the best reasons anyone can in reason demand are those that *everyone* can demand. For from the point of view of Reason, no one has a position of special privilege until there are special reasons why he should be granted them . . . But if the coercive social order were to be for the good of everyone alike, then anyone would have as good a reason as anyone else for regarding the coercive rules as reasons to act as they require. But then everyone has reason as good as *everyone* can demand, and that surely is adequate reason, since there could be no better reason for everyone.' Professor Baier does not explain why one should choose to be rational in his sense, if or when it is manifestly contrary to self-interest to do so.

Professor Gauthier also appears to depart from these conceptions of rationality (or did in 1974), although he professes to accept the standard social scientists' 'expected utility maximization' conception of rational choice.[2] He thinks it is rational to act morally if and only if it is rational to prefer cooperation to a state of nature. He asserts it is rational to opt for cooperation only if it will bring the chooser at least as much utility as he could have secured for himself in a state of nature, plus a proportion of his optimal social increment (which is assigned the number 1 if his state-of-nature utility is assigned 0, and is the utility he would enjoy if all others cooperated, on a basis marginally attractive to them as compared with their state of nature, to produce for him as much utility as possible), equal to that of everyone else (the number between 0 and 1 being the same for all), the proportions being made as high as possible for the total system. Gauthier claims that morality can avoid conflict with rational requirements only if we conceive of it in this way. I suggest his concept of rationality is not the standard one, at least unless he thinks the demand for an equal proportion of one's optimal social increment is the best bargain one can make; it reads more like a requirement of justice. Incidentally, Gautheir does not explain why it is not rational to be a free-rider in society if one can (and we must recall that the rules of morality are not coercively enforced).

Both these lines of thinking, however, seem to me important; they deserve, and will get, further exploration in the years ahead.

I have left myself little space in which to comment on Professor Gewirth's provocative claims. Gewirth's ethical theory[3] utilizes a very astringent notion of 'rational': as accepting observed facts and the principles of deductive and inductive logic. Moral philosophers will not contest that we ought to be rational in that sense. It would clearly be a tremendous coup if Gewirth could show it is irrational in this sense not to accept important moral principles. He claims to show this. I remain unpersuaded, but of course cannot do justice to his elaborate argument in a few sentences. But I will venture this comment. Gewirth correctly affirms that agents want their motivating goals and also want freedom to act and their own purpose-fulfillment generally; he wants the latter two as necessary to any goal-achievement. Gewirth then argues that a person who understands this must claim a *right* to freedom and well-being, on the ground these are necessary for all purpose-fulfillment. The right-claim is a demand made on others, based on a reason. Other persons, of course, can make similar demands on him, based on symmetrical reasoning, and in consistency he must concede that these demands are as valid against him as his against others. What I do not see is why these reciprocal prudentially-based demands are demands which the persons addressed are in any way bound to honor. So I fail to see how Gewirth's theory gets off the ground. I suggest that if we are to find a 'rational' basis for morality, not to mention for criticism of desires and actions generally, we must move to some less astringent, and therefore more controversial, conception of rationality.[5]

247

NOTES

1 Kurt Baier, 'Rationality, Reason and the Good,' paper read at conference at Simon Fraser University, Feb. 9, 1980.
2 David Gauthier, 'Rational Cooperation,' *Nous* 8 (1974), 53–65.
3 Alan Gewirth, *Reason and Morality*, Chicago: University of Chicago Press, 1978, pp. 89f.
4 R.D. Luce and Howard Raiffa, *Games and Decisions*, New York: Wiley, 1958, p. 97.
5 I am indebted to Allan Gibbard for helpful comments; he is not responsible for remaining errors.

15

ETHICAL THEORY IN THE TWENTY-FIRST CENTURY

Michael D. Bayles

During the past two decades, philosophers have given more and more attention to issues of 'applied ethics.' Indeed, the subspecialties multiply and divide faster than bacteria – medical ethics, business ethics, professional ethics, engineernig ethics, population ethics, academic ethics, dental ethics, agricultural ethics, and so on and on. Yet many sophisticated and sympathetic critics, both within and without philosophy, complain that applied ethics does not aid in resolving daily problems. Some critics contend that ethical theory cannot be applied; that consideration of practical problems should proceed without ethical theory. Elsewhere I have addressed the use of ethical theory in analyzing practical problems.[1] Here, I shall consider some implications of applied ethics for ethical theory. The general questions are whether, and if so how, ethical theory needs to be modified in view of the problems and recent work in applied ethics.

One might characterize the apparent aim of normative ethical theory as providing one or a few a priori principles stating necessary and sufficient conditions for evaluating all conduct of a fixed number of coexisting normal adult humans of equal moral worth in a national society who will always comply with the principles. No theory explicitly has this precise aim, but most theories have major elements of it. The purpose of this statement is to make explicit a large number of assumptions that are often made by ethical theorists. These assumptions are as follows:

1 that (a) one or a few (b) a priori principles (c) can provide

necessary and sufficient conditions (d) for evaluating all
conduct of persons;

2 that the number of persons involved does not change;
3 that the relevant persons coexist;
4 that the persons are humans;
5 that the persons are normal;
6 that the persons are adult;
7 that the persons are of equal moral worth;
8 that ethical problems occur within one society; and
9 that everyone will always comply with the principles.

The contention of this paper is that the work in applied ethics
shows that probably none of these assumptions should be made.
The primary reason for any hesitation concerns assumption 1, for it
is very difficult to prove that no such theory can be developed.
Problems in applied ethics require dropping each of the other
assumptions. Assumptions 2 and 3 cannot be made for problems of
population and the environment. Assumption 4 cannot be made for
problems of animal rights and the environment. Assumption 5
cannot be made for problems concerning mentally abnormal persons, and 6 cannot be made for questions of children's rights.
Number 7 simply assumes an important moral position regarding
racism and sexism. Assumption 8 is inadequate for problems of
world hunger and nuclear warfare. Finally, assumption 9 is obviously false and cannot be made in considering problems of punishment
and corrective justice.

The bulk of this paper expands on these points. No theory makes
all the assumptions listed above, but every ethical theory makes at
least one of them, and most make several. When all these assumptions are dropped, normative ethical theory becomes much harder.
Perhaps new styles of doing ethical theory are needed and will
develop, although they will probably be variations on some older
views. About that, I am not at all sure, but I am sure that ethical
theory at the beginning of the twenty-first century cannot make
these old assumptions and be at all adequate for the problems of
applied ethics.

MORAL COMMUNITY

Assumptions 2 to 6, and 8 concern what can be called 'the moral community' and are considered in this section. The others – 1, 7, and 9 – concern what can be called 'theory construction' and are discussed in the next section. Actually, 7 could also be treated as a problem of the moral community, but for reasons that should become clear, it is probably best treated as an assumption of theory construction. By 'the moral community' I mean the range of entities for whom moral concern is appropriate. The expression moral concern can mean concern to evaluate as having acted rightly or wrongly, or it can mean concern in determining what constitutes right or wrong conduct. This distinction can be made precise by considering obligations. The first meaning pertains to those who can have moral obligations or be moral agents. One can thus speak of the community of moral agents. The second meaning pertains to the entities whose well-being or status is relevant to determining obligations. One can thus speak of the moral community of the beneficiaries of obligations – those for whose sake the obligations exist.

Usually, beneficiaries are those to whom one might owe an obligation. Consequently, one might say the moral community of beneficiaries consists of all those beings that can have rights. The classes of bearers of rights and of beneficiaries of obligations will be the same if, and only if, every right entails an obligation and every obligation is owed to someone and entails a right. The correlativity of rights and obligations is a highly disputed point. In any case, not all beneficiaries of obligations need be those to whom obligations are owed (and thus right bearers). For example, if Abrams promises to take care of Baker's dog while Baker is on vacation, Abrams's obligation is to Baker, but the dog may also be a beneficiary. Historically, the beneficiaries of life insurance were not deemed to have legal rights, only the person's estate had rights. It is, however, reasonable to assume that all moral agents can also be beneficiaries of obligations, but not vice versa.[2] Possible beneficiaries of obligations, such as animals, need not be capable of being moral agents.

The fundamental principles of the two dominant traditions in modern ethical theory – Kantianism and utilitarianism – seem to emphasize these different concepts of the moral community. Kant's theory is based on rational beings who can be moral agents – whether they can will the maxims of their actions as universal laws for all such beings. Consequently, non-rational beings have an anomalous position in the Kantian tradition. The moral community of beneficiaries seems to be the same as the community of moral agents. In contrast, the utilitarian principle emphasizes beneficiaries – all beings that can experience pleasure or pain. Some more specific differences between the traditions stems from this difference, for example, their respective conceptions of rights. The Kantian concept emphasizes the ability to claim or waive rights, while the utilitarian concept emphasizes the ability to benefit or be harmed. These general differences also underlie the difficulties each type of theory has when assumptions 4–6 are dropped.

Assumption 4, that the persons are humans, seems most appropriate for the community of moral agents. However, one could raise questions about animals as moral agents. At one time, animals were punished by law, and many owners of dogs and cats admonish and punish them. Issues of the environment and the treatment of animals clearly raise questions concerning the membership of various entities in the moral community of beneficiaries. Is the concern for the environment based simply on potential problems that might be caused humans, or is it also based on concern for the well-being of animals? One might also contend that plants, such as giant redwood trees, and even rivers and streams, have some status as beneficiaries. The assumption of the equal moral worth of animals, or speciesism as it is called, also arises. Consequently, an ethical theory adequate for these problems cannot assume that even the community of moral agents consists of human beings, let alone the moral community of beneficiaries.

Assumption 5 of the normality of members of the moral community renders an ethical theory useless for some important practical problems. In particular, important ethical questions surround mentally retarded and mentally ill persons. Ethical problems arise concerning the membership of mentally abnormal persons in the community of moral agents. Is mental illness or retardation an excuse for wrongful acts? Can mentally ill or retarded persons have obligations? All or only some of them? Traditionally, mental abnormality afforded an excuse in criminal but not in tort law, and few people believe insanity excuses all conduct. An ethical theory must provide guidance as to when mentally abnormal people can

252

and cannot be responsible for fulfilling obligations. Until very recently, mentally abnormal persons were not recognized as full members of the moral community of beneficiaries. For example, people with Down's Syndrome were often denied dental treatment. One of the current movements in mental retardation is for equal rights, which appears to raise some questions of equal worth. Other people seem to claim that there are special obligations to mentally retarded persons. In short, ethical issues about mentally abnormal persons concern their membership in the moral communities of agents and of beneficiaries.

Nor can an ethical theory assume 6 that members of the moral community are adults. The membership of children in the moral communities of agents and beneficiaries arises in practical problems. Although the issues of children as moral agents are much like those of mentally abnormal persons, there are some practical differences. For example, juvenile justice systems treat children differently from the way mentally abnormal adult offenders are treated. Consequently, a different rationale might be involved. One might think that the membership of children in the moral community of beneficiaries has always been recognized, but that is myopic. Children have often been treated as property. Even societies that recognize them as persons do not accord them the same rights as adults. Moreover, one of the most deeply dividing issues in Western societies concerns when an entity becomes a child. This is the problem of abortion. A related problem is whether a fetus can be the subject of child abuse.[3] Similar problems occur at the other end of life; when does one cease to be a member of the moral community of beneficiaries (the definition of death)?

As noted above, Kantian theories often have trouble accounting for members of the moral community of beneficiaries who are not also possible agents. All the above difficulties have plagued John Rawls's theory of justice, because he assumes that the contractors are rational heads of families.[4] Consequently, the membership of beings who are not rational or heads of families in the moral community of beneficiaries must depend on the concern of those who are. As a result, Rawls's critics have noted that on his theory, women and children may be subject to tyranny in the family, and animals and mentally retarded persons may lack rights of justice.[5] Lest it be thought Rawls is a particular exception in ethical theory, one can search in vain the writings of rational intuitionists such as

253

Prichard and Ross for significant help on these questions.[6]

Utilitarian theory, with its emphasis on the moral community of beneficiaries, has trouble determining the community of moral agents. This difficulty is shown in the standard criticism that it might be appropriate on utilitarian grounds to punish or blame an innocent person. On some versions of act utilitarianism, the appropriateness of praise or blame is determined by the utility of praising or blaming. Because of effects on others, it might be useful to praise or blame children or persons who are mentally abnormal, even when they could not have helped doing what they did. The same general difficulty can be seen from another perspective by asking who has a duty to maximize utility. Unless assumptions are made about the purpose of an ethical system (for example, to guide people in making decisions), the theory might apply to any behavior that can affect utility, whether by competent adults, incompetent mentally ill or retarded persons, children, or even animals. The statement of the theory assumes that alternative *acts* are available, but the theory does not specify a concept of act. Moreover, there seems to be a difference between the treatment of one's own acts and those of others, since praise or blame might be appropriate for involuntary behavior of others but one is unlikely to apply the utilitarian principle to one's own involuntary behavior.

None of these comments is meant to imply that Kantian or utilitarian theories cannot handle these problems. Instead, the point is that frequently they implicitly assume answers to them. For example, in using an act utilitarian principle authors often make assumptions about the requirements for being moral agents. Applied ethics, however, has clearly shown that these are contestable and important assumptions; they must become explicitly defended elements of a theory.

Another common assumption, usually by way of ignoring problems, is 8: that moral principles are for a rational society. Both Rawls and Brandt have made this assumption.[7] However, as the problem of world hunger clearly illustrates, practical problems require dropping it. Moreover, it would be mistaken to claim that only few general problems, like world hunger, require dropping this assumption. A host of problems that many people face in their daily lives require dropping it. For example, the ethics of hiring professional engineers for projects has raised problems when US engineers prohibited competitive bidding but engineers in other societies did not. Similarly, property rights in the form of patents on pharmaceuticals can be undercut if one country recognizes them and another does not. My contention is not that questions of international justice must be settled before one can address those of justice within a society, or vice versa. The claim is simply that one cannot generally assume that those are separate problems. For some practical problems one can assume that one is dealing only with problems within a single society, but they are not as common as one might think. More importantly, no ethical theory that claims to be complete can make that assumption.

Not only is it inappropriate to make assumptions about the geographical or spatial limits of the moral community, it is also inappropriate to make assumptions about its temporal extent and numerical size – assumptions 2 and 3. Many issues about nuclear war, the environment, and population growth pertain to future generations. One cannot assume that the future beings are or are not members of the moral community of beneficiaries. Instead, one must argue for such claims. The same applies to assumptions about the size of the class of beneficiaries. The size (including very existence) of future populations depends, at least in part, on the actions of presently existing people. Dropping these assumptions creates severe difficulties for both Rawlsian contractarianism and utilitarianism.[8] An ethical theory adequate for applied ethics must not assume that all members of the moral community of beneficiaries presently exist and that their numbers will not change.

Nor can one assume that all relevant moral agents coexist. Of course, any agent that can act now must exist now. But many policies and ethical principles depend on some consistency over time, a consistency that is more than acting on the same principle. A principle's prescriptions can be context dependent in such a way as to undermine its purpose if followed over time.[9] In short, the appropriateness of ethical principles may have to take into account what future moral agents will do (even following the principle).

To sum up, ethical theories must specify the moral communities of agents and beneficiaries. Most theories simply assume aspects of one or both of these communities. In the future, an adequate ethical theory for all practical problems cannot assume that the membership of either moral community consists of a fixed number of coexisting normal, adult humans in one society. Each of these specifications of the moral communities will have to be explained and justified.

III: The future of ethics

THEORY CONSTRUCTION

This section concerns assumptions and problems in theory construction – assumptions 1, 7, and 9. Calling them assumptions of theory construction is to indicate that the features play a prominent role in the justification of an ethical theory's fundamental substantive principles. The assumption of equal moral worth, 7, is included here, because it is frequently specified as a requirement of an adequate ethical theory. The other assumptions – strict compliance, a few principles specifying necessary and sufficient conditions, comprehensiveness, and the a priori character of principles – are more clearly related to the structure of arguments for theories.

One might roughly distinguish between strong and weak versions of assumption 7, of equal moral worth. For example, Rawls and Ackerman make the assumption an element of their justification procedure. Rawls's original position is deliberately designed so that each contractor is equal.[10] Of course, as noted above, this does not guarantee that noncontracting members of the moral community of beneficiaries have equal moral worth. Similarly, Ackerman's neutrality condition for dialogue is one of equal moral worth – that no person or person's conception of the good is better than anyone else's.[11] Ackerman, however, does provide arguments for this condition. A weak version of equal moral worth is found in utilitarianism. Each person counts equally only in the sense that pleasures and pains (or whatever) of equal intensity and duration count equally, no matter who or what experiences them. If some beings, say humans, are more sensitive than others, say animals, to pleasure and pain, then as experiencers they will count for more. The assumption is not really of the equal moral worth of persons, but of the equal moral worth of experiences. But it implies an equal moral worth of persons in that the experience of one person counts for no more than a similar experience of another.

Applied ethics cannot assume equal moral worth, at least in the strong version. Many of the problems of the world arise because one group does not recognize the other as of equal moral worth. Indeed, the history of the world is full of such cases – the ancient Greeks' view of Turks, the Christians' view of Jews, the Nazis' view of non-Aryans, the whites' view of blacks, and men's view of women. If one assumes equal moral worth, then the practical problems

256

become different. For example, most recent writing on racism and sexism has been about how to abolish them and bring about equality. The prior question is whether the assignment of differences in worth can be shown to be incorrect. This question has not been discussed very much. In recent theory, only R.M. Hare has bluntly faced this problem, and he had to admit that he could not conclusively show such views to be incorrect.[12] While Hare's theory has frequently been criticized for this failure, the critics have usually failed to tackle the problem themselves, simply assuming equal worth to be a requirement of an adequate theory. Those who have tried to address it have had no more success than Hare in showing the denial of equal worth to be incorrect.

Another problem in theory construction is the assumption (9) of ideal or strict compliance, that everyone will always comply with the fundamental norms. Rawls, of course, makes this assumption and restricts himself to ideal theory.[13] Ackerman makes the same assumption in the beginning, what he calls 'a perfect technology of justice,' but he then considers second best theories.[14] Utilitarians also often make this assumption. For act utilitarians, it can be the assumption that everyone in the society is an act utilitarian. Some versions of rule utilitarianism assume that everyone complies with the rules. It is embedded in the common sense question 'But what if everyone did that?'

A major difficulty with ideal compliance theory is that it omits many practical problems. For example, Rawls does not provide any significant discussion of corrective justice. If everyone acts properly, there is no need for corrective justice. The practical problems considered in applied ethics arise in the world in which we all live, and that is not a world of strict compliance. Even when the problem is not one of corrective justice, whether one assumes everyone will follow the proposed mode of conduct can make an important difference.

The common rebuttal to such charges is that one must know the ideal before one can consider the less than ideal. One must know at what one aims, because in practical problems, one should try to come as close as possible to the ideal. One will have to trade off various aspects of the ideal and choose between them.[15] This involves some difficult problems, but they cannot be faced until the ideal is known.

This rebuttal incorrectly assumes that the ideal will not vary for a society of imperfect compliance. There are good reasons seriously to doubt this claim. The substantive rules for a situation of imperfect compliance may be radically different from those for a situation of perfect compliance. For example, all justifications concerned with protecting oneself or others from unjust infringement will be omitted from a strict compliance idea. This does not merely mean justifications of self-defense and defense of others in criminal and tort law. It also means questions of nuclear deterrence and just war are not found in an ideal compliance theory. Moreover, even the addition of a justification of self-defense will not take care of problems. If one assumes that everyone will use force against others only when it is justified as self-defense, then one does not allow the defense when it is reasonable but mistaken to believe one is threatened. Allowing the defense on the basis of a reasonable belief implies that some injuries will be justified in the name of self-defense when there is no actual threat.

In general, substantive rules (even those allowing for non-compliance, as in criminal law) may not be best if accurate determinations cannot be made.[16] In short, the assumption of strict compliance makes two assumptions: (a) that people have perfect knowledge; and (b) that they will comply. If one drops these factually false assumptions, there is little reason to believe that enough will remain of an ideal compliance theory to be useful for practical problems. One cannot simply tinker with an ideal compliance theory to make it applicable to situations of less than perfect compliance. Instead, one must often rethink the entire issue.

Most ethical theories, at least theories of obligation, can be stated as providing necessary and sufficient conditions for an action being obligatory (or permissible or wrong). Yet, many problems in applied ethics seem intractable and cast doubt on this assumption (1,(c)). One can rule out many actions as wrong, but one cannot decide between two or three remaining alternatives. Often the problem stems from a lack of sufficiently precise information. One cannot determine precisely what the effects of an act will be. This problem of lack of information does not challenge the claim of ethical theories to provide necessary and sufficient conditions for evaluating conduct.

Other problems are different. They involve weighing competing values or prima facie rights or duties. One may not have an adequate theoretical basis for a choice between the values in the particular context. Not all theories are subject to this sort of theoretical difficulty. Act utilitarianism, for example, implies that there is a correct answer; either one act will produce more utility than any other, in which case it is obligatory, or two or more acts will produce the same amount and more than any others, in which case either is permissible. However, many other types of theory are subject to the problem. Besides a theory of prima facie duties, most rights-based theories, such as those of Dworkin and Gewirth, face this problem.[17] Dworkin must balance different abstract rights, and Gewirth must balance rights to freedom and to welfare. Nor does Rawls's lexical ordering of principles avoid the problem, because it arises within his principle of liberty.[18] To determine the most extensive system of equal liberties, one must balance one liberty against another. None of these theories provides a basis for specifying which right or liberty is more important in every situation.

There are two ways to handle this problem. First, one can say that in any such case either action is permissible. The theory then provides necessary and sufficient conditions for evaluating conduct, because in the difficult cases it specifies that both are permissible. However, this is a technical fix that denies agonizing moral choices. In effect, it says when a choice is agonizing, it should not be because either action is permissible. Second, one can simply recognize that ethical theories do not provide sufficient conditions for evaluating all conduct. Instead, at best they provide necessary conditions that can handle many but not all cases. This way does not imply, as the technical fix does, that there is no reason for agonizing over hard choices. It simply recognizes that ethics provides guidance, not algorithms.

A related problem is the assumption (1,(a)) that ethical theories can be stated in one or a very few principles – Ross has a half-dozen or so prima facie duties. Now there are good reasons for trying to do so, for example, simplifying and unifying the theory. There are also many disadvantages. Almost every theorist recognizes that the fundamental principles alone provide little direct guidance, perhaps the least useful being Aquinas's principle of doing good and avoiding evil.[19] Instead, the fundamental principles must be developed in considerable detail – sets of natural laws or specific rights, or even the act utilitarian's rules of thumb. In short, the fundamental principles do not provide much guidance for practical problems and, thus, are not of overwhelming use in applied ethics.

Another related assumption (1,(d)) is that a theory can be provided for evaluating all conduct.[20] Almost all ethical theorists have had this comprehensiveness as a goal. Aristotle, Aquinas, Kant, and Bentham thought that their theory would cover all ethical issues. Rawls is the most prominent contemporary theorist not to claim that his theory covers everything – only the basic structure of society.[21] Many followers of Rawls have ignored his limitation and applied his theory directly to concrete problems.

The difficulty with this assumption or goal relates to the difficulty of a few principles providing guidance. If the principles are not for all conduct but only a limited range, then they are likely to be more specific and provide more guidance. This assumption also implies that there cannot be fundamentally different principles for different groups. For example, it denies, without argument, the sometimes claimed autonomy of professional ethics. There is little reason to think that a theory cannot be of limited scope and adequate for the problems it does address.[22] Of course, it will have to be careful not to make assumptions incompatible with plausible solutions to problems not addressed.

Given the difficulties with constructing theories of one or a few principles that state necessary and sufficient conditions for evaluating all conduct it seems reasonable to decrease the emphasis on seeking them. This is not to say such a theory is not desirable, only that its value has been overemphasized. It might be more profitable to work on generating a larger number of principles that each specifies a necessary condition, or more likely, a feature or consideration that must be considered in making practical decisions and judgments in a range of problems. The theory might be more complex, but it might be more useful.

The final aspect of theory construction concerns the assumption (1,(b)) of the a priori character of principles and the relevance of empirical information. With respect to fundamental principles, empirical information is frequently not essential, although many theories do rest on general assumptions (or visions) of human nature. For some theories, such information is important; for example, natural law principles depend on various claims about human inclinations. In any case, once one begins to use a theory, even for very general problems, empirical information plays a crucial role. For example, if one wants to use Rawls's principle of liberty and develop the most extensive system of equal liberties, then empirical information about the effects of recognizing one liberty on the security of others is quite important. Similarly, much Rawlsian analysis depends on claims about effects on self-respect. These claims too require empirical support. Similarly, consequentialist views often involve empirical assumptions in their deployment. For example, R.B. Brandt argues for income supplements for the ill and handicapped, in part on the ground that their utility curves are similar to those of healthy, nonhandicapped persons.[23] However, no empirical evidence is cited for this assumption, and there is some reason to believe it is false or at least that the curves are not as similar as Brandt thinks. Some severely handicapped persons do not find their lives worth living, and it seems doubtful that people deprived of most pleasures of physical activity will have utility curves anywhere near as high as healthy, nonhandicapped people. Of course some individuals will, but the question concerns the average person.

The point is not that Brandt or others are in fact incorrect, but that they often do not provide evidence for their claims. Often, of course, no evidence is available, but this is not always the case. Prior to the twentieth century, little empirical information about society and human behavior, other than individual observation, was available. Today, however, huge quantities of empirical data are generated annually. Although the data are spotty and sometimes irrelevant to any conceivable purpose, some social science information is relevent to ethical theory. Ethical theory cannot continue as though the social sciences do not exist. Philosophers doing applied ethics have generally become aware of this point; the work being done now is much more informed than that of a decade or so ago.

Empirical information becomes especially important if one drops assumptions 1, (a), (c), (d), and 9. As noted above empirical information is more important the less general the scope of principles, so it becomes more relevant the more one focuses on developing any principles for ethical problems of limited scope. Moreover, if one drops the assumption of strict compliance, then one needs detailed information about how much information people can and do have and how they will behave in various circumstances. In an imperfect world, ethical resolutions that will not work as intended are not ethical resolutions of problems.

In sum, important assumptions have often been made in the construction of ethical theories that can no longer reasonably be made. The equal worth of human beings or members of the moral community of beneficiaries cannot be assumed, especially if one expands that community greatly. To do so is to sweep away many of the most serious ethical problems of human history. Nor does the construction of ideal compliance theories have much value if one wants a theory to provide guidance for practical problems. Although it would be desirable to have one or a few fundamental, a priori principles that provide necessary and sufficient conditions for evaluating all conduct, it seems unlikely that such a theory can be achieved. There may be more value, at least for practical guidance, in seeking to develop a large number of principles that provide necessary but not sufficient considerations for evaluating conduct in limited spheres. Development of such a theory is likely to require considerable empirical information to establish its claims.

CONCLUSION

This paper has not presented the contours of an ethical theory suitable for the twenty-first century. Instead, it has primarily characterized ethical theory by what it cannot or plausibly should not do. Development of ethical theory for the twenty-first century requires considerable effort to determine the borders of the moral community. In rejecting ideal compliance theory, it must also involve considerable knowledge of human behavior and what can be expected of people. Some of the needed information is available, but much more is needed.

One might object that no one person can be expected to know everything that is claimed to be relevant to the development of ethical theory adequate for the twenty-first century. This objection may well be correct. As characterized here, ethical theory certainly calls for interdisciplinary knowledge and training. It may require more than that. Most scientific studies, in both the natural and social sciences, now involve teams of researchers. Such a prospect may be in store for philosophy. Philosophers and social scientists may work together on studies that are partly empirical and partly conceptual and normative. Whether a team approach to philosophy will ever work, I do not know, but it would not surprise me to start seeing multi-authored works in ethical theory. A few such efforts have already been made in applied ethics, so some may be in store for ethical theory. In short, not only the character of ethical theory, but that of ethical theorists may change in the twenty-first century.

NOTES

1 'Moral Theory and Application,' *Social Theory and Practice* 10 (1984).
2 One might possibly imagine beings whose well-being or status could not be affected by conduct and so could be the bearers of obligations but never beneficiaries. See H.L.A. Hart, *The Concept of Law* (Oxford: Clarendon Press, 1961), p. 190.
3 See Edward W. Keyserlingk, 'The Unborn Child' Right to Prenatal Care,' *Health Law in Canada*, 3, 1 (1982): 10–21 and 3, 2)1982): 31–41.
4 John Rawls, *A Theory of Justice* (Cambridge, Mass: Harvard University Press, 1971), pp. 142–3, 292.
5 Jane English, 'Justice Between Generations,' *Philosophical Studies*, 31 (1977): 93–5; Michael S. Pritchard and Wade L. Robinson, 'Justice and the Treatment of Animals: A Critique of Rawls,' *Environmental Ethics* 3 (1981): 55–61; Daniel Wikler, 'Moral Theory and Mental Retardation,' presented at Fifth Congress, International Association for the Scientific Study of Mental Retardation, Jerusalem, August 3, 1979.
6 H.A. Prichard, *Moral Obligation* (Oxford: Clarendon Press, 1949); W.D. Ross, *The Right and the Good* (Oxford: Clarendon Press, 1930)and *Foundations of Ethics* (Oxford: Clarendon Press, 1939).
7 Rawls, *Theory of Justice*, pp. 7–8, R.B. Brandt, 'Some Merits of One Form of Rule-Utilitarianism,' in *Readings in Contemporary Ethical Theory*, Kenneth Pahel and Marvin Schiller (eds) (Englewood Cliffs, N.J.: Prentice-Hall, 1970), p. 291.
8 See Michael D. Bayles, *Morality and Population Policy* (University of Alabama Press, 1980), Appendices 1 and 2.
9 See Peter Singer, 'A Utilitarian Population Principle,' and Derek Parfit, 'On Doing the Best for Our Children,' in *Ethics and Population*, Michael D. Bayles (ed.) (Cambridge, Mass.: Schenkman, 1976), pp. 81–99 and 100–15 respectively.
10 Rawls, *Theory of Justice*, p. 19.
11 Bruce A. Ackerman, *Social Justice in the Liberal State* (New Haven and London: Yale University Press, 1980), p.11.
12 R.M. Hare. *Freedom and Reason* (Oxford: Clarendon Press, 1963), Chapter 9.
13 Rawls, *Theory of Justice*, p. 145.
14 Ackerman, *Social Justice*, pp. 21, 23, for example.
15 See Ackerman, *Social Justice*, p. 23.
16 See Gordon Tullock, *Trials on Trial* (New York: Columbia University Press, 1980), pp. 34–46.

17 Ronald Dworkin, *Taking Rights Seriously* (Cambridge, Mass: Harvard University Press, 1977); Alan Gewirth, *Reason and Morality* (University of Chicago Press, 1978).
18 Rawls, *Theory of Justice*, p. 302.
19 St Thomas Aquinas, *Summa Theologica*, I-II, q. 94, ad. 2.
20 See also James S. Fishkin, *Beyond Subjective Morality* (New Haven: Yale University Press, 1984), p. 61. Fishkin's claims that people assume an adequate ethical theory must provide an answer to all moral problems. This seems to combine assumptions 1, (c), and 1, (d) in the text.
21 Rawls, *Theory of Justice*, pp. 7–11.
22 See Fishkin, *Beyond Subjective Morality*, pp. 134–5.
23 R.B. Brandt, *A Theory of the Good and the Right* (Oxford: Clarendon Press, 1979), pp. 316–19. Brandt is much better than any other theorist in calling on and using empirical information, even though one might challenge his selection and reading of it.

16

HOW MEDICINE SAVED THE LIFE OF ETHICS

Stephen Toulmin

During the first 60 years or so of the twentieth century, two things characterized the discussion of ethical issues in the United States, and to some extent other English-speaking countries also. On the one hand, the theoretical analyses of moral philosophers concentrated on questions of so-called metaethics. Most professional philosophers assumed that their proper business was not to take sides on substantive ethical questions but rather to consider in a more formal way what kinds of issues and judgments are properly classified as moral in the first place. On the other hand, in less academic circles, ethical debates repeatedly ran into stalemate. A hard-line group of dogmatists, who appealed either to a code of universal rules or to the authority of a religious system or teacher, confronted a rival group of relativists, and subjectivists, who found in the anthropological and psychological diversity of human attitudes evidence to justify a corresponding diversity in moral convictions and feelings.[1]

For those who sought some 'rational' way of settling ethical disagreements, there developed a period of frustration and perplexity.[2] Faced with the spectacle of rival camps taking up sharper opposed ethical positions (e.g. toward premarital sex or anti-Semitism), they turned in vain to the philosophers for guidance. Hoping for intelligent and perceptive comments on the actual substance of such issues, they were offered only analytical classifications, which sought to locate the realm of moral issues, not to decide them.

Two novel factors contributed to this standoff by making the issue

265

of subjectivity an active and urgent one. For a start, developments in psychology – not least, the public impact of the new psychoanalytic movement – focused attention on the role of feelings in our experience and so reinforced the suspicion that moral opinions have to do more with our emotional reactions to that experience than with our actions in it [3]. So, those opinions came to appear less matters of reason than matters of taste, falling under the old tag, *quot homines. tot sententiae*. This view of ethics was strengthened by the arguments of the ethnographers and anthropologists, who emphasized the differences to be found between the practices and attitudes of different peoples rather than the common core of problems, institutions, and patterns of life that they share. To cap it all, the anthropologist Edward Westermarck took over Albert Einstein's term 'relativity' from physics and discussed the moral implications of anthropology under the title of *Ethical Relativity* [4].

Between them, the new twentieth-century behavioral and social sciences were widely regarded as supporting subjectivist and relativist postitions in ethics; this in turn provoked a counterinsistence on the universal and unconditional character of moral principles; and so a battle was joined which could have no satisfactory outcome. For, in case of substantive disagreement, the absolutists had no further reasons to offer for their positions: all they could do was shout more insistently or bring up heavier theological guns. In return, the relativists could only turn away and shrug their shoulders. The final answers to ethical problems thus came, on one side, from unquestioned principles and authoritative commands; on the other, from variable and diverse wishes, feelings, or attitudes; and no agreed procedure for settling disagreements by reasonble argument was acceptable to both sides.

How did the fresh attention that philosophers began paying to the ethics of medicine, beginning around 1960, move the ethical debate beyond this standoff? It did so in four different ways. In place of the earlier concern with attitudes, feelings, and wishes, it substituted a new preoccupation with situations, needs, and interests; it required writers on applied ethics to go beyond the discussion of general principles and rules to a more scrupulous analysis of the particular kinds of 'cases' in which they find their application; it redirected that analysis to the professional enterprises within which so many human tasks and duties typically arise; and, finally, it pointed philosophers back to the ideas of 'equity,' 'resaonableness,' and 'human relationships,' which played central roles in the *Ethics* of Aristotle but subsequently dropped out of sight [5, esp. 5.10.1136b30–1137b32]. Here, those four points may be considered in turn.

THE OBJECTIVITY OF INTERESTS

The topics that preoccupied psychologists and anthropologists alike during the first half of the twentieth century were foreign to the concerns of physicians, and they tended to distract attention from those shared features of human nature which define the physiological aspects of human medicine and so help to determine the associated ethical demands. To begin with, the novel anthropological discoveries that exerted most charm over the general public were those customs, or modes of behavior, which appeared odd, unexpected, or even bizarre, as compared with the normal patterns of life familiar in modern industrial societies. The distinctive features of unfamiliar cultures (rain dances, witch doctors, initiation ceremonies, taboos, and the like) captured the imaginations of general readers far more powerfully than those which manifested the common heritage of humanity: the universal need to eat and drink, the shared interest in tending wounds and injuries, and so on. Theoretically, likewise, field anthropologists focused primarily on the differences among cultures, leaving the universals of social structure to the sister science of sociology. In their eyes, the essential thing was to explain the modes of life and activity typical of any culture in terms appropriate to that particular culture, not in terms brought in from outside with the anthropologist's own cultural baggage.

As a result, the whole field of medicine was something of a stumbling block to anthropology. If one studied the procedures employed in handling cases of tuberculosis among, say, pygmies in the Kalahari Desert, it might well turn out that they did not recognize this affliction as being, by Western standards, a true 'disease.' In that case it might – anthropologically speaking – be inappropriate to comment on their procedures in medical terms at all. On the contrary, witch doctoring must be appraised in 'ethnomedical' terms, by standards adapted to the conception of witch doctoring current inside the culture in question.

III: The future of ethics

For those who were concerned with the internal systematicity of a given culture, this might be an acceptable method. In adopting it, however, one was obliged to set aside some of the basic presuppositions of the modern Western (and international) profession of medicine: notably, the assumption that human beings in all cultures share, in most respects, common bodily frames and physiological functions. While the epidemiology of, say, heart disease may in some respects be significantly affected by such cultural factors as diet, the evils of heart disease speak no particular language, and to that extent the efficacy of different procedures for dealing with that condition can be appraised in transcultural terms.

So, the *cross*-cultural study of epidemiology and kindred subjects – what may be called 'comparative medicine' – has to be distinguished sharply from the *intra*cultural study of 'ethnomedicine.' The latter is concerned with the attitudes, customs, and feelings current within exotic cultures in the face of those afflictions that we ourselves know to be diseases, whether or not the people concerned so perceive them. The former, by contrast, is concerned with the treatments available in different countries or cultures, regardless of the special attitudes, customs, or feelings that may cluster around those conditions locally, in one place or another. Fieldworkers from the World Heath Organization, for instance, are concerned with comparative medicine and are not deterred from investigating the links between, say, eye disease and polluted water supplies just because members of the affected community do not recognize these links. The central subject matter of medicine thus comprises those objective, universal conditions, afflictions, and needs that can affect human beings in *every* culture, as contrasted with those relative, subjective conditions, complaints, and wishes that are topics for anthropological study in *any given* culture.

Now we are in a position to see how needlessly moral philosophers thrust themselves into the arms of the 'ethical relativists' when they adopted anthropology as their example and foundation. An ethics built around cultural differences quickly became an ethics of local attitudes. The same fate overtook those philosophers who sought their example and foundation in the new ideas of early twentieth-century psychology. For they were quickly led into seeing ethical disagreements between one human being and another as rooted in their personal responses to and feelings about the topics in debate; as a result, questions about the soundness of rival moral views were submerged by questions about their origins.

Contrast, for instance, the statement, 'She regards premarital sex as wrong *because* her own straitlaced upbringing left her jealous of, and censorious toward, today's less puritanical young' – which offers us a psychological account of the causes by which the ethical view in question was supposedly generated – with the statement, 'She regards it as wrong because of the unhappiness which the current wave of teenage pregnancies is creating for mothers and offspring alike' – which states the interests with which the view is concerned and the reasons by which it is supported. Modeling ethics on psychology thus once again diverts attention from genuine interests and focuses them instead on labile, personal feelings.

The new attention to applied ethics (particularly medical ethics) has done much to dispel the miasma of subjectivity that was cast around ethics as a result of its association with anthropology and psychology. At least within broad limits, an ethics of 'needs' and 'interests' is objective and generalizable in a way that an ethics of 'wishes' and 'attitudes' cannot be. Stated crudely, the question of whether one person's actions put another person's health at risk is normally a question of ascertainable fact, to which there is a straightforward 'yes' or 'no' answer, not a question of fashion, custom, or taste, about which (as the saying goes) 'there is no arguing.' This being so, the objections to that person's actions can be presented and discussed in 'objective' terms. So, proper attention to the example of medicine has helped to pave the way for a reintroduction of 'objective' standards of good and harm and for a return to methods of practical reasoning about moral issues that are not available to either the dogmatists or the relativists.

THE IMPORTANCE OF CASES

One writer who was already contributing to the renewed discussion of applied ethics as early as the 1950s was Joseph Fletcher of the University of Virginia, who has recently been the object of harsh criticism from more dogmatic thinkers for introducing the phrase 'situation ethics.'[3] To judge from his critics' tone, you might think that he was the spokesman for laxity and amorality, whereas he belongs, in fact, to a very respectable line of Protestant (specifically, Episcopalian) moral theologians. A main influence on him in his

269

youth was Bishop Kenneth Kirk, whose book on *Conscience and Its Problems*, published in 1927 [9], was one of the few systematic works by an early twentieth-century Protestant theologian to employ the 'case method' more usually associated with the Catholic casuists. Via Kirk, Fletcher thus became an inheritor of the older Evangelical tradition of Frederick Dennison Maurice.[4]

Like his predecessors in the consideration of 'cases of conscience,' Kirk was less concerned to discuss conduct in terms of abstract rules and principles than he was to address in concrete detail the moral quandaries in which real people actually find themselves. Like his distinguished predecessors – from Aristotle and Hermagoras to Boethius, Aquinas, and the seventeenth-century Jesuits – he understood very well the force of the old maxim, 'circumstances alter cases.' As that maxim indicates, we can understand fully what is at stake in any human situation and how it creates moral problems for the agents involved in it only if we know the precise circumstances 'both of the agent and of the act': if we lack that knowledge, we are in no position to say anything of substance about the situation, and all our appeals to general rules and principles will be mere hot air. So, in retrospect, Joseph Fletcher's introduction of the phrase 'situation ethics' can be viewed as one further chapter in a history of 'the ethics of cases,' as contrasted with 'the ethics of rules and principles'; this is another area in which the ethics of medicine has recently given philosophers some useful pointers for the analysis of moral issues.

Let me here mention one of these, which comes out of my own personal experience. From 1975 to 1978 I worked as a consultant and staff member with the National Commission for the Protection of Human Subjects of Biomedical and Behavioral Research, based in Washington, D.C.; I was struck by the extent to which the commissioners were able to reach agreement in making recommendations about ethical issues of great complexity and delicacy.[5] If the earlier theorists had been right, and ethical considerations really depended on variable cultural attitudes or labile personal feelings, one would have expected 11 people of such different backgrounds as the members of the commission to be far more divided over such moral questions than they ever proved to be in actual fact. Even on such thorny subjects as research involving prisoners, mental patients, and human fetuses, it did not take the commissioners long to identify the crucial issues that they needed to address, and, after patient analysis of these issues, any residual differences of opinion were rarely more than marginal, with different commissioners inclined to be somewhat more conservative, or somewhat more liberal, in their recommendations. Never, as I recall, did their deliberations end in deadlock, with supporters of rival principles locking horns and refusing to budge. The problems that had to be argued through at length arose, not on the level of the principles themselves, but at the point of applying them: when difficult moral balances had to be struck between, for example, the general claims of medical discovery and its future beneficiaries and the present welfare or autonomy of individual research subjects.

How was the commission's consensus possible? It rested precisely on this last feature of their agenda: namely, its close concentration on specific types of problematic cases. Faced with 'hard cases,' they inquired what particular conflicts of claim or interest were exemplified in them, and they usually ended by balancing off those claims in very similar ways. Only when the individual members of the commission went on to explain their own particular 'reasons' for supporting the general consensus did they begin to go seriously different ways. For, then, commissioners from different backgrounds and faiths 'justified' their votes by appealing to general views and abstract principles which differed far more deeply than their opinions about particular substantive questions. Instead of 'deducing' their opinions about particular cases from general principles that could lend strength and conviction to those specific opinions, they showed a far greater certitude about particular cases than they ever achieved about general matters.

This outcome of the commission's work should not come as any great surprise to physicians who have reflected deeply about the nature of clinical judgment in medicine. In traditional case morality, as in medical practice, the first indispensable step is to assemble a rich enough 'case history.' Until that has been done, the wise physician will suspend judgment. If he is too quick to let theoretical considerations influence his clinical analysis, they may prejudice the collection of a full and accurate case record and so distract him from what later turn out to have been crucial clues. Nor would this outcome have been any surprise to Aristotle, either. Ethics and clinical medicine are both prime examples of the concrete fields of thought and reasoning in which (as he insisted) the theoretical rigor of geometrical argument is unattainable: fields in which we should

271

above all strive to be *reasonable* rather than insisting on a kind of *exactness* that 'the nature of the case' does not allow [5, 1.3.1094b12–27].

This same understanding of the differences between practical and theoretical reasoning was taken over by Aquinas, who built it into his own account of 'natural law' and 'case morality,' and so it became part of the established teaching of Catholic moral theologians. As such, it was in harmony with the pastoral practices of the confessional [12, D.3, Q.5, A.2, Solutio]. Thus, Aquinas's own version of the fundamental maxim was framed as an injunction to the confessor – 'like a prudent physician' – to take into account *peccatoris circumstantiae atque peccati*, that is, 'the circumstances both of the sinner and of the sin.' Later, however, the alleged readiness of confessors to soften their judgments in the light of irrelevant 'circumstances' exposed them to criticism. In particular, the seventeenth-century French Jesuits were attacked by their Jansenist coreligionists on the ground that they 'made allowances' in favor of rich and high-born penitents that they denied to those who were less well favored. And, when the Jansenist Arnauld was brought before an ecclesiastical court on a charge of heterodoxy, his friend Pascal launched a vigorous counter attack on the Jesuit casuists of his time by publishing the series of anonymous *Lettres provinciales* which from that time on gave 'casuistry' its unsavory reputation.[6]

By taking one step further, indeed, we may view the problems of clinical medicine and the problems of applied ethics as two varieties of a common species. Defined in purely general terms, such ethical categories as 'cruelty' and 'kindness,' 'laziness' and 'conscientiousness,' have a certain abstract, truistical quality: before they can acquire any specific relevance, we have to identify some actual person, or piece of conduct, as 'kind' or 'cruel,' 'conscientious' or 'lazy,' and there is often disagreement even about that preliminary step. Similarly, in medicine; if described in general terms alone, diseases too are 'abstract entities,' and they acquire a practical relevance only for those who have learned the diagnostic art of identifying real-life cases as being cases of one disease rather than another.

In its form (if not entirely in its point) the art of practical judgment in ethics thus resembles the art of clinical diagnosis and prescription. In both fields, theoretical generalities are helpful to us only up to a point, and their actual application to particular cases demands, also, a human capacity to recognize the slight but significant features that mark off, say, a 'case' of minor muscular strain from a life-threatening disease or a 'case' of decent reticence from one of cowardly silence. Once brought to the bedside, so to say, applied ethics and clinical medicine use just the same Aristotelean kinds of 'practical reasoning,' and a correct choice of therapeutic procedure in medicine is the *right* treatment to pursue, not just as a matter of technique but for ethical reasons also.

In the last decades of the nineteenth-century, F.H. Bradley of Oxford University expounded an ethical position that placed 'duties' in the center of the philosophical picture, and the recent concern of moral philosophers with applied ethics (most specifically, medical ethics) has given them a new insight into his arguments also. It was a mistake (Bradley argued) to discuss moral obligations purely in universalistic terms, as though nobody was subject to moral claims unless they applied to everybody – unless we could, according to the Kantian formula, 'will them to become universal laws.' On the contrary, different people are subject to different moral claims, depending on where they 'stand' toward the other people with whom they have to deal, for example, their families, colleagues, and fellow citizens [13].

As the modern discussion of medical ethics has taught us, professional affiliations and concerns play a significant part in shaping a physician's obligations and commitments, and this insight has stimulated detailed discussions both about professionalism in general and, more specifically, about the relevance of 'the physician/patient relationship' to the medical practitioner's duties and obligations.[8]

Once embarked on, the subject of professionalism has proved to be rich and fruitful. It has led, for instance, to a renewed interest in Max Weber's sociological analysis of vocation (*Beruf*) and bureaucracy, and this in turn has had implications of two kinds for the ethics of the professions. For, on the one hand, the manner in which professionals perceive their position as providers of service influences both their sense of calling and also the obligations which they acknowledge on that account. And, on the other hand, the professionalization of medicine, law, and similar activities has exposed practitioners to new conflicts of interest between, for example, the individual physician's duties to a patient and his loyalty to the profession, as when his conduct is criticized as 'unprofessional' for harming, not his clients, but rather his colleagues.

In recent years, as a result, moral philosophers have begun to look specifically and in greater detail at the situations within which ethical problems typically arise and to pay closer attention to the human relationships that are embodied in those situations. In ethics, as elsewhere, the tradition of radical individualism for too long encouraged people to overlook the 'mediating structures' and 'intermediate institutions' (family, profession, voluntary associations, etc.) which stand between the individual agent and the larger scale context of his actions. So, in political theory, the obligations of the individual toward the state was seen as the only problem worth focusing on; meanwhile, in moral theory, the difference of status (or station) which in practice expose us to different sets of obligations (or duties) were ignored in favor of a theory of justice (or rights) that deliberately concealed these differences behind a 'veil of ignorance.'[9]

On this alternative view, the only just – even, properly speaking, the only moral – obligations are those that apply to us all equally, regardless of our standing. By undertaking the tasks of a profession, an agent will no doubt accept certain special duties, but so it will be for us all. The obligation to perform those duties is 'just' or 'moral' only because it exemplifies more general and universalizable obligations of trust, which require us to do what we have undertaken to do. So, any exclusive emphasis on the universal aspects of morality can end by distracting attention from just those things which the student of applied ethics finds most absorbing – namely, the specific tasks and obligations that any profession lays on its practitioners.

Most recently, Alasdair MacIntyre has pursued these considerations further in his new book, *After Virtue* [16]. MacIntyre argues that the public discussion of ethical issues has fallen into a kind of Babel, which largely springs from our losing any sense of the ways in which *community* creates obligations for us. One thing that can help restore that lost sense of community is the recognition that, at the present time, our professional commitments have taken on many of the roles that our communal commitments used to play. Even people who find moral philosophy generally unintelligible usually acknowledge and respect the specific ethical demands associated with their own professions or jobs, and this offers us some kind of a foundation on which to begin reconstructing our view of ethics. For it reminds us that we are in no position to fashion individual lives for ourselves, purely *as individuals*. Rather, we find ourselves born into communities in which the available ways of acting are largely laid out in advance: in which human activity takes on different *Lebensformen*, or 'forms of life' (of which the professions are one special case), and our obligations are shaped by the requirements of those forms.

EQUITY AND INTIMACY

Two final themes have also attracted special attention as a result of the new interaction between medicine and philosophy. Both themes were presented in clear enough terms by Aristotle in the *Nicomachean Ethics*. But, as so often happens, the full force of Aristotle's concepts and arguments was overlooked by subsequent generations of philosophers, who came to ethics with very different preoccupations. Aristotle's own Greek terms for these notions are *epieikeia* and *philia*, which are commonly translated as 'reasonableness' and 'friendship,' but I shall argue here that they correspond more closely to the modern terms, 'equity' and 'personal relationship' [5].

Modern readers sometimes have difficulty with the style of Aristotle's *Ethics* and lose patience with the book, because they suspect the author of evading philosophical questions that they have their own reasons for regarding as central. Suppose, for instance, that we go to Aristotle's text in the hope of finding some account of the things that mark off 'right' from 'wrong': if we attempt to press this question, Aristotle will always slip out of our grasp. What makes one course of action better than another? We can answer that question, he replies, only if we first consider what kind of a person the agent is and what relationships he stands in toward the other people who are involved in his actions; he sets about explaining why the kinds of relationship, and the kinds of conduct, that are possible as between 'large-spirited human beings' who share the same social standing are simply not possible as between, say, master and servant, or parent and child [5].

The bond of *philia* between free and equal friends is of one kind, that between father and son of another kind, that between master and slave of a third, and there is no common scale in which we can measure the corresponding kinds of conduct. By emphasizing this

275

point, Aristotle draws attention to an important point about the manner in which 'actions' are classified, even before we say anything ethical about them. Within two different relationships the very same deeds, or the very same words, may – from the ethical point of view – represent quite different *acts* or *actions*. Words that would be a perfectly proper command from an officer to an enlisted man or a straightforward order from a master to a servant, might be a humiliation if uttered by a father to a son, or an insult if exchanged between friends. A judge may likewise have a positive duty to say, from the bench, things that he would never dream of saying in a situation where he was no longer acting *ex officio*, while a physician may have occasion, and even be obliged, to do things to a patient in the course of a medical consultation that he would never be permitted to do in any other context.

With this as background, we can turn to Aristotle's ideas about *epieikeia* ('reasonableness' or 'equity'). As to this notion, Aristotle pioneered the general doctrine that principles never settle ethical issues by themselves: that is, that we can grasp the moral force of principles only by studying the ways in which they are applied to, and within, particular situations. The need for such a practical approach is most obvious, in judicial practice, in the exercise of 'equitable jurisdiction,' where the courts are required to decide cases by appeal, not to specific, well-defined laws or statutes, but to general considerations of fairness, of 'maxims of equity.' In these situations, the courts do not have the benefit of carefully drawn rules, which have been formulated with the specific aim that they should be precise and self-explanatory: rather, they are guided by rough proverbial mottoes – phrases about 'clean hands' and the like. The questions at issue in such cases are, in other words, very broad questions – for example, about what would be *just* or *reasonable* as between two or more individuals when all the available facts about their respective situations have been taken into account [17–19]. Similar patterns of situations and arguments are, of course, to be found in everday ethics also, and the Aristotelean idea of *epieikeia* is a direct intellectual ancestor of a central notion (still referred to as 'epikeia') in the Roman Catholic traditions of moral theology and pastoral care [11].

In ethics and law alike, the two ideas of *philia* ('friendship' or 'relationship') and *epieikeia* (or 'equity') are closely connected. The expectations that we place on people's lines of conduct will differ markedly depending on who is affected and what relationships the parties stand in toward one another. Far from regarding it as 'fair' or 'just' to deal with everybody in a precisely *equal* fashion, as the 'veil of ignorance' might suggest, we consider it perfectly *equitable*, or *reasonable*, to show some degree of partiality, or favor, in dealing with close friends and relatives whose special needs and concerns we understand. What father, for instance, does not have an eye to his children's individual personalities and tastes? And, apart from downright 'favoritism,' who would regard such differences of treatment as unjust? Nor, surely, can it be morally offensive to discriminate, within reason, between close friends and distant acquaintances, colleagues and business rivals, neighbours and strangers? We are who we are: we stand in the human relationships we do, and our specific moral duties and obligations can be discussed in practice *only* at the point at which these questions of personal standing and relationship have been recognized and taken into the account.

CONCLUSION

From the mid-nineteenth century on, then, British and American moral philosophers treated ethics as a field for general theoretical inquiries and paid little attention to issues of application or particular types of cases. The philosopher who did most to inaugurate this new phase was Henry Sidgwick, and, from an autobiographical note, we know that he was reacting against the work of his contemporary, William Whewell [20, 21]. Whewell had written a textbook for use by undergraduates at Cambridge University that resembled in many respects a traditional manual of casuistics, containing separate sections on the ethics of promises or contracts, family and community, benevolence, and so on [22]. For his part, Sidgwick found Whewell's discussion too messy: there must be some way of introducing into the subject the kinds of rigor, order, and certainty associated with, for example, mathematical reasoning. So, ignoring all of Aristotle's cautions about the differences between the practical modes of reasoning appropriate to ethics and the formal modes appropriate to mathematics, he set out to expound the theoretical principles (or 'methods') of ethics in a systematic form.

By the early twentieth century, the new program for moral philosophy had been narrowed down still further, so initiating the era of 'metaethics.' The philosopher's task was no longer to organize our moral beliefs into comprehensive systems: that would have meant *taking sides* over substantive issues. Rather, it was his duty to stand back from the fray and hold the ring while partisans of different views argued out their differences in accordance with the general rules for the conduct of 'rational debate,' or the expression of 'moral attitudes,' as defined in *metaethical* terms. And this was still the general state of affairs in Anglo-American moral philosophy in the late 1950s and the early 1960s, when public attention began to turn to questions of medical ethics. By this time, the central concerns of the philosophers had become so abstract and general – above all, so definitional or analytical – that they had, in effect, lost all touch with the concrete and particular issues that arise in actual practice, whether in medicine or elsewhere.

Once this demand for intelligent discussion of the ethical problems of medical practice and research obliged them to pay fresh attention to applied ethics, however, philosophers found their subject 'coming alive again' under their hands. But, now it was no longer a field of academic, theoretical, even mandarin investigation alone. Instead, it had to be debated in practical, concrete, even political terms, and before long moral philosophers (or, as they barbarously began to be called, 'ethicists')[10] found that they were as liable as the economists to be called on to write 'op ed' pieces for the *New York Times*, or to testify before congressional committees.

Have philosophers wholly risen to this new occasion? Have they done enough to modify their previous methods of analysis to meet these new practical needs? About those questions there can still be several opinions. Certainly, it would be foolhardy to claim that the discussion of 'bioethics' has reached a definitive form, or to rule out the possibility that novel methods will earn a place in the field in the years ahead. At this very moment, indeed, the style of current discussion appears to be shifting away from attempts to relate problematic cases to general theories – whether those of Kant, Rawls, or the utilitarians – to a more direct analysis of the practical cases themselves, using methods more like those of traditional 'case morality.' (See, e.g., the discussion in a recent issue of the *Hastings Center Report* of the moral issues that are liable to arise in cases of sex-change surgery [23, pp. 8–13].)

Whatever the future may bring, however, these 20 years of interaction with medicine, law, and the other professions have had

How medicine saved the life of ethics

spectacular and irreversible effects on the methods and content of philosophical ethics. By reintroducing into ethical debate the vexed topics raised by *particular cases*, they have obliged philosophers to address once again the Aristotelean problems of *practical reasoning*, which had been on the sidelines for too long. In this sense, we may indeed say that, during the last 20 years, medicine has 'saved the life of ethics,' and that it has given back to ethics a seriousness and human relevance which it had seemed – at least, in the writings of the interwar years – to have lost for good.

NOTES

This paper is one outcome of a research project undertaken in collaboration with Dr. Albert R. Jonsen, of the University of California at San Francisco, with the support of a grant from the National Endowment for the Humanities, no. RO–0086–79–1466.

*Committee on Social Thought, Department of Philosophy and Divinity School, University of Chicago.

1 For a further exploration of the standoff, see [1].
2 It was, in fact, just this problem which presented itself to me when I wrote my doctoral dissertation [2].
3 Just how much of a pioneer Joseph Fletcher was in opening up the modern discussion of the ethics of medicine is clear from the early publication date (1954) of his first publications on this subject [6–8].
4 It was Albert Jonsen who drew my attention to the work of Kenneth Kirk and his great forerunner, the mid-nineteenth-century Evangelical teacher, F.D. Maurice [10]. For further discussion consult A.R. Jonsen [11].
5 The work of the national commissions generated a whole series of government publications – mainly reports and recommendations on the ethical aspects of research involving research subjects from specially 'vulnerable' groups having diminished autonomy, such as young children and prisoners. I have written a fuller discussion of the commission's work for a forthcoming Hastings Center book on the 'closure' of disputes about matters of technical policy. As a member of the commission, A.R. Jonsen was also struck by the casuistical character of its work, and this led to the research project of which this paper is one product.
6 The *Lettres provincales* were published periodically, and anonymously, in 1656–57, but it did not take long for their authorship to be discovered, and they have remained perhaps the best-known documents on the

279

subject of 'case reasoning' in ethics. The intellectual relationships between the vigorous attack on the laxity of the Jesuits' case morality contained in the *Lettres* and the larger program of seventeenth-century philosophy deserves closer study than it has yet received.

7 For the word 'casuistry,' see the entry in the complete *Oxford English Dictionary*, which revealingly points out how many English nouns ending in 'ry' (e.g., 'Sophistry,' 'wizardry,' and 'Propery') are dyslogistic. It seems to be no accident that the earliest use of the word 'casuistry' cited in the *OED* dates only from 1725 – i.e., after Pascal's attack on the Jesuit casuists. This helps to explain, and confirm, the current derogatory tone of the word.

8 See Bledstein's discussion [14, p. 107] of the nineteenth-century confusion between codes of ethics and codes of etiquette within such professional societies as the American Medical Association.

9 I borrow this phrase a trifle unfairly from John Rawls [15], but I have argued at greater length in [1] that *any* unbalanced emphasis on 'universality' divorced from 'equity' is a recipe for the ethics of relations between strangers and leaves untouched those important issues that arise between people who are linked by more complex relationships.

10 Once again, the *Oxford English Dictionary* has a point to make. It includes the word 'ethicist' but leaves it without the dignity of a definition, beyond the bare etymology, 'ethics + ist.'

REFERENCES

1 Toulim, S. The tyranny of principles. *Hastings Cent. Rep.* 11:6, 1981.

2 Toulmin, S. *The Place of Reason in Ethics*. Cambridge: Cambridge University Press, 1949.

3 Stevenson, C.L. *Ethics and Language*. New Haven, Conn.: Yale University Press, 1944.

4 Westermarck, E. *Ethical Relativity*. New York: Harcourt Brace, 1932.

5 Aristotle. *Nicomachean Ethics*.

6 Fletcher, J. *Morals and Medicine*. Princeton, N.J.: Princeton University Press, 1954.

7 Fletcher, J. *Situation Ethics*. Philadelphia: Westminster, 1966.

8 Fletcher, J. *Humanhood*. Buffalo, N.Y.: Prometheus, 1979.

9 Kirk, K. *Conscience and Its Problems*, 1927.

10 Maurice, F. *Conscience: Lectures on Casuistry Delivered in the University of Cambridge*, London, 1872.

11 Jonsen, A.R. Can an ethicist be a consultant? In *Frontiers in Medical Ethics*, edited by A. Abernathy. Cambridge: Bollingen. 1980.

12 Aquinas, Thomas. *Commentarium Libro Tertio Sententiarum*.

13 Bradley, F. *Ethical Studies*. London, 1876.

14 Bledstein, B. *The Culture of Professionalism*. New York: Norton, 1976.
15 Rawls, J. *A Theory of Justice*. Cambridge, Mass: Harvard University Press, 1971.
16 MacIntyre, A. *After Virtue*. South Bend, Ind.: Notre Dame University Press, 1981.
17 Davis, K. *Discretionary Justice*. Urbana: University of Illinois Press, 1969.
18 Newman, R. *Equity and Law*. Dobbs Ferry, N.Y.: Oceana, 1961.
19 Hamburger, M. *Morals and Law: The Growth of Aristotle's Legal Theory*. New Haven, Conn.: Yale University Press, 1951.
20 Sidgwick, H. *The Methods of Ethics*, Introduction to 6th ed., London and New York: Macmillan, 1901.
21 Schneewind, J. *Sidgwick's Ethics and Victorian Moral Philosophy*. Oxford and New York: Oxford University Press, 1977.
22 Whewell, W. *The Elements of Morality*, 4th ed. Cambridge: Bell, 1864.
23 Marriage, morality and sex change surgery: four traditions in case ethics. *Hastings Cent. Rep.*, August 1981.

17

ETHICS, SCIENCE, AND MORAL PHILOSOPHY

Marcus G. Singer

Ethics has been understood and practiced in different ways at different times. Some of these differences are the result merely of changes in fashion, others result from changes in intellectual climate or developments in science or technology, others mark a genuine development in the subject. Our times have seen a number of important changes in the practice and conception of ethics, to the point where some practitioners have come to think of it as capable of developing into a separate and somehow unified discipline, independent of philosophy, and possibly into a science. The question whether ethics is a science, like the question whether philosophy is, has been raised repeatedly in the history of thought, ever since science came to be thought of as providing a paradigm of intellectual or cognitive respectability. There seems good reason now for raising it again. In what follows I delineate some recent changes in ethics and consider anew the question whether ethics is, or ought to be, a science.

Philosophers automatically think of ethics as identical with moral philosophy. But there is a sense of ethics gaining currency in which it is not a branch of philosophy but a new, independent subject, exercising the skills of physicians, psychologists, lawyers, economists, sociologists, scientists and others who would not normally think of themselves as doing philosophy. This does not mean that there will be no more moral philosophy. Far from it. But moral philosophy itself is changing.

In the practice of ethics construed as distinct from moral philosophy the philosophical questions are being begged, but so are they in the various sciences in the interest of getting on with it. And there is a sense of urgency about, for ethical problems are thought of as part and parcel of the problems of medicine, law, science, technology, and the environment – which need to be solved, not discussed for ever and ever with greater and greater refinement of apparatus and technique but with no progress toward a workable solution. This is what is happening, and if it does not happen with philosophers involved in the process, it will happen without them. However, we find that more and more philosophers are becoming involved in this process *as philosophers* and not just as citizens in what many now think of as 'applied ethics.'

Ethics as a branch of philosophy is now not simply identical with ethics as a branch of study, in which are studied problems of conduct and character as they relate to either another branch of study (say medicine or biology) or to a practical discipline (say the practice of medicine or law). Ethics is now coming to be thought of as a branch of many studies or theoretical disciplines, and by some as a unitary (though not a philosophical) discipline intersecting the institutions of law, medicine, science, technology. This is where the change and ferment is occurring.

I RECENT TRENDS

Here are the most important changes that have occurred in ethics recently, some of them still occurring.

1 Moral philosophy is becoming more intertwined with political, social, and legal philosophy, as it was in the period of utilitarian ascendancy in the nineteenth century. Perhaps the most striking change in this respect is the much closer relation to philosophy of law, which has been undergoing its own revival and may by now be established as an autonomous branch of philosophy. One would have to go back to the time of Austin, Bentham, and Kant to find anything similar.

2 The notion of rights is now at the center of ethics. The traditional concepts of ethics have been right and wrong; duty, obligation, and 'ought'; good and bad and evil; value and desirability; moral value and moral worth; virtue, ideals, and virtues; and agency, self, and personality. Rights entered in only through the question of the relation between rights and duties, that is, because

of duties. That duties are more fundamental than rights is still no doubt the standard view amongst moral philosophers, but rights are nonetheless now at the forefront of discussion.

3 A related development of note is an upsurge of interest in *autonomy* and the appearance of works attempting in varying ways to base all of ethics and politics on some conception of autonomy. The notion of autonomy was introduced into ethics by Kant, but I can offhand recall no significant use of the notion in ethics by other than Kantian commentators until very recent years. Now there is a torrent of works by autonomists, so that now one of the basic problems is what autonomy is. The word 'autonomy' had its original home in English in political contexts, where autonomy is the autonomy of states, not of citizens; here curiously enough autonomy is closely allied to sovereignty. In Kant's usage, autonomy is of the will, the rational will, and was contrasted with what he called heteronomy. *Now* autonomy, or so it sometimes seems, can be of anything – as the autonomy of ethics, of aesthetics, of science, of philosophy, as well as of the person – and is, in various writers' hands, a basic right, a basic duty or obligation, a fundamental value, the highest good, a fundamental principle for the reorganization of society, or merely the equivalent of liberty or freedom; and for some advanced thinkers it is the antinomy of sovereignty. It is in any case a word to conjure with.[1]

4 There has been a great revival of applied or practical ethics, and theoretical or pure or abstract ethics is more and more thought of as having value only as it can throw light on the problems of applied ethics. Thus we have on an unprecedented scale studies, programs, workshops, conferences on medical ethics, bioethics, engineering ethics, business ethics, professional ethics. In 1978 a four-volume *Encyclopedia of Bioethics* was published (barely ten years after the term 'bioethics' had been coined). The remarkable growth of bioethics goes along with developments in biology, biotechnology, and genetic engineering, and suggests that there will be a similar development in the ethics of science – physics, chemistry, social science, psychology.

5 There is a growing awareness in the various sciences of the ethical problems connected with scientific research. This is especially notable in research involving human subjects, and it is quite a change from the attitudes of the earlier part of the century to have scientists and psychologists themselves taking the lead in consider-

ing the ethical import of their research. There is also a new field, 'environmental ethics.' Though in some respects this is just another sample of applied ethics, it has as its special point of difference that it does not relate to any one discipline and that it deals with the medium in which all other research goes on.

6 Along with 'applied ethics' goes a renewed interest in what some philosophers would call 'normative ethics,' to distinguish it from 'metaethics,' which had for so long been regarded by so many philosophers as morally or normatively neutral and as the only study of ethics that philosophers could legitimately and philosophically pursue. Indeed, the idea of scientific or philosophical neutrality, for so long taken as an ideal, is now itself regarded with suspicion.

7 There has been a rejuvenation of interest in questions of justice, which for a number of years had been relegated to political and legal philosophy and played little or no role in the discussions influenced by Moore, Ross, and Prichard.[2]

8 There is beginning to be a concern with needs, as distinct from mere desires, wants, and interests. Given the importance of the distinction between needs and wants in everyday moral thinking, it may seem amazing that more attention has not been paid to this concept in ethics, but ethical treatises are relatively free from consideration of it, and it is certainly not wanted, or needed, by utilitarianism.

9 We are seeing a reunion of sorts between ethics and economics, akin to that which existed in the period of classical utilitarianism. Utility theory has been an important branch of economics since Bentham, and has in this century gone its own economic way not disturbed by nor disturbing the course of ethical theory. This is now changing. Such disciplines as game theory and decision theory are attracting the attention of increasing numbers of moral philosophers. The theory of justice and the theory of morality are regarded by some as parts of 'the theory of rational choice.' Thus is the lure of mathematics exercised again on moral philosophers, who find in game and decision theory what seems a congenial and exciting way of applying mathematics to ethics.

10 There is also a renewal of interest in moral psychology, hence a return of sorts to some of the central concerns of eighteenth-century British moral philosophers. Philosophy of mind, as it is now called, is equivalent to older mental philosophy and philosophy of

the passions as discussed by Hume and Reid, and moral psychology plays an essential role in Rawls's *Theory of Justice*. This goes along with a renewal of interest in 'character ethics,' virtues and vices and the nature of persons, and a denigration of such questions as 'What ought I to do?' as the central focus in ethics. [3]

11 Not a development actually *in* ethics, but one with respect to ethics, and of a class that has been with us with periodic waxing and waning since Darwin if not Spencer, is sociobiology, an attempt to apply biological and genetic techniques and theories to the understanding of society. Sociobiology is the latest in a seemingly endless series of attempts to apply science to ethics and in this way answer or dispose of the problems of ethics and make ethics into a science. But sociobiology can also, like bioethics, be accounted a testimony to the tremendous changes occurring in the biological sciences, with their unexampled implications for biotechnology and genetic engineering. If human beings can be produced in the laboratory, then presumably moral agents and persons can, and some therefore wonder whether if biology can change the character of persons it can change the character of morality.

The most important philosophical stimulus for a number of these changes was John Rawls's monumental book *A Theory of Justice*. [4] Rawls's work has provoked discussion not just among philosophers but also among lawyers, legal scholars, political scientists, economists, and social theorists. This is a remarkable phenomenon, which has left its mark on ethics, if not indelibly then certainly for a long time. Not all of the changes listed before, however, can be traced to this work. The great interest in medical ethics developed independently of Rawls's book, and in fact antedated it. The Institute of Society, Ethics and the Life Sciences was organized in 1969, and in doing so answered to concerns that already existed. And events in the country and in the world are responsible for a great many of these renewed interests and concerns. The Civil Rights Movement of the 1960s, the disaster of Vietnam, the standing possibility of nuclear devastation, new attitudes and feelings about sex and marriage and the family, concerns about abortion and Affirmative Action and Preferential Treatment, rebellions against capitalism and 'the Establishment,' demands of ethnic and other minority groups and women for equality of treatment and opportunity, concerns about pollution, overpopulation, the environment, and the effects of technology and industry on health and the very livability of the world in which we live, crises about energy, nuclear power, inflation, and unemployment, increasing crime and increasing barbarism and violence, the ending of legal and even social restrictions on pornography, the sweep through the former colonial worlds of various liberation movements both genuine and so-called, political ferment and ruthless repression in Africa, Asia, and Latin America, continuing and escalating conflicts in the Middle East and renewed turmoil and apparently hopeless strife in Northern Ireland, new concerns and insistent demands about the rights or the 'liberation' of animals, children, patients, handicapped persons, the elderly, and a new penchant for christening any demand as a violated right – all this in a period of unprecedented change in science, technology, politics and international relations, together with instant information provided by television, satellite transmissions, and computer technology, which bring home to people – literally home to them – sudden death, slaughter, barbaric cruelties, institutionalized torture, mass starvations and mass migrations of helpless and homeless refugees, have had people reeling under the impact of all this information of what the world is like and wondering how if at all anything constructive can be done about it and if there is in the end any hope for humanity on this planet. All this and more, along with moralizing on an unprecedented scale, plays a role in the transformation of ethical concerns and interests, and hence of ethics itself.

II IS ETHICS A SCIENCE?

Is ethics, in developing in these ways, a science? Ought it to be? Clearly a distinction is called for between different senses of ethics, between different things and activities that go by that name. A clear and distinct, relevant and usable sense must be attached to the term 'science,' true to science as it is and can be and also capable of rewarding speculation, for it becomes apparent early on that here the appeal to ordinary use is of no use. Our question is not just philosophical but ethical. What I shall argue is that ethics stands for several distinct though related disciplines and activities, and while in some of these sense ethics is not a science and cannot be, in others it either already is or ought to be. The branches of this thesis are these: (1) Ethics in the sense of moral philosophy is not a science but a branch of philosophy. (2) However, ethics in the sense of casuistry, dealing with problems case by case, guided by accepted principles, settled precedents, and agreed-on ends, certainly can be a science, if it is not already, at least to the extent that jurisprudence is. (3) Further, ethics in the sense of the ethics or casuistry of science, operating from accepted principles and agreed-on ends, not only can be a science but ought to be, for there is need for such a discipline to deal with the ethical problems growing out of the practice of science itself. (4) It may be of little moment, except for purposes of funding and prestige, whether ethics in the senses delineated be called a science. Yet the reasons for regarding it as a science are in the end pragmatic and moral, and do not derive from the nature of things.

We can determine nothing to the point from the meaning or use of the term 'science.' It is used too variously, too loosely, and too unsystematically, and its various associations, resembling on occasion nothing more than an emotional afflatus, have too often made of it a treasure to be coveted. One can get any conclusion one wants by utilizing a suitable definition of science, and the word is elastic enough to accommodate this. Thus it does not at all jar with usage to speak of ethics as a science, or of 'ethical science' (on the model, say, of 'political science'), or of 'the science of ethics' (on the model, say, of 'the science of economics' – note the whimsical 'the science of boxing'). But such expressions and such usage constitute only a loose use, a mere way of speaking, in which the word 'science' is used to mean no more than a special study or scholarly discipline or a special technique based on study and practice in which one can acquire expertise. And when the question whether ethics is a science is raised explicitly and specifically we cannot be content with a mere *façon de parler*.

On the other hand, we must also be on our guard against the sort of metaphysical imperialism that denominates the philosophy of some particular school as itself a science because based on science ('Marxism is the only scientific philosophy,' 'Logical empiricism is the only scientific philosophy') and the ethical theory, whatever it is, of that particular ideology as the only scientific ethics because based on or derived from the axioms, the laws, or 'the method' of the science.

If we take our question literally as asking about ethics here and now and in the light of its traditions of over two thousand years, then it seems clear enough that ethics is not a science, since ethics is a branch of philosophy and philosophy is not a science. I take it as *manifest* that philosophy is not a science, in any strict, definite, and distinguishable sense of the term. If philosophy is a science, then what is not?

But this argument that ethics is not a science because it is a branch of philosophy would imply that logic is not a science and hence presents a dilemma. It seems equally manifest that logic is a science. If logic is not a science, then what is? This illustrates the difficulty of trying to decide such questions by philosophical arguments from essences and classifications, and indicates that we must approach the matter more circumspectly.

It *could* be argued that logic in the sense in which it is a science is not (or no longer) a branch of philosophy, any more than mathematics is. From this point of view, it is of no great import that logic continues to be taught and studied and developed in philosophy departments of universities. After all, logic has for some time now also been taught and studied and developed in departments of mathematics; on this count it would equally follow that logic is a branch of mathematics. It is also worth noting that the sense of logic in which it is still properly a branch of philosophy and not an autonomous science now often goes under the name of philosophical logic or philosophy of logic. Before the relatively recent and revolutionary developments resulting in the development of logic as a science such a distinction was not even thought of. But logic itself is now no more properly a branch of philosophy than, say, psychology is, or mathematics itself.

There may be something in this. But it is troublesome, since it ignores the central role of logic in philosophy itself and also ignores the fact that although logic has from the very beginning been regarded as a science, this has not by itself been regarded as a reason for not regarding it as a branch of philosophy. Clearly there is something wrong with the metaphor of 'a branch of.' Why should a subject not itself a science not have a branch that is? At the same time the argument that ethics is a branch of philosophy and hence not a science has at least some force, for ethics is a branch of philosophy in the sense that it is a philosophical discipline – moral philosophy. What we are running into here is the breaking down of departmental and disciplinary boundaries as subjects change and develop. Thus we have logic as both a branch of philosophy and a branch of mathematics, which shows that in logic, philosophy and mathematics meet and there is no clear demarcation between them. The existence of interdisciplinary sciences, such as biophysics, physical chemistry, astrophysics, and ecology, shows the tenuous nature of rigid philosophical definitions of fields and distinctions among them. The sciences are living, growing and developing and cannot be hemmed in or restrained by classificatory schemes, which at best can provide a rough guide to the terrain at a given period and which date very rapidly.

Consider the analogy with psychology. Psychology once was a branch of philosophy and developed into a science and was thence no longer a branch of philosophy. Instead we have as branches of philosophy philosophical psychology, philosophy of psychology, and philosophy of mind. This is but one instance of many. Philosophy through the ages has performed this mothering and nesting function. And for every science that has left the nest there is a philosophical counterpart. This indeed is just why there is an essential yet essentially vague distinction between philosophy and science, and why philosophy or a philosophical subject is not itself a science. For a discipline or mode of inquiry to be a science, it must have a background of accepted results, an accrual of funded knowledge. This is not to say that every science must be equally developed, but only that it must have achieved some success, in fact and not in metaphysical propaganda, so that practitioners can start from an already developed frontier. One who sets out to study a science sets out from where the science is at the particular time, not from the beginning. In philosophy, not only can one always go back to the beginning, but there are always philosophers who are doing so and urging others to do so as well. This is why the history of philosophy plays such an important role in the development and teaching of the subject. The history of science plays no similar role in science, though it does in the philosophy of science.

Now every (or nearly every) science has its philosophical part – its more theoretical, speculative, or methodological part – and the investigators in this theoretical part of the science often are engaged in activities and inquiries that are indistinguishable from those of a philosopher. At the same time we find that philosophy, or rather a particular branch of philosophy, such as logic, philosophy of science, or philosophy of language, can have its more settled, developed, and successful – its more scientific – part and that the practitioners there are often engaged in activities and inquiries indistinguishable from those of a scientist, even to the point of accruing a fund of demonstrated knowledge. We have also found on occasion something like a revolution in science, a revolution of theory or interpretation, resulting from the researches and specula-tions of some philosophical scientist or scientific philosopher. We also find on occasion that some branch of philosophy has become even unto a science, in character and form and activity and success if not in name and departmental autonomy. It becomes apparent, then, why the various attempts that have been made to draw a hard and fast line between philosophy and science have never succeeded. It is because there is none. It also becomes apparent why the various attempts to establish philosophy as a science have been so unsuc-cessful, for there is an ineradicable distinction which such attempts ignore and distort. Philosophy and science are distinct but not wholly distinct. They overlap, and necessarily so.

If the question then is whether there is anything essential to the nature of ethics that prevents it from developing into a science, the answer immediately presents itself: yes and no; it depends. Ethics, as the study of the principles, standards, and methods for distin-guishing right from wrong and good from bad, though a branch of philosophy, nonetheless can have branches capable of developing into a science. Philosophical questions about principles or methods – what they are, their scope and limits, whether there are any, even whether there is any genuine distinction between right and wrong – always will arise, and there is no way of constructing a science for preventing this. No degree of success in the natural sciences has managed to dampen sceptical or philosophical questions about reality and appearance, truth and falsity, certainty and uncertainty, or what knowledge really is, and there is no reason to believe that ethical or normative science would be any more successful at this. But this suggests that, while ethics as a branch of philosophy is not a science, there is a sense of ethics in which it can be. There is nothing essential to the nature of ethics that can prevent such a development from taking place. What we should expect is that scientific ethics would have its philosophical part and that moral philosophy would have its empirical, scientific part, and this in fact we do find.

Consider the sense in which 'ethics' is used to refer not to a branch of study but to a code of conduct. It is in this sense that we use the term when we speak of a given person's ethics or the ethics of a profession or a group. Note that there is a familiar distinction between judging conduct immoral and judging it unethical. The judgment of conduct as ethical or unethical appeals to a code that is felt to depend somehow on the will and agreement of human beings, whereas the judgment of conduct as moral or immoral does not appeal to a code or set of principles felt to be changeable in this way. This is shown by the fact that while it makes sense to say 'That is not unethical, but it ought to be' it does not make sense to say 'That is not immoral, but it ought to be.' This point marks off an important distinction between (i) morality and the principles of morality (the subject of philosophy) and (ii) ethics in the sense of a code of conduct and in the sense of a theoretical discipline dealing with the formulation, application, and revision of the code of conduct. The principles of a code of ethics rest on agreement of some kind and can be changed by agreement or negotiation. The principles of morality (the subject of moral philosophy) are independent of such agreement, and it is a presupposition of moral judgment in the context of moral judgments that these principles would be recognized as such by all reasonable persons with a sense of right and wrong.

Now the members of a certain group, a professional society, say physicians, or scientists, can agree on a set of principles and on the ends they are seeking to achieve by their characteristic activity, and questions arising under this code can be decided by appeal to those principles and those ends. The backlog of decisions, so far as there is record or memory of them, will be precedents containing implicitly the principles on which they were decided. No doubt the principles themselves, perhaps even the agreed-on ends, will alter in the process. This process is one that resembles in the relevant respects that of deciding cases in a legal system. There are recognized and accepted procedures for revising the principles, as there are procedures for accepting them, and further experience in dealing with such problems will generate intelligence in the understanding and application of the code itself.

I can see no reason why this activity of applying the principles of a code to cases arising under them could not be a science. Philosophical considerations will play a role here analogous to the role they play in law and in the established sciences themselves. Furthermore, moral considerations, in the sense delineated before, will obtrude themselves occasionally as they do in law and the established sciences, and the activity of considering the import of these will be extrascientific. Thus the principle occasionally put forward that 'the scientist owes regard first, last, and all the time to the truth alone without regard for consequences' comes to appear doubtful even to its proponents as it becomes clearer what the consequences of this credo are.[5] What becomes clear is that, if it is a hitherto accepted principle in the ethical outlook of scientists, it ought not to be. The exact working out of its limits and of the proper role of the attainment of truth and the growth of knowledge in science then becomes an important and indeed an essential question for ethical-scientific inquiry to deal with. The tracing out of the consequences of such a credo for the course of scientific research and for the world at large is clearly a scientific task. The determination of what principles should govern scientific activity is then a task for the ethics of science, and it is not an activity or an inquiry that can sensibly or morally be divorced from science itself. If it is not already a task for science it ought to be, and, since there is nothing in the nature of science or of ethics or of the world in which we live to prevent it, it can be. This discipline would be at once a branch of philosophy and a branch of science, and, insofar as it is or would be a branch of science, it is or would be a science.

The appropriate analogy here is with medical or clinical ethics. I am not referring here merely to the specific principles of medical ethics adopted, say, by the American Medical Association, nor am I referring specifically to the 'Opinions and Reports of the Judicial Council,' though such opinions provide an instance of the casuistry I have been speaking of, but rather to the discipline of clinical ethics which has developed and has had to develop as an adjunct to clinical practice. As I conceive it, medical or clinical ethics is a branch of medicine, dealing with the ethical-moral problems arising in and out of the practice of medicine as well as those arising about the practice or institution of medicine itself. It is not and ought not to be considered to be a branch of moral philosophy, for its aim is to deal with the problems that arise in the practice of medicine, not the problems that arise in the practice of philosophy, though there will always be much to philosophize about in contemplating and study-ing this activity. Similarly the ethics of science, parallel to medical ethics, which has already begun to develop as an adjunct to science itself, ought to develop as a branch of science, for its aim is to deal with the ethical-moral problems arising in and out of the practice of science and about the practice and consequences of science itself.

293

III: The future of ethics

As Freeman Dyson has put it, 'The best way to approach the ethical problems associated with science is to study real dilemmas faced by real scientists.'[6] The alternative is textbook ethics, in which students are put to studying often ingenious and intricate but still textbook dilemmas faced by textbook scientists, and these will be in every sense of the word unreal. But I do not mean to suggest, in speaking of the ethics of science as a branch of science, that its activities and inquiries are to be carried on solely by scientists and not by philosophers and others as well. Almost by the nature of the case it would be interdisciplinary.

The claim that scientific inquiry is to be allowed to proceed to the solution of its own problems, no matter what the consequences, because knowledge is the sort of thing worth accumulating for its own sake, is a claim that cannot be supported by ethics or philosophy because the growth and maximization of knowledge by itself and without reference to any further or wider consequence is not a self-evident and self-certifying ideal. There are normative limits to scientific research, limits that have only become apparent in recent years – since Hiroshima. The determination of these limits is a task for science itself, of that branch of science I am calling the ethics of science. Research on human subjects is the most prominent example of such research. Recombinant DNA research is the most dramatic and the most mysterious. But the most serious philosophically is so far the least heralded: nuclear reactions in laboratories for experimental purposes. Everyone has heard, especially since Three Mile Island, of the problems and risks connected with the use of nuclear energy for purposes of generating power. But few have thought of the similar problems and risks of generating excess radioactivity and disposing of radioactive wastes connected with nuclear fission in laboratories. If scientific research itself is having an adverse effect on the atmosphere, the environment, the lives of human beings, and if it consequently is having an impact on the survival of life on this planet and therefore of course on the continuation of science itself, than scientific research must be somehow restricted, and the extent and scope of this restriction ought to be determined by science itself, rather than by legislation, court orders, religious taboos, or mob hysteria.

The ethical science I am talking about would be and would have to be a normative science. It is not a matter of describing more exactly what is occurring or predicting more precisely what will,

294

though such information may be vital to any such endeavor, but of laying down norms for determining what may be done, what ought not to be done, and perhaps even what ought to be done. But there is no contradiction in the notion of a normative science, any more than there is in the notion of a normative judgment.

III FUTURE PROSPECTS

Is there one unitary discipline, ethics, somehow involved in these otherwise apparently diverse areas of environment, ecology, science, medicine, biology, engineering, technology, law, government, and business? Or is talk of environmental ethics, medical ethics, and so on merely talk about questions of a certain kind, though one and the same kind, which arise in these diverse areas and undertakings? The question I am raising here is surely one for ethics in the larger sense in which it is a branch of philosophy. It involves among other things the question whether the same rules and principles are involved in making moral judgments in each and all of these diverse areas and undertakings, or whether the rules, principles, and concepts appropriate and applicable in, say, medical ethics are peculiar to it and not transferable without vital shifts in emphasis, meaning, and probative force to environmental ethics, engineering ethics, and so on through the whole vast array. This is not a question that can be answered a priori; it must wait for reasonable settlement until each of these areas has been explored further and until a better grasp is achieved of the underlying structure of ethical or moral problems in each of these areas of human endeavor.

Of all these species of applied ethics, the most developed is medical ethics, or the wider field that has come to be called bioethics. An industry that has grown to such a size in such a short time and has gotten itself politically and economically embedded is unlikely to be just a fad, and the interest in the subject cannot be supposed to be provided by only out-of-work philosophers. There is something in the enterprise itself that attracts and intrigues professionals and practitioners. It is physicians, researchers and scientists themselves who have manifested this interest, for they have come to think that they must pay attention to previously ignored ethical and moral aspects of their work. But this activity is not just in the area of applied ethics, having no effect on philosophy itself. The activities sponsored by the Hastings Center are often indistinguishable in character and quality from the activities of philosophers. One can find articles in its *Reports* on all sorts of philosophical questions having bearings on ethics.

However, there is a danger that needs noticing. One wonders about the audience for all these new journals, five or more in the past decade in medical ethics alone. Is it just those who work in medical ethics, or does it also include practitioners? This concern has been expressed in an editorial in *The New England Journal of Medicine*:

> No one can doubt the importance of publishing philosophic
> reflections on medical practice and research. . . . However,
> what is the purpose of these journals? With whom do they seek
> to communicate? . . . One likes to assume . . . that the ultimate
> purpose of articles discussing the relations of medicine . . . and
> ethics is not only the production of scholarly dissertations but
> also the hope that the medical practitioner or researcher will be
> made more aware of, and responsive to, the philosophic and
> moral problems he increasingly faces today. Yet the more articles
> on philosophic subjects are so written . . . and published, that
> they appeal primarily to a group of subspecialty experts . . . the
> less will they affect the physician who deals with patients . . . [7]

The prediction of practical fruitlessness implicit in this statement may be unfounded, but the concern is not unreasonable. The practical justification for such theoretical activities as these must itself be pragmatic. Will these applied ethics areas have effects on medicine (law, the environment, engineering, and so on), and will the effects be beneficial? In an article in another major medical journal, which may be taken as almost a response to these worries, Dr Mark Siegler claims that 'If clinical ethics . . . can be shown to improve medical care, the resistance to medical ethics will be effectively stifled . . . Medical ethics will become an integrated aspect of professional life . . . when it is no longer artificially divorced from the practice of medicine itself.'[8]

The moral is that these applied ethics fields must be integrated into the areas to which they are applied. Dr Siegler takes it for granted that 'clinical ethics . . . can . . . improve medical care' and that this 'can be shown,' and the implicit assumption of all this activity in applied ethics areas is that they will improve medicine, law, engineering, government, the environment, and life on earth. But this of course is the historic mission of ethics.

NOTES

* This paper is an amalgamation, with some modification and interpolations, of portions (but not the whole) of two previously published papers: 'Recent Trends and Future Prospects in Ethics,' *Metaphilosophy*, vol. 12, 1981; and 'Is Ethics a Science? Ought it to Be?', *Zygon*, vol. 15, 1980.

1 The present writer has had an opportunity to pay his respects to this vogue notion in 'Reconstructing the Groundwork,' *Ethics*, vol. 93, 1983, pp. 566–78.

2 G.E. Moore, *Principia Ethica* (Cambridge University Press, 1903); W.D. Ross, *The Right and the Good* (Oxford: Clarendon Press, 1930); H. A. Prichard, *Moral Obligation* (Oxford: Clarendon Press, 1949); and E.F. Carritt, *The Theory of Morals* (Oxford University Press, 1928) are representative and excellent examples of this tradition.

3 John Laird, 'Act-Ethics and Agent-Ethics,' *Mind*, vol. 55 (1946), pp. 114-42, is a forerunner of this recent revival. A more recent work worth remarking on here is A.I. Melden's *Right and Persons* (Berkeley: University of California Press, 1977), a work in the vanguard of a new and different approach in moral philosophy (though only new and different in relation to the dominant tendencies of the past century or so), which would deemphasize the importance of considering what one ought to do, what Edmund Pincoffs, with malice and foresight aforethought, termed 'Quandary Ethics' (*Mind*, vol. 80, 1971). Melden insists on the importance of rights for understanding the moral relations of persons and vice-versa, and how rights must be adequately understood if we are to have an adequate understanding of moral reasoning. Others, such as Philippa Foot, insist that 'a sound moral philosophy start from a theory of the virtues and vices' (*Virtues and Vices* (Berkeley: University of California Press, 1978), p.xi).

4 John Rawls, *A Theory of Justice* (Cambridge, Mass: Harvard University Press, 1971). Cf. Brian Barry, *The Liberal Theory of Justice* (Oxford: Clarendon Press, 1973), R.P. Wolff, *Understanding Rawls* (Princeton University Press, 1977), Norman Daniels (ed.), *Reading Rawls* (New York: Basic Books, n.d.), H. Gene Blocker and Elizabeth H. Smith (eds), *John Rawls's Theory of Social Justice* (Athens, Ohio: Ohio University Press, 1980); also the present writer's 'The Methods of Justice: Reflections on Rawls,' *The Journal of Value Inquiry*, vol. x,

1976, and 'Justice, Theory, and a Theory of Justice,' *Philosophy of Science*, vol. 44, 1977.

5 I quote this as it was stated by R.B. Lindsay, who for other purposes formulated it without recommending it in 'The Survival of Physical Science,' *The Scientic Monthly* LXXIV, 3, March 1952, pp. 140-1.

6 Freeman Dyson, 'Disturbing the Universe,' *The New Yorker*, August 6, 1979, p. 38.

7 F.J. Ingelfinger, 'Specialty Journals in Philosophy and Ethics,' *The New England Journal of Medicine*, vol. 295, December 2, 1976, pp. 1317-18.

8 Mark Siegler, 'A Legacy of Osler: Teaching Clinical Ethics at the Bedside,' *Journal of the American Medical Association*, vol. 239, March 6, 1978, p. 953.

18

MORAL PHILOSOPHY AND THE FUTURE

William K. Frankena

This essay is a somewhat programmatic review of contemporary moral philosophy in relation to the future moral standard of our society. The occasion for writing it is the recent widespread concern about our moral standards, that is, about the general moral norms, principles, rules, or values governing (or not governing) our behavior, and about the way our moral education should go. My conviction is that recent moral philosophers have had a good deal to say that is relevant to these concerns, not just when they have been writing about practical moral problems as they have been doing more and more, but even when they have been writing books of ethical theory. My aim is to explain something of what this is and to make some comments about it.

I

Most moral philosophers have presented us with constructive pictures of morality and, by implication at least, of moral education. They have advocated a thorough use of reflection and critical thinking and have been convinced of the necessity and possibility of discovering moral standards that are in some sense rationally justifiable. This is especially true of recent British and American moral philosophy, which I shall mainly have in mind in what follows. Even earlier, however, philosophers characteristically looked for something that could reasonably be taken as basic in morality – some principle, end, virtue, method, 'original position,' or point of view, by reference to which it can be determined, either directly or indirectly, what it is morally right, rational or good to do or be. They have looked for a rational method – let us say *the* Method – to use in moral reasoning and judging. Moreover, at least recently in Britain and America, they have generally given up any belief that it can begin with or uncover moral knowledge that is either innate (in reason or conscience), self-evident or otherwise a priori – let alone revealed. It is true, as we shall see, that they have different conceptions of what the Method is and of the way in which it is to be applied – e.g. some are act-utilitarians, some are rule or principle utilitarians, and some are non-utilitarians – and also that many of them are non-methodological relativists, believing that, while there is, indeed, a rational Method for answering ethical questions, it is not such as enables us always to decide between conflicting views. Still, they agree that there is such a Method.

Such Methods obviously must be described in abstract and general terms and my review of them must likewise be rather abstract and general; I hope, however, that it will be intelligible, without being too schematic to be helpful. In reviewing them, part of my purpose will be to bring out the conceptions of moral education they seem to imply, since, as Michael Oakeshott points out,

> Every form of the moral life . . . depends upon education. And the character of each form is reflected in the kind of education required to nurture and maintain it. [1]

Today, some of these Methods still take as basic some substantive End or Principle, e.g. the general welfare, the amelioration of the human predicament, respect for persons, the law of love, or the principle of utility. Most of them, however, involve the idea of a basic 'original position' or 'moral point of view' by the taking of which the more substantive goals, principles, practices, and judgments of morality are to be arrived at and certified. In one way or another Kurt Baier, R.B. Brandt, J.N. Findlay, R. Firth, R.M. Hare, John Rawls, P.W. Taylor, and myself, espouse Methods of this type. These are of three main sorts: (a) benevolent or impartial spectator theories, (b) rational contractor or 'social contract' theories, and (c) universal prescriptivist theories. The main difference between the three sorts lies in the way in which they define or characterize the original position or moral point of view, and theories of each sort may also describe this in somewhat different ways, e.g. some theories of the first kind say that the spectator in question is to be benevolent, others that he or she is to be impartial.

Obviously, for each view of the nature of the Method, there will be a related view of moral education, since, if there is such a Method, it must be a primary aim of moral education to teach all or some of us this Method and to foster in all of us a disposition to live by its conclusions. The ends and means of moral education may overlap or be similar for different Methods, but they will also differ in certain respects. However, what mainly interests me here is another point, namely, that whatever the Method may be (or almost whatever), it may still be applied in rather diverse ways, and that much the same options about this are open under each method. Most of them have been advocated by some recent moral philosopher or other, and each of them has implications for moral education. These options and their educational implications I shall now review, I fear rather sketchily.

II

Suppose that we are convinced that a certain Method is the one to use in an examined morality. Then the first question is whether we should regard this Method as a method for *individuals*, i.e. as the method by which an individual is to determine how he should act; as a method for *institutions*, i.e. as the method by which society is to determine what social institutions it should have or set up, including perhaps a socially sanctioned moral code (a 'positive social morality' or PSM), the understanding being that individuals are to guide themselves, not by using the Method, but by the rules of these institutions; or *both* as a method for individuals and as a method for institutions. The second question, if we hold that our Method is for individuals, is whether it is to be used *directly* to determine what one should do in a particular situation, as it is e.g., in act-agapism or act-utilitarianism, or *indirectly*, i.e. whether or not it is to be used to find what I shall call Gens (standards, principles, norms, rules, etc.) like 'Treat people equally' or 'Do not lie,' by which one is then to determine what one should do in concrete cases. If a Method is to be used indirectly in this way, then moral reasoning is a two-storey affair, as, e.g. in rule-utilitarianism, otherwise it is a single -storey business. If a Method is to be taken as a method for institutions, then morality necessarily involves two storeys, since institutions consist of Gens of a certain kind (i.e. rules), but the storeys will be of a somewhat different sort. I shall, however, present the different types of answers to these two questions as if they formed a single spectrum.

At one end of this spectrum is an extreme form of what I shall call Actarianism. It is one of the many kinds of things so confusingly and confusedly called 'situation ethics' (some of which are not ethics at all); but there is an even more extreme kind of situation ethics that denies there is any such Method as we are talking about, insisting that morality is or should be a matter of wholly unguided personal decision or intuition in particular cases. The present theory holds that there is a Method to guide particular judgments, and that it is a method for individuals, but it is like the more extreme view in holding also that no Gens, not even rules of thumb, are to intervene between the Method and the particular judgment, nothing is to intervene except the relevant facts relating to the case. Some of these facts may be general, but at any rate no intermediate *moral* Gen is to play a part in moral reasoning and deliberation, only the Method and the facts. Among the facts, of course, may be facts about the rules and institutions obtaining in one's society, perhaps even facts about a prevailing moral code consisting of Gens, and these facts may have to be taken into consideration along with others, but, even so, the Gens, Rules, etc., are not themselves to be used directly as bases for determining what to do.

This view may be taken by an act-agapist or act-utilitarian who is willing to be that situational. For it, a Method is a method for individuals to be used only to reach particular conclusions and to do so directly. An action is right in a situation if and only if it is dictated directly by the Method plus the relevant facts, and an action is to be *judged* right only if it is seen as being so dictated. The view may, however, take two forms, both of which represent interesting options. According to the first, morality is a purely personal matter; one is not to praise, blame, or otherwise apply moral sanctions (as distinct from legal ones) to the actions of others. 'Judge not, that ye be not judged.' Many so-called 'new morality' spokespersons seem to hold this position. On the other form of the view, acts of praising or blaming others, etc., are permissible, but one must *each time* decide whether or not to engage in such an act by looking to see if doing so is itself dictated by the Method plus the facts. One must distinguish between the rightness of an action and the rightness of praising or blaming it (or of otherwise punishing or rewarding it) but in both cases the rightness is to be determined by a direct application of the Method in each particular situation; no Gens are to intervene in either case, not even rules of thumb.

It is important to notice here that, on the second form of this rather extreme Actarian view, it might sometimes be right to praise or sanction action in accordance with a certain rule or Gen, even if this is stronger than a rule of thumb – e.g. a law or a social rule – or even to advocate such a rule or Gen, provided, of course, that in each case the act of praising, sanctioning, or advocating is itself directly dictated by the Method and the facts. Even on this view, then, it would be possible for individuals to support a system of laws or a PSM, though only in those particular situations in which an act of doing so is required by the Method espoused. An action would, however, never *be* morally right because it is required by the law or the moral code, but only because it is called for, or at least permitted, by the Method. It should not even be *judged* to be right simply because it is required or permitted by the law or social code.

As for moral education – it would on both forms of this theory consist in teaching the Method and a disposition to act according to its conclusions together with a disposition to get the facts straight about the situations one is faced with. This is true because, although such a view may allow one individual to address a Gen to another because doing so is called for by the method, it cannot allow any individual to determine what he or she should do simply by appealing to a Gen (other than the Method itself).

It is, however, hard to see how morality and moral education can do without moral Gens in this way, and, in fact, the view just described is too extreme even for Joseph Fletcher: he calls it antinomianism as distinct from situationalism, which for him admits rules of thumb or 'maxims' into the application of the law of love. [2] It is even harder to see how, in its second version, one can refrain from using the words 'morally right' and 'morally wrong' in any of the Gens one may, perhaps correctly, regard it as right to advocate, sanction, or teach, as the theory requires one to do. Rather more plausible, then, is a somewhat less extreme view, also Actarian, one which allows us to formulate and act on Gens of a certain sort, viz. rules of thumb, maxims, or what Rawls has called 'summary rules.' It also allows us to teach such Gens to others, especially to the young, for use when time is short or when ignorance of fact is not remediable. These Gens would be built up by inductive generalization from previous cases in which the Method has declared a certain action to be right or wrong; they would in effect say that, in situations of a certain sort, the Method has judged that one should or should not do so-and-so and probably will so judge next time.[3] Notice that, on this more modified form of Actarianism, an action will still *be* right if and only if it is required or at least permitted by the Method in the light of the facts, but it may sometimes be *judged* to be right or rather probably right, even when it is not itself seen as called for or permitted by the Method. An action may also be overtly *said* to be right, even when it *is* not (and is judged not to be), if the act of saying so is called for by the Method on that occasion (or is suggested by a rule of thumb based on previous use of the Method). For on this kind of view, lying (or whatever) may sometimes be right, if found so by use of the Method; a rule of not lying can have only the force of a rule of thumb, even if it is sometimes right to treat it as if it were stronger. An action or its agent may, however, be judged to be *good*, whether it is right or not, if it is motivated by moral concern – and may be *said* to be good if saying so is right, whether the act or agent is actually good or not.

III

Just as in moral theology there has been much criticism of Fletcher and situation ethics, so in philosophy there has been much criticism of these extreme actarian Methods, usually in the form of attacks on act-utilitarianism. Often the critics accept the basic Method (e.g. the principle of utility, or the law of love), but disagree with this kind of theory about how it is to be applied. One thing that troubles them, of course, is the point just mentioned about lying. More generally, there is a conviction, not only that Gens are needed in the moral regulation of conduct and in moral education, but also that rules of thumb are not strong enough to do the job. It is not just that time is often too short for the Method to be applied directly; there is also the fact that not following a rule of thumb can hardly generate feelings of compunction, the fact that people are often under stress or temptation, the fact that they are often ignorant, stupid, or careless and irresponsible in their thinking, and the fact that, even when they are not, their thinking may go awry because of bias or self deception, often unconscious, due to desire or self-interest. These facts lead many, myself included, to doubt the wisdom of views that leave an individual's judgments and decisions so entirely to his own application of a Method in each situation he is in, and to look for a form of morality in which there are Gens about what is right or wrong, which are stronger than rules of thumb and taught and perhaps even sanctioned as such, whether regarded as absolute or not.

Even if we take this anti-situationalist position, however, a number of options are still open to us. We have a choice between taking our Method, whatever it is, as a method for individuals and taking it as a method for institutions. We must also decide between the view that an action is right and only if it is itself dictated by our Method plus the relevant facts, and the view that it is right if or because it is required by our intermediate Gens. And we must decide whether morality is or should be a purely personal business *or* take, at least in part, the form of a socially sanctioned moral code or PSM. There is also the question whether intermediate Gens should be regarded as absolute or as prima facie in W. D. Ross's sense (though still more stringent than rules of thumb), but I shall leave it to one side except for one or two references. Depending on how we answer these questions, we will be espousing one or another of the following theories.

At the opposite end of our spectrum from the theories discussed here in section III there are or may be a family of interesting views, which must be described here, though they are not very widely held today. For them morality is not a personal business at all; it is a matter of social codes and institutions. They are not only Genarian as versus Actarian,[4] they are social and institutional in a special sense. For them an action is right if and only if it conforms to the moral code and moral institutions of the society in question. They hold, however, that there is a single Method which in some sense underlies the evolution and variation of social codes and institutions. They even believe that the evolution of these codes and institutions involves a kind of reflective application of this method but they think of this reflection mainly as an activity of something like a general, social, or universal mind, and as being largely implicit and unconscious, at least until it is made explicit by some philosopher appearing rather late in the process; it may on occasion

305

peak in the thinking and activity of some reformer serving as its instrument, but in general it is not of the conscious, individualistic sort usually favored by philosophers. The views of Hegel and his followers come readily to mind as examples; today the position of W.H. Walsh at least approximates to being a theory of this type.[5] But what is sometimes now called actual-rule-utilitarianism must also be listed here; it holds that individuals should conform to the institutions of society but believes that these tend to arise and change as they are seen by society to be or not to be conducive to the general welfare (Hegel thought they arise and change as they are seen by universal mind to be or not to be conducive to freedom or self-realization).

As for the moral education of the young, it will on such views consist largely in the teaching and internalization of the Gens incorporated in social codes and institutions. There will not be explicit teaching of the Method, for individuals are not to use it to guide their actions, since they are to be guided by existing codes and institutions, nor are individuals given much room for themselves to use the Method to criticize and change these codes and institutions. They need not even spend much time trying to think out a blueprint for a reform of moral education, as I am proposing we do, since this is presumably taken care of by the ruminations of the social or universal mind. In practice, then, these last theories are very much like those who propose that we do nothing about 'the present crisis' or at most work harder to pass on our present social norms – except that some of them tell us what the process is all about when it is effectively over, while others believe that a revolution may on occasion be called for by the dialectic of history. But I am here assuming that such views are mistaken.

IV

More common in British and American philosophy at present is a type of theory that is also genarian and, in a sense, institutional, but much more individualistic. The nicest example is a certain kind of ideal-rule-utilitarianism, perhaps best expounded by R. B. Brandt.[6] It takes the Method to be a method for determining what moral code and moral institutions a society should have, and contends that an action is right if and only if it conforms to the Gens that would be institutionalized in those codes and institutions. However, unlike the Hegelian theory, it gives to the individual the job of using the Method to decide on the ideal set of rules for society to have (teach, sanction, etc), with the understanding that *this* is what he is to live and judge by in practice (and not by a direct application of the Method in each situation), and that he is to do his bit to make it the code of his society – until he sees reason to revise it. The reflection involved is more conscious and individual than on the Hegelian view, but its function is also to work out and realize a set of social rules and institutions, not to determine directly what one should do in particular cases. Like the Hegelian theory this one takes the idea of a PSM as central, but it does not tell the individual to live by the prevailing one, or even to live by it except where he or she can 'persuade' it to change (as Socrates held in the *Crito*), but rather to think out an ideal PSM and act according to it, while also acting to persuade his or her society to adopt it, applying sanctions in accordance with it, etc.

To my mind, this is the most satisfactory of the conceptions of morality so far reviewed. It says, roughly, that one should judge and act on the moral code which, using the Method (e.g. the principle of utility or some other method), one perceives as ideal for one's society. Moral education will, then, have two aspects: one, the teaching of the Method to everyone, at least to those capable of grasping it and living by its conclusions, the other, the teaching of a code of moral rules seen as ideal through a use of the Method, plus a disposition to act according to them, feel compunction on violating them, disapprove of others' violating them, etc. There are, however, still other views to look at. They are of rather different sorts but we may think of them as occupying the middle portion of our spectrum, between the theories just discussed and the rather extreme actarian ones reviewed earlier. Some of them take the Method to be a method for individuals, but they insist that morality must or should involve Gens that are stronger than rules of thumb, and that we are normally to act according to these Gens, rather than applying the Method directly. At the same time they maintain that the Gens must somehow be themselves justified by appeal to the Method, though not necessarily in the way rules of thumb are. The Gens one should normally act on are not necessarily those that prevail in society; they are, rather, those generated by an appeal to the Method in conjunction with the facts. But some of these theories hold that these Gens should be given the form of social rules (a PSM) while others do not, arguing that morality is a personal affair, and some of them allow that sometimes an individual may or must apply the Method directly in order to determine what to do. All of them agree that one may often judge an action to be right or wrong by reference to some set of intermediate Gens and act accordingly; what they differ about is whether these Gens should be incorporated in a PSM, and especially whether an action *is* right if and only if it conforms to them. As for *saying* that it is right when it is not and is not judged to be right, most proponents of these views would regard this as violating a Gen telling us that lying is wrong.

One of them is best illustrated by the more recent works of R. M. Hare, though it need not be so utilitarian as he seems inclined to be. [8] As a result of a difficult piece of argument, which I shall not try to recount (and do not find convincing), Hare thinks of the Method as equivalent to a kind of act-utilitarian reasoning that issues in particular moral judgments (or rather, since he holds these must be universalizable, in principles of unlimited specificity about what to do in a certain situation), and he maintains, as I understand him, that an action is right if and only if it is dictated by correct act-utilitarian thinking, whether it conforms to any of our usual moral Gens or not. This distinguishes his position from that of rule-utilitarians like Brandt, with whom Hare otherwise largely agrees, and makes Hare an actarian in my sense rather than a genarian. However, he also contends, for such reasons as were indicated earlier, that morality cannot be simply a matter of everyone's trying to apply the Method directly; we must try to generate, teach, and sanction a set of standards of limited specificity, such as we usually think of in morality. And normally we should simply live by these Gens, rather than try to apply the Method, though there may be occasions when we must resort to it, e.g. in new or in conflict situations, so that we must, if possible, have a grasp of the Method and an ability to use it. This set of Gens may not coincide with the prevailing ones, but they should be given the form of a socially-sanctioned moral code, insofar at least as this is necessary and as we can agree about the Gens to be included. The Gens must, however, be selected and tested by the Method, i.e., for Hare, by act-utilitarian (not rule-utilitarian) reasoning; they must be those whose general acceptance in our lives will lead to the nearest possible approximation to the prescriptions of correct act-utilitarian thinking, since an action *is* right if and only if it is prescribed by the Method directly, i.e. by such thinking.

This is an actarian view, but one that entails a belief that morality should include a PSM and not be a purely personal matter, at least not while human beings are as they now are. As Hare thinks of it, it involves a kind of 'double intellectual life' or two levels of moral thinking: Level I thinking, which is pretty much a matter of applying the rules one has been taught or taught one-self, feels compunction about violating, etc., and Level II thinking, which is a direct use of the Method (however this is conceived), and is to be used in selecting, testing, and revising these rules, in cases for which one has as yet no rules, and perhaps in a 'cool hour,' when one has the time and the necessary factual knowledge and is not under stress or in danger of error or self-deception. The task of moral education on such a view is to dispose and equip one – or everyone capable of it – for leading such a two-level moral life.

A very different kind of conception of morality is best illustrated by the view put forward not long ago by G. J. Warnock.[8] This is a genarian but non-institutional conception. Like rule-utilitarianism, it says not only that an action may be *judged* right if it conforms to certain Gens, but that it is right if and only if it conforms to them. Like rule-utilitarianism too, it holds that these Gens must be justified by appeal to the Method, i.e., for Warnock, by a consideration of what is needed for 'the amelioration of the human predicament.' However, the view rejects the idea that morality should take the form of a positive social code of rules supported by moral sanctions, etc.; it thinks of its intermediate Gens, not as quasi-legal rules, but as simply 'moral views' or 'principles,' though not as mere rules of thumb. In this sense, it regards morality as a personal affair of accepting and acting on one or more (Warnock thinks four) principles. These principles, however, are thought of as established by a procedure analogous to that of rule-utilitarianism, not, as in Hare's scheme, to that of act-utilitarianism. Moral education, then, will not involve the use of rules and social sanctions, but the fostering of a concern for the amelioration of the human predicament (or whatever, depending on how the Method is conceived) and a kind of instruction in the use of certain Gens thought of as justified by the Method and hopefully actually so justifiable. As it were, on this view, morality and moral education are conceived in liberty and dedicated to the proposition that they should ameliorate the human predicament (or whatever).

Actarians will object that, like rule-utilitarianism, such a view entails a species of 'rule-worship,' or rather, Gen-worship, since it takes the right to be determined by certain Gens, rather than by a direct application of a Method to a particular situation. It seems to me, however, to be very nearly a vision of what morality ideally ought to be like, though I have doubts about Warnock's form of this vision. What troubles me about it is a conviction that a realistic morality and moral education, while not consisting entirely of a PSM, must include such an institutionalized and/or socially sanctioned system of rules along, perhaps, with other sorts of standards, ideals, or 'values' – given such facts about human nature as were mentioned before. I think, therefore, that we must in practice choose between Brandt's type of view and Hare's though not necessarily in their utilitarian versions – unless some combination theory is more satisfactory.

V

I have been discussing rather pure types of theories about the Method and its application. It is, however, possible to complicate them in various ways, and it may be that such more complex theories are more adequate than any of the pure theories. One such theory was presented years ago by H.L.A. Hart, P.F. Strawson, and J. O. Urmson;[9] according to them morality is or should be partly a matter of positive social morality and partly a matter of personal ideals, moral views, or principles. For them both parts of morality involve intermediate Gens that are not mere rules of thumb, but perhaps one could think of one part in genarian and of the other in actarian or situational ones. The most widely discussed recent combination theory, however, is that of John Rawls and D.A.J. Richards.[10] This adopts a rational contractor (or hypothetical social contract) conception of the original position and hence of the Method, and maintains that this Method is to be used to decide on principles, not to determine directly what is right in a particular situation (which is rather to be determined by reference to the principles), and that it is to be used to decide both on principles for individuals and principles for institutions. It is therefore a genarian theory, but more complex than the previous ones. It could be that the principle of utility would be chosen by such rational contractors, both for individuals and for institutions, but the proponents of this theory argue that in fact it would not, and they see their Method as an alternative to the utilitarianism so widely adopted by other recent American and British moral philosophers. In any case, they hold that the right action is the action that conforms to the principles such social contractors would agree to in the original position. They might also claim, though I am not sure they would, that such contractors would set up a PSM; at least they could argue that this is one of the institutions such contractors would devise or that, once chosen, principles for individuals or some of their corollaries should be embodied in positive social rules reinforced by internal and external moral sanctions. If so, then a PSM would figure in moral education, otherwise, not; in any case, moral education would presumably include (a) getting across the idea of taking a certain original position and of choosing Gens from this position; (b) teaching certain Gens as those one would choose from this position; and (c) fostering the dispositions needed to motivate one to live accordingly, e.g. a sense of justice.

In my opinion, some such complex non-utilitarian theory, one which favors having a PSM, is the line we should take. With this comment I conclude my rather sketchy review of recent theories of morality and moral standards. My purpose has been to exhibit them as offering alternatives we might take in answering the question what we should do about the present situation with respect to moral standards, or as alternatives for reconceiving the moral education of society. I hope to have shown that recent British and American moral philosophy has much to say that is interesting and constructive from this point of view.

VI

So far I have been classifying and describing the main views prevailing in British and American moral philosophy about the Method of ethics, as well as about certain very abstract and general questions concerning its application, together with their implications for the theory of moral education. My chief point has been that, for a given view about the Method of ethics, there may be and have been very different conceptions of its use. I have also done something to indicate which of these views and conceptions seem most plausible to me. Now I would like to add a section about the application of a Method to other practical moral problems besides that of moral education. In doing so I shall continue in a very general and abstract vein, but I hope that this will nevertheless be of some use to those who are thinking about the ethics of business, law, medicine, or the treatment of the environment.

One of my reasons for doing this is that I believe a study of such practical issues as those of medical or bio-ethics may help one to choose between the views sketched above. One cannot or should not decide finally for or against a certain view of the Method of ethics and its applications, e.g. act-utilitarianism, without a careful consideration of its implications for the resolution of such practical issues. In this sense, methods are to be tested, not only by theoretical consideration, but by their practical consequences. At the same time, however, I doubt that one should try to resolve practical issues in entire isolation from any consideration of such theoretical questions as are involved in the choice between the views about Method that have been sketched. If a view about Method must be tested by its practical consequences, so must an answer to practical questions also be tested by its relation to a theoretically defensible conception of Method. Too many writers on contemporary moral problems forget this, even philosophical ones. Ideally, one should work on abstract general theory and practical issues in a reciprocal way, as, for example, Brandt and Hare have been doing.

To go on, I must refer back to what I said in the first paragraph of section II. There I stated that, if one is inclined to accept a certain view about the Method of ethics, then the next question is whether one should regard it as a method for individuals to use in determining what they should or should not be or do, as a method for society to use in determining what institutions to have and how to shape them, *or* as *both* a method for individuals and a method for institutions. Let me now say something more about this question. Historically, most moral philosophers have held that the answer to our question is *both*. Plato and Aristotle, for example, explicitly united ethics and politics. Some important twentieth-century moral philosophers, however, have seemed to limit ethics to the question of what an individual should do, thus by implication apparently committing themselves to the view that the method of ethics, whatever it is, is to be taken only as a method by which individuals are to determine what they morally should be or do, e.g. G. E. Moore and W. D. Ross.

There is, however, a third answer to our question, as I indicated earlier – that the Method is not to be used directly by an individual to determine what he or she should do but only by society to determine what its institutions should be, the individual then determining what she or he should do only by consulting the rules of the institutions thus set up. On this view the *direct* application of a Method consists entirely of using it to determine what the rules that constitute our social institutions should be, not at all in using it to determine what one should do. How would this work out?

One of the institutions normally present in a society is that of the law, human civil law. Let us suppose, as against the anarchists, that the existence of a legal system can be justified by use of the Method. Then one further application of it would consist of using it to determine what the laws should be, what they should forbid, permit, and require, e.g. whether they should forbid, permit, or require abortion, and if so under what circumstances. This is one of the questions involved in our contemporary debates, and it should be noticed that it is not directly a question of what an individual should or should not do but of what our laws should be.

On the view being described, however, morality is itself a social institution, like law in many respects but also different. Each society has a more or less prevailing moral code or 'moral value system,' not the same as its code of etiquette. Locke called this its 'law of opinion or reputation,' more recent writers call it a 'positive social morality.' It is an informal quasi-legal code of rules, precepts, and ideals that is taught by the society and supported by non-legal sanctions like praise and blame, so that its members come to judge themselves and others in terms of it. One's conscience may be more, but it is at least an internalized social morality of this sort, secular or religious. Now, just as one may question the morality of a law or a legal system, one may also ask about the morality of the moral code of one's society; both sorts of questions have been raised in connection with racial and sexual discrimination and the treatment of animals, not to mention abortion again. Some new moralists and social reformers have even asked whether a society should have, or has a right to have, such a PSM at all; but at least there is the question what it should incorporate, what it should require, prohibit, or permit, what rights and duties it should recognize, what virtues it should foster. In fact, perhaps our contemporary discussions in bio-ethics and elsewhere should be viewed in part as attempts to reach a better consensus about what should go into our social morality and what should not. Answering such questions, then, constitutes a second kind of application of a Method, but again it should be noticed that such questions are not directly about what individuals should do or not do but about what our positive social morality should be, i.e. about what kind of conduct we should praise and blame, esteem or disesteem, or support by moral rather than legal sanctions. As, in the case of law, an individual will not know what to do or not do until legal rules have been laid down, so in morality, for the view in question, an individual will not know what to do or not do until moral rules have been formulated.

Law and a PSM are not, however, the only institutions a society may have; others are the family, the professions or vocations, private property, etc. These instutions also involve rules, and, while some of these will overlap with those of law or social morality, not all of them will; some will be specific to the institution, e.g. the rules of a book club or of a craft guild. Thus a third kind of application of a Method will be the question of what institutions a society should have besides law and a PSM, and what the rules of such additional institutions should be.

On the view in question, then, a Method of ethics is to be used directly only to answer the three sets of questions indicated; it is not to be used straight out by an individual to determine what he or she should do. However, the view does provide an individual with an answer to this question also; one is to do or be only what is required or permitted by the rules of the institutions that are approved by the Method. In this sense, the application of a Method is two-storeyed in the way indicated earlier. The view may be thought of as falling between those I ascribed to Hegel and to Brandt, less conservative than the former, and less individualistic than the latter.

To my mind it seems clear that a Method of ethics should be used in these three ways; i.e. as a basis for designing, assessing, and criticizing our institutions in moral terms. Like most moral philosophers, however, I keep the feeling that a moral theory should allow room for an individual to use the Method directly in determining what he or she morally should do or be. In other words, I believe that a Method should be regarded as both a method for institutions and for individuals. It seems to me that the question what an individual morally ought to do or not do is not just the same question as what the law, a PSM, and other institutions should require, forbid, or permit; it may be, it seems to me, that a person morally ought to do something that should not be required of her or him by law, by the moral code of one's society, or by the rules of any social institution. I believe, in other words, that morality is not just one social institution among others; it is also (a) a basis for making judgments about social institutions and (b) a basis for judging directly what persons should or should not be or do.

I also believe, though I cannot argue this here, that a society should have institutions of the three kinds referred to: law, a PSM, and others. If this and what I have just said is correct, then there are four kinds of practical questions that a Method of ethics may and should be used to answer:

1 What should our laws require, forbid, or permit?
2 What should our PSM require, forbid, permit, encourage, etc.?
3 What should be the rules and ideals of other social institutions?
4 What morally ought or ought not an individual to do or be?

Questions of all these kinds appear in contemporary discussions in bio-ethics and other areas, often without being distinguished clearly or at all, but they are different and the differences ought to be kept in mind. It may be that they should be differently answered, at least at some point. The law should not enforce all promises, even though breaking promises is morally wrong; perhaps the same thing is true of social morality. Maybe both law and social morality should permit abortions in certain cases even if it is wrong to have or perform an abortion in such cases. Some moral matters should perhaps be left to an individual and his or her conscience or God.

NOTES

1 M. Oakeshott, *Rationalism in Politics* (London: Methuen, 1962), p.62.
2 J. Fletcher, *Situation Ethics* (Philadelphia: The Westminster Press, 1966), pp. 1–39.
3 For an earlier view that holds approximately this, see Adam Smith, *The*

III: The future of ethics

Theory of Moral Sentiments, 1759, Part III, Chapters II, III.

4 On an actarian view what is right or wrong in a particular situation is to be determined by an individual by a direct use of the Method (itself a kind of Gen), e.g. by the principle of utility. On a genarian view, this is not so; what is right or wrong is to be determined, at least sometimes, by reference to Gens of Limited specificity that are stronger than rules of thumb but are determined by a use of the Method.

5 See W. H. Walsh, *Hegelian Ethics* (New York: St Martin's Press, 1969), pp. 17, 77. For present purposes I include Marxists among Hegel's followers, as well as Walsh.

6 See e.g. 'Toward a Credible Form of Utilitarianism,' in *Morality and the Language of Conduct*, H.N. Castaneda and G. Nakhnikian (eds), (Detroit: Wayne State University Press, 1963), pp. 107–43; also *A Theory of the Good and the Right* (Oxford: Clarendon Press, 1979).

7 See especially, 'Principles,' *Proc. Aristotelian Society* 72 (1972-73), pp. 1-18; 'Ethical Theory and Utilitarianism,' in *Contemporary British Philosophy*, Fourth Series (London: Allen & Unwin, 1976), pp. 113-31; also *Moral Thinking* (Oxford: Clarendon Press, 1981).

8 See *The Object of Morality* (London: Methuen, 1971).

9 See H.L.A. Hart, *The Concept of Law* (Oxford: Clarendon Press, 1961); P.F. Strawson, 'Social Morality and Individual Ideal,' *Philosophy* XXXVI (1961), pp. 1-17; J. O. Urmson, 'Saints and Heroes,' in *Essays in Moral Philosophy*, A. I. Melden (ed.) (Seattle: University of Washington Press, 1958), pp. 198-216.

10 See John Rawls, *A Theory of Justice* (Cambridge, Mass.: Harvard University Press, 1971); D. A. J. Richards, *A Theory of Reasons for Actions* (Oxford: Clarendon Press, 1971).

19

ETHICAL THEORY AND MORAL PRACTICE: ON THE TERMS OF THEIR RELATION*

Abraham Edel

Why is there so much controversy about the turn to normative or substantive ethics that is often called 'applied ethics'? If ethics is a practical discipline it should include dealing with practical moral problems. Instead, some philosophers call it a radical departure and some professionals an unwarranted invasion of their expertise. Yet in the history of ethics the great moral philosophers whom we commend to our students explicitly connected their theory to critique of and recommendations for the institutions, policies, and practical problems of their time. Plato's *Republic* scarcely draws a line between ethics and social policy. Aristotle's *Politics* is continuous with his *Ethics*. Aquinas, Hobbes, Hume, Adam Smith, Bentham and even Kant are no different in this respect. Issues of war, economy, distribution, promise-keeping, contracts, international relations, crime and punishment, show up all along. Adam Smith's *The Theory of the Moral Sentiments* and *The Wealth of Nations* are not in his eyes separate departments of ethics and economics; both belong to the one course of the 'moral sciences.'

Novelty is not itself novel in the history of ethics. Current applied ethics indeed got into swing with bioethics where new technologies like organ transplants generated problems. Aristotle had nothing like that to worry about, though he did speculate about what would happen to slavery under an imagined automation; nor did Bentham raise questions of pollution in his enthusiasm for technical invention. Yet Athenian democracy, which provoked moral problems for Plato, was new in its time. And some of the questions of seventeenth-century ethics – in Hobbes and Locke – clearly

317

pre-suppose the rise of a unified national state which itself was (in Europe) a recent growth.

Accelerating concern with practical moral problems expresses the need of a world of technological and social change for widespread institutional and moral readjustment. The sense of an abrupt departure in moral philosophy expresses the more local fact that for some four decades ethical theory had been experimenting with an isolation which divorced theory from moral judgment. Only with respect to this isolation could the resumption of a traditional continuity of theoretical and practical be suspect. Hence proper appreciation of the practical turn requires a brief view of the isolationist experiment.

This experiment emerged in the central analytic schools of our century, beginning with logical positivism before World War II. Positivism rested on a basic trichotomy that made separate domains out of logic, fact, and value. Positivist moral philosophy found traditional ethical theories to be a *mélange* of moral values, empirical assumptions, and conceptual elements. It relegated the empirical to science and regarded values as purely expressive or emotive. Moral philosophy proper (ethical theorizing) would then lie in a logical-linguistic analysis of moral discourse which was value-free except for the methodological values of clarity and consistency, and enmeshed in no specific factual or scientific assumptions. This pure new discipline was called *metaethics*.

Positivist bases of metaethics were shaken in subsequent philosophical controversy, by internal criticism as well as external assault. The analytical ordinary language (Oxford) approach became uncomfortable with formalist conceptions of logic and analysis, with broad abstract ideas of value and fact. Its influence in moral philosophy was even greater than the earlier positivist; yet is stayed the course and cherished its independence as analysis. Overt criticisms of metaethics were, however, not uncommon: implicit empirical assumptions and value attitudes were uncovered within the proposed metaethical schemes themselves.[1] Some arguments for continuity of the theoretical and the practical looked back to Dewey, who had seen no fundamental difference between ethical theorizing and moral reflection in which an individual seeks general principles to direct his conduct.[2] Theory simply extends reflective morality to deal with problems of decision under uncertainty as to what is right, as compared to customary morality acting on the basis of accepted precepts. Uncertainty requires more subtle conceptual instruments and more elaborated theory.

The present demand that ethical theory help in moral problems sets such help as a criterion of success or failure in ethical theory itself. The benefits of the isolationist episode in moral philosophy did not include ways of dealing with practice nor of addressing the complexities of moral experience. In the remainder of this paper I want therefore to examine five lines of theory directed to these ends.[3] Some are critical of contemporary moral philosophy (whether analytic or traditional), and some of incipient tendencies in current applied ethics. Others, however, try to provide fresh instruments for reestablishing connection between theoretical and practical.

TOWARD A NETWORK ANALYSIS FOR ETHICS

Analytic ethics presented a polarization of methods.[4] Positivism sought large-scale formal deductive systems that reconstructed and refined the language of ethics; it disparaged the looseness of ordinary language as a heritage of obscurity. Ordinary language analysis, on the contrary, found linguistic uses rich, variegated, and subtly differentiated.[5] If positivism bundled all moral terms into affective attitudes, as a dumping-ground for the non-empirical and the non-logical, it nevertheless inspired imposing efforts to build systems of deontic and axiological logic; yet then it paid little attention to their use and the interpretation of their fundamental terms in practice.[6] Ordinary language analysis immeasurably clarified shades of moral terms in different contexts of use. It exposed the *naiveté* of asking for a single formula for what 'ought' means, finding uses that were decisional, prescriptive, evaluative, etc.[7] But it limited context to the linguistic, ignoring the cultural, social, and historical. In general it looked into meanings that contemporary language had already established, the status-quo patterns of the existing dialect. It neglected linguistic change and thrust aside technical language. And on the whole it paid attention to single terms rather than the relation of terms or how they operated together in a given field.

Is it possible to integrate gains from both movements – the formalist respect for construction and refinement and the informalist attentiveness to diversity and context? It requires a shift of attention in both. For formalists the shift would be from mathematical emphasis on deductive systems to scientific emphasis on concepts undergoing refinement in terms of their role in concrete investigations, with an eye on their connections and division of labor, and all this with an experimental attitude. For informalists, already attuned to context, the shift is only from linguistic context alone to broader ranges including cultural, social, and historical contexts; also from an analysis of single terms to the study of groups in their interrelations.

Such revision would yield two important methods for addressing the complexity of moral experience: a network of concepts operating interrelatedly, and a rich interpretation of concepts instead of their isolation and abstractness. Compare, for example, the different outcome in such concepts as liberty, equality, community, individual. Liberty considered alone yields familiar alternatives of legal and political freedom, economic freedom, negative as against positive freedom, inner or external freedom. Equality alone begets political, social, economic equality; equality of opportunity versus equality of results. Community careens between totalitarian threat and prudential altruism; in between are natural affection toward others and the sense of loyalty. Such analyses generate suspiciously abstract artificial problems: liberty versus equality, individual versus society, political versus economic, etc. Now attention to a network and to fuller context would address specific social-historical-cultural problems of a given period and trace the way the concepts appropriated parts and aspects of the problems and the proposed solutions: why specific movements enlisted under a banner of equality instead of liberty (what division of labor between the concepts characterized that period); what opposing classes or social groupings enlisted under which banner for what concrete objectives; with what typical activities was individualism identified and what constituted being an individual. Evaluation thus shifts from acceptance of one or another ideal to assessment of the specific pattern of life, its goods and evils and problems, its potentials and its dead-ends.[8]

A similar contrast can be found in different ways of ethical theory. Network analysis will not give separate treatments of good, right, virtue, and then debate which is prior in an ethical theory – whether to go in for teleology, deontology, or aretaics; whether to reduce the other concepts to a preferred one by some definitional schema. Instead, it will analyze them together in relation to the aspects of life in which each arises and plays a role; it will identify interlocking roles and problems giving rise to temptations for elevating one or another. Such analysis does not conjure away problems of duty versus interest; it pinpoints specific issues that give rise to specific moral conflicts, to be resolved not by appeal to a formula of duty or interest but by facing the underlying decisions that are routed into such a dichotomy. Dewey's mature ethical theory illustrates such an approach. [9] Basic attention is to forces in human life that generate morality; the matrix of appetite and desire with conflicts that call for solution and reconciliation; the interpersonal relations and claims integral to group life; mutual responses and appreciations that build character and personality. The good is then seen to express the need for evaluative criteria in the appetitive group; the right for regulative patterns in the interpersonal; virtue for the value patterning of character. Reconciliation of conceptual relations among the three reflects the patterning of relations among the forces and processes; it requires moral decision in specific conflicts, not decision by definition of the moral terms and their relations. Such moral decision consists in the concrete elaboration of standards for assessing needs and rules and character-patterns in terms of the central problems of the period as generated by the mode of life, the conditions and consequences.

Such analysis is by no means easy, but it is clearly what is required by the efforts to restructure ethical concepts to do the work of practical ethics.

BEYOND MICROETHICS

An individualistic model is enshrined in contemporary ethical theory and much of social science: group values and laws are built up from the interaction of individuals as atomic units. The individual's good is usually equated ultimately with his preferences. The great problem of ethical theory, whatever the school, is to achieve dependable passage from individual to social goods – whether through utilitarian devices, Kantian legislation of autonomous individual will, or sympathic and altruistic impulses of the normal man.

321

Earlier ethical theory reached beyond the individual in several ways. The good might be a *species good*, giving the individual a standard by which to judge his preferences; or an *institutional good*, in which the individual had a well-defined role and obligations; or an initially specified *public or social good* mandating general support. The great tide of individualism rolled over all this in the last few centuries. Only when it had conquered, when even the individual appeared in ethical and social theory as a mass of preferences with problems of their consistency and reconciliation, did the question of what it is to be an individual, to be a self, itself become urgent. Major energies are still devoted to the passage from individual to social – on individualistic terms.

Contrary tendencies have begun to appear. In its later days, analytic ethics discerned an institutional component in the theory of obligation. It abandoned the attempt, for example, to justify keeping a promise by having the individual reckon good consequences or appeal to intuitions about duty. Instead, it analyzed keeping a promise as itself a 'practice' where a practice differs only in degree from an institution.[10] The institution could be justified by general benefits or in some other way, but not by the individual's preferential reckoning of each particular promise. This way of dealing with obligation in institutions, roles, and public matters signals a move beyond an individualistic model in some parts of ethics. A comparable shift is from utilitarian concepts of general happiness, with a summative connotation, to the *quality of life* of a community. All such moves may be read as attempts to establish macroethics alongside of microethics.

To admit macroethics is to treat some ethical questions in a framework of institutional and public goods, not by individual summation. In ordinary life we recognize this readily enough. One could list: setting up a constitution to last for generations, national defense, clean air, wholesome water supply, land conservation, a flourishing economy, a pattern of distributive justice, maintenance of some family structure, cultural institutions. For the most part, in building or maintaining an institution, arguments take inherent obligations for granted. If they are questioned we reconsider the desirability of the institution and propose reforms, but not in individualistic terms.

Important theoretical issues lie beyond this point; how far institutional and public goods are determined by conditions of society, under what conditions an item moves into the list or out of it, modes of reasoning to be employed in macroethics and how the conflict of public goods is to be handled, extent to which questions in micro-ethics presuppose prior solutions to questions in macroethics. The recognition of macroethics is a modest step. It does not turn all ethics into social ethics or threaten individual moral autonomy. The contrast of social and individual may not have all the importance that has commonly been assigned to it. A person is after all both social in makeup and individual in action. The contrast of macro-ethics and microethics goes along a different dimension.[11]

Macroethics raises pertinent questions for applied ethics as prac-ticed today. Applied ethics tends to focus on the individual's dilemmas as individual problems. Yet often the dilemma is pro-voked by 'rules of the game' in some area of professional ethics. For example, the lawyer faces a dilemma of confidentiality or the nurse questions what is allowable on one's own inititative. But the source of the dilemmas may be the institutional rules and changed condi-tions under which they operate: confidentiality refers to the client but the change from an individual to a corporation as client produces conflicting obligations; the scope of a nurse's decision rests on an authority structure in which the doctor is dominant, a doctor who is no longer the old-style family practitioner who knows the patient well but an occasional visitor on rounds. Here clearly a source of the dilemma is the institutional setting; its rules and policies are what require attention. In general, problems of practic-al ethics, when treated as individual dilemmas alone, throw an excessive burden on microethics. There is a certain drama in looking to the court-room, the scene of legal duels, or to the hospital, the scene of surgery and cure. But law includes the whole framework of rules that ensure smooth working in other institu-tions; and medicine (or if it rejects anything but curing, then public health) helps people keep in shape and not be sick. Practical ethics has therefore to pay attention to institutional policies and their reassessment as well as to individual dilemmas, and to policies as involved within individual dilemmas. Experiences here will show how far the macroethical is a necessary framework of the mic-roethical.

THE CONFRONTATION OF ETHICAL SCHOOLS

What roles do ethical theories play in facing practical moral problems? Does the agent have to align himself with one as against another? Let us compare the conflict of schools in general theoretical battle with their services to the person or group on a practical dilemma.

The favorite tactic in theoretical battle is a 'crash argument,' a counter-instance in which the formulae of the ethical theory under attack yield an intuitively horrifying result. Against utilitarianism cases are constructed in which the greatest happiness of the greatest number calls on a person to break a death-bed promise to a friend, or a judge to condemn knowingly an innocent man, or a doctor to raid the body of a slightly ill patient for organs to save the lives of several seriously ill patients (better one death than several). Such horror stories can, however, be framed for any ethical theory, by attention to borderline cases; Kant once wrote that a person ought not to tell a lie even to save a life.

Horror stories show not that an ethical theory is to be thrown out as incorrect or inadequate, but that there are limits to what it can solve. We have to discover those limits, not necessarily to abandon the theory if it works well within the limits. A carpenter confident his saw can handle any wood may be disappointed when it fails to cut some harder wood. He does not throw the saw away, nor does a scientist abandon a fruitful theory when it fails for extreme cases. Ethical theories too have to be reformulated and refined as knowledge and experience and reflection upon them accumulate.

The claims of an ethical theory may be criticized in more systematic ways. Assumptions about the state of the world and the nature of human beings may turn out incorrect or no longer applicable, or hold under only very limited conditions. Values that permeate it may be only some among the wider range of people's values and ideals. Procedures it requires for practical use may be lacking or insufficiently precise or incapable of effective application. Moreover, an ethical theory may have excellent vision in one direction but be short-sighted in its scope. For example, late Stoic ethics assumed almost total insecurity of life; it invested wholly in inner withdrawal and self-control, completely accepting what chance brought in the outer world. Such total adulation of 'autonomy' involved cutting

324

oneself off from deep interpersonal affective relations, even while
going through the form of the usual associations. Certainly today it
fits some situations well: death, holocaust, nuclear disaster. But
normal life now allows greater control of environment and society;
it provides an advanced technology and admits of reasonable
calculations about advancing social welfare. A utilitarian ethic
coupled with understanding of risks and probabilities can operate
successfully as guide in many areas without dogmatic universal
pretensions.

In facing dilemmas of practical decision an ethical theory clearly
does not provide axioms from which duties can be deduced *in more
geometrico*. Nor does the agent say, 'I am a partisan of theory t1 and
therefore . . .' This would assimilate ethical theories to dogmatic
cults. On the contrary, an ethical theory throws light on the
situation in which the decision is to be made. It calls attention to
factors that but for its perspective might have been overlooked or
underemphasized. It helps formulate questions to be explored.
Kant asks us to consider whether we would universalize the maxim
of our action; it certainly adds a dimension to our insight to think of
ourselves as making institutions or enstating practices. Others look
at long-range consequences of action; or the implications for the
sort of person we shall become; or the strength of our commitments;
or our continuities with tradition, our sense of the past; or the
strength of our communal bonds.

Different paths still lie open in the confrontation of theories.
Some call for an ethical eclecticism, some for moving to a fresh
meta-level of comparison of theories, some to estimations of greater reliability for one over another theory in virtue of its scope and
applicability, some to a frank instrumentalism with respect to
theories as such – which then calls for criteria to determine jurisdiction for theories in particular cases. All of these give greater weight
to the particular situation of decision, to an analysis of its complexities and to the processes of decision.

As to the future of the confrontation of theories, at least three
paths lie open. One is further refinement of each line of theory, to
unfold the complexities of structure and enhance its capabilities.
Whether in such development and in response to tasks generated by
other theories there would be considerable convergence of theories
remains an open, by no means remote, possibility. A second path is
to bridge the confrontation by finding more basic values and

principles – for example, democratic values – underlying all their contemporary forms. A third path is analytic undercutting of present confrontation by tracing differences to non-ethical sources, such as different implicit accounts of human nature or theories of human action.[12] Such approaches would support a new attitude to ethical theory itself, as an advancing frontier in which growth of knowledge and shaping of human purposes and refinement of analysis operate in human experience to facilitate moral decision.

IS 'APPLIED ETHICS' A MISLEADING IDEA?

'Applied ethics' may refer to a province or a process. As province it designates particular or professional fields that call for their own special ethical regulations. As process it signifies the way in which an ethical theory is used or a common morality invoked to provide a special code or resolve a particular moral complexity.

It is a mistake to think of professional fields being any more applied ethics than ordinary moral situations. Why should a doctor considering whether to lie to a patient about the seriousness of his condition or an advertiser wondering about the limits of truth in praising his products or a TV network in doubt whether a docudrama confuses truth with entertaining fiction be classified as applied ethics while a father wondering if he should answer his child's embarrassing questions truthfully or ambiguously and a friend tempted to shade the truth to spare another's feeling are ordinary morality? If the existence of a specialized area makes the former group applied ethics, then we can construe the latter group as concerned with family ethics and friendship ethics. Of course some areas will require knowledge of specialized conditions, but the relation to the moral view of lying is the same. As a province, so-called applied ethics is a misleading name for practical moral problems.

If 'applied ethics' refers to the process of invoking an ethical theory, then our previous consideration of confrontation of theories shows it to be more complex than the simple ideal of application suggests. It is rather a case of helping enlighten conduct by adding significant perspectives to understanding the situation. It may involve some element of rule following, but even that is more like using knowledge in many ways than deducing or deriving results for special conditions. This holds too for applying a common morality (code or ideal) to a problem. The process can be seen magnified in judicial decision, which exhibits the same complexity in a more structured situation. Views of judicial decision as applying the law used to regard the law as major premise, the facts of the case as minor premise, and the decision as logical conclusion. That indeed had the appearance of straightforward application. But intensive jurisprudential and philosophical literature has shown the complex processing behind the scenes. The particular case has first to be brought within the scope of one or another body of law, which involves a selective structuring. Then a law to govern the case has to be selected from the roster of laws for that area, and reasons have to be given why that particular law is preferred to rivals. There are also background standards as to what kind of reasons are permissible. The successfully selected law has then to be interpreted, and there are different kinds of interpretation (e.g. grammatical, historical, systematic). Even after that criteria are needed to judge relevance in presenting the facts of the case, selected from a wider mass of facts. This in turn depends on knowledge of different kinds of possible connections. Taken as a whole, this does not give the appearance of 'application' in its usual sense.

Perhaps 'application,' even in 'applied science,' requires more careful articulation and the substitution of a more refined vocabulary.[13] In ethics at least, it misleads in suggesting an antecedent system that settles practical questions 'in principle' and invites quasi-automatic solutions. Again, by covering over the background in which the processing of the case takes place, we fail to follow up on the way in which the practical decision reacts on the codes and theories that are being 'applied'. We fall victim to the same divorce of theory and practice that characterized the separation of metaethics and normative ethics.

All in all, we would be better off if we dropped the appelation of 'applied ethics' and studied ways in which theory and morality enlighten decision and the ways in which they all interact.

HISTORICAL CONTEXTS AND MORAL CHANGE

Our world is undergoing great changes – in technology, social institutions, knowledge, personal attitudes, even morality.

(Although occasional traditionalists interpret moral change as deterioration, there is no doubt that new views about conduct and feeling are offered as moral refinement and moral sensitivity.) Much current concern about practical ethics stems from uncertainty in facing new situations. By contrast with all this, moral philosophy still cherishes a timeless quality; it looks for final formulae of justice, unchanging structures of liberty, permanent principles of right and wrong, almost eternal rights and responsibilities. There is little diachronic interpretation of ethical ideas, nor even the recognition that the synchronic is a temporal cross-section of a changing process.

Philosophical movements of our century have gradually forced ethical theory to recognize the many dimensions of the act or situation that is under moral judgment or decision. The dimensions are internal features without reference to which the act is insufficiently described and the evaluation may go astray.

The recognition of decision as central has been primary. Different philosophical schools moved in this direction. Some (Sartre's existentialism) directly posited decision at every point in ethical judgment, not just at the end; the very formulation of a problem is decisionally constituted, for opposing rules selected out of a mass of possibilities generate the conflict, and every principle invoked in deciding is itself the object of choice. Analytic ethics moved in the same direction more deviously; it located a prescriptive element within the ethical utterance itself, not as a supplementary act. In sum, decision is not voluntaristic acceptance of a previously contemplated ethical judgment; it is the judgment being completed. And meanwhile, logicians and mathematicians and statisticians worked on the process of decision itself and the factors that enter into it; the complexities they revealed – appeals to frequencies of experience or subjective beliefs or postulates of indifference – showed the tie-in within decision to the major philosophical ideas that had hitherto permeated the analysis of ethical judgment itself. Attempts to put choice or will or decision in the center of ethics are, of course, an old story, at least back to medieval struggles of voluntarism with rationalism. The new element in the twentieth century is the analysis of decision once it is located at the center.

Further dimensions emerged in the analysis of the act or situation that is under judgment or ethical review. Much of it was directed against the simplistic search for atomic facts or behavioral physicalistic units. Behind the analytic recognition that when we judge it is of something 'under a description,' behind the debates about 'essences,' 'types', 'sortals', lay the recognition of the constructive work that goes into getting judgment or decision under way – the dressing of the object, as it were, for its appearance in court.

Perhaps the most immediately successful effort to broaden the description of the act or situation under moral judgment came from the phenomenological movement. Phenomenological description insists on the prior importance, before judging, of understanding the meaning of the act or situation to the agent.[14] Take a standard example, usually brought up against ethical relativism. In olden days the Eskimo abandoned aged incapacitated parents, and we readily see this as cruelty or ingratitude. But is this what it meant to them? Further study shows it was unavoidable, for in order to survive the family had to be constantly on the move. To take incapacitated parents along would jeopardize survival; parents expected abandonment and asked for it, the culture even providing reassuring myths. With this knowledge, we see the situation in a wholly different way. It is more like our view of an overcrowded lifeboat in which someone has to go overboard, or like sacrifice in war. (We too have our theories of 'lifeboat ethics' and our concepts of 'triage.') The insistence on phenomenological description was carried into interesting explorations in psychiatry, education, interpersonal relations, and social psychology.

Beyond phenomenological horizons, cultural and social studies gathered materials that were still to be brought into the inner sanctum of ethics. What kept them out was the same isolation of ethics we noted in dealing with metaethics. The cultural and social were construed not as dimensions within the description ethics requires, but as scientific study of causal factors; it would be a 'genetic fallacy' to give them a part in evaluation or judgments of adequacy. This bias was countered in part by analysis of the alleged fallacy.[15] More effective perhaps were the inroads made by cultural description and the study of cultural patterning within moral concepts. One can barely approach specific or lower-level ideas in morals – say, of work or love, dishonesty or adultery – without looking to the patterning of economy or of family. Similarly for components of an ethical theory: for example, resting moral obligation on religious authority or on contract, selecting guilt or shame or pride or sympathy to do the heavy work of morality. As the social sciences allowed themselves at mid-century to enter the study of values and as social psychology and personality theory presented a richer picture of the self, it became possible in ethics to integrate the cultural and social within the exploration of moral judgment.

These various dimensions, however, only hovered on the brink of the temporal. It is one thing to probe the cultural and social aspects of a present situation to get the fuller view of the object of moral judgment. But need one go to the past, the development in time of the present situation, in order to understand it? To omit the cultural may be to omit variables necessary for judgment. How can the same be said for history? One of the obstacles to involving the historical was the traditional model of science, that prediction (or control, if possible) requires only laws and description of the present state. Yet even within science place had to be found for the temporal character of evolutionary and of geological explanation. In human affairs knowledge of historical development is necessary on a much wider scale: for example, if there are economic cycles, at what stage of the cycle are we now? If a drought or disease or threat to agriculture has been spreading, what is its rate of growth? The present is extended to include some of the past.

That historical development of a moral problem may be part of its description, necessary for its solution, can be suggested by brief illustrations. Take the many moral problems clustering about the ideal of equality, removal of discriminations, issues of affirmative action. If the ideal of equality is reduced to a justifiable formula regarding the state of individuals, we focus on equal treatment, equal opportunities, equal results, proportions or quotas, reverse discrimination. If equality is studied in historical development, we observe the step-by-step growth of efforts of submerged groups to participate in the social and cultural operations of society and to share its material and cultural gains. Present problems in removing discrimination are seen in terms of the stage reached in such efforts: quotas are assessed not as an effort to achieve an ideal formula of justice, say a due proportion for Blacks and women in employment, but as a temporary instrument to make a breakthrough in a present stalemate, when other effective instruments are unavailable. This historical view of the moral elements thus serves to refocus the present problem for moral judgment. The same effect is secured in controversies over individual and social means for dealing with welfare problems: historically, emphasis falls on changes in economic and social conditions that made older methods of individual compassion and charity, individual search for employment and enterprise, insufficient to cope with large-scale economic processes and depressions. Moral judgment is thus attuned to alternative means and their consequences rather than to simply a general formula relating the individual and the social. We may wonder whether even intense moral struggles found in matters of contraception and abortion can be sufficiently clarified for moral judgment without seeing their historical development in the growing movement for liberation of women from age-old subordination and discrimination, stimulated by the growth of other liberation movements and the greater availability of technical and medical knowledge. Without such an historical picture opposition of two principles in abstract form – right to life and right to choose – does not carry us far.

It is not being suggested that the historical view is required in all moral issues. An historical perspective is sometimes advanced today in indirect form: for example, that intelligibility in human affairs requires the self or the group being seen as actors in some narrative. Since we cannot know ahead where the historical dimension will prove particularly relevant, it should be placed alongside the phenomenological and socio-cultural in any diagnosis preparatory to moral judgment.

Even if the historical is granted a place in moral judgments, the question remains whether it is relevant for ethical theory. This too can best be examined briefly by example. Take the vigorous contemporary controversy over utilitarianism. This is usually done by formulating the theses of the theory and, as indicated earlier, either conjecturing counter-instances or probing presuppositions about human nature and permanent human values, or by evaluating the practicability of procedures for putting the theory to work. Usually no distinction is made between different periods of historical development; Bentham and Mill are combined into a unified doctrine with wrinkles and differences ironed out or theoretically adjudicated (for instance on whether pleasures are to be qualitatively as well as quantitatively distinguished). Now how can historical analysis of 'the greatest happiness of the greatest number' be helpful? In Bentham's situation power lay with an entrenched landed minority. Bentham did not require a more subtle principle as instrument simply because the underlying issue at the time was bringing greater numbers, particularly the growing industrial class, into political participation. Bentham could also accept the economics of Adam Smith and the primacy of security over equality and abundance as ways of opening up freer trade and advancing productivity. James Mill could still follow Bentham's lead because he had full confidence that the leadership of the new middle class would be accepted by the mass of the people. But John Stuart Mill wrote after the Chartist movement and the rise of socialist ideas. He could no longer give a blank cheque to what will bring the greatest happiness to the greatest number; so he refined the theory to stress protection of individual liberties and made the debate between competitive individualism and socialism an empirical issue of what works out best.

Twentieth-century consideration of social and economic change had the same focus: it could still be cast as raising the standard of living (increasing the greatest happiness of the greatest number) – especially in welfare movements of the 1930s when the great depression brought majority suffering and threatened even those who had hitherto been self-supporting. In the United States, however, after World War II, it seemed for a short historical period that the welfare of the majority at least (if not of the greatest possible number) had been achieved. Moral attention now turned to those still dispossessed, to achieving gains for minorities. The succession of liberation movements could hardly have been expected to be content with the fact that the majority was well off. In social and ethical theory a central issue became formulated as the conditions under which there should be institutional change. Some clung to Pareto's older formula, only such change as will make no one worse off than he was before. Rawls offered a more refined version: acceptable change requires improving the lot of the most disadvantaged. Others seek even more refined formulations. Suspicion that utilitarian formulae cannot cope with the issue is evident even earlier in the renewed theory of human rights. Such rights characterize individuals: the individual makes claims, not in terms of group statistics. Of course different formulae may be used for different aspects of life. If macroethical concerns are given a greater role, 'quality of life' may, as noted earlier, replace or supplement 'greatest happiness' within a utilitarian view.

Whether this specific historical 'narrative' is correct does not concern us now. It will at least illustrate what the historical dimension may do in helping evaluate ethical theory as well as moral judgment. Current concern with practical moral problems will probably strengthen study of the historical dimension largely because differences in initial formulation of problems often constitute the crux of decision.

CONCLUSION: THE IMPACT OF ETHICAL THEORY

We began with the suggestion that demands of practical ethics would force an altered view of ethical theory. The topics discussed indicate lines of further theoretical inquiry. The first would provide a mode of analysis in which the concepts of a theory would be collectively tested and refined through their relations with the conditions of practice. The second would liberalize ethical theory be removing the shackles of a single (and tyrannical) model. The third would dislodge the fixed and universal pretensions of an ethical theory and give it rather the role of an enriching perspective. The fourth would recognize the complexity of decision processes and free inquiry into them from constraints of a narrow concept of application. The fifth would round out the dimensions of ethical inquiry, enabling it to make fuller use of the knowledge acquired in cultural, social, and historical disciplines; by immersing ethical inquiry in the temporal it would open the way to the largely unexplored area of moral change.

The resultant impact on theory is to open doors and offer opportunities. The full work of a more mature moral philosophy remains to be done. Theory and practice are brought closer together, not to transfer power from a theory separately established and then dictating practice to a practice that determines theory or chooses perspectives to suit its convenience. For what is of convenience itself reflects a theory of the relation of theory and practice. The prominence of practical decision is thus not itself a theoretical answer. A more definite answer requires greater exploration of the multiple relations revealed in the analysis of decision itself. To this, the growth of experience in attention to moral practice may be expected to contribute greatly – if for no other reason because the diversity of moral problems rooted in the complexities of our present life will provide a panoply of intricacies for reflection in moral philosophy.

NOTES

* This paper was given as the presidential address to the American society for Value Inquiry, December 29, 1984.

1 Such criticisms varied for different metaethical schemes. Thus emotive theory was criticized for: assuming emotion to be noncognitive; neglecting the purposive component in the affective (which would introduce a cognitive element, allowing a true-false assessment); carrying in its formulation a proselytizing value individualism; conveying an irrational mood.

2 John Dewey and James H. Tufts, *Ethics*, revised edition, New York, Henry Holt, 1932, pp. 173-6.

3 Some of these themes have been previously explored in a number of studies. See especially, Abraham Edel, 'Comments on Frankena's *Philosophy and Moral Standards*, in *Two Centuries of Philosophy in America*, ed. Peter Caws, Basil Blackwell 1980, pp. 329-39; also Edel, *Exploring Fact and Value*, New Brunswick, N.J., Transaction Books, 1980, Chapter 9.

4 For a characterization of these methods, see P.F. Strawson, 'Construction and Analysis' in *The Revolution in Philosophy*, by A.J. Ayer *et al* London, Macmillan, 1956, pp. 97-110.

5 For a comparison of the analytic modes within a general overview of modes of analysis, see Abraham Edel, *Analyzing Concepts in Social Science*, New Brunswick, N.J., Transaction Books, 1979, Introduction, especially sections V and VII.

6 For an analysis of the seriousness of this problem by one of the major architects of deontic logic, see G.H. Von Wright, *Norm and Action*, London, Routledge & Kegan Paul, 1963, Chapter VIII.

7 Cf. P.H. Nowell-Smith, *Ethics*, London, Penguin, 1954, Chapter 13; and Paul W. Taylor, *Normative Discourse*, Englewood Cliffs, N.J., Prentice-Hall, 1961, Chapter 7.

8 For a fuller examination, see Edel, *Exploring Fact and Value*, op. cit., pp. 181-6.

9 Dewey, op. cit., Chapters XI-XIII. See also his 'Three Independent Factors in Morals' translated from the French by Jo Ann Boydston, in *Educational Theory*, XVI, 3 (July 1966), pp. 197-209.

10 For such an analysis, see John Rawls, 'Two Concepts of Rules' in *Philosophical Review*, XIV, 3 (1955), pp. 3-32. For a similar approach to other ethical ideas, see Philippa R. Foot, 'Approval and Disapproval' in *Law, Morality and Society*, ed. P.M.S. Hacker and J. Raz, Oxford, Clarendon Press, 1977, pp. 229-46.

11 John Dewey offers the categories of *public* and *private* to do the work mistakenly ascribed to *social* and *individual*. See his *The Public and Its Problems* (1927), reprinted, Denver, Allen Swallow; also in *John Dewey: The Later Works*, ed. Jo Ann Boydston, vol. 2, Carbondale and Edwardsville, Southern Illinois University Press.

12 An excellent example of this is Andrew Oldenquist, 'Rules and Consequences,' in *Mind* LXXV, 289 (April 1966), pp. 180-92. Oldenquist
questions the sharp contrast of teleological and deontological ethics.

13 For a fuller treatment, cf. Abraham Edel, 'Ethics Applied *or* Conduct
Enlightened?' Ninth Wayne Leys Memorial Lecture, University of
Illinois at Carbondale, March 10, 1983.

14 The classic article employing phenomenological psychology to argue
against ethical relativity is Karl Duncker, 'Ethical Relativity? (An
Inquiry into the Psychology of Ethics),' in *Mind*, New Series, XLVIII,
189 (January 1939).

15 Cf. Abraham Edel, *Method in Ethical Theory*, Indianapolis, Bobbs-
Merrill, 1963, Chapter XI ('Genetic Inquiry and Truth Determination').